The Neolithic Revolution in the Near East

D1562835

The Neolithic Revolution in the Near East

Transforming the Human Landscape

Alan H. Simmons

With a Foreword by Ofer Bar-Yosef

The University of Arizona Press   Tucson

The University of Arizona Press
© 2007 The Arizona Board of Regents
All rights reserved

www.uapress.arizona.edu

First paperback printing 2010

Library of Congress Cataloging-in-Publication Data
Simmons, Alan H.
  The neolithic revolution in the Near East : transforming the human
landscape / Alan H. Simmons ; with a foreword by Ofer Bar-Yosef.
    p. cm.
  Includes bibliographical references and index.
  ISBN 978-0-8165-2966-7 (pbk.: alk. paper)
  1. Neolithic period — Middle East — Case studies. 2. Hunting,
Prehistoric — Middle East — Case studies. 3. Hunting and gathering
societies — Middle East — Case studies. 4. Agriculture, Prehistoric —
Middle East — Case studies. 5. Domestication — Middle East — Case
studies. 6. Pottery, Prehistoric — Middle East — Case studies. 7. Middle
East — Antiquities — Case studies. I. Title.
GN776.32.N4S56 2007
939'.4 — dc22   2006020256

Manufactured in the United States of America on acid-free, archival
quality paper and processed chlorine free.

15 14 13 12 11   7 6 5 4 3 2

Frontispiece: A modern farmer in Lebanon.

Contents

List of Illustrations

Figures

All photographs by Alan H. Simmons except as otherwise noted in the individual photo captions.

Tables

Foreword

The Neolithic Revolution was a major threshold in human evolution. While opinions may diverge concerning why it happened, where it started, and how it spread, there is no doubt that the ensuing economic changes caused by the establishment of farming communities and the emergence of pastoral societies had a major impact on the history of planet Earth.

The socioeconomic transition from foraging to farming left its imprint on the collective human memory, expressed in various parts of the world in mythological stories. Judging by the myths, the shift from the seemingly leisurely lifeways of hunting and gathering to toiling on the land, sowing, planting, harvesting, and storing surplus grain, was a major shift in the role of both work and gender in society. In the biblical story it is retold as the expulsion of Adam and Eve from the Garden of Eden. Thus, the transition in lifeways caused by the Neolithic Revolution resulted in deep-seated cultural shock retained in the oral history of the populations of the Near East.

This region, geographically known as southwestern Asia, was one of the first centers where intentional cultivation of annual plants began. Sedentary villages participated in this socioeconomic change by tending and domesticating goats, sheep, cattle, and pigs. We are not certain who among the local groups of foragers initiated this transition during the terminal Pleistocene or early Holocene or whether it was done in one small core area or two. However, scholars often attribute the pioneering efforts of incipient cultivation to the Natufian, a complex society of hunter-gatherers, known from the southern Levant and their descendants. Furthermore, we still lack a good body of knowledge concerning the last foragers in northern Syria and southeast Turkey, a region known as the northern Levant.

The investigation of the emergence of farming communities began during the nineteenth century when scholars became interested in social evolution. Basing their investigations on documented mythologies as well as on information provided by Roman and later historians, they looked for the root of agricultural societies. Among those scholars was George P. Marsh, an American researcher, who in his book *Man and Nature*, published in 1864, stated that "the action of man upon the organic world tends to subvert the original balance of its species, and while it reduces the numbers of some of them, or even extirpates them altogether, it multiplies other forms of animal and vegetable life."

Indeed, long before systematic excavations were conducted, the Swiss botanist Alphonse de Candolle indicated in 1883 that the main loci for the emergence of cultivation were China, southwest Asia, and Egypt, as well as Meso- and South America. He suggested that the search should concentrate on the original centers of cultivated plants.

Interestingly, one of the first practitioners of archaeology who set out to find concrete evidence for the origins of agriculture was R. Pumpelly, an American geologist whose pioneering work in central Asia in the early years of the twentieth century stimulated others. Pumpelly discovered that a large Pleistocene lake, the residual of which is Lake Aral, dried out and was followed by the establishment of farming villages. He thus recognized the importance of Pleistocene climatic fluctuations and their potential impact on the environment and on human behavior. In his view, the gradual drying of central Asia motivated isolated populations to initiate cultivation. Hence, by introducing the climatic factor as a reason for when and why farming was initiated, he influenced the ensuing studies by V. Gordon Childe. Needless to say, climatic fluctuations and degraded environments continue to play a major role in building models that explain the transition to agriculture.

However, it was not in central Asia that the efforts to disclose what happened in prehistory took place. The interest in the archaeology of the Near East was and is common among European and American scholars, and appears to be related first and foremost to the teaching of the Bible. From various schools of archaeology came excavators who were active in exposing the evidence for the Neolithic Revolution. Worth noting is that no other region in the entire world enjoys so many different schools of archaeology involved in the search. In most countries, only locals do archaeology, but the situation in the Near East is unique. As an archaeologist I can testify to the importance of this multinational involvement of both foreigners and local researchers. It is not just that the excavations are conducted in a variety of ways, opening large or small areas, submitting samples to a host of radiocarbon laboratories, employing archaeobotanists and archaeozoologists trained in various schools, but that there are varied stimulating interpretations that emerge from the either explicitly or implicitly expressed assumptions held by the different teams. This is also the strength of this volume — that contradicting ideas or interpretations of the Neolithic Revolution are explicitly presented. Readers will benefit from the summaries and the treatments of particular sites and, when in doubt, can find the primary evidence in the exhaustive list of references.

The detailed story of the Neolithic Revolution in southwestern Asia and, in particular, in the Levant is told step by step in this volume by Alan Simmons, one of the energetic excavators of Neolithic sites in the Levant. The author employs updated data sets accumulated in the last two decades to weave this new picture grounded in observations from the field and the laboratories. I must admit that it is a hard task throughout the years to follow all the published papers. Aside from the newsletter *Neolithics* coedited by H. G. Gebel and G. Rollefson, which brings updated news from recent field projects, papers by various authors are spread throughout many journals and edited volumes.

By describing the archaeological evidence and including the controversies among scholars, the author provides room for readers and researchers to rethink or at least try to test their own ideas. The sequence that begins with the Natufian culture, where several small hamlets were probably sedentary, meaning that humans stayed for a large portion of the year in one place, is often considered the first step in the emergence of Neolithic villages. That this was a socially and economically difficult process is clearly indicated by the evidence. One can also imagine that among individuals in each community there were those who enjoyed the conditions of the better-established economy where surplus accumulated, and that there were others who suffered from the change. While the indications of physical conflicts are few, it is easy to assume that permanent villages of the Early Neolithic known as the Pre-Pottery Neolithic A (PPNA), led to intra- and intergroup conflicts. Having a population of 350–450 people in each large village meant that the entire mating system was in place, and the search for mates became easier when compared to the Natufian dispersed settlement pattern. These Neolithic farmers continued to hunt and gather, but for that purpose had to rely on task groups. Several of these forayed far from their base camp, and meeting other hunting parties (whether peaceful or not) resulted in the use of the same types of the newly designed arrowheads across the Levant.

The next phase in the evolution of farming in southwestern Asia described in detail by Simmons is the flourishing of village society. This period is known as the Pre-Pottery Neolithic B (PPNB), although ceramics appear in some sites during its last few centuries. Exposed areas in most sites in the southern Levant are relatively small, although larger exposures are available in the northern Levant and from a somewhat later time from Anatolia. In the southern Levant the larger sites are located east of the Jordan Valley, thus raising the issue of why no similar megasites were discovered in the well-watered areas west of the Jordan Valley. The economy flourished, the social entities grew, animals were domesticated, and a process of budding-off communities characterizes the entire region.

On Cyprus, and later in Crete, people who migrated there with their domestic tools planted crops and tended and kept animals, including the fallow deer that were strategically targeted game, and changed the face of these islands. While the forms of the employed seacraft are as yet unknown, the evidence for the migration reflects the presence of leadership and by extension the emergence of an elite. On the mainland, societal changes were even clearer, not only by the presence of plastered skulls, but in particular by the appearance of central cultic places.

Perhaps the most striking discoveries of the last decade are the centers where rituals, ceremonies, and public gatherings took place. The foremost example is the large site of Göbekli Tepe in southeast Turkey, where the carved T-shaped stone pillars indicate major investments and centrally organized operations. Not less amazing are the efforts conducted to fill the buildings in this site when for some reason it went out of use. A similar process of filling abandoned houses was practiced in many villages. While the reasons for these acts are unknown, it seems that the social pressures caused by the Neolithic Revolution and the rapidly increasing population were alleviated by the emergence of organized rituals.

When we add to these discoveries the knowledge concerning exchange or trade routes, the formation of social interactions within a geographic sphere that incorporated farmers-herders as well as foragers, who occupied the deserts, and the ensuing appearance of real pastoral communities, we recognize the hallmarks of the foundations of Near Eastern civilizations.

The final chapter of this book is thought-provoking. Readers are faced with a panoply of updated hypotheses for explaining the driving forces that motivated the entire Neolithic Revolution. New questions, neatly phrased by Simmons, require more fieldwork and additional laboratory analyses that may or may not be followed by the conservation and preservation of sites and finds. Academic reflections on whether we need better models or improved evidence are brought forth. All of us who work in this region are fully aware that the vagaries of daily life in different countries are far from the academic arena. Even in places where violence does not take place, modern development—building dams, expanding towns and cities, reclaiming land for agriculture—is taking its toll on the antiquities. Sites disappear when bulldozers move in or are flooded by water when a newly constructed dam is completed. Looting occurs too, but most plunderers target sites and graves of later periods. This is no consolation, however, because we should do better in making authorities and governments aware that the understanding of human evolution in the Near East does not include only the emergence of the monotheistic religions, but also the foundations for the historic process that are rooted in the Neolithic Revolution.

Ofer Bar-Yosef
Department of Anthropology, Harvard University

Preface to the Paperback Edition

I am delighted with the reissue of this volume in paperback. Since the original publication in 2007, I have been honored by the numerous and (generally!) positive reviews that the book has garnered, and I was humbled that it received the G. Ernest Wright Award from the American Schools of Oriental Research in 2009. This paperback edition is not a revision, although since 2007, investigations into the Neolithic of the Near East have maintained a quick pace, and new discoveries and interpretations continue to make this research particularly relevant. This is a testament to the enduring interest in the origins and consequences of our modern domestic subsistence base. While I could already do a revised version to add new data, many of the research themes that I addressed in 2007 are the same today. I would, however, like to take this opportunity to provide just a few critical updates.

The island of Cyprus continues to surprise us with increasingly early and sophisticated Neolithic remains. Perhaps most significantly, the Pre-Pottery Neolithic A (PPNA) hinted at in the 2007 volume has now been confirmed at Ayia Varvarva *Asprokremnos* (Sturt Manning, Carole McCartney, Bernd Kromer, and Sarah Stewart, The Earlier Neolithic in Cyprus: Recognition and Dating of a Pre-Pottery Neolithic A Occupation, *Antiquity* 84:693–706, 2010). In addition, a major volume on the intriguing early Neolithic site of *Shillourokambos* is about to be published, and my own investigations at *Ais Yiorkis*, another early Neolithic site, continue to yield unexpected results. All this research attests to the seafaring and colonization skills of Neolithic people at a far earlier date than previously thought.

Another area that continues to yield incredible remains is Turkey, which of course has a long history of research on the Neolithic at sites such as Çatalhöyük and Çayönü, to name but two. Current investigations are providing considerable insight into the Neolithic world, from rich PPNA occupations onward. Certainly the intriguing ceremonial site of Göbekli Tepe remains perplexing to archaeologists with its scale and elaborate art; tantalizingly, surveys in its general area suggest that it might not be unique. One thing that Turkey continues to demonstrate is that the concept of a "Levantine-centric" Neolithic is outdated, if indeed it was ever valid (although the present book does in fact focus on the Levant). It is increasingly clear that there were multiple regions of Neolithic development throughout the Near East, and one intriguing question is the degree of interaction between them. As more and more research is conducted, it also is becoming apparent that our concepts of "domestication" need to be refined. Indeed, it is now likely that both plants and animals in many cases were "co-domesticated," despite the conventional wisdom that plants were domesticated before animals.

And of course research into the Neolithic in the Levant continues at a frantic pace. Both Israel and Jordan continue to provide more and more insight into the Neolithic, and one can hope (albeit optimistically) that additional stability might come to places such as Lebanon, Syria, and the Palestinian Authority, all of which we know have rich Neolithic heritages. Given the current political situation, it is unlikely that too much research (at least western-based) will occur in countries such as Iran and Iraq, which is a pity, given that we know these regions have substantial and important Neolithic remains. One can also hope that research in countries such as Saudi Arabia and the emirates might produce unanticipated Neolithic discoveries.

Finally, issues of preservation and site presentation continue to be major issues. Development continues at an alarming pace in most Near Eastern countries, and with that come the challenges, opportunities, and responsibilities to protect and preserve the irreplaceable vestiges of what ultimately resulted in modern society.

Acknowledgments

In writing a summary such as this, it dawned on me on how many people I am grateful to. There is no way that I can begin to include all of them here, but I can offer thanks to many. I always knew I wanted to study archaeology, so even as a freshman at the University of Colorado I immediately became an anthropology major, and learned an awful lot of archaeology from Dave (and Barbara) Breternitz, Frank Eddy, and Bob Lister. In graduate school, I worked first with Bruce Schroeder at the University of Toronto. My education continued at Southern Methodist University under the patient tutelage of Tony Marks and Fred Wendorf, as well as David Friedel and Joel Shiner. While there, I also first met Ofer Bar-Yosef when he was a visiting professor, and he has had a profound impact on my archaeological thoughts. My first "real" job in archaeology (one that paid a full-time salary!) was at the University of Arizona, working for Jeff Reid. While at Arizona, I also had the opportunity to meet many other archaeologists, such as Bill Deaver, who had an influence on me. Over the years, innumerable colleagues have both argued and agreed with me, and they have sculpted my perspectives on archaeology. In particular, I want to single out Gary Rollefson, who gave me the opportunity to return to the Near East after what seemed like a long absence and work at 'Ain Ghazal. Other colleagues who have given much in the way of countless discussions and arguments on archaeology, as well as their data, include Ted Banning, Anna Belfer-Cohen, Hans-Dieter Bienert, Pierre and Patricia Bikai, Brian Byrd, Geoff Clark, Tom Davis, Bert DeVries, Harold Dibble, Dave Doyel, Bill Finlayson, Joe Gallagher, Hans Georg Gebel, Nigel Goring-Morris, Alfred Johnson, Zeidan Kafafi, the late Ju'ma Kareem, Ian Kuijt, Alain and Odille LeBrun, Burton MacDonald, David McCreery, Mohammad Najjar, Deb Olszewski, Eddie Peltenburg, David Pearlman, Leslie Quintero, David

Rupp, Stuart Swiny, Alex Wasse, and Phil Wilke. To these, I have to add those specialists whose contributions to interdisciplinary research have greatly aided in our quest to learn more about the Neolithic. These include Sue Colledge, Paul Croft, the late Jonathan Davis, Bill Farrand, the late Don Graybill, Julie Hansen, Rolfe Mandel, Reinder Neef, Dave Rhode, Linda Scott Cummings, and Peter Wigand. I also want to thank Darden Hood of Beta-Analytic for answering several radiocarbon questions for me and assisting greatly with calibrations. There are many, many more. I would be remiss not to thank all of the students who have volunteered on various projects, because without them, much of the research documented in this book never could have been done. I would like to thank Ramzy Ladah for his patience in preparing most of the maps in this book. Other students who have especially helped with comments, editing, and research include Misty Fields, Nathan Harper, Jeff Parkin, Kasey O'Horo, and Doss Powell. Finally, the students in a new University of Nevada, Las Vegas graduate seminar, "Origins of Agriculture," co-taught by Barbara Roth and myself, provided considerable insight.

Virtually none of the research documented in this book could have been done without the incredible support from various departments of an-tiquities. I have often heard some archaeologists complain about foreign bureaucracies. In my experience, if one follows the rules, such complaints have a way of disappearing. It is all too easy to forget that we are guests in many of the countries that we work in, and when I hear of some bu-reaucratic problem, one thought I have is this: how difficult would U.S. agencies make it for foreign archaeologists to work in this country? We are also lucky in the Near East to have affiliates of the American Schools of Oriental Research to facilitate our research in many countries. In par-ticular, I would like to thank Vathy Moustouki in Cyprus for her help and friendship over the past many years. Some of the most important people to acknowledge here are the people who live in many of the places that archaeologists work. I have been very lucky to make lasting friends amongst these people. Most recently this includes Onisiferos Loucades and his family in Cyprus and Abu Fuaz and his family in Jordan. My col-leagues at the University of Nevada, Las Vegas have also been supportive. I would like to thank Chris Szuter and Allyson Carter at the University of Arizona Press. Chris constantly cajoled me at every Society for American Archaeology meeting that I went to with, "When are you going to write that Neolithic book?" and Allyson patiently guided me through this process when I finally decided to do it. I also want to thank Lisa Williams for her skillful copyediting and good humor. Animals apparently were first domesticated during the Neolithic, and I would be remiss not to mention felines Omar and Mikey and the late canine Crash, whose constant curiosity caused me to think more than once on the meanings of domestication. Finally, and most importantly, Renée Corona-Kolvet was a constant source of both criticism and inspiration, and kept me on the right track.

The Neolithic Revolution in the Near East

Chapter 1

Thirty Years in the Trenches

I have been doing archaeology for a long time, and much of it has been in the Near East. This book is based on over 30 years of fieldwork there, starting as an undergraduate in 1971 at sites far more recent than the Neolithic. By 1974, however, I had my first taste of Neolithic archaeology and was hooked. To many, the volatile Near East is perhaps best known by the seemingly endless cycles of violence between modern states. Such events do little justice to this fascinating region, where so much of the human record has occurred.

The Near East has been the scene of archaeological inquiry for over a century. One reason for this is that it was the hub of some of the most spectacular complex societies known to the ancient world. Another is that the birth of Christianity, Islam, and Judaism occurred here, and ever since archaeology became a discipline, many have hoped to confirm written records with archaeological data. Hence, "biblical archaeology" has a long and storied history in the region. There is, however, an equally fascinating story to be told from archaeological "deep time," preceding written records. People of one sort or another have lived in the Near East for over a million years; thus, it is no surprise that the prehistoric archaeology there is one of the richest in the world. Around 10,000 years ago, a dramatic transformation occurred in parts of the Near East that forever affected the human experience. These were the economic and social changes from hunting and gathering subsistence strategies, which characterized over 99 percent of our long tenure on Earth, to ones emphasizing food production and settling down in small villages. This was not an easy transition, nor was it a universal one. Once it occurred, though, it changed the course of human history. Usually known as the "Neolithic Revolution," it is what this book is about.

What Is the Neolithic?

The "Neolithic" defies easy definition. Most scholars concur that it was an economic transformation that involved the domestication of wild food resources and the establishment of permanent settlements. It is not that simple, however, since there were at least semisedentary settlements in the Near East and elsewhere prior to domestication. Conversely, domesticated plants initially occur in some places, such as parts of the American Southwest, without the development of villages. So, what is a "Neolithic way of life"? There is no universally accepted definition: a flexible range of behavior is embedded in the concept of "Neolithic." Furthermore, although the Neolithic often is considered a chronological marker, it actually occurred in different areas over a span of several thousand years. There was no single "Neolithic Revolution," but rather a series of independent, albeit relatively rare, events that developed separately in a few parts of the world and then diffused to other regions.

Archaeologists like to define cultural periods based on material remains, on things we can see. The domestication process, unfortunately, often does not lend itself well to visibility, especially since economic remains often are poorly preserved. Thus, the Neolithic frequently is defined as a technological transformation, involving artifacts presumably related to agriculture. Identifying such items, however, is tricky. For example, in the Near East, one of the most diagnostic Neolithic artifact classes is projectile points, which might seem more appropriate for cultures relying on hunting rather than on domestic resources. Material definitions of the Neolithic also rely on architecture, with the hallmark signature being permanent villages (fig. 1.1).

While it is undeniable that the Neolithic was an economic and technological milestone, it also was a dramatic social and symbolic transformation. Ultimately, the most significant impacts of the Neolithic dictated a change in how humans interacted with one another and with the environment that has molded the world in which we now live. It is difficult to extract social behavior from the archaeological record. Many scholars are now attempting to do just this, however, to explain the perhaps unanswerable question of why the Neolithic happened in the first place, and what its consequences were. These represent some of the most inno-

I.I   The village of Dana near the Wadi Feinan of Jordan. This village, now partially abandoned, likely resembles many Neolithic settlements. The PPNB community of Ghwair I is located a short distance away.

vative approaches in contemporary archaeological investigations of the Neolithic.

Thus, in answer to "What is the Neolithic?" I offer the following. It was, certainly, an economic transformation, but not so much in *what* was domesticated as in *how* people used and viewed food in a different way. This required technological innovations, many of which are preserved in the archaeological record, and many others that are more subtle. Any time that economic patterns and the material items that humans are so fond of surrounding ourselves with are changed, there are bound to be social consequences as well. All of these activities are part of the "Neolithic package," but it is impossible to establish a list of universal criteria, because even in the same parts of the world, this package varied depending upon a host of local circumstances. Despite differing trajectories, one consequence of the Neolithic was expanding populations, which provided the foundation for the subsequent development of increasingly complex societies. In the Near East, the archaeological manifestations of this are the magnificent urban societies that have captured the imaginations of generations of archaeologists and the public. But make no mistake, the ultimate impacts of the Neolithic are reflected in the world in which we live today.

Scope of the Book

Why write a book about the Near Eastern Neolithic? There is a vast literature on this subject. The most comprehensive work, James Mellaart's *Neolithic of the Near East* (1975), is over a quarter of a century old. This was truly a landmark, covering the entire Near East as well as the eastern Mediterranean island of Cyprus. At about the same time, Purushottam Singh (1974) published a similar but more site-oriented account of the Near Eastern Neolithic.

Since the 1970s, there have been other significant works. Particularly important is the impressive culmination of the late Jacques Cauvin's career, originally published in French in 1994. Fortunately for the anglophone world, this was translated into English by Trevor Watkins (Cauvin 2000a). Cauvin masterfully provided a perspective on the Neolithic that is geographically wide, descriptive, and perhaps most importantly, theoretically oriented. While many may disagree with his views on symbolic aspects of the Neolithic as well as his diffusionist perspective, no one can deny the significance of this work. Other important recent European works are Aurenche and Kozłowski (1999) and Kozłowski and Aurenche (2005), the latter of which was not available for thorough review at the time of this writing, but which examines Neolithic cultures and boundaries using a somewhat "old school" series of maps and trait lists.

This book is not an updated version of previous works. Given the amount of research over the past three decades, that would now be a nearly impossible task without multiple volumes. Nor do I pursue a specific theoretical orientation, although my overall perspective is anthropological and processual. I have tried to present a variety of the often conflicting arguments that scholars have used in their approaches to understanding the Neolithic. What I want to convey is the diversity of people who lived in the Near East from approximately 13,000 to 7,000 years ago. I incorporate a variety of theoretical views, providing an overview of dominant, and often competing, models, punctuated by more detailed examination of specific issues representing contemporary research trends. I also have chosen a perspective that reflects my long involvement with the Neolithic. Given the vast amount written, both from a theoretical perspective and from site-specific description, this has not been an easy task. I have had to achieve a sometimes uncomfortable balance between archaeological data and explanation, but only by coupling on-the-ground data with explicit theoretical inquiries can we ever hope to really know more about the Neolithic. The result, I hope, is one that will appeal to professional archaeologists, students, and anyone interested in the Neolithic Revolution.

Largely because of the enormous database, I restrict most discussion to the Levantine portion of the Near East to make the task more manageable (fig. 1.2). I do this aware of recent criticism of a Levantine primacy model (e.g., *Neolithics* 2003:32–37, 2004:21–52). The fact remains, however, that the Levant is the best-known region. I have gone to great pains to provide primary sources, since many of these are often obscure or limited-distribution regional publications. I rely strongly on the newsletter *Neolithics*, edited by Gary Rollefson and Hans Georg Gebel, which provides current summaries of new investigations. Several summary works are heavily used as well. There are bound to be those I have not cited whom I should have, and to them I apologize. Inevitably, new works were published as this one was being edited; while I have not been able to thoroughly incorporate these, I have cited them as appropriate.

Some Comments on Chronology

Chronology is critically important to understanding the Neolithic. Unfortunately, a considerable amount of confusion exists between using calibrated (that is, calendar years) and uncalibrated (that is, radiocarbon year) dates. In this book, I primarily use dates that are uncalibrated. While calibrated dates are preferable, most summaries use uncalibrated ones to avoid confusion (although Aurenche et al. [2001] have attempted the complex task of calibration for the Near Eastern Neolithic, as has Byrd [2005a:244–252] for the very early Neolithic). When calibrations are applied to yield calendar years, there is some considerable complexity, largely due to the time span in which the Neolithic falls. Hence, correction curves for this time frame can result in calibrated dates some 2,200

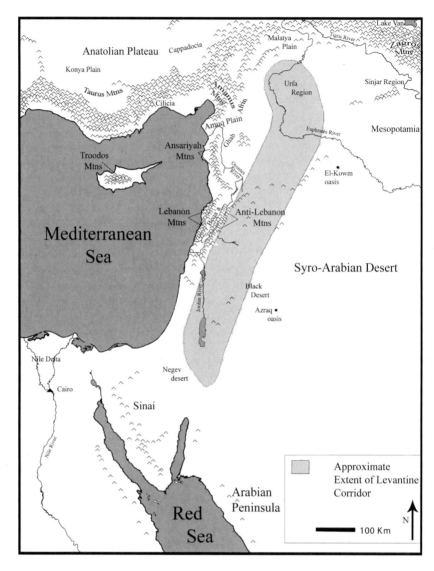

1.2 Map of the Levant, showing major features, including the Levantine Corridor.

to 1,200 years older than the uncalibrated versions. Furthermore, some discrepancies occur due to the actual number of dates used in the calibrations, as well as from variations in different calibration programs. For these reasons, most dates here are presented in uncalibrated BP (Before Present) form, although for period summaries, calibrated estimates also are provided (using INTCAL 98).

Structure of the Book

Following this introduction, chapter 2 provides a selective summary of theories on the Neolithic. Chapter 3 gives the environmental backdrop against which the Neolithic occurred. Chapters 4 through 9 are data chapters and are of necessity selective in their discussions of sites and levels of detail. Most chapters start with a brief overview, followed by sections on history and terminology, geographic range, material culture, physical anthropology, social structure and organization, ritual behavior, and regional interactions. They conclude with a concise summary. The exceptions are chapter 7, where a more narrative approach addressing the "megasite" phenomenon in Jordan is used, and chapter 9, where intriguing new research on the eastern Mediterranean island of Cyprus is rewriting our conception of the extent and impact of the Near Eastern Neolithic. Most chapters also contain at least one case study, all based on various projects in which I have had the good fortune to participate.

Chapter 4 introduces the Natufian culture, setting up the cultural and environmental framework for subsequent discussion on the Neolithic. Chapter 5 addresses the first fully recognized Neolithic culture, the Pre-Pottery Neolithic A (PPNA), where we document the establishment of the first permanent villages. In chapter 6, the Pre-Pottery Neolithic B (PPNB), representing the florescence of Neolithic culture in the Levant, is summarized. This is followed by chapter 7, where more detail is given to late PPNB and Pre-Pottery Neolithic C (PPNC) developments that witnessed the formation and demise of the megasites. Chapter 8 deals with the Pottery Neolithic (PN) and settlement realignment following the collapse of the Levantine megasites. Chapter 9 addresses the Neolithic colonization of Cyprus. Finally, chapter 10 is a summary, addressing the current state of knowledge on the Neolithic. In particular, it deals with theoretical improvements, data gaps, data trends, and site preservation.

Chapter 2

Theories on Why People Became Food Producers

For most of the human experience, humans subsisted on wild resources. Then, at the end of the Pleistocene, some groups took a momentous first step in exercising more control over their food, eventually culminating in the domestication of both plants and animals. Anthropologists and archaeologists have long wondered and debated why this happened. What caused the disruption of an indisputably effective hunting-and-gathering lifestyle and the move to one that likely entailed more work, more social complexity, and potential health hazards? Open any introductory textbook on archaeology, and there will be a discussion on the transition to food production (hereafter, "the transition"). There is a huge literature, with many suggested causes for the Neolithic Revolution.

Discussion of many of these ideas can be found in numerous articles and several edited volumes that I cannot even begin to do justice to here. Some outstanding contributions, however, include Cowan and Watson (1992), Gebauer and Price (1992), Harris (1996), Harris and Hillman (1989), Price and Gebauer (1995), Redman (1978), Reed (1977), and Ucko and Dimbleby (1969). Two excellent generalized treatments are Bellwood (2005) and Smith (1995). For the Near East specifically, Cappers and Bottema's (2002) volume contains a wealth of information. In this chapter I summarize a range of theoretical contexts and conceptual frameworks for understanding the Neolithic.

I have broken down the development of transition models into several periods, roughly following the development of modern archaeology. Many models are globally focused, although most contain Near Eastern examples, and several deal with the region specifically. Discussion here is restricted to pristine or primary domestication as opposed to secondary domestication (Watson 1995:35). The former refers to in situ development, while the latter reflects situations where domesticates were brought into areas in which they did not naturally occur.

A Potpourri of Models

Early Speculations

Scholars have pondered the transition to agriculture since at least the nineteenth century, as summarized by Gary Wright (1971). Early theories were armchair speculations not hampered by archaeological data. A common thought was that agriculture "happened," often being invented by a single great (usually male) mind. Related perspectives were that agriculture was simply part of an inevitable progress of humanity, something that was destined to occur, almost as if by divine intervention. One of the few nineteenth-century scholars to recognize that information from botany, philology, geography, and archaeology had to be integrated to understand agricultural origins was the Swiss botanist de Candolle. Using the limited data then available, he attempted to define where most of the world's crops were first domesticated. Roth was another early scholar who examined the origin of food production in detail, proposing six necessary conditions for the event: suitable climate and soil, security (i.e., stable government), capital and labor, freedom from animal pests, fixed settlements (i.e., sedentism), and economic necessity (Wright 1971:450–451).

Even into the early twentieth century most theorizing on the transition was based on virtually no archaeological data. Some scholars, though, had the initial stirring of theoretical models more sophisticated than those of their nineteenth-century predecessors. The writings of Brooks, Peake and Fleure, and Pumpelly, among others (see Wright 1971 for citations), influenced one of the most significant figures in early Near Eastern archaeology, Vere Gordon Childe.

Early Theoretical Approaches

Childe (1936) coined the term "Neolithic Revolution," and his classic model of the transition often is known as the Oasis-Propinquity Theory. He incorporated the work of earlier scholars, proposing a sudden and drastic change in economies. A basic assumption was that major climatic change at the end of the Pleistocene caused the drying of broad areas, changing them into deserts. Accordingly, plants and animals were dying or becoming scarce. This was true except for desert oases and river valleys. Here, in the only places left with water, humans, animals, and plants clustered and were forced to live in proximity. Childe proposed that people soon realized that some animals were more useful than others, so they protected them. They also would have been forced to try new plant foods, both for themselves and to feed the animals. By trial and error, they eventually domesticated these, and the Neolithic Revolution was born. Although Childe's model is frequently cited as one for the origins of agriculture, in fact he concentrated more on animal domestication and was vague about the beginnings of plant domestication (Watson 1995:23).

Childe's model was widely embraced at the time. He integrated existing environmental, technological, and economic evidence into a synthetic regional model, albeit one with a decidedly environmental deterministic perspective. This is to be admired even today, considering that many of Childe's peers either were conducting fieldwork and focusing on local cultural chronologies or were proposing sweeping theories (Henry 1989:5–6). In a sense, Childe was proposing "middle range" theory far in advance of his time.

Years later, Carl Sauer (1952) took a different approach, emphasizing the ecology of food production. He viewed the transition as a change in the way culture and environment interacted, suggesting that agriculture did not develop from a lack of food, and that hearths of domestication should be sought in areas of marked ecological diversity. Sauer proposed that Southeast Asia was a major center of domestication, and that root crops—tubers—were the main cultigens.

Early Data-Based Approaches

Innovative as they may have been, both Childe's and Sauer's models suffered from a lack of robust archaeological data. One of the first concerted scientific attempts to understand the origins of agriculture came not from an archaeologist, but from a Soviet biologist and geneticist, Nikolai Vavilov, whose efforts in the 1930s set a baseline for future research. He and his colleagues mapped out the distribution and degree of genetic diversity of several crops throughout the world, noting that in some areas high levels of variation occurred, while elsewhere there was much less diversity. This led Vavilov to conclude that regions where a domesticate showed the greatest diversity would also be where it was first domesticated. He ultimately identified seven world centers, including the Near East, of cultivated plants. While we now know that many of Vavilov's ideas were flawed, his contributions are nonetheless important, especially from a biological perspective (Smith 1995:5–8).

Bruce Smith (1995:8) believes that a parallel tradition of investigation into the transition, one much better known to archaeologists, was that of the late Robert and Linda Braidwood. The Braidwoods, of the Oriental Institute of the University of Chicago, were true pioneers in applying problem-oriented interdisciplinary research to archaeological data. Not satisfied with the then-dominant model proposed by Childe, R. Braidwood sought the origins of agriculture elsewhere (Braidwood 1960; Braidwood and Howe 1960), setting out to explicitly test the oasis hypothesis. The Iraq-Jarmo project started in 1948 and continued until 1955, when worsening political conditions made it impossible to work in Iraq. Braidwood then continued his research in both western Iran and southeastern Turkey. Geomorphological and paleoclimatic data from these projects (although now greatly revised, H. E. Wright 1993) found no support for Childe's claim of desiccation, and Braidwood proposed what has come to be known as the Hilly Flanks Theory (Watson 1995:24–26).

Smith (1995:8–11) cites three key elements of Braidwood's approach. First, he reasoned that the best place to find archaeological evidence for the transition would be in the natural habitat zones where potential domesticates occurred in the wild. He believed this "nuclear zone" was in the foothills (or "hilly flanks") of the Zagros Mountains. Second, Braidwood had to find archaeological sites that were transitional from hunting-and-gathering camps to sedentary farming villages. This ultimately led him to focus on two sites only 2 km apart, Karim Shahir and Jarmo. The former was a seasonal hunter-gatherer settlement, while Jarmo was a permanent farming village. Both gave Braidwood's team the evidence they needed for the transition to food production. Indeed, shortly after the discovery of Jarmo, Braidwood entered into a spirited debate with Kathleen Kenyon, excavator of Jericho, on who had the "earliest" village (Braidwood 1957; Kenyon 1957a). Finally, a third element of Braidwood's investigations was perhaps the most significant. Realizing the need for true interdisciplinary research, he incorporated a wide range of scientists from the biological and earth sciences. Their report (Braidwood and Howe 1960) remains a model to emulate.

Braidwood's model essentially proposed that the causes of domestication were cultural, not environmental, although it had a strong ecological flavor. He viewed food production as the culmination of the ever-increasing cultural specialization. People in the hilly flanks became so familiar with their habitats that they began to domesticate plants and animals that naturally lived there. The process involved a "settling in" by groups who came to understand and manipulate plants and animals around them. Domestication then diffused from the nuclear areas. Domestication had not occurred earlier primarily because "culture was not ready" (Braidwood and Willey 1962:342). Thus, domestication was a natural result of cultural evolution, with an implicit causal force being human nature (Braidwood 1960, 1975). The Braidwoods' research set the stage for subsequent studies, and while the hilly flanks no longer contain some of the earliest Neolithic settlements, this is inconsequential to their contributions.

Processual, Postprocessual, and Contemporary Ideas

With the advent of processual, or "new," archaeology, many scholars turned their attention to explanatory, if often conflicting, models. Many of these used the Near East as their primary data source. Most, however, were broader in scope, what Watson (1995:21–22) has summarized as inherently deductive "covering law" (CL) models. Typically, early processual models are variants on themes of broad-spectrum subsistence, demographics related to population growth and expansion, resource stress, climatic change, or combinations of these (cf. Henry 1989:27, 2002:15). Most involved the interplay between agricultural intensification, environmental change, land use, and humans. A basic premise was that larger populations led to the need for agriculture, and not the reverse. This was contrary to many older views that essentially saw domestication as coming first, leading to population increase. We now are confident that, in the Near East at least, it was sedentism during the Early Natufian that created the need for agriculture. Sedentary lifestyles, as opposed to mobile settlement patterns, resulted in higher populations for a variety of rea-

sons, including less spacing of childbirths, increased life expectancy and
fertility (at least with early settlements), a more regular diet, and the need
for more people to assist in seasonal harvests of wild plants (Bellwood
2005:18, 23; Simmons 1980:70). These larger populations ultimately depleted resources and stressed carrying capacities. This led to increased
experimentation with an already intensive use of wild grains, ultimately
resulting in domestication.

One of the earliest processual models for the transition was that of
Lewis Binford (1968), who looked at long-term trends stressing demographic factors. He argued that once people (the Early Natufian in the
Levant) became sedentary, populations inevitably increased, leading to
an increasing use of locally available plant foods, such as cereals, that had
previously been considered marginal. From this intensive use of cereals,
and the technology associated with their processing, a regular cycle of
planting and harvesting occurred, ultimately resulting in domestication.
Of course, Binford still had to explain why Early Natufian people became
sedentary in the first place. He attributes this to the rising sea levels at the
end of the Pleistocene, which reduced the Mediterranean coastline (essentially the "Natufian core") and also created new water-oriented habitats,
with an array of aquatic and waterfowl resources. This rich environment
provided the opportunity for sedentism without domestication. However,
with increasing aridity, new stresses were placed on expanding populations, causing the carrying capacity to be approached and forcing some
groups to "bud off" into more marginal areas. Populations thus increased
in marginal areas, and previously underused resources, such as strands of
wild cereals, became more important.

A principal component of many early processual models was that relatively lush areas, such as the Mediterranean zone, could support people
with just wild resources. Often cited are Harlan's (1967) classic experiment, in which he showed that it was possible to collect 2.5 kg of einkorn
wheat per hour. He then concluded that a family of four could harvest
a metric ton, enough to last for a year. Likewise, Zohary (1969:56) suggested that during a wet year, untended wild emmer wheat and wild barley could yield 500–800 kg of grain per hectare (2.4 acres). Thus, many
wondered how and why cereals became domesticated if in their wild form
they could feed relatively large populations. Such questions were really
not answered, but many felt that it was precisely this abundance in the

wild that made many of these cereals "predisposed" to subsequent domestication and even higher yields.

Around the same time, Kent Flannery (1968) proposed a model for Mesoamerican maize domestication based on general systems theory. Central components included the concept of scheduling seasonally available resources. A balanced use of resources would allow people to continue the same procurement system every year. By having alternate sets of resources, they could fall back on one when another, for some reason (cultural or natural), was not available. This could continue indefinitely, but if there were resources that tended to increase in productivity when exploited, they would become more important at the expense of others. Flannery suggested this happened with the wild ancestor of maize, whose genetic plasticity allowed it to respond to intense exploitation. This was the initial kick making it possible to develop a growing dependence on, and ultimate domestication of, maize at the expense of the seasonal procurement of other resources.

A variation of this model that Flannery (1969) applied to the Near East was termed the "broad spectrum subsistence" model. Originally based on some of Braidwood's concepts, Flannery proposed that at the end of the Epipaleolithic a wide variety of resources were used, leading to sedentism and population growth. While wild cereals may have been plentiful in their natural habitat zones, they were second- or third-choice foods because they required more energy to find and process. The chief benefit of a cereal-based diet, however, was that it could support higher populations. As marginal zones became more densely populated, people began to specialize more, planting crops intentionally to ensure an adequate food supply. Flannery felt that farming represented a decision to work harder and eat less desirable foods, and thus people likely adopted agriculture not because they wanted to but rather because they were forced to (cf. Flannery 1973:308).

Flannery (1972) also proposed a model for the origins of villages in both the Near East and Mesoamerica that was more reliant upon social factors. His argument centered around two types of societies, the first based on communal sharing that gradually evolved into the second, based on nuclear families with private storage facilities. These are reflected by different settlement types, often based on circular structures in the former and rectangular ones in the latter. Flannery's (2002) updated discussion includes extended families and also acknowledges that one model alone is insufficient to explain the shift to nuclear families.

Another resource stress model is Brian Hayden's (1981); he believed that periodic episodes of resource stress caused by climatic conditions affected populations in two ways. First, there was an effort to balance the morbidity/mortality related to stress with the cost of maintaining the population at acceptable levels. Second, people attempted to minimize resource stress through increasing the reliability of exploited resources. This involves technological innovations and causes either an increased diversification of exploitation in poor resource areas or a more specialized exploitation in richer areas.

David Rindos (1984) viewed the transition as the unintended result of a long-term coevolution of plants and humans. He outlined a domestication continuum, the culmination of which is what we typically call Neolithic economies. An important component of his model is that he seemed to exclude human intentionality as a factor, although Watson (1995:32–33) notes that this may not have been his actual intent. She believes that Rindos simply was emphasizing that agriculture could not have been consciously "invented" by any specific group. That is, it is doubtful that people in the process of domesticating plants and animals realized that they were doing so.

Richard Redding (1988) offered a thoughtful and elegant model for the origins of food production that develops a universal generalization of the broad-spectrum argument. He used a Darwinian evolutionary paradigm stressing the importance of population growth as a factor conducive to food production. His explanation relied on an interaction of population growth and fluctuations in food resources. Redding assumed that local hunter/gatherer populations grew and stressed their resource bases, thereby forcing groups to adopt tactics to cope with stress. He viewed these tactics in evolutionary terms consisting of four stages. The first relates to mechanisms for alleviating stress in the form of population regulation, emigration, and mobility. The second stage involves diversification of the resource base, while the third relates to storage. The fourth stage is plant and animal domestication. Each stage builds successively upon earlier stages.

Redding argued that as populations grew, behaviors that limited reproduction became advantageous or a change in subsistence strategies to food production occurred. The former would occur when fluctuations in resources were predictable, less frequent, and less severe. Food production, on the other hand, would be favored in areas in which fluctuations were less predictable, more frequent, and more severe (Redding 1988:83). In this sense, his argument, as applied to the Near East at least, involves some degree of climatic instability.

Other population stress models with broad applicability typically argue that populations increased to levels that exceeded wild food resources. One example is Cohen's (1977) model, using aspects of Boserup's (1965) land depletion ideas. He argued that population growth forced the adoption of alternative subsistence strategies, and ultimately agriculture. He viewed this as a somewhat inevitable consequence of the human condition. Additional demographic stress models included Hassan (1981), Smith (1976), and Smith and Cuyler Young (1983), and each offered unique approaches toward attempting to explain why people chose, or were forced, to domesticate plants and animals.

Rosenberg (1998) recently updated the population pressure model. He proposes that the primary advantage of sedentism is increased access to the most productive portions of a territory in the context of increasing competition. He argues that population and resource imbalances derive from the inherent tendency of populations to grow, as first noted by Malthus. Rosenberg presents a thoughtful model based on evolutionary processes. Yet the lack of consensus among contemporary scholars points to the complexity of such models, as can be gauged by the range of comments that were published in concert with his paper.

Most demographic models in one way or another focused on ecological aspects of the transition. Rarely were purely social considerations given direct attention. As processual archaeology advanced, however, some scholars proposed models not related to demographic or environmental stress. For example, Bender (1978) emphasized social variables. She suggested that the success of food production was the ability of select individuals to accumulate food surpluses and transform these into valued items. Bender felt that social changes acted independent of technology and economy to create pressures on production.

Another social theory falls under the rubric of competitive feasting based on ethnographic "Big Man" rivalry. This model views food as power and has been characterized, both by proponents (Hayden 1995:282) and critics (Smith 2001:218–221), as a "food fight" model. It has been most

eloquently expressed by Hayden in a series of evolving articles (summarized in 2001, 2003). Whether or not feasting was a driver for the origins
of food production, no one can deny the importance of food in life, past or
present. Somewhat surprisingly, relatively little attention has been given
to the social customs by which Neolithic peoples in the Near East actually
prepared and consumed food (Wright 2000). Given that the Neolithic re-
volved around food in one way or another, it seems somehow appropriate
that feasting be considered as a reason for its origin.

Hayden provides a fascinating alternative to many traditional processual explanations for food production. His central thesis is that some
groups of complex hunters and gatherers were able to create an abundant and stable resource base. Within these groups, highly motivated
individuals used competitive feasting as a means of developing and con-
solidating power. Hayden believes that it was within this context that
the first domestication occurred, with prestige food items being used
by "accumulators" to outclass their rivals. For the Near East, Hayden
(1990:45–47) believes that the accumulator/feasting complex was present
by the Natufian. He argues that the cereals ultimately domesticated were
highly valued due to their carbohydrate content. He also notes another
possibility for the importance of cereals, citing Katz and Voigt (1986):
they were used to produce beer. Alcohol or other intoxicants are central
to many feasting events throughout the world. Hayden argues that this
model does not result in an immediate Neolithic Revolution, largely because it takes time to change existing patterns of sharing food and because the first domesticated foods would have been delicacies that would
be labor-intensive to obtain and would not have been significant parts of
daily nutrition (Hayden 1990:57–62, 1992:13).

The last several years have seen the emergence of a postprocessual
paradigm within archaeology. As with processual archaeology, there is
no one explicit postprocessual model for agricultural origins. In general
terms, though, such approaches have focused on a somewhat fuzzy concept of "human agency," or on what Hodder (1990:20–43) has called
the "domestication of society," with an emphasis on the term *domus*. To
Hodder, the domus not only involves practical activities carried out in the
house, but it also has an abstract meaning in which the use of the house
is a metaphor for social and economic strategies and relations of power.
In such formulations, *domus* is contrasted to *agrios*, or the wild and sav-
age (Hodder 1990:41–45, 86). Other scholars also have concentrated on

the significance of "the house" (see Banning 2003), and many of their deliberations are based on Wilson's *The Domestication of the Human Species* (1988), in which he argues that once people became sedentary, they were "domesticated" and fundamentally changed both social organization and, likely, their psychological perceptions of their worlds. In a similar vein, Tilley (1996), discussing the Scandinavian Neolithic, argues that food domestication occurred due to its social and ideological significance rather than for purely economic reasons. To many postprocessualists, then, the Neolithic was an ideological phenomenon, a new way of thinking in which the primary material manifestations were funerary and ritual monuments (Rowley-Conwy 2004:83, citing several authors).

Perhaps the most significant postprocessually influenced application for the Near Eastern Neolithic is Jacques Cauvin's (2000a) landmark book. He believed that the Neolithic Revolution was one of symbols rather than economics, a religious experience nothing less than the "birth of the gods." Even Hodder (2001) has some issues with this perspective, but it is a valuable one to consider in the overall significance of how and why the Neolithic occurred.

Contemporary models for food production often represent a blend of several theoretical perspectives. For example, Bellwood (2005) has addressed the issue of food production from a global perspective, although most of his work is concerned with the spread of agriculture rather than its origins. He does address origins, however, combining aspects of several explanatory models. He ultimately favors some sort of climatic trigger for its origins. He feels that agriculture could not have occurred anywhere without deliberate planting and a regular annual cycle of cultivation. This, in turn, likely would not have happened without the postglacial amelioration and Holocene stabilization of warm and rainy climates in areas where food production eventually developed (Bellwood 2005:19). He notes, though, that the Holocene climate "was clearly the *ultimate enabler* of early farming, but it was not the *proximate cause*" (Bellwood 2005:20). Bellwood also seems to favor a concept revolving around the idea of "affluent hunter/gatherers" in which economic wealth and feasting combined with a shift toward sedentism, but he notes that this alone was not enough. Maybe affluence was overshadowed by the threat of episodes of environmental stress, specifically the Younger Dryas (see chapter 3) being perhaps associated with experiments in farming. Thus, he notes that a "combined explanation of affluence alternating with mild environmental stress, especially in 'risky' but highly productive early Holocene environments with periodic fluctuation in food supply, is becoming widely favored by many archaeologists today as one explanation for the shift to early agriculture" (Bellwood 2005:24). Bellwood also addresses food production from a perspective that requires neither affluence or stress, but rather focuses on a gradualist and Darwinist view (following Rindos's arguments as well), in which plants are believed to have coevolved with humans.

Of course, theories on why domestication occurred are not restricted solely to anthropologists. Perhaps the most eloquent contemporary spokesperson to address this is Diamond (1997, 2002). He takes an unabashedly geographic explanatory paradigm in examining domestication from a global perspective, noting that this event involved unforeseen consequences in both plant/animal and human behavior. While such an approach inevitably results in errors of detail, Diamond has presented one of the most cogent and sophisticated treatments not only of the origin of food production, but more importantly of its consequences. He suggests that hunter/gatherer behavior began to change at the end of the Pleistocene because of an increasingly unpredictable climate, followed by more stable early Holocene conditions (thereby invoking climatic change as a major factor in domestication). For Diamond, food production ultimately resulted from a constellation of linked developments. First there was a decline in the availability of wild foods, especially animals. Decreases in big-game species, which were hunters' first-choice preys, were brought about by an improvement in hunting skills and/or climatic change. This resulted in an increasing human occupation of available habitats in order to decrease the risk of unpredictability. A second factor is inversely related to the first: there was an increase in the availability of domesticable wild plants, which made steps to domestication more rewarding. Due to variations in food supplies, people began to broaden their diet to second- and third-choice foods (that is, the "broad spectrum revolution" of Flannery). Another variable was the development of technology to collect, process, and store foods. A fourth was the two-way link between the rise in human population densities and the rise in food production — as populations grew, food production became increasingly favored. A final variable is the ongoing competition among human societies such that those with more effective technologies prevailed. By sheer numbers and technological advancements, food producers were able to kill or displace hunter/gatherers. Against this backdrop of gradual change, a trigger may have been late Pleistocene climatic changes in temperature, rainfall, and unpredictability (Diamond 1997: 110–112, 2002:704).

A key component of Diamond's argument relates to geographic variation in areas where domestication arose. He identifies several geographic advantages that allowed the Fertile Crescent to develop early food production (Diamond 1997:134–138). He argues that "early peoples of the Fertile Crescent could quickly assemble a potent and balanced biological package for intensive food production. . . . the crops and animals of the Fertile Crescent's first farmers came to meet humanity's basic economic needs: carbohydrate, protein, fat, clothing, traction, and transport" (Diamond 1997:141–142). He also proposes that in Eurasia the spread of domestication occurred on an east-west axis, being facilitated by the same latitudes that required fewer evolutionary changes in the adaptation of domesticates. Thus, in the Fertile Crescent, once a wild plant had been domesticated, it spread rapidly so that further independent domestication was preempted (Diamond 2002:704–705). While this is an eloquent argument, when one looks at likely sources of domestication in the Near East, some, in fact, occur along the north-south axis of the Levant. Likely what Diamond is referring to, however, is a bigger picture in which domesticates, once they reached Anatolia, spread westward to Europe. As such, his argument is compelling.

Diamond also addresses the expansion of food production. He proposes that agriculture spread in two ways. Less common was for hunters and gatherers outside of agricultural homelands to acquire crops. More common, according to Diamond, was that local hunter/gatherers had no opportunity to acquire crops before they were overrun or replaced by farmers, who expanded out of homelands, "exploiting their demographic, technological, political, and military advantages over the hunter-gatherers" (Diamond 2002:702–703). This argument closely follows Bellwood's, noted earlier. In the Near East, however, it is not strongly supported by archaeological data indicating actual population migrations replacing local, nonagricultural peoples. Likely a more correct version lies between local adoption of agriculture and some degree of population movement.

The thrust of Diamond's arguments relates to the consequences of food production, which he believes have largely shaped the modern world, both for better and for worse. He notes that while advantages exist in food production, such as sedentism and an explosion of technology, there also are dire consequences. A major one is the evolution of epidemic infectious diseases such as smallpox and measles (often transmitted to humans from domestic animals) and the development of so-called crowd-diseases that did not exist prior to agriculture, since they can sustain themselves only in large, dense populations. These diseases often kill their victims quickly; however, those who recover develop a lifelong immunity (Diamond 2002:703–704). In Diamond's arguments, this is exactly what happened with early farmers: they developed immunities, but when they spread into new geographic areas, these diseases took a disastrous toll on indigenous populations.

The spread of agriculture also is addressed by Diamond and Bellwood (2003), who note that the largest movements and replacements of human populations since the end of the last ice age resulted from the geographically uneven rise of food production. Food production conferred enormous advantages to farmers over hunter/gatherers living outside of farming homelands. One of these was that farming provides higher food yield per area; thus, food production can support higher populations. Another advantage is that most hunter/gatherers are mobile, but most farmers are sedentary and can accumulate stored food surpluses, which are necessary for subsequent development. A third advantage is that, as noted above, farmers developed immunities to infectious diseases, whereas hunter/gatherers did not. Diamond and Bellwood note that the study of the expansion of food production by necessity is interdisciplinary in nature. Evidence for pre-Columbian expansions comes from five independent sources: archaeology, records of plant and animal domestication, human skeletal remains, modern human genes (as well as ancient human DNA), and linguistics. Their basic hypothesis is that prehistoric agriculture dispersed hand in hand with human genes and languages (Diamond and Bellwood 2003:597–598).

Near Eastern—Specific Models

Many models for the transition have focused specifically on the Near East, and recent research has been fine-tuned, attempting the difficult marriage of theory with actual supporting evidence. One example is Mc-

Corriston and Hole (1991), who stress environmental factors as critical in understanding the transition. They also incorporate technology, social innovation, anthropogenic processes, and settlement patterns, arguing that at the end of the Pleistocene a strongly seasonal climate emerged with hyper-arid summers that selected for annual species of cereals and legumes. Technology for processing such foods already existed, but the newly emerging long dry season required food storage, which encouraged sedentism. This resulted in a depletion of wild resources within local environments, establishing preconditions for the development of agriculture.

Moore and Hillman (1992) also present a climatically driven model based on a pollen core from Lake Huleh (and supported by pollen cores from elsewhere) and on plant remains from Tel Abu Hureyra in Syria. They argue that the Younger Dryas resulted in a retreat of forest and an increase in steppe. This, in turn, required that the inhabitants of Abu Hureyra (and presumably other sites) modify their plant-gathering strategies. They believe that the stresses induced by the Younger Dryas led to widespread dislocation in settlement patterns. The transition from the Natufian to the Neolithic roughly coincided with the end of the Younger Dryas, and the new Neolithic settlement pattern resulted in fewer sites, but these were located in areas suitable for agriculture. They feel that this was no coincidence and that the disruption set in motion by the Younger Dryas was a powerful incentive to develop new subsistence modes, one of which was the development of agriculture.

Henry (1989:27–55, 2002) has proposed a composite model accommodating environmental, economic, and demographic variables. It is a two-part construction, with the first component resulting in sedentism and the second in domestication. A distinguishing feature of his model is that climatic changes were triggering mechanisms that led to the development of complex foraging and subsequently prompted the adoption of agriculture. He stresses the need for consistently applied archaeological data that can be used as proxy paleodemographic information. These include site density, site area, artifact density, and thickness of deposits.

While other models see populations as being "forced" or "pushed" into agriculture, Henry sees a favorable climatic change as having initially "pulled" Early Natufian populations into intensified harvesting of plants found in the Mediterranean woodlands. It therefore encouraged sedentary lifeways, population growth, and expansion. Subsequently, another climatic change, this time unfavorable, caused a retreat of the Mediterranean zone and an advance of the steppe and desert, creating a situation of declining resources in the face of growing and expanding populations. These conditions overloaded the complex and inherently unstable foraging system of the Natufians. This brought on alternative adaptive responses, as reflected by the Late Natufian. Ultimately, people living around the Mediterranean zone adopted agriculture; those who occupied the more arid and marginal environments returned to a simple foraging pattern. Thus, early Neolithic peoples inherited some 2,000 years of agricultural pre-adaptation from the Natufians, who had already harvested, stored, and processed wild cereals and probably had the requisite knowledge for cultivating them. Initial cereal cultivation would have only supplemented an economy still based upon hunting and gathering. People continued to rely on gazelle as a source of protein, but Henry believes that nutritional stress was probably common in the PPNA and was not alleviated until the domestication of goats and sheep during the PPNB, which also represented a tremendous population expansion.

Finally, Bar-Yosef and his colleagues have been prolific in writing about the Neolithic, proposing variations of models that tend to rely on climatic or environmental changes, coupled with social variables. In so doing, they have marshaled an impressive array of interdisciplinary evidence to provide very cogent arguments. Notably, unlike many scholars who proposed a gradual transition to agriculture, they invoke the concept of punctuated equilibrium, in which the change was relatively rapid, a response to abrupt climatic change (see also Byrd [2005a] for a similar argument for a quick transition in the Near East, but one that occurred during optimal climatic conditions, and Fish and Fish [1991:398–399] for a broader perspective). Essentially, they believe that the development of agriculture involved several threshold events, stressing the coexistence of early farmers with hunter-gatherers. They feel that sedentism was a prerequisite for cereal cultivation, and that both were critical conditions for the emergence of animal husbandry, while at the same time incorporating social aspects relating to property (Bar-Yosef and Meadow 1995:41, 68–69). While environmental changes are powerful influences in their models, they believe that the emergence of food production was "the result of social decisions motivated by the wish to maintain an optimal subsistence strategy for semi-sedentary and sedentary groups" (Bar-Yosef and Belfer-Cohen 2002:62).

Discussion

It is clear that while we may have a general appreciation of the processes involved in the transition to food production, there are several competing models with many questions remaining unanswered. It is unlikely that there ever will be one broad "covering law" theory developed for this complex process, something Flannery (1973:272) noted over three decades ago. Furthermore, his (1973:308) admonition that to "search for 'the first domestic plant' . . . is probably fruitless" is still valid today.

In light of archaeological data accumulated over the past several decades, it is easy to debunk earlier models, which were based on limited fieldwork. In broadest terms, the Oasis-Propinquity model is far too simple for the facts. There is no evidence of drastic or catastrophic climatic changes in the early Neolithic; furthermore, we do not find most early sites in major river valleys and oases (Jericho is an exception). Despite using real archaeological data, Braidwood's Hilly Flanks model also cannot be supported, primarily because the earliest Neolithic sites are not located in the foothills. Another problem is that it is difficult to archaeologically test the concept of human nature and the assumption that domestication is a higher and naturally better mode of life, both implicit in Braidwood's model.

Processual theories have not escaped criticism either. Henry (1989: 3–25) examines many of the broad-spectrum subsistence, population growth/expansion, and resource stress models. He is generally critical of these, demonstrating how they do not fit the archaeological data. For example, while Binford's model offers a plausible explanation for the transition, it is unproven and highly speculative. Archaeological data do not show a population increase in the optimal Mediterranean core area, nor do the first Neolithic villages develop in truly marginal zones. Flannery's Near Eastern model seems more robust, but Henry criticizes the broad-spectrum concept. Although there might have been a broad spectrum of resources available to Natufians, the overwhelming majority of subsistence actually appears to have come from the specialized exploitation of a few species, rather than the opposite. Indeed, an argument can be made that Neolithic economies were in many ways more broad-spectrum. Henry also takes Cohen to task, indicating that the Levantine data simply do not fit his model, and that Cohen's use of relative number of sites as a measure of population change does not work, for a variety of archaeological reasons, such as site size and erosion.

Edwards (1989) also has criticized Flannery's broad-spectrum model. He claims that this model cannot be documented in zooarchaeological data from the Levant, where, according to his analysis, diversified fauna have occurred since the Middle Paleolithic, not just the Epipaleolithic. He thus believes that the broad spectrum model is inappropriate as a general evolutionary phase in the Levant. His methodology, however, as well as his omission of discussion on plant foods, has been cogently questioned by Neeley and Clark (1993).

Social models also have not escaped criticism. Bruce Smith (2001: 218–221) effectively dismantles Hayden's "food fight" theory, viewing it as a "fact-free" model in which "the supremacy of free will and human intentionality . . . [allows] humans [to] create their own domesticates and shape their own destiny" (Smith 2001:219). Finally, postprocessual models likewise often are not in accord with archaeological facts, at least as we perceive them. Thus Cauvin's (2000a) "symbolic revolution" concept has been criticized (e.g., Hodder 2001; Rollefson 2001a). While it may have considerable merit as an intellectual concept, it too is essentially "fact-free," or at least "fact-deprived." It further suffers from an implicit assumption that pre-Neolithic peoples somehow were not quite fully modern in their mental capabilities, a concept out of tune with much current anthropological thought.

While universal agreements do not exist, we now know much more about both the transition to food production and its consequences than we did a mere decade ago. Smith (1995:36–37) notes several technological innovations that have advanced our search for why domestic economies were adopted. These include what he calls "the recovery revolution," representing a concerted interdisciplinary attempt to retrieve appropriate data. Until recently, this has not been as common as might be expected. Smith (1995:37–47) also cites direct dating of organic remains as an important technological innovation. This includes the ability to directly radiocarbon date minute samples, including individual seeds, using accelerator mass spectrometry (AMS). Other technological innovations include the study of the micromorphology of organisms using the scanning electron microscope, better-defined ancient and modern pollen sequences, and the most recent innovation, searching for relationships between domesticates and their wild progenitors at the molecular level, using DNA analyses for genetic "fingerprinting." Indeed, "biomolecular archaeology" (e.g., Jones et al. 1996) holds considerable and exciting promise for future studies. None of this technology comes cheaply. Most archaeological projects operate under restricted budgets, requiring careful selection of specialized techniques. Despite such limitations, however, ever-expanding scientific techniques have gone a long way in bettering our understanding of the complex processes involved in the transition.

Is there, then, any consensus of the characteristics associated with the emergence of agriculture? The simple answer is "no," although some scholars feel that there is a core of recurring traits, as summarized by Hayden (1995:277–280). These include sedentism, storage facilities, high population density, high resource diversity, appropriate harvesting and processing technology, and good potential domesticates. Other factors that may be significant include competition, ownership of production and resource localities, changes in climate or vegetation, and population pressure. But even these cannot be consistently and satisfactorily applied. Trait lists are dangerous, because they tend to become dogmatic.

As just one example of why trait lists likely will never be powerful explanatory devices, consider a cautionary tale, albeit from a case of secondary domestication in the American Southwest. Some of the earliest evidence for domestication occurs in northwestern New Mexico, where domesticates apparently formed a supplemental food resource that did not greatly affect culture until much later in time. That is, there is no evidence for clear sedentism, population pressure, or population density (Simmons 1986), three of the criteria outlined above. This is all the more reason why the search for a universal model may be fruitless.

Conclusions

So, where does this put us? Will we ever be able to pinpoint why people turned to domestic economies? There is no doubt that as both archaeological research expands and new analysis techniques are developed, we will see refined models. Smith (2001:215–218) provides an insightful discussion of the transition and proposes that there are two types of explanations presently in vogue. These are intellectual and scientific. Intellectuals propose grand theories that can lack relevant facts. These scholars use theory from anthropology and other disciplines to build broad explanations that are largely deductive and derivative. Scientists, on the other hand, are lower-level particularists concerned with documenting hard facts at regional and subregional scales. They are empiricists who build solid supporting arguments for their small-scale explanations. This is, of course, a false dichotomy in many respects, and there are several scholars who fall into both categories. Nonetheless, it provides a useful context from which explanations for the transition can be better understood.

While acknowledging the merits of both positions, Smith (2001:221–226) clearly favors the latter, suggesting that appropriate models for the transition fall into what he calls "regional scale between the lines theories." The entry requirements for such models are simple. First, instead of being universal, these models are scaled at regional to subregional levels. Second, what Smith means by "working between the lines" is that a few basic rules of regional-scale data recognition must be followed. This includes evaluating all available and relevant empirical information, both positive and negative. By following these criteria, Smith believes that the potential for future research on both the origins and consequences of food production will be challenging and rewarding.

In light of the above discussion, what theoretical approach does this work take? I profess no specific orientation, preferring to incorporate multiple explanations. Regardless of one's position, however, a careful consideration of verifiable archaeological data must be coupled with sound theoretical reasoning. In this context, I recently asked Brian Hayden if he considered his feasting model postprocessual. He does not. Instead, he prefers to think of it as "advanced processualism" (Brian Hayden, personal communication 2004). This is a term I like. If I had to categorize my position, I would call it the same. I do, however, believe that population pressure and ecological constraints as well as opportunities remain significant variables.

Chapter 3

Environmental Context

The Near East, or Southwest Asia, is a huge area, exceeding 5 million km² (Cressey 1960:3). This region stretches from northeast Africa and Afghanistan, Turkey, and the Arabian coasts, and contains an immense amount of environmental diversity with many different landscapes. Covering the Neolithic of this enormous region exceeds the scope of this book, and as noted in chapter 1, I focus primarily on the Levant. This chapter summarizes the modern Levantine environment and then looks at past environmental conditions during the Neolithic time frame.

The Modern Environment

I define the Levant somewhat broadly, following Colledge's (2001:1) and Bar-Yosef's (1998a) leads, the latter of whom calls it the "Mediterranean Levant." It encompasses the area east of the Mediterranean Sea and is bounded in the north by the Taurus and Zagros mountains. In the northeast, the boundary is the Euphrates River Valley, and in the south and southeast, the Negev, Sinai, and Syro-Arabian deserts. The Levant has a north-south length running some 1,100 km and an east-west width of 250–350 km; it can be subdivided into three general zones. These are the northern Levant, which includes parts of southeastern Turkey and the Euphrates Valley; the central Levant, consisting primarily of Syria and Lebanon; and the southern Levant, which comprises Israel and Jordan (see fig. 1.2). Within this region, there exists a multitude of diverse environments. While these three subdivisions are somewhat arbitrary, they conform to many major developments that occurred during the Neolithic. In addition to the continental Levant, Cyprus is here considered as part of the Levant.

The Levant is longitudinally divided into six general topographic

Table 3.1   Levantine topographic zones, from west to east

Continental shelf*
Coastal plain*
Western hills/mountains
Jordan (Rift) Valley
Jordanian Plateau
Steppe/desert lowlands

Sources: From Henry (1989:57–58); Horowitz (1979:11); and Zohary (1973:4–10).
*Presently underwater, but exposed at various times in the past.

zones, generally running in a north-south direction (table 3.1). Each has different geomorphic, edaphic, climatic, and vegetational attributes, with the richest environments generally in the west. In the central Levant, these features are less clearly defined than they are in the south. In the former, the coastal plain is only partially developed, and in some places mountains slope immediately to the sea, with virtually no coastal zone. Further south, however, the coastal plain broadens, reaching a maximum width of ca. 60 km in the Negev Desert. The northern Levant includes the southern flanks of the Taurus and Zagros Mountains, and the western geography of the north is defined by parallel chains of mountains. The northernmost of these is the Amanus, in the Hatay province of Turkey. To the south are the Ansariyah and Zawiyah ranges, with the Ghab depression between them. The Homs gap separates those ranges from the Lebanon and Anti-Lebanon Mountains, in turn separated by the Beqaa Valley. The Lebanon Mountains run southward to the Sinai plateau and are cut by two valleys, the Esdraelon and Beersheva plains. The highest points are the Lebanon Mountains, peaking at over 3,000 m. The Rift or Jordan Valley is less continuous in the north than in the south. From the Amuq Plain in northern Syria, it runs south alongside the Orontes Valley, across the Homs-Hama Plain to the Beqaa Valley. Beyond this it forms part of the Litani River. To the east of the Jordan Valley are the Anti-Lebanon Mountains, whose eastern faces slope down to the Syrian Desert. Farther south, the Jordan Valley includes the Jordan River, the Dead Sea (the lowest point on earth, at nearly 400 m below sea level), and, even farther south, the Wadi Araba that leads to the Gulf of Aqaba (Akkermans and Schwartz 2003:2–4; Colledge 2001:1).

The coastal zone is covered by sandy-calcareous and alluvial soils and mobile sand dunes (Zohary 1962:10–19, 1973:40–51). The mountain highlands are composed of Jurassic and Cretaceous limestone and sandstone formations. The limestones and dolomites of the Upper Cretaceous strata provide the fertile terra rossa soils of the region. Around Lake Tiberias (or the Sea of Galilee), volcanic lava flows border the lake. These stretch from the Jebel ed-Druz, in southern Syria, southeast across to Saudi Arabia. Fertile alluvial soils border the rivers within the Jordan Valley. To the east of the Jordan Valley, the Syrian Desert is composed of calcareous Eocene and Miocene deposits. In the southern Levant, the Jordan Valley cuts through the Nubo-Arabian crystalline block, consisting of igneous rock overlain by Nubian sandstone. The area around the Dead Sea is composed primarily of saline deposits derived from the ancient Lake Lisan. To the east of the Jordan Valley in this southern region rises the Jordanian (or Trans-Jordanian) Plateau, reaching heights to 1,700 m. The substrata of the plateau are composed of calcareous hammadas, granites, and Nubian sandstone. Further east, the plateau merges into the Syrian and Arabian deserts. Soil development is largely impeded in the steppe and desert regions (Colledge 2001:1).

The climate of much of the Levant is a Mediterranean one, characterized by mild, rainy winters and long, dry, hot summers. Today, two annual patterns of winter storm tracks prevail. The first carries humidity from the Mediterranean Sea to the southern Levant. The second arrives from northern Europe and turns to the northern Levant, leaving the southern portion dry (Bar-Yosef 1998a:160). Although various authors sometimes use slightly different divisions, essentially there are five climatic variants in the Levant associated with four major phytogeographical, or vegetational, zones (table 3.2). The Mediterranean zone in the western Levant is the richest, with more than 100 edible fruits, seeds, leaves, and tubers. Annual precipitation in this zone varies between 350 to 1,200 mm. To the east, precipitation and resource diversity drops significantly. Moisture is an important ecological variable, and the amount of precipitation determines vegetation, which is also affected by the degree of seasonal regularity in moisture distribution (Colledge 2001:2; Zohary 1973:16–18).

A diverse fauna exists in the Levant, or at least used to before modern overhunting. Generally, as with the plant communities, fauna is richest in the Mediterranean zone, and dwindles as one moves east. Although rarely

Table 3.2 Climatic and vegetation characteristics of the Levant

Climatic Variant	Location	Associated Vegetation Zone
Eu-Mediterranean	Coast and western slopes	Eu-Mediterranean
Semicontinental	Interior plains and plateau	Irano-Turanian
Mountain	Northern Levant	Oro-Mediterranean
Saharan	Southern Levant	Saharo-Arabian (Saharo-Sindian)
Xero-tropical	Southern Levant	Sudanian

Sources: From Colledge (2001:1–3, summarizing Zohary [1973:22–28] and Henry [1989:63–64]).

seen today, game animals include three species of gazelle, wild cattle, fallow deer, roe deer, wild boar, wild goat, and ibex (Bar-Yosef 1998a:160–161). The richness of faunal communities in the historical record is well attested to by numerous biblical references to a huge array of creatures, including lions and hippopotami.

The Levant bridges Africa, Asia, and Europe, and at least the coastal zone has at times been colonized by biotic communities indigenous to each of those regions. The pronounced topographic and climatic variations of the Levant also have created environmental refuges for plant and animal relics of earlier periods. As a consequence, the Levant enjoys a remarkably complex mosaic of environmental settings, particularly given that it is dominated by a generally arid climate. Thus, forest, steppe, and desert zones occur adjacent to one another. The distributions of these major biotic communities are easily changed by slight modifications in precipitation and temperature patterns, a pattern that likely also occurred in the past (Henry 1989:57).

Within the Levant, there are two terms used continuously in this work. The first is the *Mediterranean core area*, which refers to the rich ecological zones along the coastal plains and up to the foothills. A second term is used in dual ways in many works. This is the *Levantine Corridor*, and it is important since several significant events affecting the Neolithic occurred within its confines. The broader definition of the Levantine Corridor often is synonymous with the Levant itself; it refers to a corridor linking Africa with the Near East. A second usage of the *Levantine Corridor* is more appropriate to the present work, and it refers to a relatively narrow corridor stretching from the northern Negev and southwest Jordan to southern

Anatolia. Although definitions differ slightly, this corridor essentially is one that includes the Jordan (Rift) Valley and is bordered, to the west, by mountains and to the east by desert (see fig. 1.2).

Cyprus typically is not included within the Levant, but it was part of the Levantine Neolithic world. It covers some 9,550 km² and is the third-largest island in the Mediterranean Sea. It lies about 65 km south of Turkey and 105 km west of Syria and is sometimes visible from high elevations on the mainland. The highest point is Mount Khionistra (Olympus) in the Troodos, at an elevation of 1,950 m. The complex but well-documented geological history of Cyprus indicates that there was no post-Miocene landbridge connecting it with the mainland, and that the island is oceanic in origin. As with the mainland, Cyprus's climate is an arid Mediterranean type. Annual rainfall for the entire island is, on average, about 500 mm. Diversity in topography and microclimates has resulted in an unexpectedly large range of plant communities (Knapp et al. 1994:395; Simmons 1999:6–8).

Although rich in flora, the indigenous fauna is much more impoverished. Most of the species presently on the island were introduced by humans. The most notable prehuman endemic fauna were the Cypriot pygmy hippopotamus and pygmy elephant. There are only ten "indigenous" mammalian species, all presumably introduced by humans. These are the moufflon, fox, hare, rat, shrew, hedgehog, two forms of mice, Persian fallow deer, and wild boar (Boekschoten and Sondaar 1972; Swiny 1988).

Paleoenvironmental Reconstructions

A critical question that has plagued researchers for decades is whether the Neolithic occurred during periods of climatic deterioration or amelioration. This is not an easily resolved issue. Paleoenvironmental and paleoclimatic reconstruction is an immensely complex topic. Many discussions are based on global events and thus may not directly apply to the Near East. Much information is derived from a series of multi-proxy data. Particularly significant have been records of oxygen isotope fluctuations recorded in ice cores and deep sea cores. For example, high-resolution proxy climatic data from Greenland (especially the Greenland Ice Sheet Project 2) and Antarctica ice cores indicate that

climate changes were both rapid and extreme during the terminal Pleistocene and the early Holocene (Alley et al. 2003; Severinghaus and
Brook 1999). Other sources of information include terrestrial vegetation reconstructions based on pollen cores, often from lakes, geomorphological sequences, biogeographic interpretations of fluctuating faunal
spectra, dendrochronology, and faunal, botanical, and pollen data from
archaeological sites (Bar-Yosef 1998a:161). These various techniques
often produce conflicting results and thus must be interpreted judiciously.

Although the modern geomorphology and shorelines of the Levant differ from terminal Pleistocene conditions, overall topography has
changed little over the last 13,000 years (Henry 1989:58). It would, however, be a mistake to use environmental conditions of the modern Levant
as an analogy for the past. Substantial vegetation changes have occurred,
due both to climatic shifts and to humanly caused ecological degradation
that likely started in earnest during the Neolithic. The Near East was not
always the dry place that it is today.

Before the 1980s, Near Eastern environmental syntheses were limited, but now there is much more information, and paleoenvironmental
investigations "begin to reveal an increasingly complex rhythm of climatic
and environmental change, with many more distinct phases and sharp
oscillations discernible. Indeed, the evidence on global climatic change . . .
indicates many and very rapid changes of climate" (Watkins 1998:264).
While an enormous and specialized paleoenvironmental literature exists,
synthetic studies, such as Horowitz's (1979) treatment of the Quaternary
of Israel, are rare. Recent environmental works that cover much of the
Near East include Bar-Yosef and Kra (1994) and Wilkinson's (2003) important study of archaeological landscapes. It is important to remember
that precise dates of paleoclimatic reconstructions must still be viewed
as best estimates, and that conditions were not the same even within the
Near East (cf. Watkins 1998:263).

In general terms, the Levant during the terminal Pleistocene–early
Holocene, from ca. 18,000–9000 BP, consisted of a fluctuating spatial
distribution of an oak-dominated parkland and woodland (that is, the
Mediterranean vegetation zone) that provided a high biomass of available foods. This vegetation belt mostly covered the Mediterranean coastal
plains and hilly ranges, as well as a few oases, and diminished in productivity to the east. Decadal and centennial fluctuations of precipitation,

more so than temperature changes, likely were responsible for the expansion and contraction of vegetation zones. Floral resources were seasonal, with seeds most abundant from April to June and fruits from September to November. Under these conditions, decreasing annual precipitation and shifts in the distribution of rains that diminished yields of wild fruits, seeds, and game animals would have mainly stressed the steppe and desert zones. In contrast, resources in the Mediterranean area would have been more stable (Bar-Yosef 1998a:159–161).

During the terminal Pleistocene, climatic conditions were relatively unstable, and by the early Holocene, several lines of data indicate marked seasonality. This was reflected by a shift from a cold winter/hot summer and perennial rainfall continental pattern to a Mediterranean climate characterized by warm winter/hot summer and seasonal rainfall patterns. In such a regime, annuals outcompete many perennials, and these were a large component of the flora. They included plants that ultimately were domesticated. Prolonged summer aridity and temperatures higher than today's resulted in seasonal stress on several resources (Cooperative Holocene Mapping Project [COHMAP] 1988). At roughly the same time, a series of lakes that had formed on the Jordanian Plateau and wadis east of the Jordan Valley, in the Sinai, and in the Jordan Valley during the terminal Pleistocene either shrank or disappeared completely. This included Lisan Lake in the Jordan Valley, which at various times throughout the Pleistocene expanded and contracted (McCorriston and Hole 1991:47–49, 52). The modern remnants of the Lisan are the Dead Sea and the Sea of Galilee.

The impact of such climatic change cannot be underestimated. Certainly its role on later Near Eastern cultures seems undeniable (e.g., parts of Fagan [2004] and Weiss [2000]). As seen in chapter 2, climatic variations have often been cited as being responsible for Neolithic cultural change. This is important, since the environment forms a formidable backdrop against which cultures must adapt. Many models focus on climate change as a device for stimulating agricultural *origins*, although this is by no means universally agreed upon (e.g., Tchernov [1998], who prefers human agency). Climatic change also is often invoked to explain dramatic cultural change *after* farming and herding had become established economic systems, such as the end of the PPN. The role of climate is a difficult issue to resolve, and it often seems that protagonists feel compelled

Table 3.3 Estimated paleoenvironmental reconstruction

Approximate Dates (BP, uncalibrated)/Event	Conditions	Approximate Cultural Correlate
20,000–14,500 (LGM)	Cold and dry; hilly coastal areas have winter precipitation and forests	Kebaran
14,500–13,500	Precipitation slowly increases	Geometric Kebaran; Mushabian
13,500–13,000	More rapid precipitation increase	Early Natufian
13,000–12,800?	Short cold dry pulse	
11,500	Peak of precipitation	
11,000–10,000 (Younger Dryas)	Cold and dry; retractions of favorable Mediterranean vegetation	Late Natufian; Harifian
10,300	Return of pluvial conditions; very wet in northern Levant and Anatolia, but precipitation in central and southern Levant does not reach previous peak	PPNA
10,000–9000	Increase in precipitation, especially in northern and eastern Near East	
9000–8000	Rainfall higher than present day, but decreasing precipitation toward 8,000	PPNB
7400–7200	Sudden cooling and decrease in rainfall intensity; similar to Younger Dryas?	End of PPN
7200–6000	Generally more favorable than today	PN
6000–onward	Warmer and drier than previously but similar to today	End of PN— post-Neolithic

Sources: Based primarily on Bar-Yosef (1995:518, 1998a:161); Bar-Mathews et al. (1999); and Weiss (2000:75).

to totally support either cultural or climatic causations for major changes. This is unfortunate and can lead to modern versions of environmental determinism, rather than to a more proper understanding of the complex interplay between human societies and the environments in which they live. With that said, let us examine paleoenvironmental reconstructions for the roughly 6,000 years covered in this book (table 3.3), with the realization that not all of the Near East was equally affected by various climatic events, and that various data sets sometimes provide conflicting information.

Natufian (ca. 12,800–10,200 BP)

The early portion of the Epipaleolithic occurred during the Late Glacial Maximum (LGM), a period around 20,000–14,500 years ago, during which it was generally cold and dry, but the coastal regions were forested and had winter precipitation. After 14,500 years ago, however, climatic conditions greatly improved, resulting in an abundance of resources. This was possibly interrupted by another cold and dry, if short (ca. 200 years?) period around 13,000 BP, at the onset of the Allerød-Bølling climatic regime. The Allerød-Bølling (ca. 13,000–12,500 BP) itself, however, represented a marked increase in temperature and rainfall. Such favorable conditions may have provided part of the stimulus for Early Natufian groups to establish some degree of sedentism. Most scholars feel that the emergence of the Late Natufian likely occurred in tandem with the beginning of the Younger Dryas (Bar-Yosef 2002a:130, 2002b:116) (but see Stutz's [2004:27] recent use of calibrated dates suggesting that the Late Natufian in fact emerged prior to the Younger Dryas). The Younger Dryas, dated to ca. 11,000–10,000 BP, was a severe crisis resulting in dramatic cooling and drying in many areas of the Near East. It was followed by a return to a warmer and moister Holocene optimum (Bar-Yosef 1995:517, 1998a:161, 173).

According to Richerson et al. (2001:394), the Younger Dryas climate was significantly more variable than both the preceding Allerød-Bølling and the succeeding Holocene. Its impacts likely were dramatic on both people and the plants that they ultimately cultivated. This event resulted in a contraction of the Mediterranean zone and a reduction in the natural geographic distribution, and thus production of, C3 plants, such as cereals (Bar-Yosef 1998a:168). As such, the Younger Dryas often has been invoked as both forcing Late Natufian populations to return to more mobile lifeways and as having stimulated the Neolithic Revolution by forcing the systematic cultivation of some cereals in the face of reduced availability of these and other resources (e.g., Bar-Yosef 1995:517–519, 1998a:168–169, 174; Hillman et al. 2001; McCorriston and Hole 1991).

These views, however, are not universally embraced. For example, Bottema (2002) notes that wild cereals are not typical Mediterranean plants, and his analyses indicate an increase of cereal-type pollens in the Zagros Mountains and the Levantine lowlands during the Younger Dryas, rather than a decrease. In addition, Grosman and Belfer-Cohen (2002) point out the possibility of warmer and cooler oscillations within the Younger Dryas, and thus they caution against assuming universally adverse conditions. As Watkins (1998:266) notes, "In short, the evidence for the environmental impact of the Younger Dryas is ambivalent: it certainly does not appear to have been uniform, and the impact across the spectrum of plant and animal species also seems to have varied."

PPNA (ca. 10,500–9500 BP)

The deteriorating conditions of the Younger Dryas likely continued into the early PPNA, but best estimates are that much of the period correlates well with the Preboreal warming event around 9500 BP (Severinghaus and Brook 1999). This involved increased annual temperature and rainfall. Recent detailed analyses of a 60,000-year record of speleothems (stable isotopic records obtained from cave deposits) from Soreq Cave in central Israel provide very specific paleoenvironmental data indicating that rainfall was much higher than in the present-day deserts and semi-arid regions of the Levant during much of this time (Bar-Mathews et al. 1997:165–166; Bar-Mathews et al. 1999:166).

Thus, early PPNA village life flourished after rapid climatic improvements following the Younger Dryas. These improvements had human consequences: the food-rich Mediterranean woodland and forest steppe expanded, and there was increased seasonality, with more winter rain and greater summer aridity. The rapid return of wetter conditions also triggered the expansion of lakes and ponds. This presented new opportunities for human populations, since rich, easily exploitable resources became more abundant and widespread.

PPNB and PPNC (ca. 9500–7500 BP)

By ca. 9000 BP, a Mediterranean climatic regime apparently was well established in the Levant (Roberts and Wright 1993:201). Current evidence indicates that the PPNB enjoyed climatic conditions only slightly less favorable than those ushered in during the PPNA. Overall, paleoclimatic data indicate decreasing precipitation starting around 9,000 years ago (Bar-Yosef 1995:518). Along with the precipitation decrease was an apparent increase in temperature, summer humidity, and summer-intense rainfall, unlike the pattern today (Banning 1998:200; Rossignol-Strick 1993). Thus, in some areas a significant amount of summer rainfall likely would have increased grazing opportunities, especially in the semi-arid zones. This, however, likely would not have had too much of an effect on the growth of winter cereals important to PPNB peoples (Bar-Yosef and Meadow 1995:45). Landform changes are important to consider as well. At the onset of the Holocene, the coastal plain was still considerably larger than at present. A gradual rise in sea levels after the LGM until the mid-Holocene reduced the flat sandy coastal plain to a stretch 5–20 km wide and 500 km long (Bar-Yosef 1998a:161). By 8700 BP, however, the sea was still some 20 m below present levels. It was not until the Chalcolithic that levels approached their modern configuration (Kuijt and Goring-Morris 2002:365).

Soreq Cave speleothems provide more specific detail. They indicate that ca. 7,000–10,000 years ago, rainfall was 675–950 mm, nearly twice that of the present. These data are corroborated by other environmental information for high precipitation, suggesting that the Dead Sea rose to its maximum level and that there was a large population of freshwater fauna in lakes in Israel. Rainfall may have been heavy throughout the year, rather than on a seasonal (or monsoonal) basis. Such large volumes often resulted in flooding, causing either the removal of soil cover or a failure of rainwater to stay in the soil long enough to dissolve significant amounts of soil CO_2. These same data, however, also suggest a brief arid and cooling event, with a simultaneous decrease in rainfall intensity, at around 8,000–8,200 years ago (Bar-Mathews et al. 1997:165–166, 1999:91).

This latter event is critical, since some believe that it roughly corresponds to the end of the PPN and the beginning of the PN. There are, however, chronological concerns relating to calibration that confuse the issue. The 8,000–8,200 span represents calendar years. Converted to un-calibrated dates, often used by archaeologists in the Near East (and pri-marily used in this book), the arid and cooling event occurred 7400–7200 BP (see additional discussion in chapter 7). The speleothem data are sup-ported by other lines of evidence suggesting a brief but severe deterio-ration at around 8,000 calendar years ago that are along the magnitude of the Younger Dryas. These include the GISP2 ice core studies; pollen cores in Greece, Turkey, and the Levant; Negev snail isotope variability; low Dead Sea levels; and geochemistry from Lake Van. The result was relatively abrupt aridification in many parts of the world, including the Near East (Bar-Yosef and Bar-Yosef Mayer 2002:362; Weiss 2000:75–76, and citations therein). Direct archaeological data to corroborate this scenario are limited, but archaeobotanical information from PPNC Atlit-Yam also indicate colder (but more humid) conditions around 7500 BP (Kislev et al. 2004).

PN (ca. 8000/7500–6000 BP)

There are limited paleoenvironmental data for the PN. Certainly conditions improved after the crisis described above. It appears that early in the PN, temperature and summer humidity may have dropped (Rossignol-Strick 1993). In general, climatic conditions during the PN were somewhat more favorable than today's regime. This would mean that there were more perennial sources of water and that woodlands were more extensive than today. Remnants of Pleistocene lakes, however, were likely shrinking in some areas. Speleothem and other data indicate that from ca. 6000 BP onward, climatic and temperature conditions were warmer and drier than earlier time periods, and were similar to today's. There were, however, some short variations, indicating the instability of the Mediterranean climate during the Holocene (Bar-Mathews et al. 1997: 166; Bar-Mathews et al. 1999:91).

Cyprus

Comprehensive paleoenvironmental analyses for Cyprus are limited (summarized by Simmons 1999:11–14). Hence, we must assume that the overall pattern observed on the mainland also pertained to the island. A critical issue relating to the colonization of Cyprus is that of shoreline reconstructions in relation to sea-level changes. Most researchers believe that the main postglacial rises in sea level occurred around 15,000/14,000 and 9,000 years ago, but there is no direct evidence for the period when the island was initially occupied, around 12,000 years ago. The assumption, however, is of a lower sea level, and thus a slightly greater land mass and decreased distance from the mainland. By ca. 5000 BP, the present configuration had been reached.

For terrestrial reconstruction, historical information suggests an island greatly different from today's. Modern Cyprus consists of a severely eroded landscape, largely culturally induced by overgrazing and overcultivation. If the comments of Eratosthenes (275–195 BC) are to be believed, however, much of Cyprus was heavily forested in antiquity. The nature of this climax vegetation probably was oak-pine Mediterranean woodland, and thus it is likely that this characterized the Neolithic (Simmons 1999:12). Of potential domesticates, only wild barley is native to the island and had not been found at any archaeological site until investigations at Parekklisha *Shillourokambos* (Wilcox 2003:234). Thus, the domesticated plants and animals in Neolithic contexts on the island were most certainly imported from the mainland.

Conclusions

The Near East is a remarkably varied landscape, and even though the Levant represents only a portion of this vast region, it too exhibits incredible diversity. Much of the Near East today is environmentally degraded, but 10,000 years ago it was a substantially different land. The end of the Pleistocene and the beginning of the Holocene represents a time of dramatic climatic and temperature fluctuations, resulting in the expansion and contraction of favorable environments suitable for early farming. Many of these changes occurred rapidly and would have had human consequences over generations.

We noted earlier that a critical question to ask of the Neolithic Revolution is whether it occurred during a time of climatic optimum or stress. There is no easy answer to this, but Byrd (2005a:241–244), mustering an impressive array of paleoclimatic data with calibrated radiocarbon determinations, makes a strong case that both sedentism and village life occurred in resource-rich areas under optimal conditions. Based on presently available data, it does appear that the first experimentations with sedentary living, but not agriculture, started during the Early Natufian under optimal environmental conditions. The dramatic cooling and drying of the Younger Dryas may be partially linked to the general dispersal of many Late Natufian groups to a more mobile settlement pattern. During the PPN, however, when the domestication of both plants and animals occurred, environmental conditions were optimal, often better than those prevailing today. Around 8,000 calendar years ago, another short but dramatic cooling and drying phase took place. By approximately 7,000 years ago, during the PN, environmental conditions approximated those of today.

In short, the climate provides an important context for human adaptations, giving a range of choices as well as constraints. Alone, though, it was unlikely to have determined the course of human action. Bar-Yosef (1995:519–520) believes that "the effects of the rapid environmental fluctuations during the terminal Pleistocene triggered the socioeconomic responses of the Neolithic Revolution." On the other hand, Watkins (1998:266), commenting on the adoption of cultivation during the improved conditions following the Younger Dryas, wonders, "Why is this happening at a time of improving natural conditions and greater availability of the preferred food plants?" Both perspectives likely have considerable merit.

Case Study I   **Neolithic Cobble Layers**

A major settlement disruption occurred at the end of the PPN, around 7500 BP (or ca. 8,250 calendar years ago). There is considerable discussion of whether the primary drivers of this event were humanly induced or climatic. As we have seen, throughout the PPN an overall favorable climatic regime dominated. There also is evidence, based on general circulation models of the atmosphere, that the Indian Ocean monsoonal system penetrated portions of the southern Levant from ca. 10,200 to 8,000 years ago, resulting in intense summer rainfall, and then receded, resulting in drought conditions at approximately the time of the PPN's demise, or shortly thereafter (cf. COHMAP 1988; Kutzbach and Guetter 1986; Kutzbach et al. 1993; Street and Grove 1979).

3.1 Cobble layers at Wadi Shuʿeib, Jordan. Cobbles are visible above and below a plastered floor being pointed out by geomorphologist Rolfe Mandel.

Note that the Soreq Cave data also suggest drier conditions around 8,000 years ago.

Actual evidence for this monsoonal incursion is scant but tantalizing. It comes from several Jordanian hillside villages with indications of slope instability, which appears as fine-grained colluvium and slopewash interlayered with cultural debris. Most dramatic are data from sites such as ʿAin Ghazal and Wadi Shuʿeib, which contain both PPN and PN components, as well as settlements containing only PN components, such as Abu Thawwab, where we have observed densely packed layers of comparatively well-sorted cobbles in the deposits (fig. 3.1). Such deposits also may be present at Basta and other Neolithic settlements. These occur stratigraphically between the PPN and PN levels at ʿAin Ghazal and Wadi Shuʿeib (Simmons and Mandel 1988).

During excavation, we were perplexed as to the meaning of these layers, which seemed to cover large areas of the sites. One interpretation was that they were intentionally laid down as a sort of foundation for construction, although this was not a satisfying conclusion, since many of the cobbles occurred within structures, not underneath them. As an alternate interpretation, my late colleague Jonathan Davis proposed a model based on regional archaeological, climatic, and geological data. We suggested that the cobbles were the physical manifestation of the increased monsoonal pattern. That is, they were evidence for erosion and could be attributed to debris flow caused by torrential thunderstorms, thereby constituting plausible evidence of an early Holocene monsoonal incursion into the Levant.

We suggested that in their zeal to increase arable land and obtain fuel and building materials, Neolithic people cut down the very vegetation that previously had served as a retardant to erosion. Without the vegetation, there was no resistance to more active slopewash activated by strong summer rains. Increased precipitation throughout the PPN had a cumulative effect, washing large layers of colluvial cobbles onto sites. Although precipitation likely decreased by around 7400 BP, the damage had been done.

The cobble layers thus represent concrete geoarchaeological evidence for humanly induced environmental degradation in conjunction with heavy summer precipitation. This occurred against a backdrop of deteriorating climatic conditions. The combination of drought, preceded by the impacts of expanded human population, intensive agriculture and herding, and deforestation, together caused an environmental crisis that likely contributed to the collapse of the PPN and, in one way or another, has dominated human adaptation in the region ever since (Davis et al. 1990).

Not everyone agreed with this interpretation, and documentation of these layers in other sites located in different regions is needed, as is a better understanding of the extent and timing of the rains. Unfortunately, Jonathan's untimely death precluded his continuation of this study, but the model he proposed, while speculative, remains an excellent example of interdisciplinary collaboration in modern archaeology. Even more importantly, it shows that relying solely on climatic or human reasons for environmental degradation is too simplistic, and that a more realistic scenario is one in which a complex interplay of both components results in a particular outcome.

Chapter 4

The Natufian

The First Villagers? — Small Steps with Big Consequences

A prerequisite for investigating the origin of the Neolithic Revolution . . . is to review the archaeological evidence from the Natufian culture and its contemporary entities.
(Bar-Yosef 2002a:132–33)

Overview

The Near Eastern Neolithic had to start somewhere. Most scholars place this threshold as occurring during the Natufian. While explaining the precise *why* of the Neolithic Revolution is elusive, we do know that at the end of the last ice age, there was a tremendous amount of diversity in the Near Eastern archaeological record. The period between the Upper Paleolithic and the Neolithic is conventionally designated as the Epipaleolithic, which began around 20,000 years ago and ended about 10,000 years ago. There is considerable disagreement on many aspects of the end of the Epipaleolithic, which includes the Natufian. Indeed, in one of the most comprehensive works yet published (Bar-Yosef and Valla 1991), the concluding chapter (Perlès and Phillips 1991:637) poses the question: "What is the Natufian?" There is, however, general consensus that the Natufian set the stage for the "bumpy ride" to the Neolithic (Bar-Yosef and Belfer-Cohen 2000).

It was during the Natufian that something pretty close to villages was established in parts of the Near East. Years of research on the origins of food production have often posed a "chicken and egg" question: what came first, sedentism or domestication? The answer to this question is variable, and it appears to be regionally specific, even when comparing generally similar arid environments, as the Fishes (Fish and Fish 1991) did for the Near East and the American Southwest. In the Near East, however, the issue seems resolved. During the Natufian, there is evidence for some degree of sedentism without major plant or animal domestication.

Before the Natufian—An Overview of Early and Middle Epipaleolithic Cultures

Several Epipaleolithic entities, including the Natufian, were initially defined in the early part of the previous century. Near Eastern archaeology was in many ways in its formative years, and emphasis was on the remains of biblical and classical antiquity. Prehistory was at best considered a poor stepchild, and in retrospect it is amazing to realize just how significant the early contributions were. This is particularly true considering that many of the early prehistorians were also "men of the cloth," and many people questioned a prebiblical human history. It is even more remarkable that several others of these pioneers were women, working in the Near East at a time when professional women were rare (e.g., Davies and Charles 1999; Wallach 1999). One of these women scholars was Dorothy Garrod, whom we can thank for the discovery and definition of the Natufian.

It is impossible to consider the Natufian without at least a brief understanding of other Epipaleolithic entities. The systematic study of the Epipaleolithic did not occur until after World War I, when several investigations documented a bewildering array of "cultures." Sites fell into what was a developing classification system for the Levant, known as the "Upper Paleolithic Stage VI," or the Kebaran (Goring-Morris 1998:141). These industries often were defined by detailed analyses of the hallmark artifacts for the Epipaleolithic: the "microliths," tools manufactured on diminutive bladelets (small blades usually less than 12 mm in width). These tiny tools, as well as the bladelet core technology associated with them, exhibit considerable temporal and regional variability.

Over the past several decades, research on the Epipaleolithic, especially in the southern Levant, has accelerated (Goring-Morris 1998). While much early research was confined to the Mediterranean coastal region, since the 1960s investigations have focused on more environmentally peripheral areas to the east. This has resulted in a huge mass of primary data of over 700 distinct assemblages. While this is an impressive database, the conceptual framework for dealing with it has not kept pace, often leading to a plethora of confusing terms. Goring-Morris (1998) divides the Levantine Epipaleolithic into three periods: Early, Middle, and Late Epipaleolithic, with the Late Epipaleolithic encompassing the Natufian. The chronological framework is anchored by over 250 radio-carbon determinations.

Subsistence-related information is crucial to understanding what led up to the Neolithic. Such data from Epipaleolithic sites have been sporadic, although an overall broad-spectrum pattern is indicated. Available data indicate that plant foods were increasingly more important than animal resources, but this conclusion is tempered by a lack of paleobotanical data. Newer techniques and concerted recovery efforts, however, have now given us better insight into plant use during the Epipaleolithic. In particular, the Early Epipaleolithic site of Ohalo II in the Jordan Valley near the Sea of Galilee (Nadel and Hershkovitz 1991) has documented 40 plant species, including large quantities of cereals, especially wild barley, and wild edible fruits. Analysis of starch grains has provided direct evidence that the barley, and possibly wild wheat, was processed and baked (Piperno et al. 2004). Paleobotanical remains in less abundance also have been recovered from other Epipaleolithic sites, indicating that Epipaleolithic peoples consumed a wide variety of seeds, nuts, berries, tubers, and rhizomes (Goring-Morris 1998:144).

Fauna are better preserved; thus, we know more about the animal portion of Epipaleolithic diets. Locally available animals were the most common species consumed. In the mountainous northern Levant, these included fallow deer, while mountain gazelle were common in the rest of the Mediterranean zone. Dorcas gazelle and ibex were hunted in the more arid zones, and goitered gazelle and wild ass on the eastern steppes. Less common were other large mammals, such as aurochs, hartebeest, and wild boar. Smaller animals included hare, fox, reptiles, tortoise, lizards, and birds (Goring-Morris 1998:144–146).

The wide range of chipped-stone variability that has allowed the definition of distinctive, often regional, groups, and the rapid pace of change in these elements reflect the interactions of small hunter-gatherer bands on the landscape. In addition to chipped stone, ground stone assumes an increasingly important role, suggesting increased processing of many of the wild plant resources referred to above. Although Epipaleolithic peoples were mobile hunters and gatherers, there is evidence for flimsy structures at some sites (Goring-Morris 1998: 153, 158; Nadel and Werker 1999), indicating at least some degree of permanence.

Epipaleolithic groups likely readjusted specific adaptations to changing physical conditions (Goring-Morris 1998: 166), although nonenvironmental factors also may have played a role. In areas with a wide array of resources, such as the coastal regions and some parts of the eastern steppes, their settlement pattern seems to reflect less mobility, shorter travel distances to resources, and larger populations. In more marginal areas, populations are inferred to have been smaller, and settlement indicates increased mobility. Many site locations reflect optimized areas that could target resources from a variety of zones. In short, Epipaleolithic peoples appear to reflect the full spectrum from forager to collector-type adaptations (cf. Binford 1980).

There are a variety of roughly contemporaneous Epipaleolithic entities outside of the Levant, although they are generally poorly documented. These groups stretch from Anatolia (e.g., Arsebük 1998:74) to the Zagros region of Iraq, especially as reflected in the Zarzian culture (Olszewski 1993a). Their rarity may be more apparent than real, simply reflecting a lack of archaeological research, due to either political instability or research priorities on other cultural periods.

The Natufian

History of Research and Terminology

Garrod (1932, 1957) first defined the Natufian near the Mediterranean coast at Shukba Cave in the Wadi en-Natuf and at Mugharet el-Wad in the Mount Carmel area. Additional investigations in Palestine in the 1920s and 1930s by Turville-Petre (1932) at Kebarah Cave, Neuville (1934, 1951) in the Judean Desert, and Rust (1950: 119–121) in western Syria confirmed the distinct character of the Natufian. By the 1950s and 1960s, sites were documented within an expanding geographic area, with most substantial sites occurring within the relatively lush western flank of the Levantine Corridor (Byrd 1989a:161–163). What made the Natufian stand out was Garrod's proposition that they represented the earliest farmers, or the "Mesolithic with agriculture" (1957:216, 226). Since its early documentation, continuing research has defined the Natufian more thoroughly (e.g., Bar-Yosef 1998a, 2002a, b; Belfer-Cohen 1991a; Byrd 1989a; Valla 1998). The two most comprehensive treatments of the Natufian are Bar-Yosef and Valla (1991) and Delage (2004), which represents a much-needed update. Unfortunately, this volume became available only during my final editing, so it cannot be thoroughly incorporated here. From a quick scan, however, Delage (2004) represents some of the most contemporary thoughts on the Natufian, with an emphasis on economic (especially faunal) aspects.

Chronology

There are over a hundred radiometric dates for the Natufian and related entities (Byrd 1984, 1989a; Goring-Morris 1998:144), although many sites are chronologically placed based upon typological or technological considerations. Overall criteria for placing the Natufian within a chronological context vary, often due to different approaches taken by scholars. Thus, within the comprehensive Maison de l'Orient (Lyon) chronology, the Natufian is not dated separately but falls within Period 1, which it shares with other entities, and dates to approximately 12,000 to 10,300 BP (Cauvin 2000a: xvii—xviii, 16, fig. 2). Likewise, Moore et al. (2000:7) adopt a neutral approach, in which the Natufian and other "cultures" fall into "Epipaleolithic 2," dated to ca. 12,500–10,000 BP. Other chronological schemes have slightly different dates, but most researchers are comfortable with placing the Natufian within the span of approximately 12,800 to 10,200 BP (ca. 15,000–12,000 cal. BP) (Bar-Yosef 1998a; Goring-Morris and Belfer-Cohen 1998; Valla 1998). Thus, in most schemes, the Natufian spans a period of some 2,500 or more years.

It is more difficult to place absolute dates on Natufian subdivisions. Indeed, there is some disagreement upon the phases themselves. Some split the Natufian into Early and Late phases, while others further include a short Final Natufian phase (Valla 1998). Comprehensive lists of dates by phase are provided by Byrd (1989a:164–165). Approximate dates for the Early Natufian are 12,800–11,250 BP, followed by the Late Natufian at 11,250–10,500 BP, and the Final Natufian at 10,500–10,200 BP. Stutz's (2004) detailed treatment of calibrated radiocarbon dates in the aforementioned Delage volume presents a slightly different chronology, with the southern Levantine Natufian dating to ca. 13,000–11,500 BP, and the Late Natufian to ca. 11,500–10,000 BP (both presented here in uncalibrated years).

Geographic Range

The Natufian was initially defined within the relatively restricted Mount Carmel–Galilee region. This resource-rich woodland belt where oak and pistachio were dominant species has frequently been referred to as the Natufian "homeland" (e.g., Bar-Yosef 1998a:162). We now know that it was much more widespread, especially during the Late Natufian (fig. 4.1). The greatest density of sites appears to be in northern and central Israel and northern Jordan, within the preferred oak and pistachio belts, which at the time likely stretched from the Middle Euphrates, through the Damascus basin into the Galilee–Judean Hills, and along the Jordan Plateau. The high mountains of Lebanon, the Anti-Lebanon Mountains, the arid areas of the Negev, and the peripheral desertic zone of the Syro-Arabian desert were marginal for Natufians, although sites do occur there. Early Natufians sporadically spread to the Irano-Turanian zone, and only in the Late Natufian were large settlements established in this belt. Smaller ephemeral sites are found in desert environments throughout the region (see various contributions in Bar-Yosef and Valla 1991).

Some researchers prefer not to use the term *Natufian* outside of the core zone and the southern Levant. For example, the impressive site of Abu Hureyra along the Middle Euphrates in Syria is not classified as Natufian by its excavators (Moore 1991:286–291, 2000b:184). Others, however, consider the early components of large Middle Euphrates valley settlements, including Abu Hureyra 1, as Natufian (e.g., Bar-Yosef 1998a; Cauvin 2000a:16, fig. 2). Likewise, whether the Natufian extends to Turkey is largely based on semantic arguments, further hampered by a general lack of Epipaleolithic research in Anatolia (M. Özdoğan 1999:226–227). Sites such as Beldibi and Delbasi on the south coast of Turkey, for example, share some general artifactual similarities with Abu Hureyra 1 (Moore 2000a:183–184). Another Turkish site is the "proto-Neolithic" settlement of Hallan Çemi, some 300 km northeast of Abu Hureyra. It was occupied during the last few hundred years of the eleventh millen-

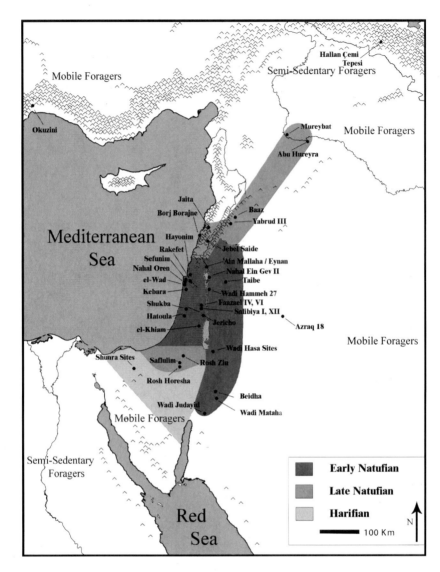

4.1 Map of selected Natufian sites. Modified from a map courtesy of Ofer Bar-Yosef.

nium BP, and, although its excavators make no claim that it is Natufian, seeing instead similarities to Iraqi cultures (Rosenberg 1999:29–30), it is roughly contemporary. Hallan Çemi, while small, contains architecture and evidence for social complexity (Rosenberg and Redding 2000).

Turning to the eastern portion of the Near East in Iran and Iraq, the term *Natufian* is ambiguous. For example, in Mellaart's early summary, he notes that in the Zagros region the Epipaleolithic Zarzian culture is followed by an approximate equivalent to the Natufian, the Zawi Chemi Shanidar phase, sometimes also known as the Karim Shahirian phase (Mellaart 1975:70). Another term that has been used for some time is *proto-Neolithic*, which is still favored by Solecki et al. (2004), who consider both the Zagros Proto-Neolithic and the Natufian as regional variants of the same broad Near Eastern tradition. This view is also advocated by Aurenche and Kozłowski (1999:31–32), who propose two large geographic zones, the Natufian in the Levant and the Zarzian in the Zagros. They favor subdividing the Zarzian into two variants, a western Zarzi and Zawi Chemi entity and an eastern Warwasi entity. They also identify a higher-elevation group north of the Zagros as the Trialetian, a very poorly documented component of a larger "Eastern Wing of the Fertile Crescent" (Kozłowski 1999).

Thus, there is a considerable geographic spread outside of the southern Levant of sites that are at least "Natufian-like." Bar-Yosef and Meadow (1995:56, fig. 3.3) map out socioeconomic entities that include both a restricted Early and an expanded Late Natufian occupation of the Levant surrounded to the south by the Harifian (a desert Natufian variant), to the immediate north and northwest by sedentary hunter-gatherers, and to the east, northeast, and northwest by mobile hunter-gatherers. While not all will agree with this model, it does provide a coherent framework.

Material Culture — Artifacts

Natufian material culture is extremely varied and rich. Its chipped stone reflects a strong microlithic industry, and these artifacts occur in remarkably high densities at many sites (Bar-Yosef 1983). Arguments on the significance of chipped stone during the Natufian (as well as the Neolithic) are immensely complex and often esoteric. Most modern studies, however, emphasize a *chaîne opératoire* (or reduction strategy) methodology. The end of the Natufian and the beginning of the Neolithic is often viewed as a major break in many aspects of the material culture. While this may be so in some perspectives, within chipped stone it is less true. Belfer-Cohen and Goring-Morris (1996) present compelling arguments that many perceived distinctions are likely due to differences in techno-typological analytical systems used by various researchers. They propose that there is considerable evidence for continuity from the Natufian to the PPNA, with differences being more of degree than of kind. They further argue that the major break occurs between the PPNA and the PPNB.

Principal Natufian "indicator fossils" are geometric microliths known as lunates. A specialized method to segment bladelets, called the "microburin technique," combined with a specific type of bifacial retouch known as Helwan to form tools, also is distinctive (Byrd 1989a:161). The frequency of the microburin technique has been used to divide the Natufian into both chronological and regional categories (Bar-Yosef 1998a:164). Alternatively, it has been suggested that this technique may reflect stylistic attributes differentiating between various social groups (Bar-Yosef and Belfer-Cohen 1989a:468). The size and type of retouch on lunates (Helwan vs. backing) also has been used to place Natufian assemblages within time and space contexts. The average length of lunates has been used as a chronological marker (Valla 1984) as well as a geographic one (Olszewski 1986).

Other tools, both microlithic and larger, also characterize Natufian assemblages. These include triangles, burins, perforators, end scrapers, core scrapers, picks, choppers, and backed bladelets and blades, some of which display sickle polish (Byrd 1989a:161). Some of these, such as picks and sickles (or "glossed pieces"), are specialized tools making their first appearance during the Natufian (Bar-Yosef 1998a:164). Extensively reduced cores are common, resulting in high frequencies of flakes along with small, broad, and short bladelets (Bar-Yosef 1998a:164). Microlithic tools usually account for 40 percent or more of assemblages (Bar-Yosef 1998a:164), and many were most likely used as composite tools, hafted into bone or wood shafts. Most of the raw material used in chipped stone manufacture was relatively local, although Anatolian obsidian is occasionally found (Bar-Yosef 1998a:165).

Of particular significance is the issue of projectile points, which are some of the most diagnostic artifacts of the subsequent Neolithic. These are absent during the Natufian, at least as distinct aerodynamically shaped and typologically identifiable entities (Belfer-Cohen and Goring-Morris 1996:223). Reasonable arguments, however, have been made that a variety of microlithic tools could have served the same function as projectile points (Anderson-Gerfaud 1983; Olszewski 1993b; Peterson 1998; Valla 1987). It is only during the contemporary Harifian phase in the Negev Desert that "proper" points occur (Harifian points) (Belfer-Cohen and Goring-Morris 1996:223).

Specific frequencies of tools may indicate regional traditions and functional and chronological differences (Belfer-Cohen and Goring-Morris 1996). Chronologically, the Early Natufian geometrics include Helwan and backed lunates, trapeze-rectangles, and triangles. By the Late Natufian, backed lunates generally dominate (Bar-Yosef 1998a:164 and citations therein). Sickle blades usually are relatively more common in the Early Natufian, and decline in the Late and Final Natufian. In the Negev, however, sickle blades first appear in the Early Natufian and become more common in the Late Natufian, declining in the Harifian. Sickle blade size also may have some chronological significance, increasing in length over time. Perforators are present only in small quantities throughout the Natufian (Belfer-Cohen and Goring-Morris 1996:223). Overall, typological variability within microliths is greater in the Early Natufian than it is in the Late Natufian (Bar-Yosef and Belfer-Cohen 1989a:470).

Regionally, frequencies of tools appear to change according to location. For example, in the Galilee and Carmel area burins are important, while in the Judean Hills–lower Jordan Valley, their frequencies are more moderate, and in the Negev they are even less common. Sickle blades are primarily found in the central Levant. Other tool types, such as retouched notches and denticulates, as well as borers and awls, are found in nearly every Natufian assemblage (Bar-Yosef and Belfer-Cohen 1989a:470).

There are, of course, other Natufian artifacts beyond chipped stone. Of these, ground stone is especially significant, particularly regarding economic parameters and implications for sedentism. The presence of these presumed agriculturally related tools, along with sickle blades, is one reason that early researchers proposed that the Natufians were the first farmers (Garrod 1932:236, 268; Neuville 1934:254), even though direct paleobotanical data were lacking. Of all the Epipaleolithic complexes, ground stone from the Natufian is the most diverse and elaborate, often occurring in large numbers, especially at larger sites (Henry 1989:195). These include a large variety of portable and not-so-portable items, such as rough fixed bedrock mortars, other mortars, a variety of bowls, cupholes, mullers, robust and delicate pestles, miniature vessels, possible serving vessels, whetstones, flat querns, heavy-duty scrapers, shaft straighteners, grooved stones, incised stones, hammerstones, and a unique type of deep mortar that is often hollowed through, referred to as "stone pipes." In addition to "built-in" bedrock mortars, other mortars often are large, exceeding 60 cm in height. The ground stone is usually manufactured on limestones, basalts, and sandstones, some of which might have had to have come from a considerable distance. Most assemblages are strikingly similar in composition, type frequencies, shapes, and styles (Bar-Yosef and Belfer-Cohen 1989a:470; Byrd 1989b:161; Valla 1998:169–171; Wright 2000:92–93). Shaft straighteners suggest the use of arrows and, thus, bows (Bar-Yosef 1998a:165).

Although many have argued that ground stone was related to various milling activities, not all functions were economic. For example, Dubreuil's (2004) microscopic analysis has shown that Natufian ground stone was used for a variety of purposes, including hide working and mineral grinding as well as food processing. She also observes that Early Natufian ground stone is more varied, while Late Natufian assemblages include more handstones and grinding slabs. Dubreuil attributes this to a greater emphasis on reducing cereal and legumes to smaller particles, allowing for more nutrients to be released.

Many ground stone artifacts also seem to reflect stylistic or artistic efforts. For example, large carved limestone slabs with geometric or meander patterns, which also occur on carved basalt bowls, have been recovered from sites such as Nahal Oren, Hayonim Cave, and Wadi Hammeh 27 (Bar-Yosef 1998a:166 and citations therein). At Hayonim Cave, these are especially abundant and include several "cutting boards" and limestone slabs with incised ladder-pattern motifs. On one large slab, a crude outline of a fish is deeply incised (Belfer-Cohen 1991:574–578). Some of the incised stones, particularly a large limestone block weighing ca. 20 kg, have been interpreted as intentional cumulative markings for seasonal notational indicators (Marshack 1997:73–87).

Many other Natufian artifacts reflect a concern with noneconomic matters, and this is nowhere more clear than in the bone craftsmanship, which Cauvin (2000a:16) compares with the Upper Paleolithic Magdalenian of Europe in its elaboration. Many sites contain bone objects made on bone shafts, teeth, and horn cores. Pointed bone implements are common and may have been used for hide working and basketry. Other bone objects include hunting and fishing tools, such as spearheads or arrows, some barbed, hooks and gorgets, and a variety of artistic representations. Probable sickle handles made either on long bones or ribs are an outstanding type. Some are decorated with animal representations. Personal ornamental artifacts include perforated teeth, sectioned bones, and various beads. Other materials also were used in the manufacture of headgear, pendants, necklaces, belts, bracelets, and earrings and included bone, greenstone, malachite and limestone (Bar-Yosef 1998a:165; Valla 1998:171).

Shells were important. These were primarily worked for ornamental purposes. In particular, dentalium shells were used to produced elongated beads, although other shell types also were worked. Most were of Mediterranean origin, although some freshwater shells were also used (Valla 1998:171–172). More exotic materials also occur, including shells from the Red Sea, a tusk shell at 'Ain Mallaha (also known as Eynan) from the Atlantic Ocean, and a freshwater bivalve from the Nile River (D. Bar-Yosef 1989, 1991).

Portable naturalistic and schematic figurines also are relatively common. These objects are made on bone and limestone. Zoomorphic figurines include tortoise, kneeling gazelles, and possibly a baboon (Bar-Yosef 1998a:167, fig. 7; Noy 1991). Several figurines depict young animals, possibly gazelles. At Nahal Oren, a limestone figurine has an owl at one end and a dog's head at the other. Also recovered was a horn core with a man's head at one end and a bovid's head at the other end. Such a combination of animal and human may be related to similar ideological changes that led to joint dog and human burials (Bar-Yosef 1998a:166; Tchernov and Valla 1997).

Despite this naturalistic art, however, human figurines are rare (Weinstein-Evron and Belfer-Cohen 1993). The exception to this is a limestone figurine from 'Ain Sakhri interpreted as a mating couple (Neuville 1933:558–560; Schmandt-Besserat 1998a:113), although its Natufian context has been questioned (Boyd and Cook 1993). Other objects are interpreted as human phalli and female representations (Schmandt-Besserat 1998a:113; Marshack 1997:75–82). Decorative motifs such as net, chevron, zigzag, and meander patterns occur on many of these. Their presence differs from site to site, and may indicate specific Natufian groups. At present, most such objects occur within the core zone (Bar-Yosef 1998a:166).

In summary, many Natufian sites contain a remarkable array of artifacts. While chipped stone constitutes the largest single artifactual category, an abundance of other items also occurs, especially at larger sites. In addition to purely functional items are artistic representations, all attesting to the richness and complexity of Natufian culture.

Material Culture — Architecture

During the Natufian we see the first evidence for substantial architecture, often with clustered units. This has important implications for sedentism and mobility. Natufian architecture typically is characterized by semisubterranean structures, or pithouses. Foundations or retaining walls often were built of dry stone walls, usually with a circular or semicircular morphology. Sometimes these walls are preserved up to a meter in height. 'Ain Mallaha (Perrot 1966a) contains perhaps the best examples of Natufian architecture. One wall there was refaced with crushed limestone coated with a red pigment, representing one of the earliest examples of the creation of an artificial construction material (Valla 1998:172). Some structures at the site have concentric circles for posts that could have supported a framework for substantial roofs. The upper portions and roofs were likely made of brush and wood, and there is little evidence for the use of mud brick or wattle and daub. Several sites contain similar structures (Bar-Yosef 1998a:163; Cauvin 2000a:15; Valla 1998:172). Structures are most common in Early Natufian sites, although at Abu Hureyra 1, they occur during the equivalent of both Early and Late Natufian (Moore et al. 2000:478).

Most structures are interpreted as domestic units; they were usually 3–6 m in diameter and contained round or square fireplaces. Structures often contain abundant room fill, but the identification of specific floors is difficult: they usually were not plastered but rather were simply packed dirt. One exception is a large (9 m in diameter) structure at 'Ain Mallaha

(House 131) that had a series of postholes preserved and clusters of artifacts on the floor (Bar-Yosef 1998a:163). Houses there were carefully laid out, being aligned along the length of the slope into which they were cut (Valla 1998:172). Not all structures were free-standing individual units or pithouses. At Hayonim Cave, a series of small, connected oval rooms was built inside the cave. Each was approximately 2.5 to 3 m in diameter and built of undressed stones (Bar-Yosef 1998a:163). At Abu Hureyra 1, the first structures are complex, multichambered pit dwellings, followed by aboveground timber-and-reed huts (Moore et al. 2000:478, fig. 14.2), although the precise form of the latter is unclear (Moore 2000a:180). Some pits there were possibly used for storage (Moore 2000b:118). Other possible storage facilities include a paved bin at Hayonim and several plastered pits or silos at 'Ain Mallaha, but overall these occur only sporadically (Bar-Yosef 1998a:163–164).

Does this degree of architectural elaboration mean that some Natufian sites were villages? The answer depends upon how one defines a village. Most sites with architecture contain only a few structures, with a maximum of six (Cauvin 2000a:17). Regardless of specific definitions, the solidity of Natufian construction and the fact that structures are often grouped together in small clusters suggests that they required more planning than preceding Epipaleolithic structures. This would, to most researchers, qualify such sites as "villages" or as small hamlets (Cauvin 2000a:15; Valla 1998:172), although the term "base camp" also is often used.

Economy

Economic transformations, from hunting and gathering strategies to those based on food production, form the core of the Neolithic Revolution. Reams have been written about the Natufian role in this transformation, but the issue really boils down to a few points. These include the following: did the Natufians domesticate plants or animals; did they intensively use wild plants or animals that were later domesticated; and does the location of their sites coincide with the natural distribution of these wild variants?

Reconstructing paleoeconomy is no easy task. Plant and animal remains provide the most direct evidence, and we know much more of Natufian faunal exploitation, since bones are better preserved. Often inferential evidence, such as abundant amounts of ground stone, is taken as a

general indicator of more intensive use of grains. Paleoeconomic reconstruction patterns require both rigorous recovery methods (such as wet
sieving and flotation) and a host of analytical approaches that include not
only traditional methodologies, such as age, sex patterns, and size (e.g.,
Ducos 1968; Zeuner 1963), but also genetic ones. Recent developments
involving skeletal analyses and residue washes from ground stone and
skeletal analyses also hold great promise in providing more direct economic evidence. Direct dating of botanical materials is always desirable,
and careful analysis of contextual relationships is important. As but one
example, Miller (2003) has convincingly demonstrated that many plant
remains from archaeological sites might not even have been economically
used by people but rather reflect animal dung burned for fuel.

Although there is no evidence for actual domestication during the
Natufian, it is useful to not only summarize key species that were domesticated during the Neolithic but also address why these species were
selected as opposed to others, as a prelude to discussion in subsequent
chapters. Smith (1995:51) lists seven primary Near Eastern domesticates.
These are sheep, goat, cattle, pig, barley, emmer wheat, and einkorn
wheat. Zohary (1999:42) adds lentil, pea, chickpea, bitter vetch, and flax
to the plant list. Broad bean and rye also could be included, although they
were not necessarily key resources. The first cultivated plants were all annuals. Of these, Zohary (1996:143–144) notes that emmer wheat, barley,
and einkorn wheat were first domesticated and other plants were added
concurrently or slightly after these cereals. The natural distribution of all
of these species excepting flax are restricted to the Mediterranean woodland or edge of the adjacent steppe or grasslands today (Garrard 1999;
Zohary and Hopf 2000). It should be noted that the primary habitats for
barley are not the same as for einkorn and emmer wheats, however; thus,
they likely were domesticated in different subregions of an arc flanking
the Fertile Crescent (Harlan and Zohary 1966:1079).

The issue of why these species were selected over others is not frequently addressed. Diamond (1997:114–156, 2002:701) provides provocative insights on this topic. For example, he notes that the ancient inhabitants of the Near East likely were intimately familiar with the plants and
animals they used (1997:145–146). They did not collect wild plants indis-
criminately, but rather selected only the most useful ones out of the scores
available. This provided the "raw material" for the unconscious first steps

toward plant domestication. He also notes that wild barley and wheat, which formed some of the most important domesticates, had many advantages over other wild plants. These include having larger seeds, being more abundant in the wild, being able to be gathered more efficiently, and having the genetic and morphological characteristics to evolve quickly. All of these properties contributed toward their importance over other wild species. Regarding animals, Diamond (1997:88) points out that once domesticated, livestock fed more people in at least four distinct ways: by furnishing meat, by providing milk and other food products, by providing fertilizer, and by pulling plows. The use of manure as both fertilizer and fuel, while perhaps not readily apparent in the archaeological record, should not be underestimated. Thus, in looking at the constellation of early domesticates, it is important to realize that these were not randomly selected, but rather represent complex interactive and evolutionary processes among humans, plants, and animals.

Most researchers view Natufian economic patterns as reflecting a broad-spectrum pattern. Certainly the location of many sites allowed access to a rich variety of resources. Fauna are abundant at many sites and often reflect regional patterns. For example, in the core zone deer, cattle, and wild boar were commonly hunted, while in more arid regions equids and goats, such as the Nubian ibex and the wild goat, were more common (Bar-Yosef and Meadow 1995:59). A large array of smaller animals also have been recovered. These include several species of snakes, lizards, tortoises, amphibians, and waterfowl and birds, including chukar; migratory or winter animals, especially duck, hedgehog, hare, squirrel, fox, badger, and wild cat; and freshwater and marine fish (Byrd 1989a:177; Henry 1989:214). At the Early/Late Natufian boundary, there appears to have been a shift to smaller game that may reflect food stress, with a change from high-ranked to low-ranked game likely related to increased mobility (Munro [and comments] 2004; Stiner and Munro 2002:196–205). Whether all of these animals were actual dietary components is sometimes questionable and depends upon context.

Despite the abundance of such creatures, the actual meat yield from many sites indicates that Natufians obtained most of their protein from one animal, the gazelle (Cope 1991; Henry 1975, 1989:214; Munro 2004). Geography, however, plays a role, with gazelle most frequent in core area sites, while at steppe and desert sites caprines and equids are common (Byrd 1989a:175). Gazelle is most commonly represented by two species: the mountain gazelle, living in mountain and forested areas, and the goitered (or Persian) gazelle, which favor the steppe and semidesert region. A third species, the dorcas gazelle, does not occur north of the Sinai and Negev until later in the Holocene (Bar-Yosef and Meadow 1995:46–47). In most cases gazelle usually makes up 40–80 percent of assemblages. When meat yield has been calculated, over 98 percent of the meat often can be accounted for by gazelle and one or two other large animals, such as cattle, boar, hartebeest, equids, fallow and red deer, sheep, and goat. This leads Henry (1989:214–215) to question the broad-spectrum model. Instead, he feels that these data point to a highly specialized strategy focused on gazelle.

Given this Natufian "gazelle culture," there have been claims that Natufians domesticated, "proto-domesticated," or at least strongly controlled gazelle (e.g., Cope 1991; Legge 1972). Many gazelle assemblages consist of high proportions (50–60 percent) of immature animals, suggesting herd culling, a common practice in animal husbandry. Some, however, have viewed these proportions differently, noting that they may reflect age profiles of natural gazelle herds (Henry 1975, 1989:215). Furthermore, many assemblages consist of roughly equal proportions of males and females (e.g., Davis 1983:60), which is not reflective of the dominance of males associated with culling. Thus, Henry believes that gazelle hunting practices were nonselective with regard to age (Henry 1989:215). This conclusion is supported by modern behavioral studies showing considerable seasonal variability in herd makeup, with some groups consisting of several young individuals. These studies suggest that it is unlikely that gazelles were ever domesticated, given that they are not a particularly gregarious ungulate (Simmons and Ilany 1975–1977). Dayan and Simberloff's (1995) and Bar-Oz et al.'s (2004) detailed analyses also found no morphological evidence of claimed gazelle dwarfing or other indicators of human control.

One animal that does appear to have been domesticated is the dog (Davis and Valla 1978; Dayan 1994; Tchernov and Valla 1997), although this assertion has been challenged (e.g., Olsen 1985:86–87; Quintero and Köhler-Rollefson 1997:570–572). They likely were domesticated for companionship and perhaps security rather than for food. While the number of dogs from Natufian sites is limited, their evolution suggests that they were the product of unconscious selection of commensal wolves around Natufian settlements, and that they were ritually incorporated into human society.

Much less specific information can be provided for plant foods in the Natufian (e.g., parts of Colledge 2001). Paleobotanic remains are rare from most Epipaleolithic sites, and Nesbitt (2002:119–120) notes that there are only three that provide abundant evidence for cereal use: Ohalo II (not Natufian), Abu Hureyra, and Mureybat. Byrd (1989a:177) adds Wadi Hammeh 27, and Hayonim Cave. Wadi Hammeh 27 yielded wild barley and a variety of legumes, including lentils, while Hayonim contained remains of wild barley, wild almond nuts, and legumes, especially lupines.

By far, the most compelling evidence of a complex economic situation comes from Abu Hureyra 1. While a wide range of animals were exploited, evidence for their domestication does not occur until the large-scale development of agriculture and expansion of the later Neolithic settlement. Persian gazelle represents approximately 80 percent of the identified bones during each period of the site's occupation (Legge and Rowley-Conwy 2000:429–432). The evidence here fits well with other Natufian sites.

It is, however, in the plant remains that some of the more controversial claims emerge. At the start of Abu Hureyra's occupation by foragers, ecological conditions were optimal, and a diverse plant resource base exceeding 250 species was exploited (Hillman 2000a, b; Hillman et al. 2001). During worsening climatic conditions brought on by the Younger Dryas, there was a decline in wild plants, especially key starch staples. There was, however, a dramatic increase in the seeds of classic weeds (small-seeded legumes, small-seeded grasses, and stony-seeded gromwells) that dominate the weed flora of dryland cultivation today. Their presence suggests the start of cultivation. Coinciding with these weedy plants are the first charred grains of morphologically domesticated rye. The earliest of these are AMS-dated to 11,140 ± 100, 10,930 ± 120, and 10,610 ± 100 BP. The occurrence of these grains led to the conclusion that they were the product of cultivation and domestication, and that rye offered several advantages over other wild cereals (Hillman 2000a:392, 397–398; Hillman et al. 2001). What is important is that these data rank as among the earliest evidence for morphologically domestic plants anywhere in the world.

This is a significant claim, one that has not gone unchallenged. Nesbitt (2002:116–120), for example, questions both the AMS dating and the context of the domestic grains, feeling they may be intrusive from over-lying Neolithic deposits. He further is concerned that only domestic seeds were identified, and not the more diagnostic chaff morphology consisting of the rachis and glumes of cereals. Nesbitt also notes that domesticated cereals have been identified at two other Natufian sites. At Mureybat, two grains of domesticated wheat and an emmer spikelet were found, but they are assumed to be intrusive, while at the cave site of Iraq ed-Dubb in central Jordan, some barley grains were considered domestic but also were likely intrusive from overlying Neolithic layers. None of these grains were AMS-dated.

Certainly such concerns are legitimate, and actual domestication should be based on more than just a few samples of domestic grains. While rye was not a primary Near Eastern domesticate, it was used as a resource continuously throughout the occupation of Abu Hureyra (de Moulins 2000; Hillman 2000b), despite Wilcox's (2002:137) suggestion that it died out. My feeling is that the Abu Hureyra 1 AMS dates are compelling evidence and that it is the intense usage of plants, regardless of whether they have reached morphologically domestic status, that is of more importance here. Clearly it appears that many plants, whether wild or domestic, or something in between, were being cultivated at the site. Cultivation, that is, clearing and tilling of soils, requires a considerable investment of energy (Harris 1989:18–19, 1990) and can be considered a critical stage in the development of agriculture. It therefore is reasonable to propose that sites such as Abu Hureyra and Mureybat represent a form of "pre- or non-domestication cultivation" (Colledge 2001:11, 2002).

There also is indirect evidence suggestive of domestication, or at least intensive harvesting, of wild plants, much of it revolving around experimental studies on sickle blades indicating the harvesting of wild cereals with other, mostly green, plants. This suggests small-scale cultivation (Unger-Hamilton 1991, 1999). Anderson (1991) also believes that micro-wear evidence indicates a subsistence strategy between gathering and cultivation. Such studies, especially when wear analyses are coupled with phytolith and starch residue studies, offer considerable promise toward better understanding some of the processes leading to domestication (e.g., papers in Anderson 1999). Bar-Yosef and Meadow, however, caution against how these studies can definitely demonstrate domestication, and believe that "intensive and extensive harvesting of wild cereals as part of an anticipated (summer) mobility pattern seems to be a more plausible and cautious interpretation for Natufian communities" (1995:59).

Olszewski (1993c) presents a provocative model using indirect evidence that suggests archaeologists have been looking at the wrong plants in addressing issues of Natufian domestication. Using ethnographic information from California as well as Natufian archaeological data, she suggests that acorns, which are very nutritious and generally outrank all cereals except einkorn wheat, were used in a domestic sense. While this conclusion is of considerable interest, it lacks much direct support in terms of paleobotanical materials and has been criticized, primarily on nutritional grounds (e.g., Lieberman and Bar-Yosef 1994; McCorriston 1994). Barlow and Heck (2002), however, provide supporting evidence, using optimal foraging concepts to show the energetic benefits of acorns.

Finally, skeletal data hint at dietary practices of Natufian peoples. Dental evidence suggests an increase in cereals, and this is confirmed by high skeletal strontium/calcium (Sr/Ca) ratios, since these are high in cereals (Smith 1991). Sillen and Lee-Thorp (1991) point to several implications from skeletal chemistry studies. First, they note that Natufians apparently ingested little in the way of marine resources. Second, Sr/Ca studies suggest a decrease in cereals from the Early to the Late Natufian. There may be some problems with these data, however, and they need to be evaluated in new contexts, especially considering both palynological data and information from global climatic shifts.

Earlier, three questions were posed for Natufian economy. The first was "Did the Natufians domesticate plants or animals?" The answer to this appears to be no, with the exception of the domesticated rye from Abu Hureyra 1, and domestic dogs. The second question was "Did the Natufians intensively use wild variants of plants or animals that were later domesticated?" Here the answer is an unqualified yes. Whether or not Natufians were broad-spectrum or specialized, several resources that they extensively exploited were later domesticated. Finally, we asked "Does the location of Natufian sites coincide with the natural distribution of these wild variants of domesticates?" Here the answer is trickier, and it appears to be a qualified yes. Based on paleoenvironmental data, many of the plants and animals that were domesticated during the Neolithic lived within zones inhabited by Natufian populations. While many scholars believe that plant domestication occurred within the Jordan Valley and adjacent regions, Lev-Yadun et al. (2000) propose, instead, that it is only in a small area near the upper reaches of the Tigris and Euphrates rivers in southeastern Turkey and northern Syria that the wild progenitors of the Neolithic founder crops all occur. This region includes Abu Hureyra and Mureybat, but few other Natufian sites. Heun et al.'s (1997) DNA fingerprinting supports Lev-Yadun et al., indicating that the progenitor of cultivated einkorn was located in the Karaçada mountain region of southeast Turkey. Other scholars (e.g., Nesbitt 2002; Wilcox 2002), however, believe that key species were domesticated in geographically independent events, and thus propose multiple centers of domestication. As noted earlier, a similar suggestion was made some time ago by Harlan and Zohary (1966:1079).

What these data seem to indicate is an economic mosaic. Some regional Natufian variants were located in areas where many founder crops occurred in the wild, while others were not. Accordingly, it seems that some but certainly not all Natufian populations set the stage for the domestication of several species of plants and, to a lesser degree, animals.

Settlement Pattern and Diversity

It is difficult to assess settlement pattern and site diversity, due to differences in defining how widespread the Natufian as a discrete entity actually was. Most agree, however, that the Early Natufian was more geographically restricted than was the Late Natufian (Bar-Yosef and Meadow 1995:56, fig. 3.3). Hamlets are primarily restricted to the core area, and are predominantly an Early Natufian phenomenon. It appears that in their later phases, the Natufians' geographic reach expanded at the expense of larger settlements. This interpretation, however, is flawed if one considers the earliest components of Abu Hureyra 1 and Mureybat as Natufian.

Natufian sites fall into three size categories—small (15–100 m²), medium (400–500 m²), and large (more than 1,000 m²). At the large and medium sites, architecture, reflecting permanent occupation, often occurs (Bar-Yosef 2002a:108; Bar-Yosef and Belfer-Cohen 1989a:468), while small sites are usually assumed to have been temporary camps. Although there are differences of opinion, Natufian settlement pattern is often regarded as consisting of a sedentary base camp with associated transitory camps. These smaller sites are frequently located around base camps in a radiating pattern (Bar-Yosef 1983; Henry 1983, 1989:219). Although this may characterize some Natufian site clusters, there is only limited archaeological support for this overall pattern. One problem is that there have been few systematic regional settlement studies that convincingly link base camps and smaller sites (Byrd 1989a:174).

It is perhaps more useful to look at site size dichotomy and geographic range in a chronological context. During the Early Natufian, sites tend to be more restricted to the Galilee and Mount Carmel regions. Major occupations include those at 'Ain Mallaha, el-Wad, Hayonim, Kebara, and Wadi Hammeh 27. Several are villages, and, interestingly, many are in caves. This suggests to Bar-Yosef and Martin (1979) that these may have been dry and thus more conducive to human occupation and storage. Most occur at relatively low elevations. Sites are usually located at the interface of either the coastal plain or the Hula basin and mountains, and are frequently near springs (Valla 1998:178).

Early Natufian sites do occur elsewhere, but usually not as villages. To the south, the coastal zone appears empty, but it is possible that post-Natufian rises in sea level may have submerged some sites. Around the Jordan Valley, some smaller sites are located at higher elevations, such as Erq el-Ahmar, while others are situated near the bottom of the valley. These include Fazael VI, Salibiya XII, and basal Jericho, if, indeed, this represents a Natufian occupation. Further to the south are high-elevation sites, such as Beidha (Byrd 1989b), Wadi Mataha (Whitcher et al. 2000), Wadi Judayid, and Tabaqa (Byrd and Colledge 1991; Valla 1998:178–179) on the Jordanian Plateau. In the Azraq region of eastern Jordan, only one site has been documented (Azraq 18), and based on typological parameters it is believed to be early to mid-Natufian (Garrard 1991). In the Negev, smaller Natufian sites are located in lowland dunes (Valla 1998:178–179).

During the Late Natufian, the core area continued to follow earlier trends, but some sites were apparently abandoned, such as Kebara and Wadi Hammeh 27. At Hayonim, the major occupation moved from the cave to the terrace. New settlements were established at Rakefet and at Nahal Oren. During this time, the geographic influence of the Natufian expands considerably. On the western edges of the mountainous zone,

Shukba Cave witnessed considerable occupation, as did Hatoula. On the eastern side, high-altitude sites are more frequent than previously, but occupations also persist in the lower Jordan Valley, at sites such as Salibiya I. In Lebanon, information is limited, but Saaide II in the Beqaa Valley represents one Late Natufian occupation (Copeland 1991; Schroeder 1991). The oases of the Syrian Desert apparently were empty, but farther north, settlements at Abu Hureyra 1 and Mureybat were established (Valla 1998:180–181). The first component of the former was founded slightly earlier than the Late Natufian, and its size is unknown, but it still contained structures and rapidly expanded to 2,000–6,000 m² by Phases 1B and 1C (Moore et al. 2000:488), during the equivalent of the Late and Final Natufian.

To the south, information is more limited. Beidha was reoccupied after a period of abandonment, and nearby Wadi Mataha apparently has a Late Natufian component. In eastern Jordan, sites are relatively plentiful but are much more modest than those in the core zone. Such desertic sites include 'Ain Rahub, Taibe, and, in the isolated Black Desert, Khallat Anaza (Betts 1991:219). In the Negev, there was considerable Late Natufian activity. Aggregated sites occur in the highlands at Rosh Zin, Rosh Horesha, and Saflulim, while small sites continue in the lower dune areas (Valla 1998:181).

The Final Natufian is the shortest phase. There is an overall decline in core zone sites, and architecture is no longer a prominent feature. Hayonim was deserted and 'Ain Mallaha only sporadically occupied. But the traditional Natufian way of life was at least partially maintained at Nahal Oren. Outside of the core area there are Final Natufian sites, such as Fazael IV in the lower Jordan Valley (Bar-Yosef et al. 1974), but it was in totally opposite geographic locations—the Negev and the Middle Euphrates—where significant developments were occurring (Valla 1998: 182).

In the Negev, an arid-adapted Natufian variant is the Harifian (Goring-Morris 1991; Scott 1977). Aggregated sites with architectural features occur both in the high uplands at sites such as Abu Salem, Ramat Harif, Shluhat Harif, and at lower elevations (Ma'aleh Ramon east and west). There also were less substantial (that is, no architecture) but still aggregated sites in the region, and smaller sites extend into the Sinai Peninsula (Valla 1998:182–183).

To the north, Mureybat is represented only from a small exposure, but it probably was occupied all year (Cauvin 1991). Valla (1998:182) states that early Mureybat (Phase 1) was the only Final Natufian site on the Euphrates, but the recent final report on Abu Hureyra 1 indicates that it, too, was occupied during this time (Moore 2000b:126–131).

What caused the decline during the Late Natufian? In a sense, this trajectory seems to contradict what might be expected, that is, an increasingly sophisticated adaptation and more sedentism leading to the Neolithic. Instead, we see a Natufian development through time in the direction of simplification, less sedentism, and more mobility (Cauvin 2000a:17; Valla 1998:182–183), although the geographic range expanded. Whether or not this signifies increased populations is not known. Munro (2004:20), in fact, believes that populations declined during the Late Natufian. Many believe that Late Natufian patterns were related to deteriorated climatic conditions associated with the Younger Dryas (e.g., Bar-Yosef 2002a:130; Moore and Hillman 1992, but see Richerson et al. [2001:395–396] and Stutz [2004:27], who suggests that the Late Natufian actually occurred prior to the Younger Dryas). Others feel that after almost two thousand years of intensive exploitation by humans in the core area, the environment was simply exhausted, while some think that existing social systems were unable to cope with expanding populations. As Valla (1998:182) notes, a likely explanation lies in a combination of factors.

Regardless, it is clear that the influence of the core area was substantially weakened in the Final Natufian. There apparently was a major disruption in society at this time. The Mount Carmel and Galilee regions seem to have been largely abandoned, with the exception of Nahal Oren. In the arid south, entities such as the Harifian developed and then apparently disappeared. Only at sites such as Mureybat and Abu Hureyra do we see evidence of a continuous human presence in the same location. Indeed, if "sedentism" is a defining characteristic of the Natufian, then these sites must be considered as the "most Natufian of all the sites in the Levant" (Valla 1998:183).

This is a good segue into the important issue of sedentism, since it has major implications for many Neolithic models. How one determines sedentism in the archaeological record has been much debated, and there are no universal reasons for *why* sedentism occurs. It is clear that there are no absolute criteria, although Bar-Yosef (2001a:5–7) provides a co-herent discussion on such markers. Likewise, Saidel (1993:76) lists five traits that can inform on sedentism: durable construction materials, labor-intensive projects, increased site size, storage facilities, and commensal-ism. Despite these, interpretations of sedentism are wide-ranging, with some arguing for forms of sedentism even during the European Upper Paleolithic (summarized by Bar-Yosef 2001a:7). Likewise, for purposes of clarity, I use the definition of sedentism that Byrd (1989a:183) prefers, which in turn is that of Rice (1975:97): "Sedentary settlement systems are those in which at least part of the population remains at the same loca-tion throughout the entire year." Note, however, that Bellwood (2005:23), citing other scholars, believes that pre-Neolithic sedentism may require residence in one location for only six to nine months.

Bar-Yosef and Meadow (1995:51) observe that it is critical to rec-ognize that there is a mobility continuum related to human occupations: people usually are not either completely mobile or completely sedentary. These scholars evaluate sedentism on biological factors rather than ar-chaeological ones, believing that certain microvertebrates in the archaeo-logical record are more sensitive indicators of sedentism. The presence of human commensals such as the house mouse, house sparrow, and rat (as well as dog?) in archaeological deposits is considered a signal of sedent-ism. Part of their rationale is that freshly dumped trash accumulating over time, as well as stored plant and animal remains, would be attractive to these animals (Bar-Yosef and Meadow 1995:51–52).

Byrd (1989a:184) feels that other lines of evidence are more produc-tive in establishing sedentism, such as the seasonality of exploited plants and animals. He argues that the degree of settlement permanence and in-tensity of occupation at Natufian sites can be quantitatively compared by examination of site structure, such as size and thickness of deposits, cul-tural features, and material culture, concluding that "no significant differ-ences exist in site structure between the early and the late Natufian . . . nor does site size vary significantly between environmental zone and chipped stone tool–derived clusters" (Byrd 1989a:184). However, the thickness of occupational deposits and chipped-stone variation do differ. Byrd de-fined three chipped-stone clusters with environmental and regional cor-relates. Cluster 1 sites, located primarily in forest and coastal areas, have higher frequencies of plant-processing artifacts, while Cluster 2 sites, in the steppe and desert, have more moderate settlement permanence and activity. More specialized activities oriented toward hunting characterize Cluster 3, the other steppe and desert group (Byrd 1989a:174–186).

It should thus be clear that sedentism must be determined by a multiplicity of approaches, including traditional artifactual and architectural elements, plant and animal seasonality indicators, robust statistical analyses, commensals, and depth of deposits. By systematically examining these issues, reasonable inferences of sedentism can be proposed.

So, a question still remains: were the Natufians sedentary? It appears that many Natufian populations were, while others were not, and still others spent a good portion of the year in one place but still moved on a seasonal basis. A reasonable examination of the constellation of evidence certainly leads to the conclusion that sedentism played a significant role during much of the Natufian.

Even if we establish that some Natufian populations were sedentary, the reasons *why* they were are far from explained. Bar-Yosef (1998a:168, citing several researchers) notes that Natufian sedentism is interpreted in a variety of ways. For example, some feel it was encouraged by the intensification of wild cereal exploitation, while others suggest that sedentism itself increased the propagation of cereals. Some interpretations revolve around the relative lushness of the environment in which sedentary communities were established, which would have encouraged less mobility. Still others note that relative sedentism could have resulted in changes in demographic structure (Valla 1998:183). Others favor social or environmental reasons. The important issue is that the sedentism witnessed during the Natufian, regardless of its causes, laid the foundation for much of what was to follow.

The People

Burials recovered from archaeological sites represent only a small portion of total populations and may be highly biased toward specific individuals or classes. Thus, reconstructions of the physical characteristics of prehistoric populations must be done cautiously. We can, however, glean important insights into these people by careful analyses. Although numerous Natufian burials have been recorded, detailed physical anthropological assessments are relatively rare. Approximately 400 skeletons have been recovered, but many are incomplete (Valla 1998:177). One of the most thorough Natufian burial studies to date is that by Belfer-Cohen et al. (1991). Eshed and colleagues (Eshed, Gopher, Gage, and Hershkovitz 2004; Eshed, Gopher, Galili, and Hershkovitz 2004) also have studied a sample of 217 Natufian remains for demographic patterns, and a sample of 103 for musculoskeletal stress markers (MSM). In addition, "proto-Neolithic" Shanidar Cave in Iraq has provided a sample of 31 individuals, although many of these are incomplete (Solecki et al. 2004).

Natufian populations are generally identified as being of Proto-Mediterranean stock (Arensburg and Rak 1979). They tended to be of low to medium stature. There is a high frequency of congenitally missing third molars, especially at Hayonim Cave. This inherited condition suggests consanguinity between the people buried there (Smith 1991, 1998:65). There is evidence for diversity between the inhabitants of different sites, although Smith (1998:65) feels this is relatively minor. For example, Natufians from 'Ain Mallaha had larger skulls and mandibles and were taller than people from other sites. In addition, people at Kebara were taller than their counterparts at el-Wad, Hayonim, Nahal Oren, and Shukba. The Hayonim and 'Ain Mallaha skeletons were more robust than those from Nahal Oren. The largest Natufians appear to be those from Erq el-Ahmar and 'Ain Mallaha, followed by Hayonim and el-Wad, and finally by Shukba and Nahal Oren (Smith 1998:65–66 and citations therein). These distinctions may be related to diet, although Smith (1998:65–66) urges caution in this conclusion due to small sample size. The full significance of the distinctions between tall and shorter Natufians is not fully understood: they could reflect genetic differences or environmental conditions. It is, however, possible that stature may suggest stress conditions, with males generally showing greater susceptibility (Belfer-Cohen et al. 1991:421–422).

Belfer-Cohen et al.'s (1991) study of 370 Natufian burials from six core area sites indicates that 21.4 percent are Early Natufian, 3 percent are intermediate, and 47 percent are Late or Final Natufian. The remaining 26 percent, from el-Wad, cannot be subdivided, although they may be from Early Natufian levels. Child burials (age 12 and younger) range from a low 16.3 percent at 'Ain Mallaha to a high of 37.8 percent at Shukba. Interestingly, the lowest proportion of children comes from the two largest sites ('Ain Mallaha and el-Wad), while smaller sites have proportionally more children. Child burials indicate a relatively high mortality of those aged five to seven years (Bar-Yosef and Belfer-Cohen 1989a:473). There is a scarcity of people over 45 years old, and such "elderly" individuals are proportionally the same between Early and Late Natufian phases. Of the adult burials, 68.6 percent are males. Of the sample that can be aged, most died between the ages of 13 and 35 years, in both the Early and the Late Natufian samples (Belfer-Cohen et al. 1991).

In general, Natufian skeletons show few diseases or deficiencies, with the most common pathology being arthritis on the joint surface of long bones and vertebrae osteophytes. The teeth are generally healthier than those of subsequent Neolithic populations. Mild hypoplasia, caries, ante-mortem tooth loss, periodontal disease, and dental calculus occur in many samples (Belfer-Cohen et al. 1991:420–421). Dental health, however, var-ies from site to site (Valla 1998:177–178), and the only significant dia-chronic trend that Smith (1991) can trace is a reduction in ramus width and an increase in dental disease over time, both of which she feels can be attributed to dietary changes, indicating a shift to foods requiring less vig-orous chewing (Smith 1998:66). This trend increases with the Neolithic, when dietary changes were dramatic. Tooth size and dental disease pat-terns in the Natufians appear to be intermediate between hunter-gatherer and agricultural populations. Over the span of the Natufian, evidence sug-gests that these people consumed a more abrasive and cariogenic diet than did previous populations, indicating they were incorporating larger quan-tities of ground cereals into their diets (Smith 1998:66). Complementing dental studies are the Sr/Ca analyses mentioned earlier, also suggesting an increased reliance on plant resources.

Finally, and perhaps quite significantly, there is virtually no sign of violence in Natufian populations (Valla 1998:178). The burials from Shanidar Cave, however, differ from the Levantine data. Here, there is a high frequency of stress markers, disease, and, perhaps significantly, trauma. The morphology of the cranial traumas is consistent with in-juries caused by digging sticks, mullers, and axes. Of note, however, is that most of the Shanidar traumas also show careful "medical" attention (Agelarakis 2004).

Henry (1989:44–45) has claimed that the Natufian unbalanced sex ratio is an indication of female infanticide, associated with stresses that occurred as their lifestyles deteriorated during the Late Natufian. But

Belfer-Cohen et al. (1991:422) suggest that the data show just the opposite trend, in that the proportion of adult females actually increased during the Late Natufian. Furthermore, they contend that agricultural models proposing stress or deteriorating health status during the Natufian are not supported by current burial data. In other words, their analysis indicates that despite some essentially day-to-day health issues, Natufian populations were not seriously stressed. Eshed and colleagues (Eshed, Gopher, Gage, and Hershkovitz 2004), however, indicate that Natufians had a higher mortality rate for individuals aged 20–40 than did Neolithic people, although they conclude that Natufian women lived longer than did men, probably because of less frequent births.

An exception to the overall lack of stress during the Natufian is the burial data from Abu Hureyra. Although the remains from the Epipaleolithic component of the site are limited, they, as well as those from the Neolithic component, show considerable pathologies, particularly on women. These include well-developed attachment areas for the muscles that raised and twisted the arms (which is not necessarily a pathology), as well as severe damage to the vertebral disk, osteoarthritis in the knees, pressures on the thigh bone in response to bending pressures, and, especially, severe damage to the big toe. These pathologies are attributed to extensive time spent grinding grain (Molleson 2000). Peterson's (2002:98–106) MSM study also lends limited support to this conclusion, although severe stresses were not noted. Likewise, Eshed's research (Eshed, Gopher, Galili, and Hershkovitz 2004:312) shows higher MSM scores (compared to Neolithic samples) of the deltoideus for females, which may relate to pounding grain in mortars. Overall, though, the Natufian mean MSM scores are lower than those for their Neolithic sample (Eshed, Gopher, Galili, and Hershkovitz 2004:311).

However the burial data are interpreted, their importance in addressing a plethora of cultural issues is obvious. It is clear that mortuary data can provide substantial information not only on sex, age, and disease, but also on social organization and ritual activity, to which we now turn.

Ritual Behavior

Determining ritual and symbolic behavior in the archaeological record is not easy. Although somewhat ambiguous, there are tantalizing hints of ritual during the Natufian (cf. Boyd 1995; Byrd and Monahan 1995;

Marshack 1997:71–87). During both the Natufian and the Neolithic there are essentially five overlapping lines of evidence informing us on potential ritual behavior. These are ritually specific artifacts; artistic representations, primarily in the form of figurines; architectural elements; mortuary data; and the spatial arrangement of different types of data sets, especially fauna.

Burials in particular provide fodder for much speculation. All villages in the Natufian core contain burials, as do many smaller sites (Bar-Yosef 1998a:164). Some graves were dug into abandoned dwellings or outside of such structures, but not under the floors of active households. Many burials were in organized cemeteries within and around villages. Graves often were in pits, and in some instances limestone slabs covered them. Some sealed graves at Nahal Oren were marked by the hollowed stone "pipes" mentioned previously, possibly serving as "tombstones," and at other sites, such as Hayonim, cupholes pecked into rocks marked graves (Bar-Yosef 1998a:164, 2002a:117).

There is considerable variability in specific Natufian mortuary practices. For example, some burials are of individuals with no apparent body orientation. In other cases, burials were deliberately placed in flexed or extended positions. There also are secondary as well as group burials, either deposited collectively or one after the other. At el-Wad, one grave contained 10 extended individuals (Garrod and Bate 1937:14–15). At Hayonim Cave, one grave had two extended individuals with a flexed infant (Valla 1998:176).

While most Natufian graves contain only bodies, some of the dead were interred with ornaments or showed evidence of decorative cloths. Distinct grave goods, such as incised head decorations, necklaces, bracelets, belts, earrings, and pendants, are rare, but when found appear to have strong symbolic meaning. Most of the decorated burials are Early Natufian (Bar-Yosef 1998a:164). At Shanidar Cave, burial goods, primarily in the form of personal ornamentation, were common, occurring in 14 of the 26 graves. They are especially prevalent with child burials but are not believed to represent hereditary status (Solecki and Solecki 2004).

Some Natufians also were buried with animals, which do not appear to represent food offerings (Valla 1998:176). Two burials, one from Hayonim Terrace and another from 'Ain Mallaha, were accompanied by presumably domestic dogs. The Hayonim burial is particularly intriguing, in that two dogs were associated with a multiple interment of three individuals within an elaborate construction (Davis and Valla 1978; Tchernov and Valla 1997).

The treatment of the dead was not restricted solely to burials. At Wadi Hammeh 27, for example, site deposits contained several burnt skull fragments (Edwards 1991:146). At 'Ain Mallaha, various body elements, such as crania, were lying on the floors of separate structures (Perrot 1966a:445). At other sites, such as Hayonim Cave and Nahal Oren, the removal of the skull, with or without the mandible, became common (Valla 1998:176–177).

Multiple or collective burials are more common during the Early Natufian, while single interments occur more frequently during the Late Natufian. Skull removal is more common at Late Natufian sites as well, foreshadowing a common Neolithic practice. Secondary burials are also more frequent during the Late Natufian. Some researchers have interpreted this as reflective of increased mobility during this time (Bar-Yosef 1998a:164), although others (e.g., Kuijt 1996, 2001) place more social significance on Late Natufian mortuary patterns.

Turning to art, it is difficult to fully interpret the meaning of many Natufian objects. Oftentimes in archaeology, when the function of an object is unknown, it is assumed to be "ritual." Symbolic artwork from the Natufian includes anthropomorphic and zoomorphic figures, geometric engravings, and body ornaments (Garfinkel 2003a:7). The variety and esoteric nature of many of these artifacts strongly suggest some ritual or symbolic behavior (Noy 1991:561). One must, however, be cautious of reading too much into such interpretations; it is possible that many ornamental objects may simply reflect "art for art's sake" rather than any deeper meaning, although Belfer-Cohen (1991b:569) believes that art objects per se are rare. In addition, such artifacts may relate to specific geographic territories (Noy 1991:557) rather than possessing any inherent ritual properties.

Another aspect of Natufian ritual behavior is tantalizingly suggested by some of the incised slabs and stones found at sites such as Hayonim. Marshack (1997:73–86) believes these represent seasonal notations, as noted earlier. These would have become increasingly important for scheduling economic activities for groups who relied on the seasonal availability of plant resources. Marshack feels that scheduled seasonal activities may have included rituals such as requesting or giving thanks for rain, and that this would have required more precise methods of notation, what amounts to a sort of calendar. Furthermore, the presence of a more formal notation structure suggests "the probable presence of a 'time-factoring' specialist—a leader, shaman, elder, or head of a kinship group" (Marshack 1997:84). Another find, a small slab with incised parallel lines, has been interpreted by Bar-Yosef and Belfer-Cohen (1999) as possibly reflecting territories or fields, suggesting the concept of ownership.

Architecturally, there also is some evidence for ritual, or at least public, buildings. For example, at 'Ain Mallaha, the large semicircular structure mentioned previously may have served such a role. At the same site, a smaller building with a rounded bench covered with lime plaster may have been used for ritual purposes, as may have some other recently uncovered Late Natufian structures. At Nahal Oren, postholes surrounding a large hearth were found within a cemetery area, thus possibly reflecting ritual activity. One room at Rosh Zin in the Negev contained a slab pavement and a limestone monolith, which could have served ritual purposes (summarized by Bar-Yosef 2002a:108–110). Finally, at Hallan Çemi there also is evidence of public buildings in the form of two large semisubterranean structures. The same site also contains high concentrations of bone and fire-cracked stone located in a central activity area that its excavators have interpreted as evidence of public feasting, as well as carved and sculpted stone artifacts believed to have had symbolic significance (Rosenberg and Redding 2000:40, 48–50).

Collectively, data from several Natufian sites suggest ritual behavior. While their meaning is elusive, that so many types of images and symboling are represented is significant (Marshack 1997:75). Certainly the mere act of burying an individual indicates symbolic activity, but humans have been buried since at least Neanderthal times, so this cannot be attributed to specific Natufian behavior. While present at smaller sites, most burials and art objects have been recovered from village sites. It seems likely that small groups of people, living together for much of the year, developed certain ritual practices or habits to deal with their new lifestyles.

Social Structure and Organization

Based on the information provided above, what can we say about Natufian social organization and structure? It is a given that sedentism brings with it increased potential for human interaction and conflict, simply due to the presence of more people in the same place at the same time. Certain social constraints are necessary once populations exceed threshold levels. Just what these levels are is unknown, but sedentary people often have more structure than do hunters and gatherers.

A common question asked of archaeological remains reflecting sedentism is "How many people lived at the site?" Unfortunately, this rather simple inquiry has no easy answer, and estimating population size in archaeology is a notoriously difficult and speculative task. Since this will be a recurrent issue in subsequent chapters, it is worth examining in some detail here. Kuijt (2000a:80–85) notes that population estimates often are made based on settlement size and depth of deposit, and rely on several important assumptions: that the structures excavated are representative of the site as a whole; that the horizontal extent of cultural materials is representative of the actual extent of the site while occupied and that occupational density is constant in all areas of the site; and that the social and economic systems for sites from different periods are similar enough to twentieth-century ethnographic studies to permit comparison. Clearly, these can be tenuous assumptions, and thus prehistoric population estimates must remain just that: estimates. These are useful for general and comparative analyses rather than as absolute figures. Given these caveats, however, many archaeologists have based population estimates on ethnographic studies such as Kramers's Iranian research, which indicates that communities average 97 adults, children, and infants within a one-hectare (or approximately 2.5 acres) agricultural village. Watson's similar research in Iran provides a figure of 83, while van Beek's Yemen study provides a much higher estimate of 294 individuals. This wide range clearly reflects the many variables that can affect population estimates and the need for caution in applying these to archaeology, but they can be useful for comparative studies of demographic shifts (Kuijt 2000a:83–85 and citations therein).

Most Natufian villages were small, consisting of up to six dwellings. Some of these structures are quite large and could have housed several families. Based on allometric growth models and the size of Natufian sites, Henry (1989:214) proposes that Natufian sites could have ranged from 45 to over 200 individuals. Large sites, such as Abu Hureyra 1, may have been home to 100–300 people (Moore et al. 2000:489). Kuijt (2000a:85), using data from several Levantine Natufian sites, suggests an estimated mean population of 59.

Moore et al. (2000:488–492) present a well-reasoned social organization reconstruction for Abu Hureyra 1. This community was a new type of settlement to the Near East: it was large, long-lived, and sedentary. The social arrangements of the people who lived there would have been influenced by this. There likely was an increase in birthrates, an incentive for developing agriculture. New forms of social organization would have been mandated by higher populations. In particular, there would have been a person or group with leadership and mediation skills who had the ability to exercise authority and regulate the village's affairs, to control access to agricultural land, and to organize the large-scale gazelle drives indicated by the faunal assemblages (although Martin [2000:28] questions the latter). It is likely that the community was divided into working bands, probably according to sex. Furthermore, the presence of exotic imported materials, while rare, would have provided opportunities for obtaining marriage partners from outside of the community.

There have been other attempts to reconstruct site-specific social structures of Natufian settlements, as summarized by Peterson (2002:21–23). For example, there is considerable debate regarding the makeup of households during the Natufian and subsequent Neolithic. Central to the discussion is the shift from circular or oval architecture during the Natufian and PPNA to rectangular architecture during the later PPNB. One of the most-cited examples here is Flannery's classic model (1972). He characterized Natufian architecture as reflecting circular hut compounds and inferred a number of social consequences of such patterns. Using ethnographic analogies, often based on floor-space requirements, he suggested that only one or two people of loose extended families would have lived in the generally small Natufian structures. Critical to his argument is that during the Natufian and PPNA, risk was assumed not at the level of the individual or nuclear family but at the group level, through pooling and widespread sharing. Food was out in the open and shared by all occupants of the settlement. Flannery's model has been criticized (e.g., Saidel 1993), but in an effective rebuttal he (1993) eloquently defended his argument.

Based on burial data some (e.g., Peterson 1994) also have argued that nuclear families are not represented. Alternately, distinct social microunits, consisting of small bands or extended families are suggested from sites such as Hayonim Cave and Kebara (Bar-Yosef and Belfer-Cohen 2002:60). Other researchers, however, believe that small Natufian dwellings were inhabited by nuclear families (Byrd 2000:80–92; Henry 1989: 214; Olszewski 1991). Peterson's (2002:22) suggestion of keeping an open mind about the composition of Natufian households is a wise one. She does not, however, rule out that Natufian groups could have been characterized by polygynous arrangements (Peterson 2002:130). Byrd (2005a: 258–260) argues that large Early Natufian structures hint at multiple families, while small Late Natufian domestic structures suggest individual families.

Along these lines, Wright's (2000:93–98) study of cooking and dining suggests that during the Early Natufian most food preparation occurred inside houses. During the Late Natufian, however, there is more evidence for activities in shared spaces. Overall, food-related activities appear to have been relatively unspecialized, and boundaries between house and communal space seem to have been fluid and unstructured. Furthermore, the general similarity of ground stone tools between sites suggests that similar rules of food sharing were recognized. Wright believes that processing and cooking would have involved small groups. Ground stone artifacts were curated, labor-intensive to produce, and decorated, suggesting a formality in food sharing and an element of social ritual, possibly even feasting.

Some of the best information on Natufian social structure comes from burials. Just as with ritual behavior, however, these data frequently result in conflicting interpretations. G. Wright (1978) examined a sample of Early Natufian burials, primarily from el-Wad, and concluded that decorated interments and those with "burial furniture" represented social stratification. He noted that burials from the el-Wad terrace differed significantly from those inside the cave. He based this on the observation that the terrace burials had children and infants buried with adults, that grave goods did not differ by age or sex, and that dentalium shell as a decoration was restricted. To Wright, these data indicated that Early Natufian society reflected ascribed status. Other researchers followed Wright's lead, suggesting that there was an evolution from egalitarian to ranked society, and that Early Natufian group burials reflect kinship relations, whereas Late Natufian single interments suggest community-wide ranking.(Henry 1989:206–209). Along these lines, Saidel (1993:93, citing

earlier arguments) notes that there is evidence for Natufian social and territorial boundaries, as suggested by different styles of headgear associated
with burials between sites.

More recent studies are critical of Wright's conclusions. Both Byrd
and Monahan (1995) and Belfer-Cohen (1995), using expanded burial
data sets, argue that there is little evidence for social stratification or ascribed status during the Natufian. They point out several flaws in Wright's
arguments, noting that at the time of his research, comprehensive burial
data were not widely available. Belfer-Cohen believes that while there are
broad similarities in Natufian treatment of the dead, sites had their own
local traditions. She concludes that evidence for social stratification, as
inferred from decorated burials, is simply nonexistent. Conversely, Bar-
Yosef (2001a:15) believes that these burial data do in fact represent some
sort of ranking.

Byrd and Monahan (1995:280–283) feel that Natufian burials represent achieved status, but more importantly, they "reflect a complex array
of ideological and cultural expressions . . . marking a variety of social identities and membership affiliations" (Byrd and Monahan 1995:280). They
continue to suggest that the emergence of on-site group burials during
the Early Natufian reflects fundamental changes in community organization. Likewise, during the Late Natufian, there was a virtual absence
of mortuary elaboration. This was coupled with a more pronounced emphasis on individual burials, frequently with skull removal, that provided
continuity with subsequent Neolithic mortuary practices.

Kuijt (1996) sees Late Natufian patterns reflecting mortuary ritual
that served to maintain a balance and cohesion among individuals and
groups who were becoming increasingly socially differentiated. Such rituals served as powerful communal acts that linked communities and limited
perception of social differentiation. He believes that Late Natufian and
subsequent PPNA communities intentionally limited and controlled the
accumulation of power and authority (Kuijt 1996:331). Others, however,
counter Kuijt's reconstruction, believing that there is little evidence for
Natufian social differentiation and that they were, in fact, organized in an
egalitarian fashion (e.g., Grindell 1998:207, 235).

Finally, can we say anything about sexual divisions of labor or gender
issues during the Natufian? The Neolithic witnessed substantial changes
in both male and female roles. During the Natufian, however, there is

not much direct evidence pointing to distinct gender divisions, although
there are tantalizing hints. Peterson (2002:22–23) has summarized some
of the models proposed, noting that Flannery (1972:25, 31) believed the
Natufian data indicated that most productive work was accomplished
by single-sex task groups, not families. Henry (1989:206–211) suggested
highly segregated Natufian labor systems. Both Peterson (2002:135–138)
and Crabtree (1991) have criticized aspects of the Flannery and Henry
models. Crabtree concludes that there is no archaeological evidence indicating male hunting and female gathering scenarios. She proposes, based
on ethnographic parallels from the Great Basin in North America, that
communal mixed sex groups conducted both hunting and gathering based
on resource seasonality.

Skeletal data offer some specific indications of gender distinctions.
Peterson (2002:98–106, 124) has conducted the most extensive analysis
and concludes that there are only limited sexually dimorphic MSM patterns during the Natufian. Her data show muscle signatures indicating
that killing game was accomplished primarily by males using projectiles,
and she proposes that some males were engaged "in habitual hunting,
preparatory target practice, [and] ritual displays of prowess and/or re-
enactments" (Peterson 2002:103). Female musculature is more tentatively
linked with processing tasks involving bilateral motions, but many strenuous activities were shared by the sexes. This leads Peterson (2002:124) to
conclude that the sexual division of labor was only weakly developed during the Natufian. This conclusion is somewhat contradicted by Molleson's
(2000) Abu Hureyra 1 analysis, which shows that women were engaged in
the severe labor of grinding, as previously discussed. Likewise, at Shanidar Cave there is limited evidence for some sort of gendered stress, but
here it is reflected by only three adult males. Their remains suggest a considerable amount of strenuous physical activities, especially in the lifting
of heavy loads on their heads and shoulders (Agelarakis 2004:176). What
these data indicate is some limited division of labor that varies by site,
with larger communities engaged in intensive plant processing showing
stronger division of labor.

There also may be gender differentiation reflected in some Natufian
burials. For example, of the four decorated Early Natufian burials from
Hayonim Cave, one is female and three are males. They are, however, un-
equally adorned, with the female and one male being the most lavishly

decorated (Belfer-Cohen 1991:580–581). Iconographically, there is little gender evidence from the Natufian. We have already noted the rarity of human figurines and images.

Thus, we are left with ambiguous information on the nature and degree of Natufian social organization. When viewing all the available information, including economic, social, and political organization indicators, some researchers have placed the Natufians within an incipient "chiefdom"-level society (Henry 1989:206–211). Others (e.g., Olszewski 1991; Byrd and Monahan 1995) dispute such characterizations. In evaluating current evidence, Bar-Yosef (2002a:112–114) believes that the Early Natufian reflects the emergence of a nonegalitarian society that changed back to a more egalitarian mode during its later phases. The reasons for this were a direct result of the impact of the Younger Dryas and consequent greater mobility during the Late Natufian, which required a "dismantling of the nonegalitarian structure" (Bar-Yosef 2002a:130). Byrd (2005a:255–262) also argues that the Natufian represented a radical departure from earlier Epipaleolithic social interactions, including major changes in community relationships and more complicated social obligations. While opinions vary, it seems clear that the Natufians represented a departure from earlier groups in several aspects, and these all point toward the development of a more complex society.

Regional Interaction

To a large extent, determining the degree of regional interaction within the Natufian again depends upon how one defines it. It is, however, unlikely that the Natufians were culturally isolated. The presence of imported materials, such as shell and obsidian, at sites where these do not naturally occur attests to exchange over relatively large geographic areas, covering many hundreds of kilometers in some cases. There also is evidence for trade in basalt over shorter but still considerable distances of up to 100 km (Weinstein-Evron et al. 1999, 2001). The nature of this trade network may never be clearly known, but certainly many Natufian people lived in an ever-expanding world.

The degree of interaction between sedentary (or semisedentary) Natufian peoples and those who maintained more mobile settlement patterns, such as the Harifians, is of interest. Were these isolated populations, or did they interact? If so, what was the nature of this interaction—did more mobile Natufian groups serve as "middlemen" for exchange networks, as Bar-Yosef (2001a:25–26) suggests for later Neolithic groups?

Summary

What is the relationship of the Natufian to the Neolithic? It seems clear that the latter cannot be understood without a comprehension of the former. In summary, we can make the following points.

1. Natufian groups can be chronologically and geographically subdivided. They were in existence for approximately 2,500 years and covered a large area of the Levantine Near East, particularly if one defines "Natufian" in a wide sense. There were contemporaneous Epipaleolithic groups in other areas of the Near East, some of which shared "Natufian-like" characteristics.

2. Some Natufian groups, especially in the core zone, were likely sedentary or semisedentary, living in small villages or hamlets. Although there are a few exceptions, most Natufian structures are interpreted as domestic dwellings.

3. The material culture of the Natufian is rich. Portable art, especially that depicting animals, is particularly impressive. At village sites, artifact density is high and varied.

4. There is limited evidence to suggest social ranking during the Natufian. Some degree of social differentiation is likely, particularly at large sites. Burials, especially during the Early Natufian, are often multiple and elaborate, containing grave goods, while during the Late Natufian these patterns disappear and are replaced by single interments. Many researchers, however, feel that mortuary patterning may reflect achieved status, rather than more formal ascribed status and social stratification.

5. Most elaboration and stability, especially in terms of sedentism and material culture, occurred during the Early Natufian, particularly in the core zone. Less elaborate and more mobile adaptations over a larger geographic area are reflected in the Late Natufian. The exception appears to be the sophisticated settlements outside of the Natufian core, such as in the Middle Euphrates valley.

6. The Natufians practiced an array of economic options and were,

minimally, complex foragers. In the rich core zone, a broad-spectrum exploitation is indicated, while resources may have been more restricted in less favorable environments. Despite the broad-spectrum nature of some Natufian adaptations, however, specialized exploitation, especially of gazelle, likely produced the majority of protein. The situation is far less clear with plant resources, although many Natufian groups appear to have harvested wild cereals in natural stands on a seasonal basis. While some Natufian groups may have practiced some forms of cultivation, there is no evidence that they actually domesticated plants or animals, with the apparent exceptions of rye and the dog.

7. Environmental conditions during the earlier Natufian were generally favorable, until the onset of the Younger Dryas around the Late Natufian. This likely resulted in smaller areas of rich resources. Deteriorating ecological conditions may have required intensification of cereal-grain exploitation, already a significant component in many Natufian subsistence strategies, thereby setting the stage for subsequent domestication during the Neolithic.

8. Cauvin (2000a:20) believes that the Natufians already had most of the necessary material accoutrements for farming, which simply needed to be put into a different structural perspective for agriculture to emerge. He feels that the significance of the Natufian is not in their being precursors to the Neolithic, but rather that the sedentism of some Natufian groups was an important step in social organization into larger communities. The Natufian developed the sociological framework that allowed the emergence of agriculture strategies. Their sedentism allowed them to "put down roots in a stable, permanent social environment, where the company of the dead . . . reinforces metaphorically the community of the living and can legitimate in some way its permanence" (Cauvin 2000a:20). Certainly there is considerable merit to this perspective, but Cauvin is perhaps overemphasizing social issues to the exclusion of both economic and environmental parameters that undoubtedly influenced both the Natufian and the Neolithic.

A Tumultuous Time

Villagers and Others During the Pre-Pottery Neolithic A

Overview

The PPNA represents the actual beginning of the Neolithic. Until recently, evidence for its very existence was limited to a few sites, but recent excavations have documented many more sites and a wide range of adaptations. Clearly demonstrated now is the establishment of true villages, the intense use of certain key economic species, and the elaboration of social organization and ritual behavior. One of the earliest documented PPNA sites is Jericho, and its degree of sophistication has both impressed and confused scholars for decades. Now that additional PPNA villages are known, Jericho is perhaps more understandable, but it still ranks as a quantum leap in complexity from previous Natufian settlements.

The PPNA

History of Research and Terminology

Substantial Neolithic deposits exceeding 6 m were initially exposed at Jericho (Tel Es Sultan) in the 1930s (Garstang and Garstang 1940), prior to the development of any systematic terminology for the period. The term *Pre-Pottery Neolithic* was initially used by Kenyon (1957b, 1981), who spent seven field seasons from 1952 to 1958 at Jericho. Following the limited Natufian encampment at the site's base, a more substantial occupation exceeding 4 m in thickness was documented. Kenyon called this the "proto-Neolithic," with major deposits above it designated as PPNA, or the "hog-back brick phase," in reference to the mud-brick style used in construction. Detailed studies of the "Proto-Neolithic" chipped stone by Crowfoot-Payne (1983) have shown that they are the same as the PPNA, and many believe that the former term should be abandoned (Bar-Yosef 1998b:190). The PPNA was followed by additional substantial deposits that Kenyon termed the PPNB.

Around the same time, Braidwood (1975:100 [1948]) proposed a more explanatory phrase — "the era of incipient cultivation and animal domestication" — to describe the early Neolithic. While this is perhaps more reflective of a processual approach, it is cumbersome, and the PPNA/ PPNB distinction has withstood the test of time. *Aceramic Neolithic* also has sometimes been used to describe the PPN.

Even in the early days of research, Jericho was not the only Levantine site with Neolithic remains. The first manifestation of the Neolithic was believed to predate the PPNA and was initially defined by Echegaray (1966) at el-Khiam terrace in the Judean Desert. This was not a village site, and there were problems with mixing of the deposits, leading some to question the integrity of Echegaray's interpretations (e.g., Garfinkel 1996). For years, the number of PPNA sites remained limited. Many, including myself (Simmons 1980:29–32), felt that there was not sufficient information to warrant a separate cultural designation, and that the PPNA should instead be considered a variant of the Final Natufian. This perspective must now be revised in light of new investigations, which have documented over two dozen PPNA sites in the southern Levant alone (Kuijt and Goring-Morris 2002:367, table II, 369–382).

Current terminology remains complex. In the Lyon system, the PPNA is usually subsumed under the geographic-neutral term "Period 2," with Period 2A reflecting the Khiamian, and Period 2B the PPNA "proper" (Cauvin 2000a:23, 35). Within Period 2B, Cauvin is quite emphatic in dividing the PPNA into three distinct geographic variants. These are the Sultanian, the Mureybatian, and the Aswadian, and they roughly correspond to the three major areas of the Levantine Corridor used here. That is, Mureybatian sites are located in the Middle Euphrates region, Aswadian ones in the Damascus Basin, and Sultanian sites in the southern Levant (Cauvin 2000a:34–50). Both the Mureybatian and Aswadian variants are not defined by many sites. The former's principal site is Mureybat, but it also includes Sheikh Hassan and the base of Çayönü (Cauvin 2000a:39). New investigations at both Tel Qaramel and Tel al-'Abr also have PPNA occupations (Akkermans and Schwartz 2003:49; Mazurowski 2000; Stordeur 2004). Tel Abu Hureyra, once considered to have a gap of up to 1,400 years that would fall in this time frame, could also be viewed as Mureybatian, since its excavators now believe that it was continuously occupied (Moore et al. 2000:104). Jerf el Ahmar is an important, recently investigated Middle Euphrates site (Stordeur et al. 1996). The Aswadian is represented primarily by only one site, Tel Aswad (Cauvin 2000a:39; Stordeur 2003a). Recent reevaluations, however, indicate that there are no PPNA deposits at Aswad, questioning the existence of the Aswadian altogether (Stordeur 2004:50). Regardless, these are important divisions in Cauvin's thoughts relating to subsequent migrations during the later PPNB. Moore (1985:14–18; Moore et al. 2000:9) prefers not to use the term *PPNA*. Instead, this period falls within what he terms Neolithic 1 of the Archaic Neolithic stage. While I prefer the geographically neutral schemes of Moore and the Lyon school, I retain usage of PPNA since it is so widely recognized.

For much of the southern Levant, Bar-Yosef (1998b:190) and many others divide the PPNA into two entities: Khiamian and Sultanian. To many contemporary researchers, the Khiamian is the earliest reflection of the PPNA. There is, however, considerable debate as to whether or not the Khiamian is a distinct entity, especially given the possibility of stratigraphic mixing when it occurs between Natufian and Sultanian levels. Some have suggested that the term should be abandoned (as with "Proto-Neolithic") (Garfinkel 1996). Others agree with this assessment, albeit more reluctantly (Kuijt and Goring-Morris 2002:369–371). However, in an article with the rather impassioned title "Save the Khiamian!" Ronen and Lechevallier (1999) argue for its retention, and many researchers appear comfortable viewing it as a brief and ill-defined, but real, entity. Furthermore, the usage of Khiamian is not solely restricted to the southern Levant. Cauvin (2000a:22–33) considers its geographic range to include the Middle Euphrates.

In chapter 4, we noted a Negev Desert–adapted version of the Final Natufian, the Harifian. Earlier research considered it as an early desert-adapted PPNA phase (Scott 1977), and Goring-Morris and Belfer-Cohen (1998:83) believe the Final Harifian was briefly contemporary with the Khiamian. Other desert-adapted "PPNA-like" entities, while sparse, include sites such as Abu Maadi in the Sinai (Bar-Yosef 1985). So, are the Khiamian, the Harifian, and the Abu Maadian the same thing? This cannot be answered conclusively, but most researchers prefer to view them as distinct regional variants of a similar phenomenon.

In putting this rather unstructured terminological morass together, I side with researchers such as Goring-Morris and Belfer-Cohen in viewing the Khiamian as a brief transitional phase between the Final Natufian and the Sultanian, having some overlap with the last vestiges of the Harifian. They feel it "represents the culmination of Late/Final Natufian trends of disintegration" (1998:82). Following this transition is the PPNA proper, represented by distinct regional variants throughout much of the Near East.

Chronology

There are over 70 PPNA radiocarbon dates from sites ranging from north of the Euphrates to the Sinai (Kuijt and Bar-Yosef 1994). Scholars have proposed a chronological range for the PPNA that varies from ca. 10,500/10,200 to 9600/9200 BP (ca. 11,700–10,500 cal. BP) (Cauvin 2000a: 23, 35; Kuijt and Goring-Morris 2002:366). These chronologies indicate a duration of between 600 to 1,300 years. The dating of PPNA subdivisions is less clear. Certainly the Khiamian was of relatively short duration, from ca. 10,500/10,200 to 10,100/10,000 BP (Bar-Yosef and Belfer-Cohen 1992:33; Cauvin 2000a:23; Goring-Morris and Belfer-Cohen 1998:82). With the PPNA proper, it is more difficult to define subphases, despite numerous radiocarbon determinations. Both regional variation and the PPNA's occurrence in an early Holocene "flat spot" for calibration make precise placement difficult (Edwards and Higham 2001:147).

Geographic Range

PPNA sites, while not as numerous as Natufian ones, are widely distributed (fig. 5.1). Villages are documented on both sides of the Jordan Valley, in the Damascus Basin (perhaps—see previous comments on Aswadian), and along the Euphrates River. In some arid Levantine zones, such as the eastern deserts of Jordan, PPNA occupation occurred, but it was not intensive (Garrard et al. 1994; Kuijt and Goring-Morris 2002:372). In other arid regions, we have already noted the partially con-

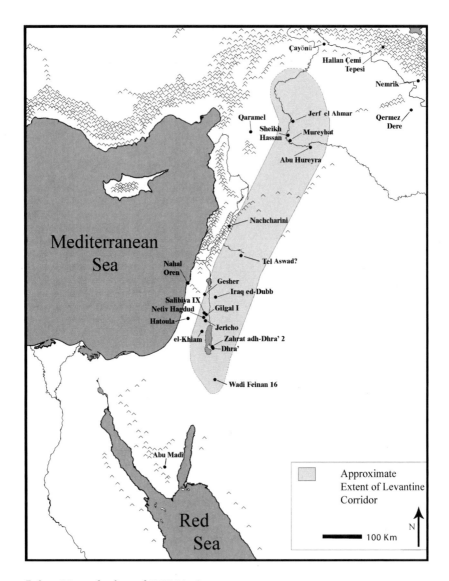

5.1 Map of selected PPNA sites.

temporary Harifian and Abu Maadi. New research in southern Jordan
has defined a constellation of at least three PPNA sites with architecture.
These are Dhra' (Finlayson et al. 2003; Kuijt and Mahasneh 1998), Zahrat Adh-Dhra' 2 (Edwards et al. 2002), and Wadi Feinan 16 (Finlayson
et al. 2000; Mithen et al. 2000), perhaps representing another geographic

variant termed the "Dead Sea Basin PPNA" (Sayej 2001). Thus, not all PPNA sites in the arid Levant were small mobile campsites.

Likewise, investigations in southern Turkey have documented another likely geographic variant. Sites are rare, with basal Çayönü, Göbekli Tepe and, possibly, Hallan Çemi representing the best examples, with other localities such as Guzitepe and Demirköy Höyük possibly containing PPNA-like materials (Biçakçi 1998:137; Esin 1999:17; Rosenberg and Peasnall 1998; Schmidt 2003). To the east in northern Iraq early components of Nemrik 9 (Kozłowski 2002) and Qermez Dere (Watkins et al. 1989) indicate distinct PPNA entities within a "Nemrikian Culture Zone" (Kozłowski 2002:98). This is part of the "Eastern Wing of the Fertile Crescent" noted in chapter 4 that includes three contemporary traditions — the Nemrikian, the Trialetian, and the Khiamian (Kozłowski 1999). The Nemrikian may show a close linkage with sites such as M'lefaat that were initially documented by Braidwood's (Braidwood and Howe 1960) pioneering studies in the "hilly flanks" of the Taurus-Zagros and north Mesopotamian plain. Even further east, in Iran, are sites such as Asiab and Ganj Dareh that were established around 10,000 BP (Peasnall 2002:229–233) and thus, at least chronologically, contain PPNA components. Hence, the PPNA was a widespread phenomenon, in contrast to earlier views of it. This large geographic spread should come as no surprise considering the extent of Late Natufian groups, many of whom undoubtedly were ancestral to the Neolithic.

Material Culture — Artifacts

The PPNA is exceptionally rich in material culture. Chipped stone reflects a continuation of Natufian elements. There is a considerable literature on these materials, and detail may be found in numerous summaries and site-specific reports, as well as detailed volumes dedicated to the PPNA and PPNB chipped stone (e.g., Gebel and Kozłowski 1994; Kozłowski and Gebel 1996; Caneva et al. 2001). Likewise, ground stone is abundant at most sites (e.g., Wright 1994, 2000). Both categories have considerable interpretative significance.

In the southern Levant, the Khiamian is strongly microlithic. It includes small lunates and sickle blades, but bifacial tools, such as axes or adzes, are rare (Bar-Yosef 1996:209). The Sultanian includes an abundant microlithic element as well, and the most distinctive artifact is the Khiam point, a small, double-notched tool first appearing during the Khiamian. This is a morphologically and aerodynamically shaped artifact that likely tipped arrows. While the Khiamian was brief, Khiam points remain a diagnostic artifact throughout the PPNA, although two other types also occur in the southern Levant: the Jordan Valley and Salibiya points (Nadel 1994:408–409; Nadel et al. 1991). Not all researchers believe that Khiam points were, in fact, projectiles. For example, at Dhra‘, a very large number of Khiam points were recovered, and microwear analysis suggests that they were used as drills or perforators rather than as projectiles (Finlayson et al. 2003:28–34).

Other Sultanian tools include sickle blades on large blades (or bifacially retouched "Beit Ta‘amir" knives), unretouched sickle blades, and many perforators and burins on small blades and flakes. Still others include lunates (although their presence could be due to assemblage mixing from earlier assemblages [Bar-Yosef 1996:209–210; Kuijt and Goring-Morris 2002:380]), retouched bladelets, and Hagdud truncations (short bladelets or small blades, truncated at both distal and proximal ends). "Nibbled" tools either are finely retouched or show signs of use and are manufactured primarily on blades. Tranchet axes-adzes ("Tahunian" axes-adzes) have working edges shaped by transverse removal. Polished celts also occur in many assemblages (Bar-Yosef 1998b:194–195). Non-tool elements include single platform blade and flake cores, many of which are exhausted (Bar-Yosef 1996:209, 1998a:194; Kuijt and Goring-Morris 2002:379–380; Nadel 1994).

Geographic variation within the PPNA is reflected in chipped stone to some degree. For example, the early part of the Mureybatian is, as to the south, considered a Khiamian industry. It is characterized by blade debitage and bipolar prismatic cores. Tools include Khiam points as well as other point types, such as Salibiya points and points with distal notches. Microborers are abundant, and geometric microliths still occur. Sickle blades, sometimes with worked bases, end scrapers, burins, and adzes also are present. By Phase II (PPNA "proper") Khiam points decrease, while tanged points with proximal notches (Helwan points) increase, and the geometrics disappear entirely. During Phase II naviform cores, which become important during the PPNB and were used to produce long, fine blades, occur among the bipolar cores. Debitage now consists of larger and thicker blades. Most projectile points have short tangs. Other tools include "daggers," sometimes made of obsidian (an imported material), sickle blades on large blades, and circular or semicircular end scrapers. Many scrapers now seem to have been used in a specialized way, set in a sleeve like a hoe (Coqueugniot 1983). There are nearly no micrcoborers. Chipped flint adzes still occur, and polished greenstone tools appear at the end of this phase (Abbès 1994; Cauvin 2000a:44; Cauvin 1994).

Geographically between the Sultanian and the Mureybatian, the Aswadian shares traits with both regions, although, as noted above, its existence is now questionable. Regardless of its status, Aswad points, however, are different from those in other regions. They are larger and more elaborate than Khiam points, having notches and a very short, wide tang with "fins" (Cauvin 2000a:39; Cauvin 1994).

As would be expected in sites with an increased dependence on plant foods, ground stone artifacts are especially abundant during the PPNA. One of the best-documented assemblages is from Nemrik 9 (Mazurowski 1997). Generally, there is a huge variety of these implements, such as pestles and shallow cuphole mortars in addition to ground or polished adzes and axes. These often are manufactured on basalts or limestones. Stone vessels were mainly rough, shallow, open bowls with relatively little variation. Finer bowls are very rare. Ground stone is typically intermediate between that of the Natufian, which it will be recalled contained many deep mortars, and the grinding querns that become common during the PPNB (Kuijt and Goring-Morris 2002:380; Wright 2000:98). Some ground stone is engraved with geometric or meander patterns, a continuation from the Natufian. Particularly impressive is an array of engraved and carved artifacts from Jerf el Ahmar, which includes intricately engraved stone vases, animal figurines, including birds of prey, geometrically decorated grooved stones (usually interpreted as shaft straighteners), and small oval stones engraved with animal motifs on one side and numerous dots on the other. The latter may reflect abstract "pictograms" as well as recording devices (Stordeur et al. 1996:1–2). Overall, though, PPNA ground stone is cruder and less decorated than during the Natufian.

Techniques used by PPNA peoples for preparing food also were different from the Natufian. Grinding slabs and small handstones used for bulk foodstuffs are much more common, implying a new emphasis on more finely ground foods, which maximize availability of nutrients by exposing more surface area of the product. Slabs with small mortar surfaces were probably used with small pestles for processing limited quantities (Wright 2000:98).

PPNA artifacts are not restricted to stone. There is a large array of other items, typical of village life. For example, the bone industry is rich and varied. There also is limited evidence for corded, spiral, and superimposed basketry technologies in the form of imprints. Corded basketry seems to establish a new tradition for the southern Levant that is not found farther north (Cauvin 2000a:36).

The PPNA has a large variety of artifacts representing images. As with the Natufian, there are enigmatic artifacts, such as incised stones and cobbles, but the more significant are animal and human figurines. These, while rare, provided Cauvin (2000a, b) with much of the data for his "revolution of symbols" model. It will be recalled that most Natufian sculpture and figurines consisted of animal forms, with human depictions being extremely rare. During the Khiamian and the PPNA, human figurines become more common, while animal representations are limited (Cauvin 2000a:25). Typical are female figures, such as seated females from Netiv Hagdud and Dhra'. Mureybat (Phase IIIA) produced eight female figurines made of stone or baked clay. There also is a zoomorphic figure, representing a raptor. At Gilgal 1 and Salibiya IX, several human and animal, primarily bird, figurines were recovered. One figurine from Salibiya IX, carved in chalk, has been interpreted as a kneeling woman, but when inverted it represents a phallus to some (Kuijt and Goring-Morris 2002:377). At Mureybat III, Nemrik 9, and Hallan Çemi, bird figurines also occur (Garfinkel 2003a:7–8). The variety of carved objects from Jerf al Ahmar has already been mentioned. Many PPNA figurines depict women in a somewhat unusual manner: they often are without breasts, navel, or genitalia, and the buttocks are frequently emphasized. Only a single example from Mureybat features a vulva (Schmandt-Besserat 1998a:113).

Cauvin feels that the "animal kingdom" is represented at PPNA Mureybat by the bull, not so much in figurines but in the presence of cattle skulls and other parts buried in houses or incorporated into features. This pattern Cauvin (2000a:25–33) attributes to the beginning of a new religion exemplified by the dualism of "the woman and the bull." Given this

perspective, it is clear that Cauvin would prefer not to see male representations at this time, although carved stone phalli have been recovered
from other PPNA sites (Kuijt and Goring-Morris 2002:377). Also, not
all researchers agree that all PPNA figurines are female; rather, many
are ambiguous or are dual-gendered representations (Schmandt-Besserat
1998a:113).

Material Culture — Architecture

It is in architecture that some PPNA sites truly stand out from their
Natufian precedents. In the southern Levant, sites consist of several scales
of occupation, ranging from camps, specialized sites, hamlets, and villages. There is clear evidence for domestic or residential architecture as
well as nonresidential architecture.

PPNA structures differ in at least one substantial manner from the
Natufian: the extensive use of plano-convex mud bricks for superstruc-
tures, whereas the Natufians likely used branches and hides. Foundations
are often of stone. Little information is available on roofing, although
roofs were probably flat. Most structures have minimal floor preparation, usually consisting of clay, sometimes overlying stone cobbles. Entrances to structures are either via steps or through a gap in one end of
a wall. The overall shape of these structures is relatively consistent, but
their size and internal organization is varied. The use of mud bricks, along
with considerable organic materials, resulted in many PPNA sites forming
mounds (or "tels"), often with substantial depth (Bar-Yosef and Belfer-
Cohen 1989b:479).

Domestic structures, as identified by ground stone and other artifacts, fire hearths, and storage features (which, it will be remembered, are
rare in Natufian dwellings), are typically oval, circular, or semicircular
(fig. 5.2). At sites such as Netiv Hagdud, Jericho, and Hatoula, domestic structures were between 5 and 8 m in diameter, while at Nahal Oren
they were smaller. Structures are either freestanding and relatively substantial, as at Jericho, Netiv Hagdud, and Hatoula, semisubterranean,
or built with one side of the structure incorporated into a terrace, as at
Dhra´, Gilgal, and Nahal Oren. Some structures consist of one large room,
while others may contain a set of two adjacent rooms with small installa-
tions around them. This latter pattern resembles that of the "compound

5.2   Reconstruction of a PPNA dwelling. Courtesy of Ian Kuijt.

arrangement" seen in some Natufian sites. In rare cases, such as Netiv
Hagdud, partitions divided the residences into different areas (Bar-Yosef
1998b:192; Kuijt and Goring-Morris 2002:373). At Dhra', one semicircular structure shows several phases of use (Finlayson et al. 2003:17–20).
There also is evidence for raised floors there, which could have been for
increased airflow or to prevent commensals from attacking stored food
(Ziegler 2003).

    Perhaps the most famous PPNA site was also one of the first inves-
tigated, Jericho. It also is among the largest, both in size and depth of
deposits. Several meters of PPNA (including the "Proto-Neolithic") deposits include over 25 building levels, and it is estimated that PPNA Jericho covered some 10 acres. While earlier structures were represented by
slight "humps" thought to be the bases of huts, later ones were substantial circular or somewhat rectilinear units. The walls were thick and well
built, and many had at least two rooms. Floors were made of beaten earth.
Many structures are relatively large, with diameters of 5 m or more, and
are semisubterranean (Kenyon 1957b:102, 1981).

A major innovation that begins in the PPNA is systematic "house cleaning" consisting of repeated clearings of floors and dumping of refuse in clearly defined trash areas outside of the structures (Bar-Yosef 1998b:192; Kuijt and Goring-Morris 2002:373). While this may tell us something about household use of space, it also eliminates detailed studies of spatial patterning of floor artifacts. Only in rare cases, such as in a burnt house at Netiv Hagdud or in abandoned rooms at Gilgal I, is there evidence for the spatial arrangement of domestic artifacts (Bar-Yosef and Gopher 1997:59; Noy 1989).

There is regional variation in domestic architecture, but the basic pattern seen at Sultanian sites is retained. At Mureybat, architecture continues in the tradition of round houses. However, in Phase IIIA, structures are larger (ca. 6 m in diameter), semisubterranean or constructed with walls of pisé. In contrast to the Sultanian, Mureybatian domestic space is strongly subdivided. For example, in one house (House 47), a raised sleeping area was constructed along an entire wall opposite the entrance, and low internal walls divide the space into small rectangular cells. One contains a hearth, while others were likely used for storage. Storage construction is also suggested by charred wood in a corridor containing an array of stone and bone tools that had not been used, as well as a wooden vessel. A flat mud roof covered this entire building. This roof rested on jointed joists, which in turn were borne on beams that radiated toward the sides from a major lintel at the end of the corridor area. Houses such as these were quite sophisticated and could be made partly contiguous with one another. There also were smaller round houses at Mureybat, including one with traces of a painted fresco decoration with geometric black and perhaps red chevrons on a white background. This ranks as among the earliest uses of art that is integral to architecture. Between houses at Mureybat there were communal open spaces containing large fire pits (Cauvin 2000a:39–41).

Toward the end of the Mureybatian (Phase IIIB), both Mureybat and Sheikh Hassan demonstrate significant architectural changes that are important for subsequent developments. This is the construction of rectangular buildings. These frequently were built of lumps of soft chalk chipped into cigar-shaped bricks bonded with mortar. They were divided internally into small square cells scarcely more than a meter square, and probably served as storage silos. The round houses, which were not subdivided, continued to exist, although these were now somewhat smaller

(3–4 m in diameter). This pattern suggests that the round houses were used for dwellings, while storage now occurred in the rectangular facilities.

At Jerf el Ahmar, impressive PPNA architecture shows a general correspondence to Mureybat. One semicircular house is transitional between a round and a rectilinear structure (Cauvin 2000a:41), and domestic architecture shows an evolution from round to rectangular forms. Aboveground rectangular domestic buildings were present, as well as subterranean rounded structures interpreted as public buildings (Stordeur 2000).

Although it is not too far from Mureybat, Tel Abu Hureyra indicates a somewhat different architectural pattern. The "intermediate period," while not well documented and representing a shrinkage of the site from both preceding and subsequent periods, dates to ca. 10,000–9400 BP. It consisted of aboveground timber-and-reed huts, similar to those from Period 1B and 1C occupations (Moore et al. 2000:478, 492–493).

In Turkey the first stage of occupation at Çayönü, which equates to the PPNA, consists of the now familiar semisubterranean round or oval huts. These were constructed of reed bundles and then wattle and daub. They became more oval through time, with plastered floors, one of which is red, and stone foundations. Groups of huts were arranged around oval open spaces. Still within the PPNA, the earliest "grill buildings" also appear. These were nearly rectangular forms with roughly parallel lines of stone laid out at wide intervals. These structures have internal divisions, partitioned for different functions. They are divided into three different sections, including a raised living floor, a rectangular central room with rounded corners, and small cells. They also frequently contained interior fireplaces (A. Özdoğan 1999:41–44).

At Hallan Çemi most structures from the lowest excavated building level (Level 3) were relatively simple and were C-shaped aboveground features approximately 2 m in diameter with walls constructed of river cobbles. By the second building level, there is more architectural differentiation. Again, these are all surface structures, but three of the four excavated units have floors paved with sandstone slabs. One of the paved structures is approximately 4 m in diameter (Rosenberg 1999:27).

To the east, over 25 structures were discovered at Nemrik 9, and these conform to expected conventions. Most are subterranean, although a few are above the ground. They are round or oval, with only houses in Phase V having a subrectangular plan. The structures are larger than many of their contemporaries, however, reaching diameters up to 5 m in the earlier phases and 7.5 m in later phases (Kozłowski 2002:27–35).

As impressive as the domestic structures are during the PPNA, it is the nondomestic architecture that is the most dramatic. Although there have been claims for such architecture throughout the Near East at this time, Kuijt and Goring-Morris (2002:373) note that, for the southern Levant at least, there is only one unequivocal example. This is, however, an impressive one, and is perhaps one of the most-cited representations of the complexity of early Neolithic life. This is the large stone tower and associated ditch and wall at PPNA Jericho (Kenyon 1957b). When originally built, the tower stood at least 8.5 m high, and was about 8 m in diameter. One side is surrounded by smaller circular and oval structures that may have been storage facilities, although they also could have been residences. There is a narrow and steep staircase that leads directly to the top of the tower, which was repaired at least once (Kuijt and Goring-Morris 2002:373–374).

Although Kenyon (1957b) argued that the tower and associated wall were built for defense, there are no other examples of similar features from contemporary sites, nor is there much evidence for conflict during the Neolithic. A commonly cited alternative explanation is that of Bar-Yosef (1986), who argued that the wall system was linked to the diversion of flash floods and that the tower might have been a shrine, an interpretation made all the more plausible by the presence of several human skeletons in the tower's interior. Ronen and Adler (2001) believe that the entire wall and tower complex were "magical," perhaps used to protect the "home" (the settlement in this case) from dangerous outside "evil spirits." Playing devil's advocate, one might wonder if there are similar features at other Neolithic sites that have not undergone the huge exposures that Kenyon excavated. Regardless of specific interpretations, however, it is clear that Jericho reflects an enormous degree of skill and planning that required considerable social organization.

There are other claims of nondomestic architecture. For example, at Mureybat, the elaborate House 47 may have been a communal building. Some of the more impressive evidence for communal or public buildings comes from Jerf el Ahmar. During the later phases of the PPNA occupation, two large, round subterranean buildings were excavated. The earlier

one is subdivided into radiating cells with raised benches and wooden pillars. Wooden pillars held a flat earthen roof laid on a wood framework.
The later building, 8 m in diameter, is transitional to the PPNB and lacks
internal subdivisions, but it has a raised bench with decorated stone slabs
that include a continuous design interpreted as a serpent. Yet another
similar possible communal building has flat upright stones decorated with
geometric designs as well as human figures engraved on some stones and
stelae that were placed transverse to the flat stones, possibly depicting the
heads of raptors. Finally, a smaller, round house, dubbed the "house of
bulls," contained several auroch skulls and horns (Stordeur 2000).

Additional evidence comes from Anatolian sites. I have already mentioned in chapter 4 the large semisubterranean structures at Hallan Çemi
that may have served nondomestic functions. By far the most impressive
and unique site, however, is Göbekli Tepe in the Urfa region. This is a
huge locality, approximately 22 acres, with a depth up to 15 m, that was
occupied during the late PPNA and PPNB. Although only a small portion has been excavated, there is no indication of daily life at the site, and
it has been interpreted as a regional meeting place for the exchange of
goods and ideas. In fact, its excavator believes that it was built not by
true Neolithic people but rather by a predominantly hunter-gatherer society (Schmidt 2001a:10). This conclusion is supported by the observation
that no domesticated plants (Neef 2003) or animals (Schmidt 2002a:24)
have been recovered. During the PPNA and early PPNB, several large
(10–30 m diameter) circular or oval enclosures containing carved upright
stelae or pillars were constructed. The elaborate motifs primarily include
animals, often life-size, that depict snakes, lions, bulls, foxes, boars, onagers, gazelle, cranes, ducks, and quadruped reptiles, as well as human
arms and landscape portrayals (fig. 5.3). The enclosures are made of concentric stone walls, connecting a circle of monolithic T-shaped pillars.
There are 25 exposed freestanding in situ monolithic pillars more than 3 m
high and weighing over 10 tons. The enclosures were completely buried
by presumably intentional backfilling (Schmidt 2001a, b, 2002a, b, 2003).
This is a pattern observed at some other sites, both with ritual and domestic structures (Özdoğan and Özdoğan 1998:589–592). It usually occurs
at Anatolian sites but also has been reported at PPNB Beidha in southern Jordan (Kirkbride 1966:16). The most spectacular example, however,
remains Göbekli, where the entire site apparently was backfilled.

5.3 Engraved pillar at Göbekli Tepe, Turkey. Photograph by Irmgard Wagner, Courtesy of Deutsches Archäologisches Institut.

Economy

We have seen that some Natufian peoples relied heavily on the intense cultivation of suites of wild plants, primarily cereals, and may have had domesticated rye. What can we say of PPNA economy? Most researchers agree that PPNA communities subsisted on cereals, legumes, wild seeds and fruits, and a variety of mammals, reptiles, birds, and fish. Procurement strategies for these resources, however, varied tremendously (Bar-Yosef and Meadow 1995:65, citing several works). It is equally important to realize that wild resources always supplemented domestic ones throughout the Neolithic.

Certainly there was intentional cultivation of key resources, some of which ultimately became domesticated. Although many believe that PPNA villages were inhabited by agriculturalists, there is, in fact, little evidence of morphological domestication during this time (Nesbitt 2002). In spite of huge advances in understanding the relationships between grain morphology and plant domestication, as well as what constitutes domestication in animals, there still is considerable and complex disagreement among scholars as to what exactly makes a species domestic, and whether morphological transitional forms can be found (e.g., Anderson 1999; Colledge 2001; Smith 1995; Zohary 1996). Nesbitt (2002) makes the point that within wild cereals, it is not unusual, statistically, to find occasional morphologically domesticated remains. In this context, given the likelihood of rapid morphological changes in plants toward domestication, Bar-Yosef and Meadow (1995:67) ask if we should even expect to find transitional forms.

Generally, there are certain characteristics that imply domestication. The rachis and glumes of cereals are critical in determining domestic status (Nesbitt 2002:116). One key trait of domesticated cereals is indehiscence, which means that the seeds do not separate from the seed heads without threshing. Tough rachis fragments, which attach the seed pods to the stem, are consistent with domestication. Other changes that occur include seed morphology, especially the enlargement of the seeds, denser clustering of seeds, and loss of delayed germination (Banning 1998:213–214; Cauvin 2000a:51–52).

What, then, is the actual evidence for domestication during the PPNA? Hillman and Davies (1990) have argued that domesticated wheat is present at Tel Aswad, Jericho, Gilgal, and Netiv Hagdud, although Kislev (1992) believes that most of the remains recovered from these sites were harvested from wild stands. Likewise, Colledge (2001:8–9) cites several domesticated plants during this period. Nesbitt (2002), however, who sees chaff morphology as a better indicator of domestication than grain shape, is critical of these claims. He notes that most of the seven PPNA sites at which relatively abundant plant remains have been recovered lack definite evidence of domestication. Whether or not the criteria used by Nesbitt are appropriate, or are perhaps too rigorous, may be debatable, but he does present a well-reasoned argument, as summarized below.

At Netiv Hagdud, a rich seed assemblage includes grain and chaff of wild barley and some wild emmer. While some domesticated-type barley internodes occur (4.1 percent), these are consistent with the harvest of wild barley. At Jerf el Ahmar, the barley, einkorn, and rye chaff is all wild. At Qermez Dere and M'lefaat, wild einkorn/rye and wild barley occur, without chaff, and there is no reason to believe that they are domesticated. Domesticated einkorn/emmer and barley grains have been identified at Iraq ed-Dubb, but Nesbitt argues that these are intrusive from later layers. Jericho has long been cited as indicative of having domestic plants (e.g., Hopf 1983), but there are only a few grain fragments from the upper PPNA levels and a single mud-brick impression of domestic einkorn. The best evidence for domestication occurs at Tel Aswad, in the form of several grains, spikelet forks, and internodes of emmer and barley from the earliest levels. The wheat chaff also is likely of domesticated-type. Overall at the site, 62 percent of the barley chaff is wild, compared to 26 percent being of domesticated-type, indicating that not all the barley was domesticated. Nesbitt, however, questions the dating context of these materials, noting that they were not directly dated, and, of course, there is the issue of whether Aswad is even PPNA. At Tel Abu Hureyra, he dismisses all of the early domesticates, as discussed in chapter 4 (Nesbitt 2002:120–121).

Given these data, Nesbitt (2002:123–125) assesses various views on agricultural origins, evaluating three often-cited perspectives. The first is that the Jordan Valley was the hearth of domestication, and that is not supported by the data. The second and perhaps most common view is that the Levant (*sensu lato*) is where initial domestication occurred. Nesbitt be-

lieves that the evidence for this model also is weak; he endorses the third
view, in which the "Fertile Crescent" as a whole has the strongest evidence
for plant domestication, but this does not occur until the PPNB. This perspective, also supported by Wilcox's (2002) careful analysis, proposes a
series of independent domestications of various crops in different parts of
the Fertile Crescent. It is directly at odds with diffusionist models from
only one or two centers of domestication.

While a multiple-origin model perhaps best fits the available data,
remember that many models for the origins of agriculture proposed that
plant domestication actually would have occurred in marginal zones outside of the area of natural distribution of wild cereals. This now seems
unlikely, as arboreal pollen evidence showing increased precipitation indicates that most sites were located with the natural habitat of the wild
cereals as they existed during the Neolithic (Bottema 2002; Lev-Yadun
et al. 2000).

If the evidence for plant domestication is weak, what of animal domestication? Following similar morphological criteria used for plants, the data
are even weaker. In contrast to the Natufian, where faunal collections are
relatively well studied, this is not the case with many PPNA assemblages
(Bar Yosef and Meadow 1995:71). Overall, trends observed during the
Natufian continued into the PPNA, especially regarding intense gazelle
exploitation. The major change in faunal exploitation does not occur until
the PPNB, when caprovines (sheep and goats—despite their distinctive
behavioral patterns, these species are sometimes lumped together unless
diagnostic elements are recovered) replace gazelle. The PPNA pattern
does vary geographically. At northern sites, cattle and caprovines were
hunted, while in the central and southern regions, gazelle were the dominant species exploited, although fallow deer, ibex, and wild boar also
occur. Smaller species also occur at most sites. For example, at Netiv Hagdud and Gilgal there is a relatively high frequency of birds and marine fish.
At Hatoula, gazelle, hare, and fox are dominant, although some cattle,
wild boar, equids, hedgehogs, and small carnivores also are present (Bar-
Yosef 1998b:196; Bar-Yosef and Meadow 1995:71). Farther north, pig
husbandry or even domestication at Hallan Çemi has been suggested
(Rosenberg et al. 1998; Rosenberg and Redding 2000:42), although this
has been disputed (e.g., Peters et al. 1999). Tchernov (1994:70), noting
that PPNA faunal assemblages vary greatly even between sites that are

geographically close, cautions that faunal diversity may well be due to sampling problems rather than biological, cultural, or geographic distinctions.

Tchernov observes that gazelles become even more significant during the PPNA than in the Natufian, citing figures of 57 percent of absolute meat weight from Hayonim Cave (Natufian) to 90 percent at Netiv Hagdud. Similar figures occur at other Natufian and PPNA sites in his analysis, but it would be interesting to see if this pattern was maintained with an even larger sample. Tchernov concludes that while there are differences between the Natufian and the PPNA, they are subtle (Tchernov 1994:70–79). What is clear is that careful studies pioneered by scholars like Tchernov must become more common. Despite the intense use of selected species, most researchers do not believe that, beyond the dog, any animals were yet morphologically domestic by the PPNA, or that animal husbandry was practiced (Bar-Yosef and Meadow 1995:72; Kuijt and Goring-Morris 2002:379).

One aspect of animal exploitation during the PPNA that deserves attention is evidence for nonconsumption use. For example, some animals, especially smaller ones like birds of prey and foxes, could have been used for "secondary products" such as pelts, feathers, and talons. Some also might well have been used for symbolic purposes (Kuijt and Goring-Morris 2002:379).

Ultimately, far more important than whether or not morphologically domesticated plants and animals were present during the PPNA is the concept that many of these species were *used* in a domestic sense. It is important to realize that morphological domestication often is the end result of a long process. Many researchers now believe that the criteria for determining domestication must be reevaluated, giving more importance to nonmorphological aspects. They note that several species may well have been "anthropologically" domesticated even if morphological changes had not yet occurred (Vigne 2001:57; Vigne et al. 2005). It is unlikely that most PPNA villagers actually thought about whether or not their plants and animals were domestic according to some scientific definition. What they did have, however, was an intense understanding of how to obtain maximal output from key resources. So, my feeling is that despite the lack of conclusively demonstrable domestic plants in the PPNA, Nesbitt (2002:124) perhaps goes too far in stating that the PPNA cannot be viewed as a farming society and that their economic, architectural, and organizational links are stronger with the Natufian. While the economic evidence may support this perspective, the architectural, artifactual, and organizational data do show an intensification over the Natufian. It may be unlikely that PPNA people had a true farming economy, but they certainly were close to it.

Settlement Pattern and Diversity

While diversity in settlement types exists for the PPNA, our knowledge is incomplete. Part of the problem of identifying a realistic settlement pattern is the historic archaeological "invisibility" of many PPNA sites (Kuijt 1994:176–180). Although the number of known sites has expanded within and beyond the central and southern Levant, most PPNA settlements are located in the Mediterranean zone, either in or adjacent to the Jordan Valley. They were rarely located in the ecotones used by the early Natufians. Typically, larger PPNA sites are in rich habitats near the margins of steppes, near marshes, along lake margins, on alluvial fans, and beside riverbanks, where considerable land could be cleared for cultivation, where deep soils would have promoted growth, and where high water tables made harvests more reliable and productive. Smaller sites outside of the Mediterranean vegetation belt likely reflect mobile hunters and gatherers (Bar-Yosef 1998b:190–192; 2002a:135; Cauvin 2000a:60).

Site size shows a clear hierarchy. The largest sites are Mureybat, Tel Aswad, and Jericho (ca. 15–6.2 acres); intermediate ones include Netiv Hagdud (ca. 3.7 acres); and smaller ones include Nahal Oren and Hatoula (ca. 1.2–.5 acres) (Bar-Yosef and Belfer-Cohen 1989a:482). Such data indicate considerable variability, with no clear concentration of size with specific geographic areas beyond the observation that the larger sites are located in more favorable ecological settings. Equally important is the range of site types. We typically tend to associate "Neolithic" with sedentary villages, but certainly during the PPNA, and the subsequent PPNB, this was not completely the case. During both periods, site types can be characterized as specialized sites, camps, hamlets, and villages (Kuijt and Goring-Morris 2002:368).

One reason that there may be fewer PPNA sites than Natufian ones is that populations decreased. More realistically, it seems likely that populations actually increased and began to aggregate for social, economic, and, possibly, ritual reasons. This resulted in the formation of substantial regional centers, such as Jericho, as well as major villages, such as Jerf al Ahmar or Mureybat. At all of these, labor investment into construction and maintenance of houses, public buildings, and storage facilities indicates that people intended to use these villages for a long time (Bar-Yosef and Meadow 1995:62).

To Kuijt (1994) a southern Levantine regional site hierarchy exists, characterized by large villages in the Jordan Valley, smaller satellite communities that were occupied year-round, and special-purpose temporary sites in adjacent ecological zones. This arrangement suggests a high degree of social and political integration at the regional level. Similar regional integrations likely existed in other parts of the Levantine Corridor and the Near East.

The People

Although there are numerous PPNA burials (e.g., 276 from Jericho alone [Cornwall 1981]), few have been published in detail, and PPNA "cemeteries" have not been documented. Data from Jericho, Netiv Hagdud, Hatoula, and Nahal Oren show that burial systems, at least in the southern Levant, were relatively standardized (Kuijt and Goring-Morris 2002:376). Over 30 years ago, Mellaart (1975:50) noted that burial data indicated the same "racial stock" as the Natufian, which he characterized as "rugged Eurafricans." There also were some "brachycephalic Alpines," but "gracile Proto-Mediterraneans" had not been reported. This latter statement seems to conflict with Natufian data, since it will be recalled that most of the populations are, in fact, considered "Proto-Mediterranean," and I suspect that Mellaart is in error here. Smith (1998:67) notes that for the PPNA, there is only one skull from Jericho for which measurements have been published, with additional cranial data available from Hatoula and Netiv Hagdud. The Jericho skull is long and narrow, and falls within the Natufian range, and the Hatoula skull most closely resembles Natufian specimens from el-Wad. PPNA mandibles from Hatoula are gracile, and tooth size is slightly smaller than in the Natufian.

Health data for the PPNA are limited. At Netiv Hagdud, a relatively large sample of 28 individuals was relatively poorly preserved, making it difficult to determine health status. There were, however, isolated instances of tooth hypoplasia (Belfer-Cohen and Arensburg 1997). Peterson's (2002) study of skeletal stress examined only PPNA samples from Hatoula (six) and Netiv Hagdud (two). In her analysis, she considers PPNA and PPNB together; thus, the results will be presented in chapter 6.

Ritual Behavior

Some of the most intriguing, as well as controversial, discussion of the PPNA relates to ritual behavior. Perhaps the most eloquent spokesperson for a radical revolution in ritualism commencing in the PPNA was Cauvin (2000a, b). He sees the PPNA as a crucial foundation period for a "revolution in symbols," an advent of divinities, and the origin of religion. Cauvin bases much of his argument on the interpretation of figurines and on specific arrangements of fauna. Essentially, he believes that a transformation in figurine art from Natufian zoomorphic depictions to PPNA female portrayals, and the presence of "bull art" "were destined to represent the divine couple, mother-goddess and bull-god, which were to persist in the Near East and the eastern Mediterranean from the Neolithic until the classic period" (Cauvin 2000b:238). Although Cauvin is the most recent advocate for this idea, he certainly was not the first. For example, over a century ago Hahn (1896) proposed that some animals, including cattle, might have been first domesticated for religious rather than economic reasons.

What is the evidence for this transformation? Cauvin cites several PPNA female figurines from sites as early as the Khiamian that range from the southern Levant to the Middle Euphrates. While relatively rare in the PPNA, female representations, and a presumed emphasis on "mother-goddesses," multiply rapidly during the subsequent PPNB. The theme of the bull is primarily restricted to the Middle Euphrates, represented by the burial of bulls' skulls (bucrania) in clay benches and horns embedded in walls at some Mureybatian sites, perhaps foreshadowing a much later emphasis on bull-related architecture at sites such as Çatalhöyük during the PN. Cauvin proposes that such burials were clearly symbolic, especially since there was only limited hunting of wild bulls during the PPNA.

To Cauvin, this iconography represents a unique ideology organized around two key symbols, the "woman and the bull." The female has already taken human form, and represents not only a fertility symbol but also "a genuine mythical personality, conceived as a supreme being and universal mother, . . . a goddess who crowned a religious system which one could describe as 'female monotheism'" (Cauvin 2000a:32). The male symbol is restricted to a still zoomorphic representation, the bull. It is important, however, to note that there are PPNA human male representations, as noted earlier. Regardless, this male/female system rapidly evolved to a more sophisticated form during the later PN (Cauvin 2000a:22–33, 2000b:237–238). While not all agree with it, Cauvin has certainly provoked considerable interest with his model.

Kuijt (1996, 2001) has attempted to understand PPNA ritual behavior from mortuary data. These indicate that southern Levantine PPNA burial pattern systems were relatively standardized, incorporating practices begun during the Natufian. These involved primary burial and secondary skull removal, as well as some distinctions in how adults and children were treated. Note, however, that while skull removal is common throughout the Neolithic, it is not ubiquitous (Kuijt and Goring-Morris 2002:376).

When adults and children were buried, frequently beneath the floors of dwellings, they were interred with no grave goods and were individual burials. Whether or not these were especially important members of the community or simply previous residents of dwellings is unknown. During burial, the location of the skulls apparently was marked, and the crania were subsequently removed, often with the mandible, after decay of the soft tissues. This pattern was practiced only on adults, not infants. The skulls were then prepared, possibly for some sort of commemorative use, and then reburied either inside or outside of structures, or outside of the settlements. The spatial relationship between the original postcranial skeletons and the reburied skulls cannot be determined. Likewise, it cannot be clearly determined whether adults and children were systematically buried in different kinds of locations, although there is some evidence for patterning. For example, at Jericho, some infants were placed in dedicatory contexts in houses, such as post foundations (Kuijt and Goring-Morris 2002:376–377).

Many early studies tended to interpret these burial patterns as reflecting the development of an ancestor cult — ritual events that were organized for the veneration of ancestors, perhaps even representing a type of symbolic reincarnation (cf. Goring-Morris 2000:116). Kuijt has as-similated these previous studies and argued that skull removal was part of a ritual belief system that focused on enhancing community cohesion and reaffirming household and community beliefs. He believes that both Late Natufian and PPNA mortuary practices integrated communities and minimized socioeconomic distinctions between individuals and kin groups at a time when economic and social changes were occurring. These practices are explained as a system of "social codes" limiting the development and centralization of power and authority. Regardless of specific interpretations, the deliberate interment of people beneath floors and the apparent continued occupation of these structures likely had some ritual or symbolic significance. We should be aware, also, that perhaps not all these burials were intentional. Rather, some structures could have been unintentionally constructed over earlier burials.

Architecture also has been used to tease out ritual behavior. We have already noted that at some sites, specialized buildings may have had ritual importance. Certainly the "house of the bulls" at Jerf al Ahmar points to the special importance of aurochs, and we have already discussed the incorporation of bull horns and skulls into Mureybatian sites. Although it is difficult to relate ritual behavior to architectural practices, there clearly are some outstanding examples that imply considerable social organization, as well as ritual behavior. One of the best examples is the tower of Jericho, where twelve individuals (three adolescents and nine adults) (Cornwall 1981:403–404) were buried within this imposing structure. Perhaps even more impressive is Göbekli, whose sole purpose appears to have been related to ritual or at least communal behavior. It likely functioned as a central gathering area for many PPNA and later PPNB communities within its catchment. Göbekli may not be alone: similar "pillar sites," such as Urfa-Yeni Yol, Hamzan Tepe, and Karahan Tepe, have been recently discovered. Like Göbekli, these also are in the Urfa region. Two domestic Anatolian sites, Nevalı Çori and Çayönü, also have some architectural parallels to Göbekli, but the "pillar sites" appear to be related solely to ritual activities. Despite the documentation of other sites, however, Göbekli is the only one in a dominating strategic position with a deep stratigraphy, and it appears to have been at the top of a hierarchally structured stratification system, surrounded by satellite sites (Schmidt 2001a, 2002b:12).

A final indication of ritual behavior resides in the constellation of faunal materials. We have already noted that the arrangement of bull skulls figures prominently in Cauvin's symbolic interpretations. Another line of faunal evidence comes from Hallan Çemi, where extremely high concentrations of animal bone and fire-cracked rock in a central activity area suggest recurrent conspicuous and formalized preparation and consumption of food, or communal feasting behavior (Rosenberg and Redding 2000:40, 52).

In reviewing the above data, what do we really know about PPNA ritual behavior? There clearly is a difference from the Natufian, but it is deceptively tempting to overread these data. Many contemporary societies tend to compartmentalize ritual behavior and separate it from everyday life. This, however, is by no means universal. Many other cultures incorporate ritual behavior into everyday life, and certainly during the Neolithic this may have been quite common. A small "shrine" found in a building does not necessarily make that building a place of worship (Banning 1998:226, 2003:19). A more realistic perspective may be that both religious and daily activities occurred together in domestic dwellings during the Neolithic, and that there were no sharp distinctions between the sacred and secular worlds (Abay 2003:21).

Social Structure and Organization

To build something such as the Jericho tower and walls or the Göbekli complex clearly requires a high degree of social organization. There is no question that by the PPNA, a set of discrete social rules and regulations must have been in place. An important element in reconstructing social behavior is a consideration of how many people lived at a given community. This is doubly important during the PPNA, where the increase in the surface area of some sites implies population increases (cf. Cauvin 2000a:63–65). We already noted the difficulty of determining population estimates, and the problem is exacerbated at PPNA sites, which are larger than Natufian ones, and have only limited excavation exposures. Nonetheless, it seems likely that a large settlement such as Jericho could have accommodated many people, although early estimates of 2,000 or more (e.g., Mellaart 1975:49) are probably unrealistic. Kuijt and Goring-Morris (2002:368) estimate community sizes of 10–30 for camps, 30–100 for hamlets, and 100–750 for villages, and these seem reasonable figures. Kuijt (2000a:81) arrives at an estimated mean population of 332, ranging from a low of 18 at Nahal Oren to a high of 735 at Jericho. As Cauvin (2000a:51) aptly notes, the large settlements and presumed social complexity reflected at major settlements are not necessarily characteristic of all PPNA sites, many of which retained what were essentially hunting-and-gathering economic strategies.

Certainly one would expect to see the most dramatic social changes occurring at larger villages. New patterns of social behavior requiring more community-wide interaction must have emerged regarding the division of labor, processing, storage, gender roles, and exchange patterns. Such intracommunity changes reflect the growing significance of ritual activities in structuring interpersonal relationships, an increased emphasis on both ownership of and access to resources, and the ability of some sort of leadership structure to organize community-wide labor activities. This was a fundamental reorganization of social life, and certainly at those sites where intense cereal harvesting was important, it must have been tied to the annual cycle of seasonality, human perceptions of the environment, and the social implications of living in larger communities (Kuijt 1994, 1996).

On an intrasite level, attempts have been made to examine social organization by analyzing architecture. Presumed public or communal structures have some social significance, simply due to labor investments required in their construction, if nothing else. At the household level, Byrd (2000) analyzes social organization using the size of domestic buildings and their implications for household sizes. The complex issue of whether PPNA households were based on nuclear families, as Byrd (2000:83, 2005a:265–266) favors, or some other composition (e.g., Flannery 1972, 2002) is unknown. Based on an analysis of several sites, Byrd concludes that there are no clear-cut patterns in interior size from the Natufian and Harifian through the PPNA. Rather, the substantial change occurs between the PPNA and the PPNB, with the latter having much larger dwellings. Some of this undoubtedly is due to the switch from circular to rectangular structures during the PPNB (Byrd 2000:74–80). It seems unlikely, however, that PPNA households at large sites such as Jericho would have mirrored Natufian ones.

On a site-specific level, Naveh (2003) takes a sociopolitical perspective at Jericho. He concludes that monumental buildings functioned in several social spheres, both at inter- and intragroup levels. He argues that prominent and long-lived structures, like the tower, could have served as markers that existed both before and after any individual's lifetime, providing a longer historical chain. This was quite different from smaller PPNA settlements, and Naveh hints that Jericho could have served as a dominant settlement with power over other communities. He further suggests that Jericho's size could have been a significant variable within the general PPNA mating system. If this was the case, such systems, at least in modern ethnographic contexts, are often bound together by social mechanisms such as bride service, bride wealth, and dowry, and Jericho's large population could have played a major role in broader economic and social contexts (Naveh 2003:93–94). While such arguments are speculative, Naveh does provide an argument worthy of thought.

The issue of social stratification is important here. There is only limited mortuary evidence indicating individual social differentiation, such as variations in burial practices, grave goods, and differential access to preferred resources, and this has led some researchers to propose egalitarian PPNA societies that lacked formalized social, ritual, or political hierarchies. Byrd (2005a:266), however, suggests that the complexities of large communities likely included enhanced roles for community leaders and possibly even elites, although he admits that there is little supporting archaeological evidence and that the existence of leaders is largely inferential. Likewise, Kuijt (1994, 1996) argues that there was ranking in some PPNA communities. Based on a careful review of the available information, especially mortuary data, he feels that while many PPNA communities lacked individual or family social differentiation, there is in fact evidence for ritual and community leaders who coordinated activities among several villages. Kuijt's model has four major components. First, it requires the maintenance of commonly shared burial and ritual practices that minimized potentially divisive social forces, such as wealth inequality. Second, these practices were established and maintained by select ritual and community leaders, whose position was likely based on seniority. Third, authority of this leadership would cover several community decision-making factors, such as collective construction projects and management of agricultural labor, but would not have permitted individual or family gain beyond certain limits. Finally, this model requires that ritual practices were centralized and deliberately maintained in regional communities, such as Jericho (Kuijt 1994:184).

Many attempts to explain the Neolithic invoke population pressure as a key variable. While one may dispute specific models, there is little doubt that the intensive cultivation of plants (whether wild or domesticated) necessitates both a substantial population base and a major restructuring of labor. To work in fields requires collaborative labor efforts at the time of sowing and, especially, at the time of harvest, since a relatively narrow window exists for collecting ripe grains. Thus, an organized mobilization of labor for at least part of the year was necessary, and would have required institutional hierarchies that exercised considerable social control over increasing populations (Cauvin 2000a:64). These increases may have been on local levels only: to Cauvin (2000a:50), populations had not yet expanded on a pan-Levantine scale.

Wright (2000:101) has inferred aspects of social organization in her study of food processing and consumption activities. She notes that many PPNA houses were supplied with fixed facilities arranged in patterned ways, and that food preparation tools were both stored and used inside houses. She suggests these were used to process and dispense foodstuffs in small amounts, perhaps as flavorings added to bulk foods and possibly reflecting declining dietary diversity. Wright believes that activities conducted in houses also took place in specific outdoor areas, possibly by work parties. In terms of food preparation, boundaries between houses and common spaces were fluid and unstructured. PPNA ground stone generally lacks the diversity, workmanship, and decoration of similar Natufian implements, leading Wright to propose that a different set of attitudes toward food and dining were in operation during the PPNA and that villages seem to have had little interest in conspicuous displays of preparing and serving food.

A related social aspect is the emerging significance of gender differentiation. In societies where fertility of the land was becoming increasingly important, it is no surprise that the roles of women would change, and certainly Cauvin has argued for their increased symbolic importance. On a more prosaic level, there is some skeletal evidence that illuminates gender distinctions. Peterson's (2002) work addresses this in the most detail, but unfortunately her sample from the PPNA is limited. She does note, however, that the "earliest farming lifestyle, then, entailed greater changes in the habitual activities of males compared to [those] of females" (Peterson 2002:107).

Finally, there is the significance of ideology, as best argued by Cauvin. His thoughts on the importance of the Neolithic as a "transformation of the mind" (Cauvin 2000a:67–72) has already been discussed. Cauvin's (2002a:66) analyses result in two major conclusions. The first is that the agricultural "initiative" was the start of a new way of life for people relative to their physical environment. The second is that the PPNA represents the time when this ideological revolution occurred. Cauvin believes that the Neolithic cannot be explained as a simple economic transformation, but rather as one during which people were dissatisfied with their traditional mode of life (that is, hunting and gathering) and wanted to dramatically transform it. This resulted in the development of a new ethos where humans questioned their role in nature and the cosmos. The emergence of divinities took human form as "The Goddess," which is depicted as a woman during the PPNA. This affected the course of much of what was to follow in subsequent creationist theologies (Cauvin 2000a:72).

We do not have a universally accepted understanding of social organization during the PPNA. Available data have lent themselves to several interpretations, often reflecting individual scholars' theoretical orientations. It seems unlikely that most PPNA communities were simple egalitarian groups. The relatively large populations associated with many PPNA villages would have required a degree of social control at a community level. This is hinted at by data from architecture, artifacts, and mortuary practices.

Regional Interaction

Compared to other Neolithic phases, there is only limited evidence for long- or short-distance trade during the PPNA. Much of this is in the form of exotic or nonlocal trade goods. The best evidence for short distance interregional trade is shell, greenstone, malachite, and bitumen. While these materials occur at most PPNA sites, they are most abundant at the large settlements, such as Jericho and Netiv Hagdud (Kuijt 1994:181).

Marine shell, mostly used as beads, from both the Mediterranean and the Red seas indicates a shift from the dentalium preferred by the Natufians to bivalves and gastropods (Bar-Yosef Mayer 1997:191). Bitumen, which occurs in the Dead Sea region (which includes Jericho) is more difficult to trace. It was likely used as an adhesive and as a sealant, and was collected and traded within the southern Levant. Indeed, it has been argued that one reason for Jericho's existence was that it was a distribution center for bitumen, as well as for salt and sulfur (Anati 1962). Better evidence for more extensive, long-distance trade and exchange is from greenstone and malachite, which occur naturally along the southern Rift Valley, and obsidian. Obsidian has been documented at sites as far south as Netiv Hagdud and Jericho and is sourced to central Turkey (Kuijt and Goring-Morris 2002:380–381).

Of course, trade items are not restricted to the southern Levant but occur at most PPNA sites throughout the Near East. For example, Cappadocian obsidian from the Göllü source on the Konya Plain occurs at Mureybat, some 400 km distant. This obsidian also occurs at Sheik Hassan, Tel Aswad, Netiv Hagdud, and Jericho. Likewise, obsidian from the Bingöl source in northeastern Turkey has been found at Hallan Çemi, Sheikh Hassan, Mureybat, and Aswad. Lake Van obsidians sourced to Nemrut Dağ composed nearly 60 percent of the total lithic material from Hallan Çemi (Chataigner et al. 1998). Although not explicitly addressed by many researchers, one also cannot rule out trade in food. But one example is Cauvin's (2000a:59) argument that rye cultivation at Mureybat could have been the result of rye seeds being brought to the site at the same time as was obsidian.

Regardless of specific interpretations, PPNA groups were not isolated. They engaged in the trade of items that were imported from over hundreds of kilometers. The exact mechanism of this exchange is not known, and it is possible that smaller sites served as intermediaries between sources and the larger villages that were the favored destinations of imported goods. It appears likely that people from these sites participated in an interlinked economic system that involved considerable regional interactions (Kuijt 1994:183).

Summary

The PPNA represents a "point of no return" for the Neolithic. Although the PPNA resembles the Natufian in many ways, it also is distinct enough to be considered a true transitional period to full sedentary farming communities. Earlier claims that the PPNA was merely a Late Natufian variant must be discarded. We now know that there were a large number of PPNA sites throughout the Near East, reflecting a wide array of activities, as summarized below.

1. The PPNA is a distinct entity composed of regionally identifiable groups. A short transition period from the Natufian—the Khiamian—appears in many parts of the Near East, although it is best known from the southern Levant. Following the Khiamian, Levantine regional variants correspond to a north-to-south zonation. Other regional manifestations that are similar to the PPNA also occur in southern Anatolia and the Zagros region.

2. A wide range of site types and functions is represented during the PPNA. Large villages likely housed hundreds of people, but much smaller hamlets and limited activity sites also occurred.

3. In at least the larger sites, intensive cultivation of plants, primarily cereals, and specialized hunting supported the population base. There is as of yet no clear evidence for morphologically domestic plants or animals during the PPNA, possibly beyond rye and the dog. Several resources, however, likely were used in a domestic manner, even if physical changes had not yet occurred.

4. Mortuary practices continued trends started in the Late Natufian and included ritualized decapitation. This pattern becomes even more formalized during the PPNB. Burials do not indicate individual social status but may reflect communal hierarchies.

5. Domestic architecture is varied, although the basic form of dwellings is circular or oval. At some sites, particularly in the north, semirectangular structures are present. Most dwellings are relatively simple, although internal subdivision occurs at some sites.

6. A few sites contain likely public architecture. In many cases, this is simply in the form of larger structures, but at Jericho and Göbekli there exist substantial public works that would have required considerable labor efforts.

7. Although evidence for social structure is elusive, it is clear that major reorganizations of those inhabiting the larger villages was under way in order to cope with expanding populations and the need for communal activities associated, minimally, with harvesting and the construction of public works.

8. Long- and short-distance trade were components of PPNA society, indicating that individual communities did not exist in cultural vacuums.

9. There was a pronounced change in ritual behavior during the PPNA, reflected by a change to human female figurines from the zoomorphic figurines that were common in the Natufian. Cattle skulls also were incorporated into some structures. The meaning of this change in ideology and symbolism is open to variable interpretations.

The PPNA was a time when many populations in the Near East were making important decisions regarding their futures. While some groups retained traditional and less complex lifestyles, others were experimenting with new ways of existence. This involved a more extensive exploitation of the environment in terms of harvesting activities, new ways of organizing social interactions, and ideological transformations. Clearly, then, the PPNA represented a "tumultuous time" for many people in the Near East.

Case Study 2   **Nachcharini Cave**

I did my first archaeological fieldwork in the Near East in Israel longer ago than I care to remember. It was 1970 and 1971, and I was an undergraduate anthropology major at the University of Colorado on a junior semester-abroad program. Those sites, however, were not Neolithic ones; the first Neolithic site that I worked on was in 1974. It did not fit the stereotypical image—rather than a huge village, it was a small and remote cave named Nachcharini. Located in the Anti-Lebanon Mountains of Lebanon, it was used during the Natufian, PPNA, and PPNB. By then, I was a new PhD student at Southern Methodist University, having completed my master's degree at the University of Toronto, and H. Bruce Schroeder of Toronto invited two other students and me to participate on the excavations.

Nachcharini was an unusual site. Although my memory is fuzzy on the details, I recall that it was used for smuggling Marlboro cigarettes from liberal Lebanon into less liberal Syria. Nachcharini was discovered when the smugglers, "excavating" pits for storing their goods, came across huge amounts of bone and chipped stone. Somehow, this information was conveyed to a local schoolteacher, which ultimately is how Schroeder found out about the site.

5.4   Nachcharini Cave, Lebanon. Bruce Schroeder (left) evaluating grid system.

I learned a lot at Nachcharini. One of these was painstakingly careful excavation. The materials at the site were densely packed (fig. 5.4), and Schroeder demanded meticulous excavation. Usually our largest excavation tools were dental picks and spoons. This was before the days of electronic distance measurers (EDMs) and other high-tech gear that is so commonly used in archaeology today, and I especially remember using narrow tubes filled with water and triangular stakes for taking precise levels.

I also learned about some of the hardships of working in remote areas. For much of the project, we lived in a Bedouin tent above the site, although we later were "promoted" to a school in a nearby village. Tent life was always interesting. I recall an annoying fly during lunches that was, finally, dispatched by one of the workmen with a .45 caliber handgun. I also remember hearing on a crackling radio that Richard Nixon had resigned . . . the broadcast was in Arabic, and our excited workmen kept saying "Nixon halas, Nixon halas" ("Nixon is finished"). Getting to the site was no easy task, and I learned how durable Land Rovers were, and how they could be repaired with all kinds of everyday items. I learned how to drive these vehicles, both aggressively by Bill Farrand, the project geomorphologist, and more gently, by Schroeder.

I also graphically became aware of the sad politics of the Near East on this project. I certainly had been aware of these during my undergraduate time in Israel, where I lived with a Lebanese family in east Jerusalem. But a more direct impact occurred at the end of the Nachcharini project. This marked the beginning of the Lebanese civil war, and I caught one of the last planes out of Beirut. This marked the beginning of another long phase of pain for this beautiful country.

Through it all, Bruce's wife, Helen, managed to (usually) keep us healthy. Try as she might, she also extolled the virtues of healthy eating to young people who simply wanted to consume vast amounts of sugar. All of us did, however, get ill to varying degrees. I was given a drug for an intestinal disorder and later learned that it had been taken off the western market because it caused, in some unspecified number of cases, brain damage. All I know is that the drug worked.

Of course, the good of the project outweighed these problems. The physical beauty of Lebanon is unmatched, as is its cultural beauty. We attended the Baalbek Festival, set amidst the ruins of that Roman city. The freshness of the fruit is a lingering taste as well (of course, this could have something to do with the aforementioned intestinal problems). I also saw the vestiges of the colonial days, when the Near East was under the control of Europeans. I have memories of our team somehow crashing a very posh party at the British embassy in Beirut, after a long session in the field with no showers. The British were not amused, but they politely entertained us. And overall, I remember the courtesy and pride of the Lebanese people. This project left a lasting imprint on me that has little to do with archaeology.

But what of the archaeology of Nachcharini? The civil war had implications for research at Nachcharini. Notes were lost, and the country was essentially closed to research for over 20 years. Nonetheless, the site remains an important example of a very specialized Neolithic occurrence. Imagine my feelings, when, just a few years ago, a young British colleague, Alexander Wasse, informed me that he was restarting the Nachcharini project! Along with a now retired Bruce Schroeder, Alex and his team have returned to this unusual site, with a new Bedouin tent (Wasse and Pirie 2001; Pirie 2001). It is a strange feeling to have been involved in the first excavations of a site in the early 1970s, and then, over 30 years later, to witness, albeit from a distance, its renewed study. As this book goes to press, I cannot help but wonder what the latest violence in Lebanon will do to both its people and its archaeology.

Chapter 6

Courses Toward Complexity

Florescence During the Pre-Pottery Neolithic B

Overview

The PPNB is the most-investigated of all the Neolithic periods and represents its florescence in much of the Near East. During the PPNB, several dramatic developments occur, including the definitive domestication of plants and animals, the elaboration of ritual behavior, widespread trade, and the recently defined megasite phenomenon (chapter 7). These developments occur over some 2,000 years, and are placed within the context of four subdivisions. A huge amount of data exists for the PPNB, and thus this chapter focuses primarily on major trends and highlights.

The PPNB

History and Terminology

As with the earlier periods, there is a considerable diversity of terminology for the PPNB. The first discoveries of Neolithic materials were made prior to World War I by colorful early archaeologists such as T. E. Lawrence (of Arabia) and Sir Leonard Woolley at Byblos and Carchmish, by Oppenheim at Tel Halaf, and Garstang at Sakçagözü, among others. While these early discoveries demonstrated that there was an intermediate stage between the Paleolithic and the great urban cultures of the Near East, little else was known (Moore 1985:3).

More serious studies began in the 1920s. In the southern Levant, Buzy's (1928) investigation of surface finds in the Wadi Tahun resulted in the term *Tahunian* for a collection that undoubtedly contained mixed materials but also included Amuq points, denticulated sickle blades, and other artifacts that would come to be identified as PPNB. *Tahunian* was a confusing term, with some researchers first suggesting that it was widely misused and should be abandoned, but then reintroducing it as an entity distinct from the PPNB (e.g., Prausnitz 1966, 1970). Certainly the most significant discovery was at Jericho. As noted in chapter 5, Garstang established a long, well-stratified Neolithic sequence, and the term *PPNB* was officially introduced into the literature by Kenyon's expanded excavations. A consequence of the early studies at Jericho was that it came to be identified as the "type site" for the Neolithic, an unfortunate occurrence, since Jericho is quite distinct from other entities.

To the north, Braidwood's early investigations also were documenting Neolithic sites. In the Amuq Valley of northern Syria, surface collections and excavations at Tel Judaidah revealed substantial evidence for Neolithic occupation. Prior to World War II, similar materials were recovered at Mersin and Tarsus in the Cilician portion of Turkey by other scholars, while in Mesopotamia (primarily Iraq) limited Neolithic occupations also were documented. After the war, research accelerated, and of particular importance was Braidwood's pioneering interdisciplinary work at Jarmo and other Iraqi sites. Also important was Mellaart's research in western Turkey (Moore 1985:3–6). Following Braidwood's research were several investigations in Iran and Iraq. Of particular note are studies in Khuzistan on the Deh Luran Plain of Iran (Hole et al. 1969), which focused on careful excavation at sites like Ali Kosh that allowed for the construction of new models for the origins of the Neolithic. While many of these sites are not PPNB *sensu stricto*, they greatly expanded our knowledge of the Neolithic (see Peasnall 2002 for a summary). Unfortunately, political considerations in Iran and Iraq since the 1970s have hampered a continuation of research into what undoubtedly was a very important core of Neolithic occupation. Likewise, it is only recently that the elaborate and expansive Neolithic of Turkey has come into clearer focus (e.g., Gérard and Thissen 2002; Özdoğan and Başgelen 1999), despite early discoveries at important sites such as Çatalhöyük, Suberde, or Çayönü. Research in the southern Levant also greatly expanded, and while Kenyon's Jericho excavations are the most famous, other scholars documented numerous PPNB communities that were much smaller than Jericho, providing a more balanced perspective.

Despite the ever-changing political climate in the Near East, research at new sites is rewriting our comprehension of the Neolithic. In particular, discoveries from Jordan, Turkey, and Cyprus have in recent years greatly expanded (and complicated) this seminal period in human history. Given the intensity of research on the Neolithic, terminology has understandably become more complex. In this book, I use *PPNB* in its widest sense. While not all regions have universally adopted this term, it is by far the most familiar. Whatever term one chooses, there is, however, no doubt that the PPNB documents a rich mosaic of Neolithic achievements.

Chronology

The chronological range of the PPNB is well secured by numerous radiocarbon determinations. Several sites in the Middle Euphrates and southeast Turkey are considered transitional between the Mureybatian PPNA and the PPNB (cf. Stordeur 2004:49). Most researchers subdivide the PPNB proper into four subphases: the Early (EPPNB), Middle (MPPNB), Late (LPPNB), and Final PPNB, now often referred to as the PPNC, a term we initially proposed for a transitional period into the PN at 'Ain Ghazal in Jordan (Rollefson 1989, 1993; Simmons et al. 1988:36). The EPPNB is not well documented, and some question its existence, seeing, instead, a transition from the PPNA into the MPPNB (Kuijt 1997), while others have suggested that it represents a temporary return to more mobile adaptations before the rapid spread of the MPPNB (Goring-Morris and Belfer-Cohen 1998:85). I retain its usage, and apply Kuijt and Goring-Morris's (2002:366) southern Levantine chronology here (table 6.1). There is some variation in the dates used by other researchers, but it is slight. Overall, the PPNB covers 2,000 to 2,100 years, beginning around 9500 BP and ending around 7500 BP.

Geographic Range

The PPNB covered much of the Near East in one variant or another (fig. 6.1). While scores of PPNB sites are documented, there still were large areas that were likely not inhabited. For example, Akkermans and Schwartz (2003:46) believe that much of Syria during the Neolithic was a relatively "empty world," with population density relatively low and settlements small and dispersed. Clearly not all researchers would agree with this perspective: the Neolithic witnessed dramatic population expansions, but in numerical terms, these likely were nowhere near the densities of later periods.

Table 6.1   Chronology for the Pre-Pottery Neolithic B

Subphase	Conventional (Uncalibrated) BP	Calibrated BP
Early PPNB	9500–9300	10,500–10,100
Middle PPNB	9300–8300	10,100–9250
Late PPNB	8300–7900	9250–8700
PPNC	7900–7500	8600–8250

Source: Based on Kuijt and Goring-Morris (2002:366).

For example, as an exercise in speculation, consider the following reconstruction. We have a relatively good idea of the minimum number of Neolithic settlements throughout the Near East. For argument's sake, assume that the PPNB included 200 modest-sized villages of 200 people each that were occupied contemporaneously. Further assume the existence of, say, 15 megasites (see chapter 7) with populations of 3,500. These admittedly weak assumptions would result in a total population of only 92,500 souls. Adding a few thousand more for non-villagers, this is still a tiny population, given the size of the Near East. Even expanded tenfold, the result is still a population under one million. While the numbers may not be important, this exercise demonstrates that Akkermans and Schwartz's point merits some serious consideration.

Regardless of specifics, the existence of a PPNB "interaction sphere" (cf. Bar-Yosef and Belfer-Cohen 1989b) is a good way to envision its influence. This does not, however, mean that we are looking at a homogeneous Near Eastern "culture." Indeed, one might argue that distinctive regional variants, perhaps reflecting some sort of "tribal" (cf. Bar-Yosef and Bar-Yosef Mayer 2002) or "ethnic" identities, were becoming established. Furthermore, while the PPNB was widespread, there were particular concentrations of different types of sites in specific geographic areas. For example, the "megasite" phenomenon seems to have been primarily (although not exclusively) concentrated in the eastern margins of the Levantine Corridor. At the same time, many desert-adapted PPNB variants coexisted in the more marginal arid zones.

Certainly the best-known reflection of the PPNB is in the Levant. The EPPNB is poorly documented, especially outside of the Middle Euphrates. This is important, because in Cauvin's (2000a) model, the "real"

6.1   Map of selected PPNB sites.

PPNB essentially originated in the Middle Euphrates and spread to both the north and the south by actual population movements. He states that "the Middle Euphrates, the only part of the Levant where the culture is indigenous, is thus its true cradle" (Cauvin 2000a:81), although Rollefson (2001a:113) questions this contention. While Cauvin proposes a migration from the Mureybat region, he also admits that the EPPNB is poorly known in Syria. At Mureybat itself, it is apparently documented in only a very small area, while it is better represented at Dja'de (Cauvin 2000a:78). Abu Hureyra 2, dated to ca. 9400–7000 BP, also chronologically overlaps with the EPPNB (Moore et al. 2000:493).

There are other EPPNB sites outside of the Middle Euphrates and the Damascus Basin (as now possibly reflected by Aswad). Examples include Mujahiya on the slopes of the Golan Heights, and perhaps er-Rahib in Wadi Yabis in northern Jordan. These, however, have undergone only limited investigation. Other sites also occur in Galilee (e.g., Horvat Galil) and the adjacent coastal plain (e.g., Nahal Oren, Michmoret, Sefunim, el-Wad), although some have argued that they actually represent the earliest phase of the MPPNB (Kuijt and Goring-Morris 2002:382–384). In the Negev and Sinai, there appears to have been a virtual abandonment for the first half of the tenth millennium BP, followed by a slight increase of small EPPNB sites interpreted as hunter-gatherer occupations at sites such as Abu Salem, Nahal Boqer, and Nahal Lavon 109 (Gopher and Goring-Morris 1998; Kuijt and Goring-Morris 2002:384).

It is curious that there are PPNA and similar occurrences in many areas where there are no subsequent EPPNB occupations. For example, in the Rift Valley, Jericho is the most famous example of the PPNA and PPNB, but the latter occurs there only as the MPPNB after an apparent hiatus. Indeed, many PPNA sites are abandoned, and PPNB ones are established on virgin soil. This apparent depopulation of the Rift is difficult to explain (Kuijt and Goring-Morris 2002:382–384) and is an area for future investigations.

Outside of the Levantine core, evidence for the EPPNB is also limited, perhaps due to differing terminologies. It is Cauvin's (2000a:75–95) belief that while the birth of the EPPNB was in northern Syria, there was a first phase of expansion extending to southeast Turkey, resulting in the "Neolithisation" of Anatolia (the "Taurus PPNB"). Göbekli continued to be occupied during the EPPNB (Schmidt 2002a:24), but perhaps the best example of an EPPNB occupation is at Çayönü. Other Turkish sites, such as Nevalı Çori and Çafer Hoyuk, also likely date to this subphase, and to the northeast, in Iraq, the EPPNB may be represented at Qermez Dere (Cauvin 2000a:81; A. Özdoğan 1999:41–47). Indeed, Kozłowski (2002:97) feels that the Nemrikian cultural zone, which en-

compasses a huge area of the central-eastern Iraqi Jezirah, has an extensive time range from ca. 10,300–8500 BP, which includes all but the latest
phases of the PPNB.

Much better data exist for the MPPNB, with sites located throughout the Near East. In the Levant, most large (up to ca. 12 acres) settlements are located in the Levantine Corridor or along its eastern edge.
Closer to the Mediterranean coast are smaller (3–4 acres) communities,
probably functioning as agricultural hamlets or villages. In the more arid
zones of the Levantine Corridor, similarly sized villages existed as well,
despite their location in marginal environments (Kuijt and Goring-Morris
2002:388).

It is worth considering this southern expression of the PPNB in a bit
more detail. Based on the presence of small, temporary sites, some authors
(e.g., Jobling and Tangri 1991:147) have proposed that the PPNB adaptation here was one characterized by seasonally mobile hunters and gatherers, as suggested for similar sites in the Sinai (e.g., Bar-Yosef 1984; Tchernov and Bar-Yosef 1982). Many such sites may also represent logistical
camps away from villages, or pastoral activity. Garrard et al. (1996:221)
note that many late PPNB inhabitants in the more arid portions made use
of a pastoral package that "would have provided a useful risk-buffer for
those engaged in marginal farming and hunting."

The problem with this line of reasoning is that southern PPNB sites
also include small but complex settlements such as Ghwair I, Beidha, and
Ba'ja, and large megasites such as Basta and 'Ain Jamman. The identification of these clearly does not support a model restricted to seasonal occupation. Despite the generally inhospitable environment of the desertic
areas, Neolithic life flourished there.

In this context, 'Ain Abū Nukhayla in the Wadi Rum of southern
Jordan represents a rather curious situation in that it is somewhat "in
between" a formalized village and smaller, seasonal PPNB localities. It
may have been a component of a settlement/subsistence pattern involving
seasonal transhumance and long-term multiseasonal occupation (Henry
et al. 2003).

Despite the presence of villages in some arid zones, there are relatively light MPPNB occupations of the more extreme environments of
the eastern Jordanian deserts and the Negev and Sinai. Sites usually are
small (250 m² or less) and often contain rounded dwellings in a "beehive"

arrangement. These were probably the remnants of mobile foragers who may have been Neolithic in chipped stone technology and typology, but not in economy (Kuijt and Goring-Morris 2002:388–389). Whether or not people occupying these sites were farmers "forced" into the more marginal environments by expanding populations in the Levantine Corridor or simply chose to maintain a hunting-gathering lifestyle, is a point of debate (e.g., Byrd 1992; Simmons 1980, 1981, and Case Study 3). Their role as "middlemen" in trade and exchange also should be considered (Bar-Yosef 2001a:25–26).

Outside of the Levant, many Neolithic communities thrived during the MPPNB. Cauvin (2000a:75–95) attributes this to a second wave of cultural diffusion from the Middle Euphrates to regions within the open forested steppe, which defines the limits for dry farming. This new extension involved both northern expansion in Anatolia and southern expansion to the southern Levant. One of the most famous Neolithic sites known, Çatalhöyük, was established during the MPPNB (Hodder and Cessford 2004:19), although it attains more significance during the PN. We have already noted Iraqi sites within the Nemrikian cultural zone beginning with the EPPNB, and the site of Jarmo—famous mainly due to its discovery by Braidwood and the subsequent debate between him and Kenyon on the significance of early villages—likely was established during the MPPNB (Banning 2002a:15). Farther east, in Iran, sites such as Ali Kosh and Tepe Guran were founded during the MPPNB (Peasnall 2002:226–235).

In Cauvin's (2000a:76) model, during the subsequent LPPNB there was a virtual explosion of the culture. The process of "Neolithisation" expanded beyond the core or nuclear zone as far as the temperate coastal areas of northern Syria, to Turkey, and into the interior areas of Iran and Iraq. Settlement in the southern Levant, however, appears to have contracted. Here, there is a concentration of megasites along the eastern edge of the Levantine Corridor. Some of these show occupational continuity from the MPPNB to the LPPNB, such as Wadi Shu'eib and 'Ain Ghazal, while farther south others were established during the LPPNB. The absence of many substantial sites (Abu Ghosh and Beisamoun being notable examples) in the western Mediterranean zone may reflect population aggregations into the megasites (cf. Simmons 2000:215–217), although site visibility may be a problem—Kuijt and Goring-Morris (2002:406) note that the formation of later period tels on top of LPPNB settlements must be considered. If, however, this is a real pattern, it reflects a major population reorientation to the eastern edge of the Corridor.

There also is LPPNB expansion into the desertic areas. This is reflected in areas such as the Azraq Basin and areas farther east in Jordan (e.g., Garrard et al. 1994) but also occurs in other desertic zones, including eastern Syria and the Negev and Sinai (Byrd 1992). Most of the desert sites continue to be small, seasonal occupations, often consisting of no more than six oval stone structures (Kuijt and Goring-Morris 2002:406).

Until the past two decades or so, many archaeologists believed that there was a chronological gap or hiatus between the LPPNB and the beginning of the PN. We now know that this is not true in all regions, with the documentation of the transitional PPNC phase in the southern Levant. While there does appear to have been a population contraction during the PPNC, continuity between the LPPNB and PPNC occurs at some megasites. This also appears to be the case at sites closer to the Mediterranean, such as Yiftahel, Tel Eli, and Beisamoun, and in the Damascus Basin, at Tel Ramad. New PPNC villages were established as well, primarily along the Mediterranean coast, such as Atlit Yam in the Mount Carmel area and Ashkelon, farther to the south. It also is possible that many sites are submerged, since during the PPNC sea levels were about 20 m lower than at present. A spectacular example is Atlit Yam (Galili et al. 1993). In the desert areas, such as eastern Jordan, the Negev, and the Sinai, there also is evidence for occupation during the PPNC, although it was not as intense as during the LPPNB (Kuijt and Goring-Morris 2002:414).

The term *PPNC* is not as widely used outside of the Levant, where there is a preference for *Final PPNB* (e.g. Bar-Yosef and Meadow 1995: 73). Whatever term is used, however, it is clear that much of the Near East continued to be occupied during this time. Thus, we can see the widespread influence of the PPNB interaction sphere that shared many cultural components and yet developed distinctive regional profiles, boundaries, and territories (cf. Kozłowski and Aurenche 2005). It is obvious that during this time the Neolithic world had reached the peak of its expansion.

Material Culture — Artifacts

We know more about chipped stone in the PPNB than for any other Neolithic period. However, within phases knowledge is uneven. In general terms, assemblages are blade-dominated, with frequent usage of naviform cores. This standardized technology resulted in a large variety of well-made tools, including very diverse projectile points (e.g., Gopher 1994) (fig. 6.2), represented by the "Big Arrowhead Industries" (Kozłowski 1999), sickle blades, drills, borers, knives, scrapers, and burins. During the PPNC, however, assemblages become less standardized.

Ground stone during the PPNB also is abundant. Vessels are finer and more diverse in size and shape than in the PPNA. They were well made but simple and usually undecorated. Shapes are open forms and include miniature bowls and plates, medium-sized globular bowls and V-shaped bowls with thick walls and flat bases, and rare examples of cups on pedestals. Platters are a PPNB innovation. Handstones and querns are common; these were primarily manufactured on sandstone, but also on basalt or limestone. Many milling tools are larger than their PPNA counterparts and would have permitted cooks to process more food in a given operation. Some grinding slabs were essentially immovable; for example, of 26 complete pieces from Beidha, the mean weight was 26.74 kg, and some weighed as much as 52 kg. Some platters at Beidha were up to 1 m in diameter. Ground implements also occur that had functions other than food grinding. These include palettes, bowls, axes or celts, probable gaming boards and many items of personal ornamentation, such as stone bracelets (Banning 1998:201–204). The presence of many such artifacts has considerable social implications relating to leisure time and individual persona. Other vessels were made of cordage, basketry, wood, stone, plaster, and early versions of pottery. Plaster vessels (whitewares, or *vaisselles blanches*) are more complex than stone vessels, with pedestal bases and sometimes incised and painted designs (Wright 2000:101–103).

The uncertainty of dating EPPNB sites makes it difficult to critically define their assemblages. In general, however, the chipped stone shows technological and typological characteristics between the PPNA and MPPNB. There is a tendency toward nonlocal chalcedonies and other fine-grained raw materials. Pyramidal cores are common, but naviform ones also occur. It will be recalled that this distinctive technique seems to

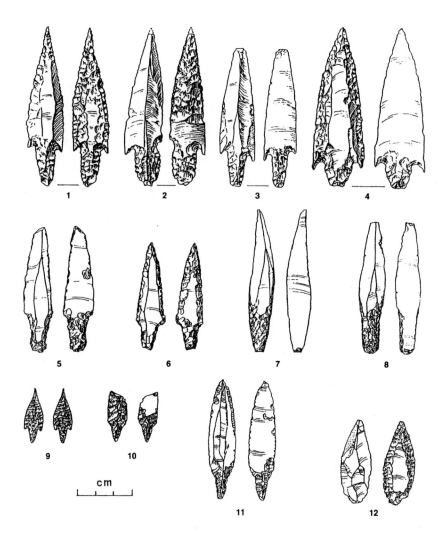

6.2 A sample of PPNB projectile points. 1–4: Jericho points; 5–6: Byblos points; 7–8: Amuq points; 9: Haparsah point; 10: Nizzanim point; 11: Byblos variant; 12: Herzliya point. Courtesy of Avi Gopher and American Schools of Oriental Research.

have originated in the Middle Euphrates region during the final Murey-batian (Cauvin 2000a:78). Points include Helwan and early Byblos types, the latter of which are larger than previous forms and become a typical PPNB type. Both naviform core technology and certain types of points may have diffused from the Middle Euphrates to other regions. Hag-dud truncations rarely appear in some, mostly northern, assemblages, and burins tend to be dihedral. Perforating tools seem to be less common and standardized than during the PPNA, and microliths all but disappear. Heavy-duty tools such as bifacial axes and chisels also were produced. Ground stone implements show considerable continuity from the PPNA, with an increasing use of querns (Kuijt and Goring-Morris 2002:386–387).

In contrast to the EPPNB, there is a huge wealth of information on MPPNB chipped stone. Assemblages are generally characterized by long, inversely retouched sickle blades, a high number of distinctive projectile point forms, such as Jericho and Byblos types and their variants, and a lesser number of Amuq points, oval axes, perforators and borers. Navi-form blade cores are common, although more opportunistic core technologies still occur. MPPNB assemblages display considerable regional and local variation. For example, a reduction of sickle blades and an increase in the percentages of projectile points and burins occurs in desertic areas in Jordan. Much intersite and intrasite variability may be related to access to raw materials, the location of settlements, and the spatial location of economic activities within settlements (Kuijt and Goring-Morris 2002:400–401). There also is some evidence for craft specialization in naviform core production at the regional level at 'Ain Ghazal (Quintero and Wilke 1995).

In ground stone, various saddle and trough querns are common, as are grinding slabs, stone bowls and platters of limestone, chalk, sand-stone, basalt, and metamorphic rocks. Handstones are frequently oval and made from a variety of raw materials. Mortars are rare, although combi-nation pounding/grinding handstones are common. Polished and grooved stones also occur, as do whetstones and palettes. Stones with multiple in-cised parallel or crossed lines, probably with symbolic significance, also are found (Kuijt and Goring-Morris 2002:402–403).

During the LPPNB, the chipped stone technology is similar to that of the MPPNB. While naviform technology decreased, there is a con-tinued emphasis on opposed-platform core systems, as well as more informal blade and flake cores. Byblos and Amuq points are the dominant types. Sickle blades continue to be important, and ground stone assemblages also show continuity from the MPPNB, although there is a wide use of limestone grinding stones. Another aspect of ground stone technology is the production of sandstone and limestone bracelets, especially at sites in southern Jordan, such as Ba'ja and Basta, which may be another example of craft specialization (Kuijt and Goring-Morris 2002:412, 425–426).

The PPNC shows some major changes in chipped stone technology and is one way of identifying this subphase (Rollefson 1993). There are changes in raw material preferences, and a reduced emphasis on naviform core technology. This may be due to the declining use of sickle blades. Smaller and lighter projectile points are another characteristic of the PPNC (Kuijt and Goring-Morris 2002:417–418). Little is known of the ground stone technology, but overall it reflects a continuation of the LPPNB.

As would be expected from sophisticated sedentary villages, there is a huge amount of nonlithic material culture. This includes a remarkable array of bone tools, stone and shell jewelry, and occasional basketry, or at least impressions of basketry. It is, however, in the symbolic realm that the PPNB stands out, particularly the MPPNB, where unique collections of tokens, masks, statues, and figurines have been recovered. Finally, an important technological contribution of the PPNB is a sophisticated pyrotechnology—the application of high temperatures to manufacture plaster from limestone. Plaster was used for a variety of purposes, especially for floor and wall finishes, sculpture, and the production of vessels (Banning 1998:204–205).

Material Culture—Architecture

Distinctive architecture, a hallmark of the PPNB (fig. 6.3), was first systematically classified by Aurenche (1981) and has been discussed in detail by several authors (e.g., summarized by Banning 2003; Banning and Byrd 1989; Byrd 1994). The major innovation from the PPNA to the PPNB is the change from circular or oval structures to well-formed rectangular rooms. There are, however, considerable regional and chronological variations. For example, in the southern Levant, "megaron" or

6.3   Reconstruction of the Neolithic community of 'Ain Ghazal,
Jordan. Courtesy Jonathan Mabry.

"pier houses" were quite common (fig. 6.4). These consisted of usually
free-standing rectangular structures with an entrance at one of the short
ends, and stone or mud brick piers, or wooden posts situated symmetrically along the axis to support the roof (Banning 2003:7; Byrd and Banning 1988). PPNB structures often are linked into several roomblocks,
frequently forming an almost "condominium" morphology. A notable activity during much of the PPNB also was extensive "remodeling" of individual structures. Some of the most distinctive architecture occurs at
sites in Turkey, such as Çayönü. This involves an evolutionary change
from PPNA round houses to rectangular structures in the PPNB that exhibit chronological development from grill plans, to channeled building
and cell-plan building plans (Banning 2003:7–9; A. Özdoğan 1999:41;
Voigt 2000:274). Despite the emphasis on rectangular structures, however, some PPNB communities consisted of circular architecture. This
pattern seems more persistent in the southern arid regions at sites like
Shaqarat Mazyad, 'Ain Abū Nukhayla, and early PPNB Beidha.

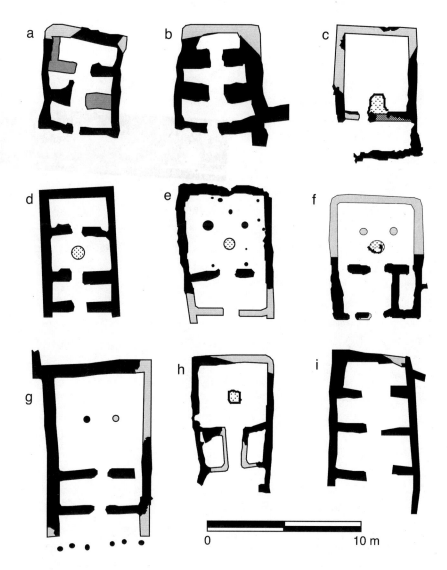

6.4 House plans of PPNB pier structures. *a*, *b*: Beidha; *c*: Beisamoun; *∂*, *e*: ʿAin Ghazal; *f*, *g*, *h*: Jericho; *i*: Yiftahel. Courtesy of E. B. Banning and American Schools of Oriental Research.

Although exposures at most EPPNB sites are limited, there is evidence for a shift from oval to small subrectangular domestic architecture
at sites such as Aswad, Horvat Galil, Abu Hudhud, and Jilat 7. EPPNB
house walls often were constructed of fieldstones, but at Aswad and Horvat Galil, rectangular mud bricks were used in conjunction with colored
lime-plaster floors, which curved up to the walls, a pattern that becomes
more common later. In the desert areas, oval structures still were predominant. Overall, the small scale of domestic structures is notable, as is the
dichotomy between house-cleaning activities. It will be recalled that one
characteristic of the PPNA was the cleaning of floors, and this continued
into the EPPNB, with the exception of the desert sites, where ash and
other debris often accumulated in structures. There presently is only limited evidence for EPPNB nondomestic architecture (Kuijt and Goring-
Morris 2002:385).

It was during the MPPNB that well-established villages with exceptionally well-made domestic structures came into existence. It is during
this time that we see the trademark of PPNB architecture in the form of
multiroomed rectangular structures. Many sites have spectacularly preserved architecture (fig. 6.5), often standing to three or more meters. A
frequent analogy is the Native American pueblos of the Southwest. The
past two decades have witnessed several detailed analyses of MPPNB
architecture as a way of understanding social organization, household
composition, economic patterns, site and regional patterning, and the relationship between domestic and nondomestic architecture (Kuijt and
Goring-Morris 2002:390–391, and citations therein).

MPPNB architecture overall was characterized by rectangular or
subrectangular structures that had an entrance at one end, were internally partitioned, and often had open internal space opposite the entrance,
with a central hearth. Walls frequently were constructed of fieldstones
that were later filled with mud and irregular stones. Floors were almost
always made of thick plaster, painted red, pink, or white, and contained
multiple postholes for roof supports. Remodeling was frequent, and structures were highly standardized in terms of length, width, and internal
layout, with rooms frequently being large and open. In the arid desertic
areas, circular structures continued to be constructed (Kuijt and Goring-
Morris 2002:390–393). It was also during the end of the MPPNB that
some megasites came into being.

6.5   Well-preserved architecture at PPNB Ghwair I, Jordan.

There is considerable evidence for nondomestic architecture at many MPPNB sites, giving us tantalizing glimpses of how communities were organized for collective purposes. One manifestation of nonresidential architecture is distinctive buildings both within and outside of settlement boundaries. These often differed from residential structures in that they were larger and had different artifact compositions, suggesting use for either ritual or community-wide purposes. Often large upright stones are found, and niches also occur in many structures, frequently interpreted as being caches for objects. Sometimes, nondomestic buildings were incorporated into residential units. There is limited evidence for large outside nondomestic structures as well, such as the stairway and possible public forum area of Ghwair I (see Case Study 4). Specialized sites such as Kfar HaHoresh in the Galilee appear to have been constructed only for mortuary purposes.

In the Taurus PPNB, substantial evidence exists for nondomestic architecture. At Çayönü, several special stone buildings are documented, including the Skull Building, the Flagstone Building, the Terrazzo Building, and the Bench Building. These span the site's occupation from EPPNB through MPPNB (A. Özdoğan 1999; Verhoeven 2002:239). At Nevalı

Çori, occupied during the EPPNB and MPPNB, three consecutive non-domestic buildings are documented. These are distinct from residential structures, and Building III is particularly impressive due to a female sculpture carved into slabs. Other sculpture includes a carved stone "totem pole" with numerous figures and other iconographic depictions (Voigt 2000:270–274). Göbekli, with no residential structures, also continued to be used.

As with the MPPNB, the standard architectural pattern during the LPPNB is the continuation of rectangular and subrectangular multi-roomed buildings containing plastered floors and walls. Remodeling continues to be common. In some regions where stone was not readily available, unfired mud brick served as the construction material. Freestanding architecture occurs, but in some larger settlements, buildings were constructed against each other. Two-story buildings also appear, and at some, ground floors often consisted of small (1.0–2.0 m²) rooms that usually lacked domestic artifacts and are frequently interpreted as storage units (Kuijt and Goring-Morris 2002:407).

In spite of this general continuity, however, substantial changes also occurred during the LPPNB, especially at the megasites. While houses during the MPPNB often had large rooms, during the LPPNB the number of rooms in structures increased, but their size decreased. Many LPPNB structures are elaborate, and some of the two-story units often contain internal stairways (Bienert 2001:110–111).

Presumed nondomestic architecture typically consists of structures that are much larger than domestic units and are located both within residential areas or slightly away from these. As one example, at 'Ain Ghazal, Rollefson (2000:174–178) identifies three types of ritual structures during the LPPNB occupation. The first are small (ca. 10 m²) apsidal buildings, three (or possibly four) of which have been documented. The second may be an evolutionary development from the apsidal buildings and consists of a small (2.5 m in diameter) circular room with a large hearth/altar installation. The third type is what Rollefson refers to as a "temple" or "sanctuary," based on the unique "furniture" found inside this large (ca. 4 × 5 m) structure. At least two occupations are suggested, and during the earlier one, three orthostats, or "standing stones," about 70 cm high were arranged symmetrically. A heavily burned "altar" also is present, as are other features. Oddly, the floor was constructed of dirt, not plaster like most other 'Ain Ghazal structures. During the later phase, remodeling occurred. A brilliant white orthostat may have an anthropomorphic shape. Other architectural features suggest that the enclosure may have been open to the sky. A low platform built inside a thin wall, along with the "altar," created two rooms. While some may question Rollefson's use of the term *temple*, it is clear that this was a unique structure.

Not all LPPNB nondomestic architecture relates to symbolic behavior, however. One striking feature that occurs at sites in the arid zones that likely are LPPNB are the desert-kites, linear stone features usually interpreted as elaborate game drives used in gazelle hunting (Betts 1989). While these are not restricted to the LPPNB, they appear most commonly during this time.

During the PPNC, most architectural evidence comes from a single site, 'Ain Ghazal. There was considerable reuse of LPPNB structures, with two primary house plans. One consists of small (ca. 3 x 4 m) rectangular structures, while the other includes semisubterranean pier and cell houses. A major change is in the use of plaster flooring, which deteriorated in quality, perhaps due to ecological reasons (see chapter 7). At Ashkelon, domestic architecture was initially thought to be semisubterranean pit dwellings, but recent excavations suggest that these were waste dumps, and that domestic architecture used mud brick and was on the surface but is poorly preserved (Kuijt and Goring-Morris 2002:415).

Information on PPNC nonresidential architecture is limited. At 'Ain Ghazal, it includes a 14-m-long massive but low wall that probably represents the separation of courtyard areas. A walled street, 2.5 m wide and extending at least 9 m, has two entrances. A "sanctuary" was originally thought to date to the PPNC but now is likely placed within the LPPNB (Rollefson 1997a:294–298, 1998a:117; 2000:179). At Atlit Yam, long walls and several wells were constructed, one of which is 7 m deep. The latter is a rare form of Neolithic architecture and has parallels in Cyprus (see chapter 9) (Kuijt and Goring-Morris 2002:415–416).

Economy

Both animal husbandry and agriculture became firmly established during the PPNB, although this did not necessarily spread to the more arid zones. At the same time, wild resources continued to be used. There are now confirmed domesticated cereals, and important crops included winter wheat, two-row and six-row barley, peas, lentils, chickpeas, vetch, and horse bean. There also was an increasing dependence on goat and sheep herding, and, to the north, cattle herding. Gazelles continued to be hunted, especially in the steppe and desert zones. Other hunted animals included deer, boar, and a variety of other mammals (Banning 2002a:8). While the PPNB witnessed a rich and diverse economic base, during the PPNC available data indicate a more restricted dietary breadth.

The issue of incontestable domestication is, of course, a major topic of debate, as previously discussed. Given available data, what can we say about when the first true domesticates appeared during the PPNB? For the EPPNB, data are relatively scarce. At Aswad, the presence of domesticated and cultivated cereals has been argued (van Zeist and Bakker-Heeres 1985) from the PPNA levels, but as summarized in chapter 5, Nesbitt's critical analysis questions the dating of these materials, and its PPNA status is dubious as well. Nesbitt also notes that the barley chaff from all phases of this site contain only 26 percent domestic type, suggesting that not all plants were domesticated (Nesbitt 2002:121).

According to Nesbitt, the first unambiguous morphological evidence of plant domestication occurs not in Cauvin's "heartland" or the southern Levant, but rather in southeast Turkey, during the EPPNB, at ca. 9200 BP, from the early levels at Nevalı Çori. Here abundant einkorn and emmer grain and chaff are present and virtually all the chaff is of domesticated type. Barley chaff is less well-preserved and possibly of wild type. Also in the same region, at Çafer Höyük, domestication is well attested to on the basis of domesticated grains of einkorn and emmer, and tough-rachised emmer spikelet forks, although secure dating is an issue. Çayönü is more problematic, since it was excavated prior to systematic flotation-recovery strategies. In the late grill building phase, from ca. 9200–9100 BP, barley is present, but its chaff is of wild type. Emmer wheat grains also appear wild, but the chaff is all of domesticated type, and einkorn grains appear domesticated as well, leading to the conclusion of domestication (Nesbitt 2002:121–122).

Given the critical criteria that Nesbitt uses for convincing evidence of domesticates, when do these actually appear in the Levantine Corridor? Nesbitt (2002:122) feels that Nahal Hemar, a specialized cave site, actually has the best current evidence of domesticated cereals in the

Levant, although the EPPNB dating is in question. Aswad (Phase II, i.e., MPPNB) also has convincing evidence, and domestic status may occur there earlier, but as noted previously, dating is a problem (Nesbitt 2002:121, 127). Often cited is the presence of domesticates from EPPNB Jilat 7, in the arid steppe zone (Garrard et al. 1996:213), but Nesbitt's (2002:128) critical eye notes that the evidence here is limited to one grain of domesticated two-grained einkorn, and two indeterminate wheat grains. Despite his cautious views, however, Nesbitt does not argue that domestication first occurred in southeastern Turkey. Rather, the evidence has as much to do with lack of publication and the rigorous application of archaeobotanical sampling. He believes that "agriculture was still emerging in the early PPNB, and that crops were still in the process of spreading through the fertile crescent . . ." (Nesbitt 2002:122).

By the MPPNB domesticated cereals are well documented at many sites, indicating that the "Neolithic package" of cereals was well established (Nesbitt 2002:122). Domestication of individual species likely was a geographically independent event and a gradual process. For example, rye appears at Abu Hureyra and later at Çan Hassan III, barley in the southern Levant and possibly in the Zagros, emmer wheat in the northern Levant (e.g., Çayönü) and possibly independently in the southern Levant (Aswad, Jericho), and einkorn in southeastern Turkey (e.g., Nevalı Çori).

What can be said of animal domestication during the PPNB? As with plants, there is considerable regional variation. Most evidence points to domestication occurring after plant domestication, and has implications for the development of pastoralism. Unlike plants, which require cultivable land and water, animals are more "portable." There is no question that the keeping and breeding of ungulates for both primary resources (meat and by-products) and secondary resources (milk, hair, fertilizer, traction) was an important element to Neolithic economy (Bar-Yosef and Meadow 1995:82–90). Indeed, the ultimate preference for sheep over goat may have been related to their greater yield of secondary products, as well as their being easier to handle and less detrimental to the environment (Peters et al. 1999:42).

Many but not all researchers agree that initial domestication of primary animal species occurred in the northern Levant and southeast Turkey, rather than in the southern Levant (Peters et al. 1999). The issue of whether many were morphologically domesticated remains unclear, and, as with plants, there is considerable disagreement among scholars as to what, exactly, constitutes animal "domestication." For example, Zeder and Hesse (2000) believe the initial goat domestication occurred around 8900 BP at Ganj Dareh in the highland Zagros, which is within their natural habitat. These were not, however, morphologically domesticated or genetically distinguishable from wild goats. Rather, Zeder and Hesse reach their conclusions based on profiles of young males slaughtered and prolonged female survivorship, which they feel makes them a managed, and therefore domesticated, population. Certainly new approaches using ancient DNA should be coupled with more traditional methodologies to determine domestic status. For example, at Abu Ghosh, DNA studies generally are in agreement with morphometric data but also point to deficiencies with the latter approach. At this site, two species of wild goat (Nubian ibex and bezoar goat) were identified by DNA, although they were not differentiated by morphometric data. This study also indicated that during the site's PPNB occupation, wild goats were undergoing the process of domestication but were not fully domestic until the PN (Bar-Gal et al. 2002).

Given data limitations and incomplete reports, this is what we know of PPNB animal domestication. While the exact mechanisms involved are unknown, many feel that an external catalyst was required and that there is not necessarily a linear progression from wild to domestic status. This may have been linked to environmental degradation, both climatically and humanly induced, that began during the Natufian (Horwitz et al. 1999:77–78). Peters et al. (1999:42–44), however, feel that sociocultural factors were more important. In any case, animal domestication should be perceived of as an end result of sedentism.

The domestication of sheep and probably goat likely first occurred in the southern Taurus piedmont during the EPPNB (although see Zeder and Hesse 2000). Caprines become more common in the northern Levant during the MPPNB, although they account for less than 30 percent of bone samples (Peters et al. 1999:43). In the southern Levant, there is an overall shift from gazelle to caprovines by the MPPNB, but it is only during the LPPNB that there is convincing evidence for domestic sheep and goat. Incipient or proto-domestication, however, began in the MPPNB, and Wasse (2000, 2002) argues for domestic goats at 'Ain Ghazal from the time of its MPPNB foundation. In any case, by the LPPNB at 'Ain Ghazal, not only are goats domesticated, but cattle and possibly sheep are as well, providing more than 80 percent of the meat protein for the site's residents (Köhler-Rollefson et al. 1988).

Unconscious selection on populations of captive animals isolated from their wild counterparts may have been a critical variable during the initial stages of domestication. Once a precedent was established with caprines, the domestication of other species rapidly followed. Overall, there is a predominance of sheep remains in northern Levantine sites, while goats are more common in the southern Levant. It is generally agreed that sheep were introduced into the southern Levant from the north, with the earliest domestic sheep occurring around 8500 BP in the Damascus Basin. Their ultimate source may have been either central or southern Turkey. In Jordan, domestic sheep occur earlier than they do to the west, in Israel, where they do not appear until the PPNC. The coexistence of both wild and domestic sheep may have occurred at Basta (Horwitz et al. 1999:76–77).

Thus, whether caprines, as well as cattle and pigs, were locally domesticated or imported into the southern Levant is a contentious issue. Some feel that goats, like sheep, were introduced to the south from either the northern Levant or the Taurus region, while others prefer an autochthonous model, showing progressive changes associated with domestication at several sites. For the more arid zones, both sheep and goats were likely introduced, rather than being domesticated locally. For domestic cattle and pigs, the evidence is even less clear. The Middle Euphrates likely was a center of cattle domestication (De Cupere and Duru 2003:116; Peters et al. 1999), with these animals documented at Tel Halula at the end of the MPPNB and possibly at nearby EPPNB Dja'de (Cauvin 2000a:217–218; Helmer et al. 2005). Thus, cattle probably were introduced to the south during the LPPNB, although, again, some prefer local domestication.

Finally, data on pigs are presently too inconclusive to draw definitive arguments on their origin. No domestic pigs are documented during the PPNB in the southern Levant, although they do occur at a few sites, such as 'Ain Ghazal and Atlit Yam, during the PPNC. It appears likely that pigs were initially domesticated in the north during the LPPNB, with probable domestic pigs first documented at sites such as Çayönü, Gritille, and Assoud. Of these, Çayönü appears to contain the earliest, at ca. 8500 BP;

there also are morphological indications of domestic pigs in the east at sites such as Jarmo by about 8000 BP (Peters et al. 1999; Smith 1995:63–64).

In summary, then, in the southern Levant, the earliest domestic animals, the caprines, are found in the core Mediterranean zone and adjacent Jordan Valley. The more arid zones may have served as target areas for the later introduction of already-domesticated animals. The Levantine Corridor, a link between the northern and southern portions of the Fertile Crescent, served as a natural route for introducing domesticates such as sheep, and possibly cattle and pigs.

Most discussion here has focused on domestic plants and animals. Not yet mentioned is the role of marine resources during the Neolithic. While substantial data are lacking, Neolithic underwater sites such as Atlit-Yam provide rare glimpses into this element. The establishment of fishing economies based on coastal villages has exciting implications not only for adding dimension to Neolithic economic practices, but also to exploration of the Mediterranean islands (Galili et al. 2004).

It also must be remembered that Neolithic peoples continued to hunt gazelle, ibex, wild goat, and sheep and to gather wild plants. This is especially true in the more arid zones (Simmons 1980, 1981). Eventually, though, domesticated plants and, especially, animals were introduced, either by actual population migrations or by adoption by indigenous desert-dwellers (Byrd 1992:53–56). It was likely during the Neolithic that classic Near Eastern patterns of pastoral nomadism became established (cf. Bar-Yosef and Khazanov 1992).

Ultimately, what is important to realize is that, as with the PPNA, PPNB people were using a variety of both wild and domesticated plants and animals. Specific species varied by location. While arguments may be made about what actually constitutes "domestication," it is clear that to support the large populations at many Neolithic sites, these resources were undoubtedly used in a domestic sense.

Settlement Pattern and Diversity

The PPNB is best exemplified by the emergence of villages (cf. Byrd 1994), but there is a large range of site types spanning enormous megasites to small specialized localities. The assumption is that most villages were occupied year-round, although some, especially smaller ones, may have been seasonal. Villages are typically located in environments favorable to farming and close to permanent springs and alluvial fans or major wadis. Even in the more arid reaches, they tend to be near major drainages. There are also a few cave occupations (Banning 2002a:2). Many PPNB settlements are partially or entirely buried in alluvium or colluvium. Oftentimes, however, they are not buried deeply. For example, 'Ain Ghazal, although nearly invisible from the surface, has only a few centimeters of surface materials covering its Neolithic deposits, which exceed 8 m in some places.

Bar-Yosef and Meadow (1995:75) provide estimates on the sizes of several sites. These range from a maximum of 30 or more acres for sites like Çatalhöyük, Abu Hureyra, or 'Ain Ghazal to only a few square meters for specialized sites. Many village sites fall within a range of 3 to 10 acres. Kuijt (2000a:84) provides estimates for MPPNB villages of between around 1.2 to 7.4 acres, and for larger "towns" during the LPPNB and PPNC of 20–30 acres. More telling are his estimated site size increases between periods: 5,000 percent over the roughly 2,000-year period from the Late Natufian to the LPPNB (Kuijt 2000a:85)! By the LPPNB, there may have been considerable crowding at many Neolithic settlements, and this, in turn, undoubtedly affected social relations. Such pressure may have contributed to the abandonment of some large LPPNB and PPNC communities in the southern and central Levant, and new settlements, founded during the PN, were often considerably smaller (Kuijt 2000a:94). A quite different trajectory, however, occurred in other areas of the Near East, where PN occupations often were substantial.

While much recent attention has focused on large PPNB sites, it is important to note that on a regional scale, they are relatively rare. They may have served as central places in both local and regional networks (Bar-Yosef 1998b:193; Rollefson 1987). Far more common were numerous villages and hamlets distributed across the landscape. These represented small agricultural communities that in many ways are not too different from similar settlements in the contemporary Near East.

Another type of site, admittedly rare, is the cave, such as Nahal Hemar in the Judean Desert (Bar-Yosef and Alon 1988). This served as a storage place for an array of ritual paraphernalia, and is interpreted as a sacred place that possibly marked a boundary between PPNB entities from the Judean Hills and the northern Negev (Bar-Yosef and Meadow 1995:82).

Small specialized sites are usually interpreted as seasonal encampments of Neolithic hunters and gatherers. In some cases, they have unusual configurations, such as at the burin sites and desert-kites in the Jordanian deserts (Betts 1988, 1989). Another site type with possible ritual significance could be that containing rock art. Unfortunately, these types of sites are rare, and when rock art occurs, it primarily is within sites rather than as isolated pieces. Some examples are the carved animal and human forms at PPNB Dhuweila, a small desert camp site in eastern Jordan (Betts 1988:379). Note that this rock art is distinct from the elaborately carved stones incorporated into architecture, as at Göbekli.

The People

Literally hundreds of human skeletons have been recovered from PPNB sites, but, as with the PPNA, there have been few systematic studies of these. Given the rapid population expansion during the PPNB, it is not surprising to find a large amount of variability in the human remains. What is perhaps somewhat surprising is that in terms of biological morphometrics, there is little evidence for local continuity between Natufian and PPN peoples, tending to support marked regional diversity (Pinhasi and Pluciennik 2004:73–74). Smith (1998:66–69) notes that PPNB crania from several sites appear to be shorter and broader than those from Natufian contexts. Facial measurements are limited and highly variable, but suggest a more elongated face than the Natufians'. PPNB mandibles tend to be longer with greater ramus height than what is characteristic of the Natufians. There is some evidence of cranial molding or deformation, but much of this might have been postmortem. Stature appears to have been similar to that of the Natufian, although some PPNB specimens from Abu Ghosh and Beisamoun were more robust than even the largest Natufians. Samples from Basta, however, are gracile.

Cauvin's (2000a:104) belief of PPNB diffusion includes actual population movement. He notes the arrival of a new population of "gracile Mediterraneans," who already existed during the Mureybatian of northern Syria, and "some brachycephalic elements" into Jericho during the PPNB. These new arrivals did not replace the "robust Mediterraneans" of the Sultanian culture, but added to this existing population to form a racially composite whole. The idea of actual population movements has a long, and not necessarily illustrious, history in archaeology, and rather than view entire new demic incursions, it is perhaps best to appreciate the amount of diversity that characterized many of these populations.

In terms of health, specimens from 'Ain Ghazal and Basta have more dental disease, especially calculus and caries, than those from the PPNA. Many PPNB samples also show an increased frequency of antemortem tooth loss from severe dental attrition in comparison with the Natufian. This condition increases with age and might suggest that people lived longer during the Neolithic. It also could imply that the diet became more abrasive, probably from increased carbohydrate consumption, as well as simply eating more ground foods. Differences in stature and skeletal robustness within the Neolithic also might have been related to differences in environmental stress and changing lifestyles. Dental hypoplasia, one estimate of environmental stress, is present in less than 50 percent of Natufian and some PPNB samples, but increases to over 90 percent at PPNA Hatoula, and then appears to increase again toward the end of the PPNB. This could indicate a temporary increase in environmental stress at the initial stages of plant domestication, followed by a lessening of stress during the earlier PPNB, and then yet another increase toward the end of the PPNB, when the quality of life is thought to have deteriorated (Smith 1998:68–69).

Considering these dental problems, new research from the Neolithic of Pakistan offers an intriguing look at an early tradition of dentistry. Nine adults from a graveyard at Mehrgarh, dating to ca. 7,500–9,000 years ago, yielded evidence of 11 drilled molar crowns. Analysis confirmed that the drilling was on living individuals, although the motive is unclear. Aesthetic functions, however, were ruled out, since the perforations exposed sensitive tooth structure, and some type of filling could have been placed in the cavities. Numerous flint drill heads occur at Mehrgarh, and experimental work with models of these indicated that a drill hole could be produced in human enamel in less than one minute (Coppa et al. 2006).

Eshed, Gopher, Gage, and Hershkovitz (2004) conducted a demographic study that included 262 Neolithic burials. As opposed to many earlier studies, which suggested increased mortality with the advent of agriculture (e.g., Cohen and Armelagos 1984), their data show a slightly increased mean age of death for the Neolithic as compared to the Natufian, thereby confirming Smith's (1998:68) similar conclusions. They do, however, show an increased mortality among females, which they attribute to increased maternal deaths.

In an analysis of 20 skeletons from three PPNB sites in the southern Sinai, burial practices shared a common ideology with more northern Levantine burials (Hershkovitz et al. 1994). That is, they were associated with dwellings or courtyards, adults' skulls were removed for secondary burials, children were treated differently, and there were no burial goods. Dental evidence and lesion frequencies point to a hunter-gatherer way of life, and there is little evidence of stress in the form of hypoplasia, inflammatory bone lesions, reduced body size, or traumatic injuries. Finally, and perhaps most interestingly, the morphology of these individuals was more gracile than other contemporary populations. While they show more resemblance to the Levantine PPNB populations than to any other circum-Mediterranean group, they also appear to have their biological roots in neither the Levant nor North Africa. Rather, is it suggested that they probably originated in the Arabian Peninsula.

At Atlit Yam, several skeletons show similarities to the nearby Natufian and Neolithic site of Nahal Oren, indicating genetic continuity; various occupational stress markers also were observed on many individuals (Hershkovitz et al. 1991; Hershkovitz and Galili 1990). These were related to activities that included deep-sea fishing, diving, and fishnet production. One individual showed a buildup of bone forming a long ridge at the opening of the ear canal, which is linked to diving that habitually exposes the ear canal to cold water. Other stress markers included cases of flattening of long bones and overdevelopment of some areas of muscle attachment, and extreme wear of the teeth of one individual, all indicative of occupational stresses. The authors conclude that males were primarily involved in fishing and other marine food exploitation, although Peterson (2002:78–80) questions some of their interpretations.

Remains from Abu Hureyra already have been discussed in chapter 4. Molleson's (2000) analysis concentrated on earlier (Natufian-equivalent) skeletons, but she also studied later Neolithic remains, although many were mixed, making specific phase attributions difficult. Overall, though, the adults were rather small and muscular, but "wiry" rather than robust. There is a physical similarity between the Neolithic and historic remains, suggesting the importance of the local environment in determining many aspects of appearance. About half of the Neolithic remains were immature, ranging from newborns to subadults. No evidence for rickets or scurvy was observed, but there were a few cases of suspected iron deficiency anemia. Evidence from one child suggested a chronic condition that could have been induced by a parasitic infection or an infantile diarrheal condition. The amount of wear on the teeth suggests that the diet was extremely hard and coarse. Finally, Molleson concludes that there were more substantial divisions of labor than initially thought, with males hunting and making tools, while females spun, wove, ground grain, and made baskets.

Peterson (2002:83–84) summarizes some other studies of Neolithic skeletal remains. At Basta, pronounced and severe degeneration in the shoulder joints occurs in three adult males. Severe arthritis is noted among six PPN adults, and degenerative changes in the vertebrae occur in five individuals at 'Ain Ghazal. Several 'Ain Ghazal individuals also have spinal pathologies described as possible cases of tuberculosis (El-Najjar et al. 1997). If true, it would represent the earliest evidence of this disease in the Old World (Peterson 2002:83). Traumatic injuries appear rare. Only three examples are identified in the Jericho population. At Basta, some adult skulls had healed fractures (Nissen et al. 1991:19). Of course, these do not necessarily imply violence; they could have been the consequences of day-to-day life. Evidence for actual violence is rare. For example, at Basta one eight- to nine-year-old male was apparently murdered by two blows to the head, the last of which was fatal (Roehrer-Ertl et al. 1988). This has been interpreted as a result of homosexual abuse by a male group (Roehrer-Ertl and Frey 1987), but this seems a rather fanciful reconstruction. At 'Ain Ghazal, one individual seems to have died a violent death. This male, buried in a trash heap, had broken bones and apparently died from a flint blade embedded into the left side of his skull (Peterson 2002:84). Curiously, this was not a projectile point, despite Cauvin's (2000a:125–126) emphasis on a PPNB "love-affair with weapons" and his speculation that the PPNB expansion may have been achieved through force of arms (although in fairness, he concludes that there is virtually no evidence for this). Along similar lines, one of the burials at Ghwair I, likely that of an elderly woman, had a projectile point imbedded in her jaw, although this may have been fortuitous (Simmons and Najjar 2003:422). At PPNA Jerf el Ahmar, a headless skeleton on the floor of a structure also suggests violence, but its interpretation is unclear (Stordeur 2000:2).

Peterson's (2002:106–112) MSM study included 34 individuals from two PPNA sites and five PPNB sites, and indicates profound changes in workloads and new patterns of muscle activity compared to the Natufian. She characterizes the sexual patterns of lateralization as converging during the Neolithic. The habitual activity spectrum for both males and females involved a number of bilateral tasks, and for females this was a continuation of the bilateral symmetry seen earlier. For the males, however, there is a significant reorientation from the strongly unilateral muscle development seen among Natufian hunters. Thus, a farming lifestyle seems to have caused greater changes in the habitual activities of males compared to those of women, with the male pattern resembling that of the females (Peterson 2002:106–107).

Tasks associated with farming, such as land clearing, timbering, cutting and hauling, were strenuous and would have required considerable effort. One of the muscle patterns in Peterson's sample supports male activities related to such tasks. She concludes that such burden-bearing tasks resulted in changes in male musculature, suggesting some reorganization of daily labor patterns. Interestingly, her analysis also indicates that these tasks were shared, with no significant differences in workload between the sexes (Peterson 2002:112, 124).

Another MSM study using a larger sample (47 Neolithic individuals) also concludes that the transition to agriculture resulted in higher loads on the upper limbs compared to Natufian populations. It further indicates that Neolithic peoples were involved in new activities and occupations. This research, unlike Peterson's, suggests that there was a gender-based division of labor in both the Natufian and the Neolithic, and that Neolithic females took over a greater proportion of subsistence activities compared to the Natufian (Eshed, Gopher, Galili, and Hershkovitz 2004).

Ritual Behavior

Out of the huge literature on the rich PPNB symbolic material culture, one of the best and most detailed discussions from a pan–Near Eastern perspective is Cauvin's (2000a, esp. 105–120), and both a recent book (Gebel et al. 2002) and an issue of *Neolithics* are completely devoted to Neolithic magic and ritual. Several articles also explicitly address Neolithic ritual and symbolic behavior (e.g., Bar-Yosef 1997; Garfinkel 1994;

Kuijt 1996; Kuijt and Chesson 2005; Mabry 2003; Rollefson 1983, 1986, 1998b; Verhoeven 2002; Voigt 2000).

We have already addressed the evidence for ritual architecture, and it is clear that many structures were special-use buildings. I want to reiterate here, however, that not all nondomestic structures were necessarily "religious" in nature—communal works, like large stairways at 'Ain Ghazal or Ghwair I, for example, did not necessarily have ritual meaning. There are, however, several examples of structures that appear to be dedicated to the dead. Perhaps the best-known is at Çayönü, where the "skull house" contained numerous burials. This was rebuilt several times, and on the floor of the original building numerous human skulls were deposited; several skeletons were found in two pits, in one case accompanied by bull skulls and horns. During subsequent rebuilding episodes, skulls and other human remains were recovered. Traces of human, auroch, and sheep blood were also found on a large stone table, and both human and auroch blood residue was present on a long flint knife. Altogether, at least 450 individuals were in the Skull Building. Burials also were in other parts of the site, including pits full of human bones. Curiously, plastered human skulls do not occur, although these are common in many PPNB contexts (A. Özdoğan 1999:51; Özdoğan and Özdoğan 1998:584; Verhoeven 2002:239; Wood 1998). In the southern Levant, Ba'ja has a possible "charnel-house" within a large structure consisting of several secondary interments (Gebel and Hermansen 1999).

Although rare, there is impressive evidence for ritual behavior from sites that were not settlements. We have already addressed the unique nature of Göbekli as a regional ritual center. In the southern Levant, Kfar HaHoresh apparently served as a regional mortuary center (see below). Ba'ja, although a village, has been interpreted in the context of a ritual landscape, largely due to its very remote setting and possible associations with water (Gebel 2002:126). On a smaller scale is Nahal Hemar cave. As previously noted, it may have been a sacred territorial boundary. It also appears to have been a storage facility for ritual artifacts, including fragments of six human skulls modeled with strips of asphalt, fragments of two stone masks, several small pieces of plaster statues, four anthropomorphic bone figurines, and a zoomorphic stone figure, possibly of a rodent. Other items that may have had ritual significance include preserved textiles and a headdress with a net pattern similar to that on the modeled skulls, a complete sickle including a decorated handle that was in a small niche, and a rich collection of plaster, greenstone, wood, and shell beads, as well as a small number of projectile points and flint knives (Bar-Yosef and Alon 1988). Garfinkel (1994:171–172), however, finds difficulties with the storage interpretation and instead believes that it functioned as the final burial place for cultic and sacred objects belonging to a local Neolithic group.

Some of the most intriguing evidence for ritual behavior comes from mortuary data. Although hundreds of skeletons have been recovered, human remains are still relatively rare in settlements, and most of the deceased were likely buried elsewhere, either in unexcavated parts of sites or in special mortuary centers, or cemeteries (Goring-Morris 2000:116). Patterns first established during the PPNA and the Natufian are elaborated upon. There was a remarkable pattern of formalized mortuary practices, and yet a large degree of variation exists within individual sites.

For the MPPNB, Kuijt and Goring-Morris (2002:394–395) note the coexistence of three interrelated mortuary patterns. These are the primary burial of adults, both males and females, in single graves, usually under the floors of domestic structures; the interment of infants in single graves; and the secondary removal of adult skulls from many, but not all, graves. These were often modified with clay, and then reburied or displayed individually or in caches. The majority of infants were placed in fill or outdoor courtyard areas with little ceremonial treatment, while in other cases infants seem to have been buried in ritual contexts, such as in subfloor foundations and as dedicatory offerings (see Case Study 4 for an unusual infant burial from Ghwair I). This pattern largely persists through the LPPNB, although there are some changes, most notably in the occurrence of grave goods (which are still rare) and the increased burial of humans with animals (Kuijt and Goring-Morris 2002:410–411). The small sample of PPNC burials hampers our understanding of mortuary practices, but there appear to have been additional modifications to the overall pattern. In particular, secondary burials become more common, as do multiple burials. Skull removal still occurs but is less frequent (Banning 1998:224; Kuijt and Goring-Morris 2002:416).

The widespread "skull cult" has generated considerable literature. Most often it is interpreted as a form of ancestor worship and/or as a method to promote social equality (Bar-Yosef 1998b:198; Bienert 1991; Kuijt 2000b). While some have argued that special treatment of the skull was reserved for males, it was, in fact, seemingly applied in roughly equal proportions to male and female adults (Goring-Morris 2000:124). Whatever its meaning, this was a complex process that usually involved burying adults in a flexed position under house floors and then re-excavating part of the burial pit, often facilitated by markers placed over the skull, and removing the skull, presumably after the flesh had decomposed (Kuijt 2001:82–86). Once removed, the skulls were treated in at least three different fashions (Garfinkel 1994:165–170). They were sometimes remodeled with plaster and other materials, such as shells or bitumen, to form an image of a human face. Whether these remodelings were meant to reflect an actual depiction of the formerly living person (cf. Kenyon 1957b:62) is not known, but in many instances the remodeling was quite elaborate. Sometimes the teeth were removed, a practice that may have had something to do with rule or seniority by elders (Arensburg and Hershkovitz 1988:57). A second treatment method was painting skulls. The third pattern is skull removal, but with no cranial treatment. Detailed studies on samples from 'Ain Ghazal have shown that what were initially interpreted as cut-marks for defleshing of crania actually represent sanding of the exterior bone surface, likely to prepare the skull as an anchor for plaster or to remove the plaster after it was applied (Bonogofsky 2001a).

Garfinkel (1994:170) proposes that the "life-cycle" for this widespread pattern includes the following steps. First, the individual was buried; second the grave was opened to remove the skull, now making it a cultic object; third, skulls were selected for specific treatments; fourth, the skull was either stored or displayed; and fifth, as skulls deteriorated, they were no longer considered suitable for ritual use and were formally reburied. Kuijt (2000b:148), believing that Garfinkel's approach is too functional, argues that cultic objects, skull caches, plastered skulls, and foundation offerings were a series of thematically interrelated components of ritual belief and community ideology that strengthened ties between multiple households (Kuijt 2000b:155–156). In this context, Goren et al. (2001) provide a compelling analysis of skull modeling and conclude that while general concepts appear to have been widely shared, there were strong site-specific traditions practiced by artisans who were locally based.

A detailed study of 57 modeled skulls from several sites has demonstrated that not all were of elderly individuals (Bonogofsky 2001b:187).

Rather, younger adults' and children's skulls also were plastered, and none of the adults demonstrated intentional postmortem evulsion of all teeth. Bonogofsky (2001b:188–189) argues for a broader interpretative range in which skulls could have been perceived as objects associated with fertility or could simply have signified individuals who were being mourned.

Decapitation is a recurrent theme throughout the Neolithic and is not restricted to burials. It also is expressed symbolically, in wall paintings at Çatalhöyük, for example, and in the decapitation of anthropomorphic figurines (Kuijt 2000b:149). While it could be argued that some of the figurines were simply broken, there is no denying that the removal of the head had substantial importance to Neolithic peoples. Thus, it is tempting to interpret such materials as ritual and symbolic "killings," although Garfinkel (1994:180) cautions against overreliance on such conclusions.

Beyond the skull cult, there are other mortuary data that provide clues to ritual behavior. We have already noted the increase in grave goods in LPPNB contexts, as well as the decrease in the skull cult during the PPNC. Clearly these suggest ritual changes over time in how the dead were treated. Adding to the mortuary database is the remarkable MPPNB site of Kfar HaHoresh (Goring-Morris 2000). The distribution of animal remains at this site is important in inferring ritual behavior. As noted earlier, the PPNA incorporation of certain animals, especially cattle, in rooms undoubtedly has some ritual significance. This pattern continues during the PPNB, and it is not unusual to find animals associated with human burials. At Kfar HaHoresh, however, a unique situation presents itself.

Kfar HaHoresh is interpreted as a unique regional funerary and cult center that served surrounding villages. This site, 1 to 2 acres in size, contains four activity zones: a funerary area consisting of lime-plastered surfaces and human graves, a cult area that includes grouped monoliths and stelae up to 1.5 m high, a midden deposit comprised of hearths and roasting pits, and a production and maintenance area. The graves contained both single and multiple burials, some of which were fully articulated, while others were secondary. A variety of grave goods and offerings included a headless gazelle carcass with a plastered human skull (Hershkovitz et al. 1995) and at least two modeled skulls (Goren et al. 2001). Another area contained a headless but otherwise articulated human skeleton overlying a pit filled with some 200 partially articulated postcranial auroch bones, representing at least six adult animals and two immature ones (Goring-Morris 2000:110). Under one plastered surface was an oval arrangement of 15 human mandibles and other remains that included a possible depiction of an animal outlined using human and animal bones (fig. 6.6)(Goring-Morris et al. 1998). Clearly, Kfar HaHoresh is an elaborate site unlike anything else yet documented in the Neolithic world.

Several PPNB artistic materials also may have had ritual significance, These include anthropomorphic and zoomorphic figurines, engraved slabs, tokens, statuary, masks, and the decoration of architectural components, which includes painted plaster floors and walls, and engraved stone pillars (Garfinkel 2003a:9). The masks, carved of limestone, are quite rare. These are life-sized, with carved eye- and mouth-holes as well as drilled holes for attachment to the face or for attaching other features to the mask (Kuijt and Goring-Morris 2002:398). The best examples are from Nahal Hemar. Statuary also is rare, with the best examples from two magnificent caches at 'Ain Ghazal (see chapter 7); although poorly preserved, four caches of statuary also were recovered in Garstang's Jericho excavations (Kuijt and Goring-Morris 2002:396-398). The ritual significance of these has been intensely debated in the literature, with prevailing interpretations usually related to ancestors, ghosts, and deities. Schmandt-Besserat (1998b:15) concludes that:

> Monumental statuary was an outcome of an agriculture lifestyle. The statues were created to bond the large population supported by farming. The monumental figures were powerful symbols that helped foster a common ideology, restructure society, enhance leadership, and amplify the need for administrating the communal resources in the early agricultural communities. These important developments eventually paved the way for state formation.

A variety of clay tokens occurs at many PPNB sites. The first were plain, mainly geometric shapes. Schmandt-Besserat (1992:161-170) believes that tokens were a new medium for conveying information, created to keep track of goods and standing for quantities of cereals and animal counts. That is, the new economy based on agriculture brought about the need for accounting. Schmandt-Besserat believes not only that tokens

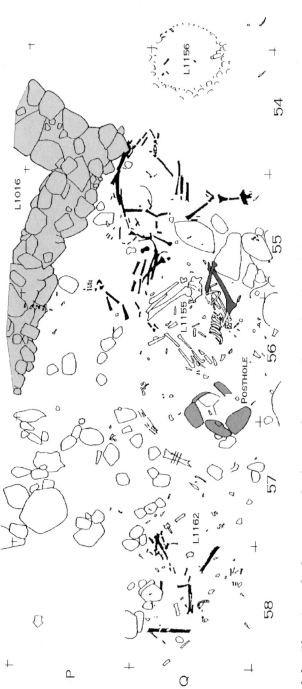

6.6 Plan view of Kfar HaHoresh, showing depiction of animal made with human bones. Courtesy Nigel Goring-Morris.

were related to accounting, but that they also influenced new social structures. She concludes that tokens can relate to cognitive skills, economy,
social structure, and communication (Schmandt-Besserat 1992:197–198).

Another particularly interesting aspect that may relate to ritual behavior is data from sites interpreted as "dance scenes" (Garfinkel 2003a,
b). At Nevalı Çori, an engraved fragment of a stone basin depicts three
figures, while at Halula, a painted floor shows 23 female figures. At Dhuweila a carved slab depicts four human figures standing in a line and holding hands. Another site, Kalavasos *Tenta* in Cyprus, has a wall painting of
a figure with uplifted hands. At el Kown 2, an incised plaster whiteware
vessel shows a very schematic human figure, and at Çatalhöyük, another
engraved plaque, originally interpreted as depicting copulating humans,
is instead viewed by Garfinkel as a dancing posture. Numerous other sites
extending into the PN also depict dancing activities in Garfinkel's innovative analysis (2003a:111–124). He believes that "from a cognitive aspect
and on an ideological plane, our dancing scenes express equality and integration between the members of a community. . . . On a practical level,
during this period there are revolutionary changes in social organization
where human societies become increasingly stratified. . . . Dancing scenes
are used as a means of concealing and camouflaging the increasing social
stratification" (Garfinkel 2003b:94).

Figurines are a common artifact, depicting both animal and human
forms. During the PPNB, the variety of figurines expands substantially,
and female figurines become especially common. To Cauvin, this reflects
the expanding role of the Earth Mother Goddess, culminating, perhaps,
in the famous Çatalhöyük goddess, a figurine that is "obese, giving birth,
seated on panthers that serve as her throne" (Cauvin 2000a:29). The Great
Goddess concept has, in fact, fallen from grace in many academic circles,
and most researchers no longer regard these figurines as symbols of early
religion (Bolger 2003:96). Many are now interpreted in more modest or
functional fashions, perhaps acting as fertility figurines or "good luck"
charms. Some have interpreted the female figurines as representing the
considerable role of women in agricultural activities (Chapman 1991:157).
Likewise, Mabry (2003:106–107) argues that these figurines were depictions of recently deceased female household members. These were treated
as elders who now symbolized lineage continuity and legitimized heri-
table claims. Kuijt and Chesson (2005) examined a range of Neolithic

figurines by subphases, pointing out that there is a higher proportion of sexual ambiguity during the MPPNB as opposed to earlier and later phases. They feel this may be related to socioeconomic aspects of life, and that both the PPNA and LPPNB/PPNC were times of increased stress in which individual and social differentiation, as presented in sexed figurines, become more important, unlike during the MPPNB when individuality was masked. Rather than assigning specific meaning to figurines, it is perhaps more profitable to note that a multiplicity of functions may be reflected by these artifacts (cf. Hodder 1990:61–65).

Not all PPNB figurines are female. While male figurines are rare, they occur, as does an array of phallic objects. Some human figurines lack sexual features and may have been used as talismans to protect their owners (Rollefson 2000:168). Many figurines are broken, often with no heads. While these may have been accidentally broken, it seems unlikely that this is the case, particularly given the prevalence of decapitated burials. These figurines could reflect ancestor veneration, or they may have been intentionally "killed" when their owners died, or were broken to prevent people outside of households from using them (Mabry 2003:105).

Many animal figurines also occur, especially bulls. A particularly vivid example is a cache of two clay bulls from 'Ain Ghazal that are pierced with bladelets, perhaps indicating a symbolic "kill" (Rollefson 2000:167). Indeed, to Cauvin (2000b:243–248), there is an increasing ascendancy of masculine symbols in conjunction with the dominance of female figurines. To him, this is so pronounced that PPNB people could be called "people of the bull" (Cauvin 2000a:123). This may be extreme, but there is no denying the importance of both female and male imagery during the PPNB.

Finally, Goring-Morris and Belfer-Cohen (2002) observe that contextual evidence suggests even mundane objects may have had symbolic importance. For example, they (2002:72) note that "game boards" could have functioned as divination devices. In a similar vein, Hermansen and Jensen (2002) believe that stone slabs in structures at MPPNB Shaqarat Mazyad could have served both practical and ritual functions, perhaps indicating that the cardinal direction "east" had some special significance. While such conclusions are intriguing, they are difficult to support, and we have to be aware of making interpretations that verge on speculation.

In summary, the PPNB is rich in symbolism. This has been interpreted in a variety of ways, from grandiose perspectives on the birth of religion, worship of the Great Mother Goddess, and connections with biblical creation myths, in Cauvin's view (see also Gimbutas 1982), to much more modest interpretations. Many scholars view the symbolic creations of the PPNB in tandem with the domestication of plants and animals that were handed down to subsequent cultures (Garfinkel 1994:180–183).

Regardless of specific interpretations of an ambiguous data set, the ritual system of the PPNB seems to have been organized around three hierarchally organized classes of ritual: individual, household, and public (Verhoeven 2002:252). Individual rituals were likely practiced in domestic contexts and are represented by human and animal figurines. They may have been linked to vitality, particularly fertility and "life force." Household rituals are indicated by burials and the skull cult, as well as animal horns in domestic spaces, and also by figurines. These rituals were primarily concerned with death. Finally, public ritual incorporated several concepts, such as communality, dominant symbolism, vitality, and human-animal linkages. Such rituals were directly related to ritual buildings as well as special ritual sites, such as Göbekli and Kfar HaHoresh. Such sites may have been visited for ritual activities by village dwellers that included communal feasting and the consumption of hunted animals, they may have been related to mobile PPNB hunters and gatherers, or they may have been the focal point of interactions between both villagers and nomads.

Social Structure and Organization

Relatively complex social organization can be inferred for the PPNB given the large-scale nature of many communities and the presence of public or communal structures (Kuijt, ed. 2000 and articles therein). Byrd's (2005b) detailed analysis of a smaller site, that of Beidha, addresses fundamental changes in the built environment over time. He proposes that throughout the Near East individual households become more independent and autonomous, that corporate bodies became formalized, and that public buildings become more important for conducting community-wide activities to integrate village life (Byrd 2005a: 266–267, 2005b). Previously, Byrd (1994) also has argued that Neolithic villages were characterized by two interrelated organizational trends: more restricted social networks for sharing and consumption, and more formalized mechanisms for community-wide integration. During both the PPNA and PPNB, ideology appears to have focused on the memory of individual family members, and property and other rights likely were inherited. Given the complex patterns of residential remodeling, postmarital residence patterns favoring location next to parents may have been typical at some sites. Critical to farmers, of course, is the issue of land ownership. Unfortunately, we have little evidence indicating whether this was at the nuclear-family level as a form of "private ownership" (Banning 1998:222).

Many researchers believe that the PPNB was characterized by the formation of nuclear families as the basis for household economy and group interaction (e.g., Flannery 1972, 2002). This conclusion often is based on ethnographic data showing that nuclear families tend to live in rectangular structures, the hallmark of PPNB architecture. Byrd (2000: 89–92), however, feels that nuclear families were already the dominant group by the Natufian. While this issue may be debated, more important to Flannery (1993:111–112) is his contention that in true villages, risk was now assumed at the level of the individual or nuclear family, unlike the group level during the Natufian and PPNA. He argues that closed site plans with private storage typify this type of organization, allowing each family to decide for itself how much or how little to produce, unlike the earlier situations, where resources were shared. Other elements used to explain the shift to rectangular dwellings include increases or decreases in the dependence on agriculture and possible shifts between polygamous and monogamous marriages (Flannery 2002:431), as well as issues relating to craft specialization, personal wealth, and the emergence of territorial and social boundaries (Saidel 1993:82–85, 93–94).

For the EPPNB, the sample size is too small to provide much evidence on social structure. Typically, sites were relatively small, hamlet-sized settlements, usually covering less than 5 acres. The situation improves with an increased sample during the MPPNB. Structures generally were built relatively close to each other, although some were separated by considerable amounts of space, and at some sites, extramural excavation has revealed large fire hearths, plaster-manufacturing facilities, and other domestic areas. Several studies have explored the nature of social arrangements in the built environment at MPPNB sites and indicate that select areas appear to have been used in a variety of both ritual and nonritual community activities. Such studies have shown considerable architectural, and presumably social, variability. This ranges from freestanding buildings separated from others by alleyways or plazas, to sites with buildings constructed next to each other, forming a high degree of architectural "packing" that does not occur again until the Bronze Age. Finally, during the PPNC, major changes occur, but interpretation is again hampered by a relatively small site sample. There is an overall decline at some megasites, although large-scale construction efforts did continue, indicating some communal social integration (Kuijt and Goring-Morris 2002: portions of 384–415).

One of the most dramatic developments throughout the PPNB was a steady increase in site size and a presumed incremental population increase. Kuijt (2000a:85) estimates mean population for MPPNB sites at 764, while for the LPPNB it is 3,293; and for the PPNC, 3,822. For individual sites in his sample, the low for the MPPNB is 45 for Kfar HaHoresh, and the high is 1,323 for 'Ain Ghazal. The former, however, is not a habitation site, and perhaps the figure of 135 for Yiftahel is more realistic. For the LPPNB, the range is 630 at 'Ain Jamman to a high of 4,116 at Basta, and for the PPNC, the figures are a low of 1,080 for 'Ain Ghazal and a high of 4,116 for Basta (Kuijt 2000a:81).

At an intrasite level, Byrd's (2000) analysis of social structure looks at room size from several Levantine PPNB sites from the Jordan Valley, southern Jordan, and the Negev and Sinai. The largest mean square footage is from sites in the Jordan Valley, at 35.3 m². Beidha, in southern Jordan, has means ranging from 29.4 to 6.9 m², and the two Negev and Sinai sites are much smaller, with mean square footage at 5.1 m². Excluding the small desert sites, this represents a substantial increase in floor space over the PPNA. Coupled with this are major changes in the organization of interior space. During the PPNB, there is a considerable degree of formal subdivision and remodeling. Domestic buildings are often highly compartmentalized, and hearths are frequently integrated within plaster floors. This is particularly evident in pier houses, where there are distinct areas for storage, processing, artifact production, sleeping, eating, and, presumably, entertaining (Byrd 2000:72–80).

Even though PPNB structures are considerably larger than earlier ones, Byrd (2000:83) does not believe that they were large enough to accommodate multiple, extended families. It appears that the concept of "dwelling," however, changed during the LPPNB, with structures housing several families, perhaps even clans (Bienert 2001:110; Rollefson 1998a:111). To what then, can the increase in structure size be attributed? Byrd (2000:85–89) proposes it is primarily due to a trend toward greater use of internal space for a variety of domestic activities, and possibly larger settlement populations. In other words, increasing floor space would have been a mechanism for coping with crowding. Coupled with this, jealousy and interhousehold disagreements may also have increased with the growth of large villages, particularly if resources were more circumscribed and if agricultural plots were subject to household ownership (Byrd 1994). Hence, the increase and formalization of interior space may have reinforced existing social order, and the general uniformity in size and shape of domestic dwellings could have promoted an egalitarian structure (Byrd 2000:85–86).

An important aspect to such arguments relates to the authority of autonomous households. Byrd (2000:85–89) believes that the increase of PPNB dwelling size reflects increased nuclear-family household autonomy. At some point, nuclear households may have become principal units of production, but the increasing size of PPNB settlements could have required the establishment of some sort of centralized authority for regulating at least some community-wide activities. Both Byrd (2000) and Kuijt (1996, 2000a, b) make compelling arguments that while communities grew throughout the PPNB, this very growth may have been the reason for the similarity in size of domestic architecture, as well as uniformity in mortuary practices, which reinforced community-wide egalitarian status, aiding household autonomy but also confirming social order within and between households (Byrd 2000:91–92).

Another aspect of social organization involves ground stone tools and their location in households. This was a time of innovation in food preparation, and Wright (2000) shows that EPPNB and MPPNB sites display new aesthetics and social rules governing food sharing. One striking feature is the new diversity of vessels, which implies specialization in the practical functions of vessels and more diverse rules of etiquette in using them. Facilities for storage, milling, and large-scale cooking were often placed in transitional zones of houses; that is, between the house and the community. Thus, persons entering a house would pass directly through milling and cooking stations in community spaces (terraces, courtyards, alleys) or in transitional "kitchen-porches" leading into houses. These arrangements were practical—large-scale cooking and milling in front of houses would make it easier to keep house interiors clean—but they also had social implications. Storage and food preparation were highly visible activities providing opportunities for social contacts between households, even though individual households controlled their own processing and storage. It is likely that households shared some facilities such as immovable grinding slabs and large fire pits, and that milling and cooking were conducted by work groups (Wright 2000:110–111).

At the same time, hearth rooms were the most secluded spaces in many PPNB houses, and Wright suggests they were the focus of household meals. Meals and artifacts used in preparing them are a central means by which social groups educate and enculturate individuals, especially the young, in proper social behavior. Meals also are a focus for hospitality (as they are today in the Near East), and Wright feels that nuclear families and lineages were central to PPNB social organization and that age was an important criterion of individual social persona. She believes that food *preparation* was an area for social interaction between households, while meal *consumption* seems to have been about privacy, the residential group, and enculturation within the lineage. If so, these habits may reflect tensions between new forms of community and traditional kinship organization (Wright 2000:111–112).

During the LPPNB, changes occurred, with larger milling tool assemblages per house and more specialized cooking facilities, such as ovens, fixed mealing bins, plaster vessels, and experiments with pottery-making. Food preparation facilities were now private, not readily visible to neighbors. Overall, a picture emerges of intensified production of food for larger groups, possibly multiple food preparers per house, larger houses, and an emphasis on privacy, including private property (Wright 2000:112–114). This leads Wright to conclude that the intensification and "privatization" of milling, cooking, storage, and dining were predominant during the LPPNB. In a sense, Wright both accommodates and elaborates on Flannery's model, since he proposed that during the PPNB eating and storage were private activities, whereas she believes that only eating was private, while preparation and storage were more public, at least until the LPPNB.

Mortuary data also have been used to predict social status. Kuijt (2000b) argues that there is some degree of social differentiation first appearing during the MPPNB in the form of cranial deformation, skull plastering and painting, and the select use of secondary skull removal and caching. Despite this, he concludes that the limited social differentiation observed during the MPPNB did not lead to successful political and economic consolidation among competing households. Kuijt (2000a:97–99) feels that during the dramatic increase in site size during the LPPNB and PPNC, while powerful individual leaders emerged, they were unable to consolidate authority and may, in fact, have been instrumental in the social fragmentation and decentralization that apparently occurred during the PN.

Certainly not all agree with the interpretation of an essentially egalitarian status of these complex PPNB villagers. One thing that does seem clear, however, is that despite increasing social complexity and concomitant stresses, Near Eastern Neolithic people were apparently reluctant to resort to extreme violence. Interestingly, this is in sharp contrast to the much later Neolithic in Europe (Guilaine and Zammit 2005:82–157). As noted previously, there is a general lack of evidence indicating community-wide violence during the PPNB. Bar-Yosef indicates (2001a:26) that Ganj Dareh in Iran is the only PPNB site in which the entire village was burned (Tel Sabi Abyad in Syria also was destroyed by fire during the subsequent PN, but this is not attributed to violence — see chapter 8). While the nuances of PPNB social organization may never be completely understood, there seems little question that their society was much more complex than previously believed.

Regional Interaction

Given the existence of an interaction sphere, both long-distance and regional trade networks are indicated for the PPNB. Individual territories can be identified on the basis of certain items of material culture, and the interaction between Neolithic villagers and hunter/gatherers has already been alluded to. Bar-Yosef (2001a:24) projects that "tribal territories" were inhabited by around 1,500–2,000 people. He (1998b:199) also notes that many material items and techniques were dispersed by the "budding off" of new communities, and by mutual exchange between neighboring villages, by intermarriage, and with kin-related groups across social and geographic boundaries. The emergence of territoriality may have been based on competition between expanding groups, during which agricultural activities exploited resources locally available, requiring the establishment of boundaries (Bar-Yosef 1998b:199–200).

There are obvious trade connections with direct exchange of various commodities between the southern and northern Levant and parts of east-central Anatolia. General PPNB similarities in many aspects of life suggest continuity over a broad area. What is somewhat unusual, however, is the near total lack of evidence for regular social or economic connections with the Nile Valley until the PN (Kuijt and Goring-Morris 2002:428).

Patterns in long-distance trade of items such as malachite, jadite, turquoise, and obsidian continued, and, as in earlier times, Anatolian obsidians predominate. The amount of obsidian found at sites varies considerably, and the trade mechanisms have often been explained in terms of a "down-the-line" distribution (Renfrew 1975), which proposes that areas within 200 km of obsidian sources will contain higher proportions of the material, and that rates fall exponentially the farther away from the source. Renfrew's model seems to be accurate for the PPNB, as obsidian is common at sites in Turkey (e.g., Balkan-Atli et al. 1999; Binder 2002) but generally becomes rarer at southern sites.

Shell continues to be important during the PPNB. Shell use is generally characterized by a decrease in *Dentalium* and an increase in *Glycymeris* and *Cardium*. PPNB sites in the Sinai tend to have more Red Sea shells than Mediterranean ones. Conversely, the farther away from the Red Sea, the lower the proportion of Red Sea shells. The distribution of both Mediterranean and Red Sea shells may indicate that PPNB hunter-gatherers in the desertic zones were trading shell for cereals with contemporary farming communities (D. Bar-Yosef 1989; Bar-Yosef Mayer 1997).

On a more theoretical level, diffusion plays a key role in Cauvin's (2000a, b) model of the "Neolithization" of the Near East, often invoking actual population movements. Many scholars feel that such arguments are antiquated, and remain unconvinced of Cauvin's model (e.g., Rollefson 2001a:113–114). Hodder (2001:109), in fact, feels that Cauvin's proposal of a "great exodus" assumes a messianic tone. Likewise, Kozłowski and Aurenche's (2005:82) concept of a "golden triangle" in the central Fertile Crescent as an area where the Neolithic first developed and then spread is open to similar criticism. This is a complex issue, and even Cauvin (2000a:98) does not posit that the PPNB spread from the Middle Euphrates northward (the "Taurus PPNB") and southward (the "Palestinian PPNB") into uninhabited regions. He allows that prior to the

PPNB, there were strong local traditions in these regions, and that they left important traces, especially in everyday life, while being incorporated into the "true" PPNB emanating from the Middle Euphrates.

A more realistic perspective may be to envision a geographically diverse group of Neolithic people, many of whom shared certain cultural patterns while at the same time establishing regional distinctions. Here Kozłowski and Aurenche's (2005) painstaking analysis proposing distinct boundaries and territories is something to seriously consider. These "cultures" or "tribes" constantly were in interaction with one another, and certainly there were population movements. In this sense, Cauvin's (2000a:104) view of PPNB acculturation resulting in ethnic admixture may be correct, but we tread on dangerous ground when speaking too strongly of ethnicity in such "deep time." The same caution must be exercised in proposing Neolithic "ethnic units" as do Kozłowski and Aurenche (2005:87–88). It seems unrealistic to invoke massive expansions of the "true PPNBers" marching forth with their splendid weaponry to colonize new regions in a "great exodus" as Cauvin's (2000a:135–206) model seems to invoke. The spread of the Neolithic clearly is a complex issue involving both population migrations and the diffusion of ideas, and researchers such as Bellwood (2005), Colledge et al. (2004), Diamond and Bellwood (2003), and Pinhasi and Pluciennik (2004) have approached this in a more systematic manner.

The idea of "Supra-Regional Concepts in Near Eastern Neolithisation" (see *Neolithics* 2003:32–37, 2004:21–52) has recently been proposed. Hole (2003) notes the need to distinguish between origins and subsequent developments, and argues in favor of multiple centers or cores of Neolithic growth, each with its specific cultural trajectory, a concept also advocated by Bar-Yosef (2002b:123) and others. Watkins (2003) argues against the "Levantine primacy" models advocated by so many researchers, which borrows strongly from a "core/periphery" perspective. Instead, he calls for an elaboration of an interaction-sphere model incorporating concepts of peer/polity interactions. Kozłowski and Aurenche's recent (2005) work also addresses this issue to some degree. Perspectives such as these provide satisfying explanatory scenarios and will form a major component of future research endeavors.

In summary, by the PPNB the Neolithic world had expanded and included most of the Near East as well as Cyprus (see chapter 9). This attests to the remarkable abilities of these peoples, some of whom were the first farmers, while others retained more traditional economic systems, although they, too, did not live in a cultural vacuum.

Summary

The PPNB represents the florescence of the Neolithic, particularly in the Levant. Human society in the Near East was radically, and perhaps irreversibly, transformed, and some of the PPNB's more auspicious aspects are summarized below.

1. The PPNB witnessed the development of true villages, in many cases of substantial size.

2. During the PPNB, the first indisputable evidence of domestication occurred, for both plants and animals. Despite the domestication of many key crops and animals, wild resources continued to play a role in Neolithic subsistence.

3. Despite the formation of village society, some PPNB peoples elected to continue a hunting and gathering economic strategy, especially in the more marginal environmental zones. In many cases, however, they, too, ultimately adopted domesticates, especially animals, and the establishment of the classic Near Eastern dichotomy of "the desert and the sown," or village dwellers and pastoral nomads, likely was established.

4. Architectural complexity is a hallmark of the PPNB. Villages often consisted of multiroom rectangular structures. In addition to domestic architecture, there is evidence for nondomestic structures with communal or ritual significance. There also are a few examples of elaborate nonresidential sites.

5. Mortuary patterns represented a continuation of patterns established earlier but became much more standardized. A "skull cult" was widespread during the PPNB. Burial patterns may also have served to regulate social tensions.

6. Whether or not PPNB societies were egalitarian or hierarchically structured is vigorously debated. While elements of egalitarianism are evident, it is likely that, at least in larger communities, there was some degree of communal leadership for certain regulatory roles.

7. The PPNB is rich in symbolism. Some scholars view the Neolithic

as essentially a religious revolution, while others see it as an increasing elaboration of society in which symbolism played an important, although not overwhelming, role. Regardless of specific interpretations, there is no doubt that PPNB people had a rich ritual life, reflected by a plethora of material items, such as figurines, masks, statues, tokens, and ritual sites.

8. The "Neolithisation" process was a complex one, and many scholars prefer models of multiple points of origin and development, rather than only a few core centers and subsequent diffusion or population migration.

9. The Neolithic world was widespread, and considerable evidence exists for trade and other social interactions across essentially the entire Near East, as well as Cyprus.

The PPNB represents one of the best-documented periods in prehistory. While data gaps certainly exist, we have a broad outline of developments that shaped the Neolithic world, and increasingly Neolithic research is focusing on elements relating to the radical social transformations that occurred during this time. One of these relates to the aggregation of large numbers of people into "megasites," to which we turn in the next chapter.

Case Study 3   **The Negev PPNB Hunters and Gatherers**

After working at Nachcharini, I had been seduced by the Neolithic. As a PhD student at Southern Methodist University, which then had a hugely active Near Eastern program under the direction of Tony Marks and Fred Wendorf, the opportunity to do a dissertation on the Neolithic of the Negev Desert presented itself. It was also during this time that I met some of the major figures in Near Eastern archaeology, including Ofer Bar-Yosef, who became in many ways my "big-chief," a term he is quite fond of.

The Negev Neolithic sites were not particularly breathtaking. The "better" ones with traces of architecture (such as Nahal Divshon [Servello 1976], had already been claimed by more senior graduate students). Nonetheless, the idea of "non-Neolithic" Neolithic sites was intriguing, and little work had been done with the numerous PPNB lithic scatters in the western Negev. After the wonderful preservation and stratigraphy at Nachcharini, these were distinctly unimpressive. However, when in search of a dissertation, one takes opportunities as they are presented, and I dutifully undertook a field season to collect adequate data for a dissertation.

I received my first research grant, in the sum of $1,776, for this project and conducted the fieldwork in 1977. This was a shoestring operation, but we got a lot done. My crew included Nigel Goring-Morris, Joel Schuldenrin, and Itzik Gilead, who went on to their own distinguished careers. This work culminated in a dissertation and the requisite spin-off article (Simmons 1980, 1981).

What I learned during this project was how to squeeze the maximum amount of data out of low-visibility sites and low budgets, skills that have been very useful as we have come to realize the large amounts of information that often are embedded in such sites (Simmons 1998a). I examined 13 sites. Little was preserved beyond chipped stone, but using site-catchment analysis (cf. Vita-Finzi and Higgs 1970), I proposed a paleosubsistence model of mobile transhumance with smaller, ephemeral sites as summer occupations of dune and plains areas, focusing on gazelle procurement. Larger sites reflected winter occupations in foothill and mountainous zones by people exploiting an array of resources that tended to exclude gazelle, which had dispersed into smaller herds. The model demonstrated that even in a relatively harsh environment such as the Negev, it was possible to sustain year-round occupation by seasonal movements and a careful exploitation of available resources.

This was a relatively simplistic model. Certainly the available technology of the time, for example, using a compensating polar planimeter to construct the catchment areas, pales in comparison to high-tech modern applications, such as geographic information systems (GIS). But the end result of the study was instructive to me, demonstrating even at this early point in my career that the Neolithic encompassed a range of economic options. This project also demonstrated the need for an interdisciplinary approach. This perspective has guided much of my subsequent research.

Case Study 4   **Ghwair I**

Fast-forwarding many years into the more recent past are our investigations at Ghwair I in southern Jordan. While I had been exposed to perhaps the extreme ranges of Neolithic sites, reflected on one hand by Nachcharini and the

Negev sites and on the other by the megasites of ʿAin Ghazal and Wadi Shuʿeib, Ghwair I placed me in a position to examine what initially appeared to be a more "typical" PPNB village. Along with Mohammad Najjar of the Jordanian Department of Antiquities, we undertook an extensive multidisciplinary investigation (Simmons and Najjar 2003, 2006).

Ghwair I is located in an extremely beautiful area in the remote Wadi Feinan system. This region has extremely hot summers, and we therefore conducted our excavations during the winter, which could get quite cold. There were times when winter rains resulted in flash floods, and snow appeared on the nearby Jordanian Plateau. The research station we called home provided an almost stereotypic archaeological field situation, consisting of tents, a concrete building center, and flimsy huts that were primitive yet comfortable.

Ghwair I was first investigated in 1993 by Najjar, and we renewed study in 1996, completing four excavation seasons, this time with more substantial funding from the National Science Foundation and the National Geographic Society, a quantum leap over my earlier grants. One objective of the project was to determine the relationship of peripheral Neolithic settlements to larger core communities. We wished to apply a modified "core/periphery" model (cf. Algaze 1989) to small sites to see if they were related, economically or socially, to the large mega-communities as dependent outposts or if they were more independent communities.

Numerous radiocarbon determinations show that, in fact, Ghwair I was occupied during the MPPNB, prior to the establishment of most megasites. This obviously negated the objective of comparing Ghwair I to the megasites, although there is chronological overlap with some of the more northern communities, such as ʿAin Ghazal and Wadi Shuʿeib. Regardless, Ghwair I was a prosperous community. The richness of the site's material culture suggests that it was largely self-sufficient and much more than an isolated and peripheral Neolithic enclave or "frontier outpost." Ghwair I yielded an enormous array of projectile points, including a cache of large, unused points. Animal and female figurines also occur, as well as objects that might reasonably be interpreted as phallic.

The site contains substantial and sophisticated architecture that belies its small size, and in some portions depth exceeds 5 m. The architectural remains are spectacularly preserved, with walls standing several meters high in some cases. There is evidence of two-story buildings in the form of internal stairways, and one room is particularly impressive in that it contains several

6.7   "Theater"/public area at Ghwair I.

wall niches, a doorway, and several features interpreted as ventilation shafts
to provide a form of prehistoric air-conditioning. Outside one room block is
a large outdoor stairway that contains possible "theater-like" aspects, suggestive of a public forum area (fig. 6.7). This includes several stepped courses of
large, carefully laid, shaped slabs fronting an open area of hard-packed earth.
The arrangement of the stones is such that several individuals could have been
seated there, in an elevated setting. The hard-packed surface is flat and could
have functioned as a "stage."

Burials provide a particularly striking example of the complexity of the
site, especially one from an elaborately treated room. This was an infant between 9 and 12 months and who likely died of a broken neck. The infant was
carefully buried mostly intact (including the cranium) beneath a plastered floor.
The baby had a single mother-of-pearl necklace or earring near the neck. This
type of burial is a pattern relatively rare for PPNB infants (although six infants, some with single bead offerings, were found at nearby Beidha [Kirkbride
1966:23]). On the floor above the burial were a number of unusual features,
including one *Bos* skull with intact horns, five goat or sheep skulls, two caches
of finely manufactured blades, and a number of other limited-production objects (fig. 6.8). This infant clearly was a very important member of the com-

6.8 Room containing a child burial at Ghwair I. Note chipped-stone cache (upper center) and animal skulls (lower right). Burial pit is below north arrow.

munity, and it is intriguing to speculate if the child died accidentally or was a sacrifice.

Only nine other burials were recovered (one an intrusive Roman). These do not conform to typical PPNB interments. Most were adults buried in crude, cobble-lined graves within the rubble of rooms. The bodies were all flexed but with no fixed orientation. They contain their crania, but the subcranial materials are poorly preserved. While these may represent secondary burials, small bones, such as phalanges, were present, indicating great care in movement. The skull of one of these individuals, a female approximately 25 years old, has been forensically reconstructed, giving us a rare glimpse of an occupant of the village (fig. 6.9).

While our interpretation of the massive outdoor stairway that doubled as a seating area and "stage" is speculative, its location indicates integrative levels beyond the household and nuclear families. If it was a public oratory area, we can only guess at its specific function. Was it for information dispersal, conflict resolution, or even entertainment? We may never know the answers to these

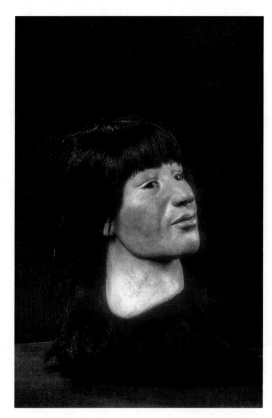

6.9   Forensic reconstruction of a ca. 25-year-old female from Ghwair I. Reconstruction done by Sharon Long.

questions, but it is probably no coincidence that the feature is situated next to the room block that contained both an elaborate structure with two internal staircases and the infant burial, further confirming the special significance of this area of the site.

Certainly, Ghwair I is not alone in possessing complex structural features. Often these are interpreted as areas where ritual or religious activity occurred. The importance of Ghwair I is that there is no evidence that this elaborate feature itself had any ritual significance. We believe it could well have served a more secular or political function, where community-wide information was relayed.

We tend to equate large sites with complexity and sophistication, but this could be misleading. What we might be seeing, instead, is a situation where the megasites were perhaps more "urban" concentrations without many of the amenities that more privileged populations may have enjoyed at smaller sites, such as Ghwair I. The elaborate nature of Ghwair I suggests a complex, perhaps elite function for the village, and its purpose may have been as a local center within southern Jordan. Certainly this degree of elaboration at this small community points to the remarkable diversity exhibited by the world's first villagers.

Chapter 7

Megasites in Jordan and the End of the PPN

Overview

Recent research in the southern Levant has shown an LPPNB and early PN cultural record east of the Jordan River that differs significantly from that of other regions (Rollefson 1989, 1996; Simmons 1995, 2000). A dramatic realignment of settlement and social relationships occurred, with populations shifting from west of the Jordan Valley to the east, particularly in highland Jordan, resulting in the establishment of a series of large settlements, the so-called megasites. Archaeologists can be guilty of interchanging words such as *town*, *village*, or *city* (Simmons 1995:119), and a variety of terms have been used to describe this phenomenon, including "site giganticism" (Rollefson 1997b:241), "central settlements" (*Neolithics* 1997; Bienert et al. 2004), "towns" (Rollefson 2001b:97; Simmons 1995), and "proto-urbanism" (Bienert 2001). Regardless of what word is used, very large communities, unlike anything seen previously, came into existence toward the end of the PPNB.

What Are the Mega-Sites?

Realizing that definitions are arbitrary, the term *megasite* is here reserved for communities exceeding 20 acres. We have already noted that a large range of site sizes existed throughout the PPNB, although most were modest, ranging from around 2 to 5 acres. Until the discovery of the Jordanian megasites, Jericho, at ca. 10 acres, was one of the largest settlements in the Levantine Neolithic.

Of course, large Neolithic sites are not restricted to the southern Levant. Substantial communities are well documented elsewhere, most notable of which is Çatalhöyük, one of the largest Neolithic sites documented, with a mound 23 m high and an extent of some 33 acres (Matthews 1996:86; Hodder and Cessford 2004:20). Likewise, Abu Hureyra covered ca. 40 acres during the PPNB (Moore et al. 2000:493). Göbekli, while not an actual settlement, also is huge, with an estimated size of 85 to 100 acres (Bar-Yosef and Bar-Yosef Mayer 2002:351). Rollefson (1987) believes that large sites served as regional centers, and recognizes a minimum of three in the Levant alone, in Syria (the Middle Euphrates), parts of Israel and the Jordan Valley (e.g., Jericho), and the Jordanian highlands (the Jordanian megasites). Certainly one might make the same argument for Turkey with sites such as Çatalhöyük, although its zenith was during the PN (see Balter 2005 for the most recent discussion of this amazing site).

What I focus on here is a more specific, regional, phenomenon, one that occurred in a relatively narrow north-south strip of the Levantine' Corridor, in what is now western Jordan. Here, several large communities stretch from central Jordan south toward the more arid reaches (fig. 7.1, table 7.1). Of these, only 'Ain Ghazal has undergone intensive excavation, and only a small percentage of it has been excavated (Rollefson et al. 1992; Simmons et al. 1988). Thus, many of the conclusions drawn from the megasites are more relevant to regional patterns than to site-specific considerations. Much of Bienert et al. (2004) addresses the Jordanian megasites, and their volume is the most up-to-date and focused discussion on the phenomenon. Unfortunately, this important volume did not appear in print until 2005, too late to thoroughly incorporate in this book.

There are many complex issues associated with these sites. A critical one is whether or not entire sites were occupied at the same time. This, of course, affects any population estimates. We initially acknowledged this problem (Simmons et al. 1988:36) when first defining the nature of 'Ain Ghazal. Nonetheless, there is no denying that the megasites were substantially larger than their earlier counterparts, and higher populations seem reasonable. These communities were distinctly different from smaller settlements closer to the Mediterranean coast and represent unique highland and desert-edge adaptations (Simmons 2000). Some, such as 'Ain Ghazal and Wadi Shu'eib, were initially founded during the late MPPNB and expanded during the LPPNB, while others were established during the LPPNB. This is important, since megasites existing during the MPPNB likely shared communications with one another

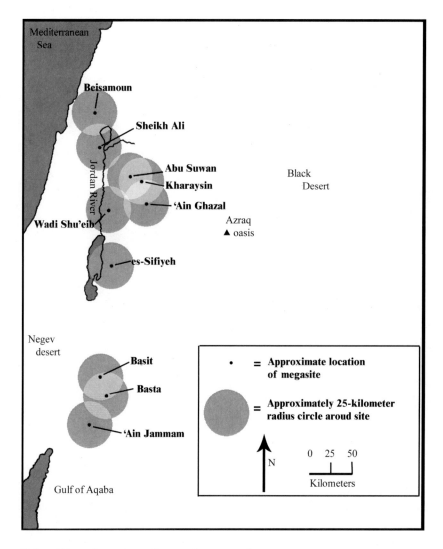

7.1   Map of southern Levantine megasites.

and smaller MPPNB settlements elsewhere, including those to the west. Indeed, as the western sites were abandoned, it may be that relatives moved to the Jordanian settlements, expanding them into megasites. On the other hand, several megasites, particularly those in the south, only came into being during the LPPNB, perhaps being recipients of over-flow populations from central (and more favorable?) locations. While this

Table 7.1 Tabulation of megasites

Site	Estimated Size (acres)	Location
Jordan sites		
ʿAin Ghazal	35–40	West-central Jordan
Wadi Shuʿeib	30–35	West-central Jordan
Basta	30–35	Southern Jordan
es-Sifiyeh	20–25	South-central Jordan
Abu Suwan*	30	West-central Jordan
Basit	20–25	Southern Jordan
ʿAin Jamman	20	Southern Jordan
Kharaysin*	85	West-central Jordan
Other sites		
Beisamoun	25–30	Northern Israel
Sheik Ali	25	Northern Israel
Ras Shamra	20	Southern Lebanon
Tel Abu Hureyra	30	Northern Syria
Çatalhöyük	30	Central Turkey
Asikli Höyük	30	Central Turkey

Note: Data are from several sources.
* Virtually no excavation has been done, and megasite status is based on survey information alone.

proposition requires actual population movements, which were criticized in the last chapter, the distances involved are not that great, and thus a stronger case can be made for localized movements.

These sites all share several general attributes. Architecturally, they are complex, consisting of agglutinated room blocks, often with several small rooms in individual structures. Two-storied structures also are common. Some have evidence for public or ritual architecture. Despite this complexity, however, many megasites have a somewhat monotonous architectural pattern. Population estimates range as high as 4,116 (Kuijt 2000a:81, table 1). They do not contain deposits as thick as Jericho's, although depths exceeding 8 m occur at some sites (e.g., Wadi Shuʿeib). Some, such as ʿAin Ghazal, Wadi Shuʿeib, and probably Basta, contain the transitional PPNC phase, and occupation continues into the PN without interruption. All appear to be abandoned after the Neolithic. This differs from many western sites, including Jericho, which was successively re-occupied beyond the Neolithic, even after periods of abandonment.

The material culture at many of the megasites is extraordinarily rich. While this has been described in numerous publications and is not re-peated here, one example does require note: nothing in the Near East has paralleled the exquisite 'Ain Ghazal statues (fig. 7.2) (Tubb and Grissom 1995). Similar, but far less complete, statues were found at Jericho during Garstang's excavations, but those from 'Ain Ghazal are notable in their preservation and workmanship. We still are unclear as to the function of these enigmatic sculptures, but their construction indicates that they were made for display. Various interpretations have included deities, ghosts, venerated ancestors, or mythical founders of the settlements, and ob-jects used during public ritual (Kuijt and Chesson 2005:168–172; Mabry 2003:104). Whatever their meaning, it is interesting that both caches were recovered buried beneath the floors of domestic, not special-use, struc-tures.

Many megasites are located in relatively fragile ecological zones, or at least adjacent to what might be termed marginal environments. 'Ain Gha-zal, for example, is in a somewhat precarious ecological setting. Despite its proximity to a major river (the Wadi Zarqa), it is situated along the minimum (250 mm) rainfall isohyet for nonirrigation agriculture and is in proximity to the eastern desert. This may have been a crucial factor for peoples who subsisted to a large degree on domesticated plants and ani-mals. Generally similar patterns occur at the other megasites, illustrating the importance of selected microhabitats along desert ecotones. Overall, though, those megasites located in the central part of Jordan likely en-joyed a better environment than those farther south.

The geographic distribution of the megasites is not random. Several clusters seem defined (see fig. 7.1), although this is tentative, based per-haps on survey bias. Regardless, for Jordan alone, current data show one cluster centered in the central-northern part of Jordan, one (represented at present by only one site, es-Sifiyeh) in the south-central part, and an-other in southern Jordan, not far from Petra. If one examines an arbitrary 25-km (radius) catchment, there is some overlap of sites in each clus-ter, but none between clusters. Expanding to the west, another cluster, in

7.2 Double-headed statue from ʿAin Ghazal. Courtesy of Gary Rollefson.

Israel, includes Beisamoun and Sheikh Ali (Tel Eli), although the latter
is poorly defined. These partially overlap with the central-northern Jordanian group. While we cannot be certain that all these settlements were
occupied contemporaneously, their "packing" is curious. If they formed
regional centers, it seems clear that there was no one center of specific importance. Rather, they appear to have interacted with one another. There
is some variation to this pattern as well, although supporting data are
not very robust. In the north, there do not appear to have been many
smaller LPPNB villages or hamlets near the megasites, although this also
could be a factor of inadequate survey. To the south, however, the situation
seems more complex, with many smaller communities existing near megasites, although again their contemporaneity is uncertain. It seems, then,
that different settlement trajectories occurred in the south as opposed to
the north. Arguments for a true "city" type of structure, organized as
a two-level hierarchical system in which some sort of interdependence
existed between a core or center (i.e., megasite) and periphery (smaller
villages), is not supported. Indeed, many researchers believe that the first
true "cities" in the Near East did not emerge until the early Bronze Age
(Bienert 2001:110), even if many of these were, in fact, smaller than the
Neolithic megasites.

Why Did the Megasites Come into Existence?

Around 8500 BP many farming villages and hamlets on the Mediterranean side of the Jordan Valley and in the valley itself were abandoned
over a relatively short period of time, with their populations dispersing to
other locales that would support an agricultural existence. As older sites
were abandoned, newer ones were established farther east in diverse ter-
rains and ecological settings, and sites that had been occupied during the
MPPNB, such as 'Ain Ghazal, expanded dramatically (Rollefson 1987,
1989, 1992:124; Rollefson and Köhler-Rollefson 1989). What caused this
population consolidation and the emergence of these megasites?

Climatic changes often are invoked to explain these population shifts.
Rollefson (1992:124, 1996:220–221), however, points out that it is unlikely that deteriorating climate was responsible, since as a regional phenomenon alternations in weather should have had similar impacts on all
sites. This is not the case. Indeed, the ecological setting of the megasites

is more marginal than in the Mediterranean zone, so if climatic deterioration caused the abandonment of the lusher western region, certainly even larger sites would not have been established in more precarious zones. Furthermore, there are few paleoenvironmental data suggesting climatic deterioration at this time (see chapter 3).

Likewise, the expected natural population growth associated with sedentary communities cannot be used to explain the establishment of the megasites. While populations undoubtedly grew throughout the Neolithic, it seems unlikely that high birthrates alone would account for such a dramatic settlement shift. The population increase associated with Neolithic economies, however, could ultimately have depleted local microenvironments and stretched carrying capacities to their maximum. A subsequent adaptive response may have been to expand farther east, to the edges of where a traditional Neolithic economy could still be practiced. This does not mean the western Levant was abandoned; clearly it was not. Large sites west of the Jordan River, such as Beisamoun, belie such a simplistic explanation and, in fact, suggest perhaps another cluster, this time west of the Jordan Valley (see fig. 7.1). Furthermore, it is unlikely that abandonment at sites such as Jericho was necessarily immediate and complete. Supporting this contention is the observation that older radiocarbon determinations from Jericho have now been rejected (Rollefson 1996:220). Certainly the PPNB at Jericho partially overlaps with that of 'Ain Ghazal, for example. A partial population restructuring could have eased pressure in the west, however, and sites such as 'Ain Ghazal could have served as population "magnets," attracting from places like Jericho. The consequence of this was that the former expanded at the expense of the latter.

While hard evidence to explain the partial abandonment of many western sites and the establishment of the megasites is scant, Rollefson (1992:124; Rollefson and Köhler-Rollefson 1989, 1992) and others have proposed complex arguments that relate to ecological and social variables. They believe that as populations expanded, the destructive effects inherent in the integrated farming and goat-herding economies practiced by MPPNB peoples eventually degraded the catchments of many settlements. This culturally induced degradation included the destruction of natural habitats for wild animals by overgrazing, by the clearing of vegetation for farming plots, and by the removal of trees for housing construction, plaster manufacture, and domestic fuel. These activities prevented effective regeneration, exposing soils to erosion, and the decrease in soil fertility and the soil loss over an extended period of constant cropping eventually made farming unproductive.

The constellation of these events ultimately resulted in some populations moving. The eastward relocation of communities facilitated the partial exploitation of new, previously underused, areas adjacent to the eastern deserts. Large sites such as 'Ain Ghazal may have attracted populations dealing with these environmental crises, resulting in a dramatic population increase centered within a few nearly urban centers (Köhler-Rollefson 1988; Köhler-Rollefson and Rollefson 1990; Rollefson 1992:124; Rollefson and Köhler-Rollefson 1989, 1992; Simmons 1995; 2000).

A move to the east was not without difficulties, however. The migration of new people into the Jordanian countryside, and their interactions with people already living there, placed new pressures on local resources, and new exploitation strategies were necessary, resulting in what Rollefson (2001b:97–98) has called the "bold experiment"—the establishment of the megasites. How was this able to happen? After all, it seems that if culturally induced environmental degradation resulted in the abandonment of western MPPNB communities, an unlikely response would be the establishment of larger communities in even more marginal environments. And yet this is apparently just what happened. One adaptation to this ecological constraint may have been the forced consolidation of populations into larger settlements. This could have allowed for scarce resources to be pooled. Such a situation would have created social pressures previously unfelt but also may have had the advantage of requiring more cooperation and the development of more efficient exploitation technologies and land use patterns.

Of course, these events cannot be explained solely in ecological terms. Kuijt (2000a, b) provides intriguing social arguments that complement environmental models. He believes that the development and maintenance of elaborate public mortuary rituals at larger communities may have attracted related households living in adjacent settlements. The simultaneous reinforcement of the authority of select ritual practitioners who organized these ceremonies and the emergence of powerful lineages and "Houses" within larger communities may have served as powerful lures to consolidate settlement into large regional and social centers. Kuijt argues that the public nature of PPNB household and community mortuary and ritual practices may have increasingly encouraged lineages to merge with other residential groups with whom they shared some preexisting social, economic, or ritual bonds (such as kinship). While Kuijt presents a compelling argument, it is not without some flaws. For example, it seems to assume that ritual and mortuary practices, which attracted populations from outlying communities, were conducted only at larger sites, such as 'Ain Ghazal, that later became megasites. This is untrue, since such activities also occurred at smaller sites.

The combination of environmental degradation, whether of human or natural origin, with social factors could have been attractive inducements to populations to form the megasites. It was thus an adaptive response that worked. Once established, a mixed herding and farming economy was sufficient to feed large numbers of people. This likely resulted in cultural adjustments in order to temper conflicting demands relating to access to farmland and pasturage, food storage, and cooperative activities such as harvesting, house and public-structure construction, trade, and specialization (Rollefson 1992:124). For over 500 years, this "bold experiment" resulted in the culmination of Neolithic cultural sophistication in the southern Levant. But at some point it, too, had to come to an end.

What Happened to the Megasites—The Collapse of the PPN or Simply a Transformation of Populations?

While the establishment of the megasites may have ingeniously allowed for continued nourishment, both in economy and cultural elaboration, the system was inherently flawed. Packing large numbers of people into megasites ultimately aggravated the problem of overexploitation, and over time farming techniques could not sustain the protracted drain on local soil conservation and fertility. By around 7500 BP, the megasites were largely depopulated, as were many smaller sites. 'Ain Ghazal, for example, lost maybe half of its population, and some sites, like Basta, apparently were totally abandoned (Rollefson 2001b:97–98). What happened?

This undoubtedly was a complicated story, one that expands far beyond the southern Levant. Essentially, we are looking at the end of the PPN and the beginning of the PN. To many scholars, the latter traditionally has been interpreted as a deterioration in the quality of life, although this is not so clear-cut (see chapter 8). But the fact remains that many megasites, as well as smaller communities, were abandoned after the PPN. On the other hand, some, notably 'Ain Ghazal and Wadi Shu'eib, continued to be occupied into the PN.

The end of the PPN was a dramatic disruption. Older models proposed that the greater part of the southern Levant was depleted of populations, the "hiatus Palestinian." The subsequent establishment of the PN was an "exodus" of new peoples from elsewhere (e.g., Mellaart 1975:68; Perrot 1968). Such scenarios, which Rollefson (1996:220–221) refers to as the "interregnum model," are no longer valid with the documentation of an in situ transition to the PN (i.e., the PPNC). The end of the PPN did result in the abandonment of many sites, but this was more apparent than real. It is more likely that regional realignments of populations who were adapting to new social and ecological constraints occurred.

Some arguments invoke major climatic deterioration to account for the abandonment, although this cannot be supported for the entire region. Certainly some (e.g., Bar-Yosef 2001a:27–28; Bar-Yosef and Bar-Yosef Mayer 2002:362) imply that rapid environmental worsening was a major variable in the collapse of the PPNB. There are problems here, however. As noted in chapter 3, there is considerable evidence for an abrupt, if brief, climate deterioration in the southern Levant, but unfortunately there often has been confusion on the timing of this event. For example, in the case of the Soreq Cave speleothems, which provide critical data for this climatic episode, the dates are not based on radiocarbon analysis, but rather on the [230]Th-U method. This is an isotopic technique, and the resulting dates are in calendar years, the equivalent of *calibrated* radiocarbon years. Thus, when Bar-Mathews et al. (1999:91) indicate the dates as ca. 8.0–8.2 ky (or BP) for the arid and cooling event, they are providing the equivalent of calibrated (that is, calendar) years. This translates to roughly *7200–7400 BP* in *uncalibrated* years. This might have been overlooked by some scholars, who may have viewed the reported *8200–8000* dates as *uncalibrated* and thus suggested a climatic deterioration around the end of the PPN, when in fact the data suggest this occurred during the PN. The PPNC ends at ca. 7500 BP; thus, with some "wiggle room" one might correlate the beginning of the climatic change with the end of the PPN. It is, however, difficult to invoke climate change for causing the end of the PPN when most of this brief deterioration likely occurred *after* the PPN. This issue points to the difficulty of confusing calibrated with uncalibrated dates, and of using consistent programs in converting the latter to the former. In any event, the chronology is a potentially weak link in invoking climatic change as the major cause for the end of the PPN, although more precise dating might resolve this issue.

Other researchers turn to humans as the culprits (e.g. Rollefson 1996), arguing that, ironically, the very sort of humanly induced ecological degradation that resulted in the formation of the megasites also likely was the reason for their downfall. Environmental mismanagement again led to reduction of crop yields. This occurred at a time when populations were expanding and required more and more food. Ultimately, these people essentially ate themselves out of their environments. But this did not happen easily. Communities such as 'Ain Ghazal and Wadi Shu'eib continued as large settlements into the PPNC and the PN.

Our best data come from 'Ain Ghazal, where the PPNB residents had a remarkably varied subsistence base consisting of both domesticated and wild plants and animals. Notable is that while the range of faunal resources was broad, the focus was on goats, a species so notoriously detrimental to vegetation that they have been referred to as "the Black Plague of the Near East" (Rollefson 1996:223). Over 50 species of animals were exploited during the site's florescence, but by the PPNC and the PN, there was a dramatic decrease in the number of species used, with caprines, pigs, and cattle predominant. Goats continue in importance, but woodland and parkland species are absent, supporting the argument that such environments were no longer present, having been cleared for either fields or timber (Rollefson 1996:223–224; Simmons et al. 1988:37–38). A similar pattern appears to exist at nearby Wadi Shu'eib.

Additional evidence for environmental deterioration comes from architecture, where Rollefson has argued that the smaller size of postholes, or their complete absence, indicates that wood resources were becoming sparse. Furthermore, the nearly insatiable quest for lime plaster, so common in the MPPNB, undoubtedly contributed to local degeneration, since lime has to be burned to form plaster. Indeed, late in the occupation of 'Ain Ghazal, the plaster is inferior, supporting the argument that fuel was becoming scarce (Rollefson 1996:223; Rollefson and Köhler-Rollefson 1989:76–82).

While these megasites witnessed a decline in the variety of exploited resources (and other elements of life?), they nonetheless continued to be occupied. Rollefson (1992:125) and others suggest that two interrelated factors served to temper the effects of environmental degradation around these sites, permitting the sustained presence of relatively large populations, at least until the end of the Neolithic.

The first relates to the ecological setting of these sites. Recall that their ecotonal locations were near areas that had previously been underexploited by MPPNB villagers, in particular, the nonarable steppes and deserts of eastern Jordan. This very setting, however, allowed for occupation during the PPNC. Hunters from the villages likely exploited these areas, providing a valuable role in subsistence. Remember, also, that there already was some PPNB occupation of these areas, and the opportunity for trade and exchange may have increased. Perhaps even more importantly, vegetation in these unarable regions could have been converted to abundant "harvests" by allowing herds of goats and sheep to be taken away from the villages to the seasonally available forage. This could lessen the harmful effects of these browsers on the fragile soils immediately adjacent to the megasites. Tapping into a previously little-used area also could have greatly increased the stable supply of meat to compensate for the diminished wild-animal resources of the badly deteriorated habitats near permanent settlements. Furthermore, the absence of some of the megasite populations during parts of the year, when they were engaged in herding in the steppe zone, could have reduced stresses on the agricultural productivity of the land around the settlements, as well as mitigated social tensions arising from crowding (Köhler-Rollefson 1988, 1992; Rollefson 1992:125, 1997a:305).

Such elements led to the second factor that allowed for continued occupation. This was the cultural modification beginning to occur at this time, in response to the stresses brought about by the long duration of demands of a growing population in a deteriorating environment. Thus, in addition to increasingly pastoral activities in the steppe, modifications were being made in the agricultural systems. Rollefson (1992:125)notes that at PPNC 'Ain Ghazal the use of sickle blades and grinding stones decreased, suggesting that harvesting and processing methods, or the types of crops grown, were changing. This also could suggest more reliance on animals.

Rollefson feels that by the early PN, perpetual farming caused drastic reductions in the crop yields on land within reasonable distances from permanent settlements. Areas for farming undoubtedly remained available in some regions, but these were near springs that could supply the needs of smaller, hamlet-sized communities only. The social organization of these smaller villages, characteristic of the PN, could once again function well on the simpler forms that characterized the earlier Neolithic. The smaller farming communities could maintain a pastoral component of the subsistence economy only if they relied on domesticated cattle and pigs, leaving goat husbandry to those populations in steppe/desert habitats. Small herds of cattle and pigs could be productive for meat, but they would not have had the dramatic habitat consequences that sheep and goats did (Rollefson 1992:125, 1997a:305).

Coupled with this scenario must have been intergroup stress brought about by the increasingly difficult farming and herding conditions, as well as by the crowding of larger populations. Several outcomes were possible, not the least of which may have been interpersonal violence. However, the overall lack of violence has already been noted and may be a testament to the efficiency of the social organization that had been forged. It apparently was robust enough to deal with deteriorating economic conditions in a nonconfrontational manner. Nonetheless, there would have been consequences of a weaker economy, and these would have had social manifestations, to which we now turn.

The rapid growth of population centers in the Jordanian highlands during the LPPNB undoubtedly created new stresses on the social fabric of these communities. Older systems based on simple kinship to maintain harmony and social identity were probably already breaking down during the MPPNB, and the huge clusters of people in LPPNB communities had to readjust to meet new demands and resolve increasing conflict. Perhaps an overall centralized authority emerged, or perhaps portions of each settlement were managed by family or clan units, even while community-oriented rituals reinforced social cohesion and identity (Rollefson 1997a:305).

One of the most elaborate social arguments dealing with the end of the PPN is Kuijt's (2000a). He acknowledges that ecological degradation was a likely factor, but he also believes the end of the PPN was linked to other complex interrelated social conditions that involved long-term demographic changes and short-term, daily, social relations within communities.

Kuijt argues that the public nature of mortuary and ritual practices within these large settlements may have increasingly encouraged household lineages to merge with other residential groups with whom they shared some preexisting social, economic, or ritual bonds. This, however, did not result in a marked expression of social differentiation indicative of positions of leadership, other than perhaps that of representative leadership from multiple households. Such merging would have created new tensions and stressful conditions at the community and lineage levels. Increased social crowding within buildings and conflicts between individual lineages over rights and obligations, and possibly even with competing ritual organizations, may have played significant roles in shaping social arrangements (Kuijt 2000a:95).

Increases in scale and density also would have challenged the existing social structure of organized labor at certain periods of the year, creating a greater need for competing and cooperating hierarchical structures for sharing information and materials. Crowding would have created social congestion, a perceived loss of control over one's immediate environment, and a reduction in privacy. All of this encouraged segmentation of physical space, which is exactly what we see in the LPPNB. This would have redefined conceptions of privacy and access. Changes in the built environment influenced and reshaped the creation of social, economic, and political relationships. If the segmentation of LPPNB architecture reflects social forces, this ultimately was inherently limited as a long-term solution, since there are physical limitations as to how close buildings can be constructed and still be functional (Kuijt 2000a:95–96). The densely packed houses at sites such as Çatalhöyük, however, might seem to contradict this somewhat.

Shifting patterns in mortuary and ritual practices may also reflect these changes. The emergence of more powerful lineages may have limited the practical ability for the community to participate in communal rituals. When such practices are conducted less frequently, the foundation for social cohesion is weakened. Furthermore, if some ritual/economic elite oversaw LPPNB ritual and mortuary practices and also managed other community activities, the erosion of ritual and mortuary practices may have led to a decrease of support for this elite. In short, the social cohesive force holding LPPNB communities together would have dissolved. With the weakening or removal of the overall ideological structure upon which this culture of village life was based, ritual systems no longer were able to maintain group solidarity. Promotion or recognition of some individuals or families over others, thereby giving them greater access to resources and privileges, would have undermined the entire system of egalitarian/communal values and beliefs seen in the MPPNB. Thus, there were now few reasons to attract families to the megasites (Kuijt 1996, 2000a:96).

So, in Kuijt's model, the collapse of the megasite lifeways can be seen as a dispersal of people to an increasing number of smaller villages. The system of social beliefs that created these communities in the first place was unable to deal with the new realities of large village life, which required greater social segmentation and resulted in people living in increasingly compressed physical conditions. Rather than develop true "rulers" necessary to deal with the complexities of megasites, these people chose to leave their large sites. Thus, at the end of the PPN communities simply were unable or unwilling to develop new means of organizing positions of leadership in the face of rapid changes. Such changing social relationships may have been related to changes within a broader set of ritualistic and social beliefs that, in combination with regional environmental changes and local ecological degradation, ultimately contributed to the abandonment of the megasites (Kuijt 2000a:95–98). Thus, the abandonment can be related to "a failed experiment in balancing antiquated systems of shared social power with the need for developing new means of organizing and directing increasingly large urban communities with competitive House leaders" (Kuijt 2000a:98).

Kuijt presents one compelling and complex explanation for what might have caused the collapse of the LPPNB system, although supporting data for some aspects of it are limited, such as the existence of ritual or economic elites. Certainly other variables should be considered as well. For example, disease and sanitation have, curiously, not been addressed too much in the Near Eastern literature (although see Groube 1996). Certainly Akkermans and Schwartz paint a rather disheartening view of village life during the Neolithic, indicating that the settlements themselves must have been unhealthy environments. . . . They were undoubtedly heavily polluted with all kinds of rotting organic matter and human waste. . . . The refuse would have attracted vermin, as well as the diseases they carried with them. Flies and mosquitoes transmit fecal-oral infections and other illnesses; rats bring hemorrhagic fevers; wild dogs and other carnivores carry rabies; and wild cats bring toxoplasmosis. Simple wounds or contaminated food also must have claimed many victims . . . diseases became constant rather than incidental threats to health. . . . Clearing . . . the land near ponds and streams . . . may have encouraged the spread of tetanus, malaria, and schistosomiasis. Stock rearing may have been another major source of human disease . . . tuberculosis can result from contact with infected cattle or through the consumption of their raw meat and milk. Many parasitic worms cycle between humans and domestic animals. . . . The Neolithic was certainly not a Garden of Eden but a world where life was difficult and people knew that they were "forever confronted with the Four Horsemen — death, famine, disease, and the malice of other men." (Akkermans and Schwartz 2003:78–79)

This likely is an overstatement. Bellwood (2005:14) notes that during the early centuries of farming, populations likely were healthy, in the sense that major epidemic diseases in humans had not yet developed, nor had major crop diseases. As noted previously, there is little evidence of such severe bodily insult on most Neolithic skeletons, although admittedly some of the afflictions cited above might not be visible on skeletal remains. Given the duration of many PPNB villages, the advantages of living in them must have outweighed the disadvantages.

Conclusions

In conclusion, the establishment and abandonment of the megasites was a complex process that we do not fully understand. Despite complex social and climatic arguments, I lean toward the ecological degradation model as playing a principal role in the dramatic changes witnessed at the end of the PPN. I realize, of course, that the trajectory that any culture follows cannot be attributed to single variables, including environmental degradation. Even Diamond (2005:11), who convincingly demonstrates that ecological mismanagement was a consistent variable in the demise of many cultures, admits, "I don't know of any case in which a society's collapse can be attributed solely to environmental damage: there are always other contributing factors." Nonetheless, he strongly argues that many past abandonments were at least partly triggered by ecological problems, in which people inadvertently destroyed the environmental resources on which their societies depended . . . a sort of unintended "ecological suicide." He indicates that population growth often forces people to adopt intensified means of agricultural production, and that unsustainable practices can lead to environmental damage usually falling within one or more of eight categories. These are: deforestation and habitat destruction, soil problems (erosion, salinization, and fertility losses), water management problems, overhunting, overfishing, the effects of introduced species on native species, human population growth, and the increased per capita impact of people (Diamond 2005:6). I would argue that the archaeological evidence suggests that some of these factors contributed substantially to the disintegration of the Jordanian megasites.

Elsewhere, I (2000:220–225) have modeled this period as consisting of three major stages. The first argues that the pattern of population aggregation and pooling of scarce resources initially was adaptive, resulting in the formation of the megasites. The second stage is disharmony, starting at the end of the LPPNB and the PPNC, where the megasite pattern began to deplete local environments, resulting in critical resource shortages that required an economic split between farmers and pastoralists. Throughout this time, strong and often competing social factors were at work, and the last stage reflects the solution. By the end of the PPN, populations could have chosen several trajectories. One of these would have been the development of more organized and powerful leaders and increased social stratification. Another, and what they apparently chose, was to retain, and in a sense revert to, the more egalitarian systems that had worked so well for so long. This is reflected by the PN.

Although a humanly induced model is preferred here, this obviously would have had social consequences, likely along the lines that Kuijt explores. Furthermore, one cannot ignore the environmental context of possibly deteriorating climatic conditions, but the timing of this is uncertain. While human causation is favored here, it is important to note that Wilkinson (2003:27–28) convincingly argues that humanly caused environmental impacts in the Near East were, in fact, late, not widely occurring until after the Bronze Age. The apparent contradiction of dense human settlement during the end of the PPN with no widespread ecological degradation is perhaps best explained in terms of scope. Because of the structure of these early settlements, human impacts essentially were localized rather than widespread. The point to consider is that even if humanly induced degradation is a favored model, it still must be viewed against climatic conditions.

It also is relevant to note that Hole (2000) believes it may be misleading to characterize "large" with any particular status or complexity, and that the concept of site hierarchy may not be appropriate for the PPN. He does not feel that there is compelling evidence that any sites, regardless of size, were political or economic centers, noting that most look pretty much like each other (Hole 2000:206). Hole's comments are well taken. Indeed, I have argued elsewhere (see Case Study 4) that the megasites may have functioned as larger "urban" entities that did not enjoy some of the social amenities that residents of smaller communities might have. Regardless of such arguments, though, it is difficult to ignore the significance of the megasites. They represent the earliest experiments with near urban living.

Many authors also implicitly hint that this experiment was a failure, by using words such as "collapse" or "fall." I prefer a more positive perspective. After all, sites such as 'Ain Ghazal were continuously occupied for around 2,000 years. To me, this suggests a remarkable resiliency and adaptability, not a failure. After all, how many modern cities can claim such antiquity?

Throughout this "bold experiment," social organization must have been particularly strained with such radical changes in both economy and personal relationships. From a period of but several hundred years, the fabric of life had gone from elaborate and large population aggregations focused on megasites to ones consisting of a splintering of populations, many of which were nomadic, at least on a semiannual basis. In the southern Levant this culminated with a return to smaller settlements during the PN (curiously, a similar pattern had occurred much earlier, between the Early and Late Natufian). Attempts at centralized authority, necessary for controlling megasites, would no longer have been necessary. A return to more clan- or tribal-oriented authority better adapted to pastoral life would now have been a more efficient control mechanism. In the course of doing so, what we see occurring may be no less than the establishment of the famed and enduring Near Eastern economic dichotomy between the "desert and the sown," or between village farmers and pastoral nomads.

Case Study 5   **The Jordanian Megasites**

A chance to work at a site such as ʿAin Ghazal comes only once in a lifetime. For me, my participation at ʿAin Ghazal and Wadi Shuʿeib was a graduation from my first experiences with limited-activity sites in the Negev . . . one could not contrast these more! My involvement with these megasites came about as much through serendipity as anything else. Once I had completed my PhD, I, like many, took positions in the United States working for a variety of cultural resource management (CRM) institutions. This gave me invaluable experience in running projects and dealing with "real-world" archaeology.

I first met Gary Rollefson in the mid-1970s, when we were both graduate students. After completing our dissertations, Gary briefly worked with me on a CRM project in New Mexico before returning to his true love of Near Eastern archaeology. In the early 1980s, at a Pecos Conference in New Mexico, Gary, a master of understatement, informed me that he had just started excavations at what looked like a "pretty interesting" PPNB site, that of ʿAin Ghazal. He invited me to join the team as co-director, along with Zeidan Kafafi of Yarmouk University in Jordan. At the time, I was director of the CRM program at the University of Kansas, and through the goodwill of the Museum of Anthropology's then-director, Alfred Johnson, I was able to accept Gary's invitation.

If ʿAin Ghazal had been in the United States, it would have been considered a CRM project, since it initially was exposed during road construction. In fact, I suspect that this perception of ʿAin Ghazal as a "salvage" project rather than "pure research" was one reason we had such difficulty in funding, but that is another story. None of us had any idea that ʿAin Ghazal would turn into the spectacular megasite that we now know it is. In fact, if it had been discovered by survey, there would have been very little indication of its magnitude. This is true of other megasites as well and indicates the potentially misleading conclusions one can come to using survey data alone (e.g., Simmons 1998a).

I was co-director with Gary and Zeidan for six years before turning my attention to Cyprus. During that time, some of the spectacular discoveries of ʿAin Ghazal were made, and I am grateful to have been a part of this exciting time in Neolithic archaeology. ʿAin Ghazal was the first Jordanian megasite identified as such. Once its extent was fully realized, the enormity of excavating with modern methods became daunting. No longer could a huge trench be put into a site, as had been done, for example, at Jericho, and we estimate that less than 1 percent of the site has been systematically investigated. Given what we found in this small sample, one cannot help but wonder what else lies beneath ʿAin Ghazal, and what was previously destroyed.

Certainly, the most impressive discovery was of the famous ʿAin Ghazal statues in 1983, and I clearly remember the day that they were found. One of our staff members, Marci Donaldson, had dutifully been excavating an abandoned house, and she noted the presence of several chunks of plaster unlike the plaster found on the floors. As she continued to excavate, she came across an unusually shaped piece of plaster that she was convinced looked like a buttock. We thought that perhaps she had been in the sun too long and was hallucinating. Sure enough, though, continued excavation exposed one of the first statues, lying face down, a somewhat ignominious reemergence into the world. This discovery caused a stir in the archaeological world, and ʿAin Ghazal was catapulted to international attention. We were suddenly visited by many dignitaries and reporters. I remember one local television program mistakenly reported that we had discovered a cache of plastered pygmy humans, rather than the 1-m-tall plaster and reed statues that these really were! Had I only known that in a few short years I would be dealing with pygmy fauna in Cyprus, I would have taken this as a sign.

Although many Near Eastern countries are reluctant to allow their antiquities out of the country due to past Western depredations, the Jordanian authorities realized the importance of the ʿAin Ghazal statues. Nothing comparable had ever been found, with the fragmentary Jericho statues being the closest analogy. They therefore allowed for the temporary removal of the statues to the Institute of Archaeology in London, where they were painstakingly restored and conserved under Kathy Tubb's excellent supervision. Shortly thereafter, another statue cache was found, not too far from the first one, and these were restored at the Smithsonian Institution before being returned to Jordan.

After the discovery of the first cache of statues, the significance of ʿAin

7.3   Excavations at Wadi Shuʿeib, Jordan.

Ghazal rapidly became apparent. It was not just the spectacular findings that
excited us the most, however. Abundant floral and faunal remains allowed for
us to develop the ecological degradation model outlined earlier. In addition,
the documentation of an unbroken sequence between the PPN and the PN
was first demonstrated at ʿAin Ghazal. I recall that Gary and I, over several
glasses of arak, were trying to figure out what to call this transition when I
suggested, somewhat in jest, the term "PPNC." The more we thought about
this term, the more we liked it, and it was introduced to the wider scientific community in a summary article published in *Science* in 1988 (Simmons
et al. 1988).

     During the ʿAin Ghazal project, we also decided to expand our study of
the megasite phenomenon to nearby Wadi Shuʿeib (fig. 7.3) in order to see if
the patterns observed at ʿAin Ghazal occurred at other sites (Simmons et al.
2001). While our investigations there were much more modest, they revealed
a sequence of occupation very similar to that at ʿAin Ghazal. Wadi Shuʿeib had
initially been recorded by Dame Diana Kirkbride, responsible for early excavations at PPNB Beidha in southern Jordan. Since she was still working in Jordan,
despite advanced age, we invited her to visit our excavations (fig. 7.4), where
she let us know in no uncertain terms that she, in fact, had discovered this

7.4   Dame Diana Kirkbride visiting Wadi Shu'eib excavations.

site (at around the time I was born). I think, though, she was happy that at last someone was systematically investigating it.

Gary and Zeidan have continued investigations at 'Ain Ghazal, and the Jordanian government is doing all that it can to protect it. But the land it is situated on is incredibly valuable, and much needs to be done before it fades back into obscurity or, worse yet, is destroyed by development. We can be hopeful that in the future, preservation plans will be developed and enforced that include an on-site museum so that visitors to Amman can witness this remarkable stage in human prehistory.

Chapter 8

The Pottery Neolithic and the Beginnings of Regional Cultures

Overview

The incorporation of ceramic technology into material culture marks the beginning of the PN period, sometimes also called the Late Neolithic. In many ways, the addition of ceramics was far less significant than other changes that occurred. While the preceding PPN shared many similarities over a wide geographic range, it was during the PN when a pan–Near East interaction sphere appears to have broken up. Instead, different parts of the Near East now follow very distinctive trajectories.

Parts of the northern Near East and Turkey elaborated on developments that had occurred earlier, but in the Levant, PN groups represent, in many ways, a less complex situation. In the north, PN cultures established a baseline that ultimately led to the creation of the classic urban societies in Mesopotamia. In the Levant, however, we see more of a rural adaptation that increasingly came under the influence of developments from both the north and the south.

The Pottery Neolithic

History of Research and Terminology

The terminology applied to various PN cultures nearly matches the confusion seen in the earlier Epipaleolithic. Much of this relates to the history of research, particularly in the Levant, and the perception that the PN was something of a "no-man's land," in that it was neglected for many years by scholars more interested in studying either the origins of food production or the subsequent Chalcolithic and Bronze Ages (cf. Gopher 1998:205).

The discovery of early pottery assemblages in the 1920s and 1940s at the basal layers of many Levantine sites, such as Jericho and Ras Shamra, pointed to the existence of a PN entity. Excavations at Byblos on the Lebanese coast by Montet and Dunand uncovered substantial Neolithic deposits that Dunand divided into three Neolithic sequences (Néolithique Ancien, Néolithique Moyen, and Néolithique Récent) (Banning 1998:193). During the early 1950s, Stekelis's (1950–1951, 1972) definition of the Yarmoukian culture at Sha'ar Hagolan on the northern bank of the Yarmouk River and Kaplan's (1958) documentation of the Wadi Rabah culture hinted at the variability of the PN. Likewise, Kenyon's Jericho excavations resulted in the subdivisions of Pottery Neolithic A and B. During the 1960s Perrot's (1966b) excavations at Munhata resulted in synthetic views of the entire Neolithic (Perrot 1968).

As Garfinkel and Miller (2002a:1–3) point out, much of this early research characterized the PN as a substantial deterioration from the PPNB, especially in the southern Levant. For example, Kenyon viewed the PN as a retrogression and the pottery-bearing newcomers as marking a sharp decline during which "the light of progress seems to flicker out. It is possible that the town-dwellers had become decadent, and fell victims to more barbarous elements" (Kenyon 1960:67–68). She also believed that the PN in the southern Levant marked a decline in comparison with contemporary developments elsewhere. While this perception has persisted in the literature, the 1980s witnessed a renewed interest in the Levantine PN, resulting in a more balanced understanding of developments (e.g., see Banning's 2002b reviews of several recent publications). Another result of this invigorated research is that the perception of an "inferior" or somehow degraded culture is no longer tenable (e.g., Banning et al. 1994).

Of course, the PN was not restricted to the Levant. In pan–Near Eastern terms, the PN falls within Moore's (1985:14) Developed Neolithic (Neolithic 3 and 4), or, in more current terms, what he refers to as Neolithic 3 (Moore et al. 2000:7). Within the Lyon scheme, the PN falls primarily within Period 6 (Cauvin 2000a: xviii). Banning (2002c) identifies several regional subtraditions. These are Amuq A-B (northwest Syria and Cilicia); Hassunan (northern Iraq, upper Tigris valley, Euphrates plain), Jarmoan (northeastern Iraq, northwestern Iran), Samarran (central and eastern Iraq on the Mesopotamian floodplain and possibly ancestral to the Sumerian civilization), Yarmoukian (central Levant) and Wadi Rabah (southern Levant). To these, one might add aspects of the Halafian and Ubaidian (Gopher 1998:205) and the Iranian variant of the Hassunan (the Zagros Neolithic Complex) (Peasnall 2002). Finally, complex developments in Turkey at sites such as Çatalhöyük and Hacilar increasingly set off this region from the rest of the Near East (Cauvin 2000a:161–164; M. Özdoğan 1999:231–232).

I concentrate here on developments in the central and southern Levant. Various local terminologies, primarily based on differences in ceramics, are confusing: Garfinkel (1999a:1–4) notes that over 50 different designations have been applied to the various cultural entities falling within the PN and the Chalcolithic. Many of these are parallel terms given to single archaeological entities. For example, a common source of bewilderment is three names given to the same entity: Pottery Neolithic A, Jericho IX, and Lodian.

Garfinkel (1999a:5–6) believes that the PN in the southern Levant consists of only one phase with three closely related and contemporaneous ceramic traditions: the Yarmoukian, Jericho IX (or PNA Jericho), and Nizzanim. He considers the Wadi Rabah as early Chalcolithic, not PN (1999a:5–6). Banning (1998:188), however, takes the opposite position, believing that many early Chalcolithic entities could be part of the late PN and noting that the distinction between the two is not very useful. Gopher (1998) also places the Wadi Rabah entity within the PN. Some researchers view the PN as consisting of three linked entities, the Yarmoukian, Jericho IX, and Wadi Rabah (Gopher 1998; Gopher and Gophna 1993). Kafafi (1987:34) prefers only two divisions, Late Neolithic 1 and Late Neolithic 2. Still others characterize the Levantine PN as a mosaic of contemporary regional cultures, consisting primarily of the Yarmoukian, Jericho IX, Nizzanim, desert variants, and two northern variants around Byblos and Amuq (Garfinkel and Miller 2002a:4). To complicate the matter further, Gopher and Gophna (1993:336–339) discuss Wadi Rabah variants, which differ primarily in details of ceramics but also have geographic significance. There is the "normative" Wadi Rabah originally defined by Kaplan, plus a more widespread series of variants. For the purposes of this discussion, I consider the primary subdivisions of the southern Levantine PN as Yarmoukian, Jericho IX, and Wadi Rabah.

Chronology

The PN is not as well dated as the PPNB, and its chronology is highly variable over different parts of the Near East. Approximate dates are 8000–6100 BP (ca. 9000–6900 cal. BP), depending upon which specific region is examined. In the Levant, a slightly later beginning around 7500 BP generally is used. Although Garfinkel views the PN as contemporaneous traditions, many others prefer some chronological overlap, with the Yarmoukian being the earliest, followed by Jericho IX and then Wadi Rabah.

For years, scholars believed that a "great Neolithic gap" or hiatus of approximately 1,000 years existed between the PPN and the PN in the Levant (Gopher and Gophna 1993:303–307; see chapter 7). Many felt that the collapse of the PPNB resulted in a virtual abandonment of much of the core Levant for a thousand years, with populations moving primarily to the northern coasts of Israel, Lebanon, and Syria. They further believed that the subsequent PN represented actual migrations of new people, thought to have come from the north (Kenyon 1960:58–68; Perrot 1968:403–404). Much of this scenario was based on poor radiocarbon chronology, however, and more current research has essentially closed this gap, primarily by documenting the PPNC in some areas as a transitional period between the PPN and PN. It now seems clear that the gap was more a result of inadequate research and an entrenched attitude by some archaeologists (Gopher and Gophna 1993:304). Rather than proposing major population migrations, shifts were likely on a smaller regional scale, and there is no need to invoke new populations as responsible for the PN.

Geographic Range

During the PPNB much of the Near East was inhabited, and this pattern continued in the PN (fig. 8.1) (Banning 2002c:40). One apparently new area with PN occupation is the "Phoenician coast" of Lebanon, Syria, and the Cilician coast of Turkey. Curiously, this rich area, with a distinct Mediterranean climate, does not appear to have witnessed much occupation during most of the PPNB. During the PN, however, several settlements are located along the Phoenician coast (Cauvin 2000a:154–155). I

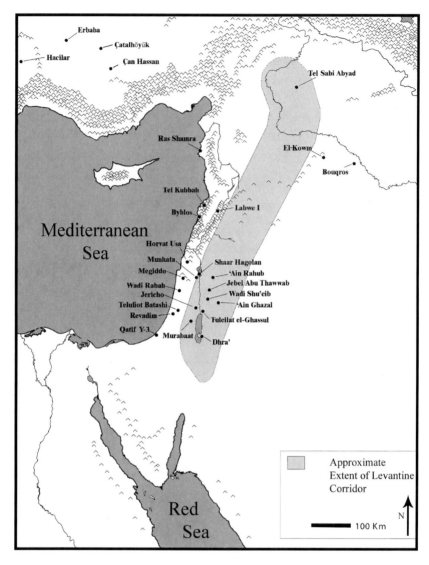

8.1   Map of selected Pottery Neolithic sites.

should note, however, that many coastal areas have not been adequately surveyed, many have been severely modified by modern development, and in many tel sites, which may have basal PPNB, occupations have not been adequately tested.

Material Culture — Artifacts

Pottery, of course, is the hallmark of the PN. Ceramics appear in the Levant with a reasonably sophisticated technology, leading earlier researchers to believe that they were imported from the north. Newer studies, however, show that local southern Levantine people were fully capable of developing their own ceramics (Banning 1998:206). Gopher (1998:215–218) does not believe that the addition of ceramics was a dramatic qualitative change, since working plaster and clay occurred during the PPN. Limited amounts of ceramics, probably experimental, have been recovered from PPNB and PPNC contexts, and of course the statuary of 'Ain Ghazal, as well as white wares, clearly shows a knowledge of working with a plastic medium.

Gopher and Goren (1998:224) believe that early pottery in the southern Levant shows a technological continuity with PPNB lime-plaster and mud products, and that a clear dichotomy exists between early undecorated and decorated pottery. The latter, common in early PN contexts, usually is made of highly calcareous pastes, resulting in functionally inefficient but easily decorable pottery. That is, decoration took precedence over function. Over time, there is a decrease in the calcareous materials in favor of mud-clay until a clearer correlation among pottery form, function, and raw material was achieved. This pattern continues into the Chalcolithic and Early Bronze Age, where utilitarian household vessels are primarily undecorated. They suggest that early pottery was not a mere improvement in cooking and storage methods, but rather an elaboration of ideological expressions, "a new type of object designed to communicate symbolic and social messages by a specific decoration. . . . Thus, we see the emergence of pottery as originating from the PPNB tradition of art objects' production . . . and believe that early pottery may be viewed more in a social context than in a daily, functional context" (Gopher and Goren 1998:224–225). While they present a compelling argument, many PN ceramic assemblages do, in fact, include a large proportion of undecorated items, but these are often not emphasized in reports (Gopher and Gophna 1993:311).

What then does this early pottery look like? There is considerable variability, dependent upon regional variants (fig. 8.2). The earliest known ceramics from the southern Levant come from Byblos and Yarmoukian assemblages (Banning 1998:208). At Byblos, Néolithique Ancien vessels were handmade and globular, and have round or concave bases. Vessel types include hemispherical or holemouth craters, bowls, and cups, holemouth jars, jars with short necks, platters, and beaker-like types. Surface decorations are rare but include cardium-shell impressions, punctate designs and incised lines defining chevrons, hatched triangles, and bands. Sometimes the decoration is highlighted with white. Vessels were usually poorly fired. Néolithique Moyen and Récent vessels include more tapered jars with high shoulders and bulging necks, similar to Wadi Rabah vessels. Flat bases occur, as do platters. Broad chevron patterns of obliquely incised lines occur on jars, and red and black slips are common, sometimes with pattern burnish (Banning 1998:208, 2002c:50).

Yarmoukian assemblages primarily include decorated bowls and jars of various sizes. There are short-pedestaled bowls, chalices, platter-basins, necked jars, and holemouth jars. Bases are usually flat or pedestaled, and handles include knobs, ledge handles, and small loop handles. Characteristic decorations are plain reverse bands incised with herringbone motifs arranged in diagonal and horizontal patterns on red slipped backgrounds and triangular, red-painted fields separated by bands. There also are vessels with painted decoration but no incisions. Yarmoukian assemblages include a large proportion of undecorated items (Gopher and Gophna 1993:311).

Jericho IX assemblages contain two elements, cruder and finer wares. The former is coarse, porous, straw-tempered handmade pottery made of light creamy ware. Main forms are bowls with rounded or straight, upright or vertical sides. Holemouth jars have inverted rims and sometimes contain cylindrical knobs and triangular knob-handles. Jars have long, straight, narrow necks, and weak shoulders. Flat trays also occur. Handles are present on many jars and large bowls. Decoration includes burnish on plain and simple red slips. The finer element consists mainly of wide, open bowls, small jars, and cups. This ware is a fine, light buff with-

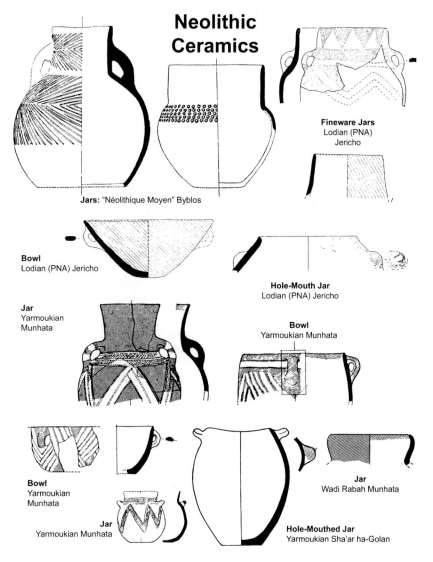

Neolithic Ceramics

Jars: "Néolithique Moyen" Byblos

Fineware Jars
Lodian (PNA)
Jericho

Bowl
Lodian (PNA) Jericho

Hole-Mouth Jar
Lodian (PNA) Jericho

Jar
Yarmoukian
Munhata

Bowl
Yarmoukian Munhata

Bowl
Yarmoukian
Munhata

Jar
Yarmoukian Munhata

Jar
Wadi Rabah Munhata

Hole-Mouthed Jar
Yarmoukian Sha'ar ha-Golan

8.2   A variety of Neolithic ceramics. Courtesy E. B. Banning and American Schools of Oriental Research.

out organic additives. On the inside faces of many vessels are geometric patterns of dark brown or red paint, with horizontal bands and chevron and lattice reserve areas unpainted. The brown or red paint was burnished (Gopher and Gophna 1993:319–323). Again, decorated pottery constitutes only a small proportion of the assemblage (Gopher 1998:211).

Wadi Rabah ceramics were still handmade, but new forms and decoration techniques appear. They also may have wheel-thrown rims. The pottery was constructed from coils with some variety in fabric composition. Decoration was applied before firing. Types of vessels include bow-rim jars, holemouth jars, carinated bowls, pedestal bowls, knob handles, and splayed loop handles. Major elements of decoration are slip, burnish, incision, impressions, combing, and applied plastic. There is a small element of painted motifs. A red painted band around the inside and outside of vessel rims also is common. Relief and applied motifs and figures include a human image on a carinated holemouth jar from 'Ain el Jarba. A small, thin, highly fired, carinated bowl of grit-free fabric, usually slipped and burnished in a deep glossy black or red also is characteristic. This often is referred to as Dark Faced Burnished Ware (DFBW), which is typical of the Amuq A-B (Gopher 1998:209–212; Gopher and Gophna 1993:327–332).

Outside of the southern Levant, other varieties of ceramics occur. Perhaps the best known is the Amuqian DFBW series. This is the hallmark of what was once thought to be a large subtradition, but now more regional variation is recognized. DFBW vessels sometimes show horizontal ledge handles below the rim and are occasionally impressed or incised with lunate, elliptical, rectangular, or other designs. Washed impressed wares and "white wares" also occur, as do unburnished black-faced wares in Amuq B (Banning 2002c:43–44).

Ceramics from the Hassunan subtradition are handmade. Hassunan Archaic Coarse Ware is fiber-tempered and consists mainly of inverted, carinated jars. Sometimes there is applied decoration of pellets or cylinders, occasionally arranged to represent eyes, breasts, or horns. Archaic Burnished Ware consists of hemispherical and inverted burnished bowls with grit temper and dark cores. Sotto ware is a well-fired, thin, grit-tempered burnished ware in red or gray. Archaic Painted Ware consists of bowls, beakers, and globular jars that are painted in red on a pinkish surface and often burnished to a gloss. Their decorations are typically vertical chevrons and groups of diagonal lines bounded by horizontal bands. Hassunan Standard wares are incised, painted, or painted and incised, and Hassunan Standard Incised Ware is the hallmark of classic Hassunan and includes large storage jars as well as tiny cups. A typical Hassunan characteristic was incision of designs while the cream slip was still wet, so that the slip did not obscure the incisions. Other ceramic objects included husking trays and clay sling balls. Jarmoan pottery is characterized by diagonal "tadpole" painting, carinated sides, or applied decoration, while Samarran pottery is fine and elaborately black-painted wares, with alternating bands of decoration separated by horizontal lines (Banning 2002c:44–46).

Of course, there are material elements to PN sites beyond ceramics. Chipped stone continues to be a major element in the cultural inventory, and there are some significant changes over the PPN. Some archaeologists have commented on the apparent deterioration in lithic technology during the PN, but this is perhaps an unfair assessment. What we do see is that the unstandardized or expedient character first observed during the PPNC continues into the PN. Bipolar core technology is still used, but in decreasing frequencies. More importantly, the technology is now dominated by flakes rather than blades. Pyramidal cores are common (Banning 1998:203). In some cases, such as Wadi Ziqlab in central Jordan, the majority of tools are simple lightly retouched flakes or expedient tools, used in "low-risk" tasks that did not require heavy investment in the production of more sophisticated tools (Siggers 1997). Obsidian, common in both PPN and PN assemblages in Anatolia, is notably rare during the PN.

The range of tools varies by phase and includes implements such as burins, bifacial knives, tabular scrapers, notches, denticulates, awls/borers, and retouched blades and flakes. A variety of projectile points and sickles are also represented. The latter were often manufactured on short, backed, and truncated blade segments, suggesting the use of composite tools as opposed to the long sickle blades of the PPNB. Frequently these contained coarse denticulations on their cutting edges. Sometimes both sides were used. This is especially true for Yarmoukian assemblages. Wadi Rabah sickle blades are different, with only tiny denticulation, nibbling, or no retouch on their cutting edges. It may be that such formalized tools with considerable labor investment were important in high-risk, critical activities, such as farming (Banning 1998:204).

Projectile points are not as common as they were during the PPNB —
and they are nearly absent in many assemblages, especially Wadi Rabah
ones. In the southern Levant, points are dominated by three types: Ha-
parsa, Nizzanim, and Herzliya points, which resemble diminutive Jericho, Byblos, and Amuq types respectively. Their small size has led some to
suggest they were used for hunting birds, although they likely had other
functions as well. Toward the end of the PN, transverse projectile points
appear (Banning 1998:204).

Heavy bifacial tools are important. Yarmoukian assemblages often
contain well-made narrow adzes. Through time, these become rarer, replaced by trapezoidal forms. As with sickle blades, considerable labor was
invested in these implements, and their likely use in clearing fields and
breaking up soil for cultivation again testifies to the importance of farming
(Banning 1998:204).

Ground stone continues to be important throughout the PN — not a
surprising observation given the emphasis on farming. There are changes
from the PPNB, primarily with the appearance of elongated grinding
slabs and two-handed grinding stones (Gopher 1998:217–218).

Non-stone items include a variety of utilitarian artifacts, such as
spindle whorls, indicating a change in spinning technology (Gopher
1998:218). Stamp seals also occur in some contexts (Banning 2002c:42).
Perhaps the most "famous" type of PN artifact, however, is the remarkable variety of incised stone and stone and clay anthropomorphic figurines, which many researchers believe had symbolic significance, often
related to fertility. In the southern Levant, these primarily occur in Yarmoukian contexts. On a wider scale, they are most famously represented
as so-called Mother Goddess figurines at Çatalhöyük.

In the southern Levant, the best examples of imagery come from
Sha'ar Hagolan (Garfinkel 1999b; Gopher and Orrelle 1996, 1998). Here,
two major groups of imagery artifacts occur: incised stones and clay figurines. The clay figurines include women and men shaped around a core.
These often are characterized as highly stylized figurines, usually of large,
obese females. The eyes are the most prominent feature. These are elongated, set diagonally, and were created by attaching clay lumps on the
face and incising them lengthwise with a deep slit. These are often called
"coffee bean eyes" or "cowrie shell eyes," harking back to a much earlier
PPNB use of these shells in some plastered skulls. Others interpret the

eyes as cereal grains or date pits, or even vulvae (Garfinkel 1999b:93; Miller 2002:226). Several figurines are quite remarkable, with minute details, such as elongated heads, diagonal eyes, noses, ears, earrings, mouths, cheeks, headdresses, garments or scarves, hands, fingers, fat folds, knees, and feet portrayed realistically, but in exaggerated fashion. Some scholars have characterized these as "the terrible mother" or "grotesque figurines," undoubtedly influenced by psychoanalytical theories, as noted by Garfinkel (1999b:92). Another category is stone and clay shaped phalli. The significance of these artifacts has been the subject of much debate and will be returned to under "Ritual Behavior."

Material Culture — Architecture

Kenyon's initial characterization of the PN as retrogressive has influenced generations of scholars. One aspect of this was the presence of circular huts or pits in the PN levels at Jericho, along with only isolated wall sections. The pits were interpreted as either dwellings or quarries for mud brick material. This contributed to the image of PN people as partially nomadic and no longer constructing substantial architecture. We now know that this is an incorrect perception. Indeed, it was during the PN that some of the largest Neolithic sites in the Near East were constructed, and these often were complex communities exhibiting considerable variability. Again, perhaps the most famous of these is Çatalhöyük, although substantial villages also were present in the Levant.

In general terms, PN architecture is actually characterized by rectangular buildings that are single- or multiple-roomed, although round structures also occur. Structures were constructed of pisé, mudbrick, or mudbrick on stone foundations. Gypsum or lime plaster is often used, but not as frequently as during the PPNB. Most structures range from 10 to 30 m^2, but some multiroom buildings were two-story, with up to 100 m^2 of living space. Large structures that may have been storehouses occur at some sites (Banning 2002c:41–42). There is considerable geographic variation in architectural and village layouts. Perhaps most distinctive is the "agglutinative plan" layout of large settlements such as Çatalhöyük, Asikli, and Çan Hassan in central Turkey, which appear to represent original Anatolian creations. The roots of this plan are in the PPNB, but it expanded during the PN. In these settlements, circulation from one house to another was not at ground level, but rather through the roofs. These sites were large agglomerations that were very tightly packed together, although Matthews (1996:86–87) suggests that substantial open areas used for rubbish did exist at Çatalhöyük. At that site, approximately every other room was some sort of domestic sanctuary that often contained frescoes and sculpted figures, as well as numerous burials. Oftentimes, the wall art depicts headless human corpses (Cauvin 2000a:161–162; Hodder and Cessford 2004:20, 35). The inclusion of sanctuaries within domestic structures further blurs the distinction between public and private architecture.

In the Amuq A-B subtradition, many settlements consisted of rectangular buildings with stone or mud-brick walls and lime-plastered floors. At the Néolithique Ancien levels at Byblos, several subrectangular plastered pits that may have been the floors of tentlike structures occur. In the Hassunan subtradition, early settlements often are small with simple pit dwellings, tent areas, and bins. These are replaced by rectilinear structures that include both small two- and three-roomed houses and some large multichambered structures that may have been communal storage facilities arranged around large plazas. Jarmoan subtradition structures typically consisted of multiroomed, rectilinear mud-brick buildings, although pit structures also occur. There was some use of gypsum plaster and terrazzo floors. Storage bins and ovens sometimes were incorporated into houses. Samarran subtradition settlements often show a standardized tripartite building plan. These have three entrances, side by side, leading into central courtyards and right and left wings. There also are "T-shaped" buildings, with a large room, small chambers, and courtyards. Cellular houses also occur at some sites (Banning 2002c:44–47).

In the southern Levant, Kenyon's original characterization of the ephemeral nature of the PN was reinforced by Stekelis's excavations at Sha'ar Hagolan, since he uncovered only semisubterranean circular huts. A similar pattern was reported for other sites, where rounded pits and limited, circular architecture seemed to characterize the Yarmoukian, giving the impression of seasonal occupation (Garfinkel and Ben-Shlomo 2002a:55). We now know that there is considerable architectural variability that strongly contradicts Kenyon's and Stekelis's original characterizations. Ironically, this is now best seen by renewed excavations at Sha'ar Hagolan (Garfinkel and Miller 2002b), which have documented

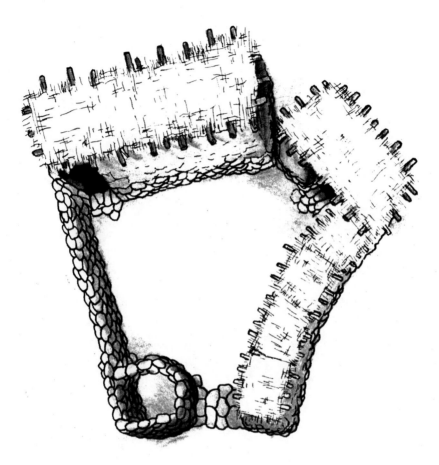

8.3   Reconstruction of a Yarmoukian dwelling at Shaʻar Hagolan,
Israel. Courtesy of Yossi Garfinkel.

extensive architecture, including a new type—the courtyard house (fig.
8.3) built along streets and alleys, as well as large structures interpreted
as communal buildings (Garfinkel and Ben-Shlomo 2002a, b).

At ʻAin Ghazal, substantial architecture during the early Yarmoukian
occupation consists of large (ca. 9 × 5 m) rectilinear houses that had mud
floors and contained multiple rooms, and a large apsidal structure remodeled from an LPPNB structure that is interpreted as a public building. Other Yarmoukian architecture includes courtyard or compound
walls, and continued usage and remodeling of a large wall and walled
street that were originally constructed during the PPNC. Toward the end

of the Yarmoukian (and final) occupation, however, there is evidence for temporary structures, possibly tents, replacing the more permanent facilities (Rollefson 1997a:298–301, 2000:181–182).

Thus, Yarmoukian architecture contains both circular and rectangular structures, including round hut-bases, rectangular huts, and a variety of pits that may have been used for storage, dumping, or pottery-firing purposes (Kafafi 2001:23). Curiously, in Jordan only three Yarmoukian sites, all in the highlands, have architectural remains: Jebel Abu Thawwab, ʿAin Ghazal, and Wadi Shuʿeib (Kafafi 2001:27).

There is less information for architectural patterns at both Jericho IX and Wadi Rabah sites. Only limited evidence for isolated sections of stone walls, plastered pits, hut-bases, and round, sunken mud-brick structures exists for Jericho IX (Gopher and Gophna 1993:322). Somewhat better data exist for Wadi Rabah sites, which contain rectangular dwellings with fieldstone foundations. Some of these are quite large and have internal subdivisions. Floors were primarily of earth, and it is uncertain what materials were used for the walls. Different sized pits also occur, including a variety of rounded, paved, and lined ones. Circular basins lined with plaster occur at some sites, as do small, irregularly spaced paved areas outside of walls (Gopher and Gophna 1993:332).

Economy

PN economic strategies were almost entirely dependent on domesticated grains and pulses, and the management of either tamed or domesticated animals. Typically, domesticates are represented by fewer species than they were during the PPN. Toward the end of the PN, the production of olive oil also may have begun in the southern Levant, and there is evidence for dairying activities, such as the presence of butter churns (Banning 2002c:41–42). This indicates an increasing emphasis on the "secondary products revolution" (Sherratt 1983). Within the Samarran subtradition, there is some evidence of irrigation from the Tigris River, where farmers may first have intentionally dug breaks and then, a bit later, artificial canals (Banning 2002c:47), allowing for the expansion of agricultural fields. This is among the first examples of irrigation in the region (see Araus et al. [1999:209], who discuss possible irrigation at PPNB Halula, but dismiss it). Of course, the use of simple irrigation techniques, such as filling animal skins with water (Bellwood 2005:57) cannot be discounted.

There also is some evidence that beer brewing may have begun during the PN, although thus far it is circumstantial. In fact, decades ago a spirited symposium between some major luminaries in the field debated whether beer rather than bread (or, as J. Sauer put it, "thirst rather than hunger" [Braidwood et al. 1953:516]) may have been the stimulus for the first domestication of cereals. While this is an intriguing idea, solid evidence was absent, and most of the symposium participants felt that the original use of cereals was as food—likely a gruel—rather than alcohol (Braidwood et al. 1953). The ensuing 50-odd years have not changed this, although Katz and Voigt (1986) make a strong hypothetical argument that beer could have been a highly nutritional resource as well as an ideal psychopharmacological substance. While acknowledging that direct evidence for beer production is presently lacking for the Neolithic, they note that such evidence could take the form of sprouted cereal grains necessary for fermentation and also may be detectable in human skeletons in the form of uric acids (Katz and Voigt 1986:33). In any event, the combination of grains and the new technology provided by ceramic vessels certainly could have allowed beer production during the PN, although the earliest solid evidence for brewing is written accounts from the Early Dynastic period in Egypt (ca. 4500 BP). Future chemical analysis of residue from pots, as well as the botanical or skeletal evidence noted above, may ultimately document beer manufacture during the Neolithic (Banning 1998:211–212; Katz and Voigt 1986).

Likewise, one might speculate on the beginning of wine making, which actually could have Upper Paleolithic origins. Residue analysis on ceramics from the Iranian Neolithic village of Hajji Firuz Tepe, dated around 7000 BP, found calcium salt from tartaric acid, which occurs naturally in large amounts only in grapes. High-performance liquid chromatography analysis pointed to a chemical component that made it virtually certain that vessels contained wine. Resin from the terebinth tree also was present, presumably used as a preservation agent, suggesting that the wine was deliberately made and not the result of unintentional fermentation of grape juice. Such wine may have been the equivalent of modern retsina. Continuing studies indicate that both red and white wine were produced. Contextual evidence suggests relatively large-scale production and consumption, and has tremendous implications relating to social relations, status, leisure time, ritual, and prestige (McGovern 2003:65–74, 302–303).

While domestic resources were primary, wild foods still played a role, although they are underreported at many sites. They probably included olive, pistachio and other nuts, and gazelle and onagers, especially in the steppe regions. For example, Umm Dabaghiyah in northern Mesopotamia may have been a specialized onager hunting and processing site. In better-forested areas, aurochs, boar, deer, fish, hares, quail and other birds, turtle, and wild sheep were part of the subsistence base. At most sites, however, hunting contributed little to the economy, although it may have had social significance (Banning 2002c:41). Pastoral nomadism, as reflected in potential herd animals such as sheep, goat, and cattle, likely was a more important form of faunal exploitation. As noted previously, this particular economic pattern may have had its roots in the final aspects of the PPN.

In the southern Levant specifically, generally similar patterns occur, although plant remains tend to be poorly preserved, possibly due to changes associated with processing or cooking methods (Banning 2002c: 49). There also appears to have been less variety in fauna, following the arguments for environmental degradation presented previously (chapter 7). During the Yarmoukian, faunal assemblages show a dominance of domesticated sheep and goat, plus cattle and pigs in smaller quantities. Some limited gazelle hunting also occurred. Yarmoukian plant usage concentrated on cereals and various legumes and flax. Submerged coastal sites indicate an emphasis on olives, but it is uncertain whether these were domesticated. Roughly similar patterns are observed for Jericho IX and Wadi Rabah sites (Gopher 1998:209–211).

Thus, what we see during the PN is essentially what Butzer (1996) and others have characterized as the basic Mediterranean agrosystem. This consists of four fundamental components—outfield cultivation of grains and legumes, infield tending of various green vegetables and condiments, orchard crops, and livestock. While the PN may not precisely match this system, amply documented from Greek and Roman sources (Butzer 1996:142), it is likely that the basic pattern became established during this time. Thus, during the PN an agropastoral economy existed that became more and more dependent on a smaller number of domesticated resources. Changes in processing and cooking brought about by the incorporation of ceramics undoubtedly are embedded in this pattern.

There was a likely increase in the use of secondary products as well. While domestic products formed the core of PN subsistence, people still used wild resources, although these no longer seem to have been of primary consequence.

Settlement Pattern and Diversity

PN sites range from huge communities to small hamlets. Limited-activity sites also are known, although these are rarer than previously. In desert and steppe areas, such sites, usually reflected by clusters of huts, may have been seasonally used, perhaps by pastoralists. Most settlements are located adjacent to arable lands. There are indications of settlement hierarchy, with small farmsteads and hamlets associated with larger villages (Banning 2002c:41).

There is considerable variability in village size. In the Amuq subtradition, site sizes generally range from 5 to 7.5 acres. Hassunan subtradition settlements often have structures scattered in no clear patterns with fairly large open areas. They range in size from ca. 2 to 5 acres. Jarmoan communities were typically ca. 2.5 to 5 acres (Banning 2002c:44–46). Several sites, however, were much larger. As noted in chapter 7, Çatalhöyük covered some 33 acres, and Abu Hureyra, which reached its maximum size during the PPNB, remained large, at ca. 17 acres, during its final occupation in the PN (Moore et al. 2000:478). Likewise, the Yarmoukian occupation at 'Ain Ghazal, only half of what it was during the LPPNB (Rollefson 1997a:298–299, n. 1), still covered some 15–20 acres and likely housed 400–500 people (Gary Rollefson, personal communication 2004). Even more impressive is Sha'ar Hagolan, if Garfinkel's (2002:258, 262) estimates of ca. 50 acres with a maximum population of 4,000 are accurate. It is interesting to contrast this site, with its relatively spacious structures and streets, to the slightly smaller Çatalhöyük, with its dense architectural packing and an estimated population of 3,500 to 8,000 people (Hodder and Cessford 2004:21; Matthews 1996:86–87).

In the southern Levant, some distinctions can be seen in settlement pattern. The Yarmoukian is spread over diverse ecological zones in a west-east direction from the Mediterranean coast to the Jordanian Plateau. The Soreq Valley is the southern border, while the Jezreel and Yarmouk valleys form the northern border, with some occurrences in the Judean Desert and the western Galilee. Jericho IX sites are primarily located

along the coastal plain and adjacent Shephelah, in the Jordan Valley between the Sea of Galilee and the Dead Sea, and to the east and southeast of the Dead Sea. Unlike the Yarmoukian, there are few Jericho IX
sites in the mountains or Jordanian Plateau, and occupation instead is
mainly in the low and hilly areas, with a more southernly extent than the
Yarmoukian. Both Yarmoukian and Jericho IX distributions overlap considerably. The normative Wadi Rabah appears in the northern valleys (the
Beqaa and Huleh valleys), in the central Jezreel and Bethsan valleys of
Israel, and along the coastal plain and Shephelah down to the Soreq Valley. Wadi Rabah variants, however, cover a wider range, including different parts of the Jordan Valley, the mountainous ridges of Israel, and the
northern Negev and the Dead Sea (if one includes the Qatifian variant
here) (Gopher 1998:214; Kafafi 1992).

Gopher (1998:214–215) notes the general similarity in the distribution of these entities, and their confinement to relatively small areas of
10,000–15,000 km². This is a considerable reduction compared to the PPN
and may be connected to the reduced role of hunting and the fact that
farming allows for subsistence in smaller territories. On the other hand,
Gopher also notes that this could simply reflect a research bias. Based
on these data, he feels that no clear site hierarchy can be identified for
the PN in the southern Levant. That is, there are no conspicuously large-
scale PN sites, particularly when compared to the late PPN, although
Gopher (1998:214) acknowledges that this could change with investigations at sites such as Tel Asawir and 'Ain el Jarba, or the basal layer of Tel
Dan. Even the well-known site of Byblos was only about one acre during its Néolithique Ancien occupation. At the time of his article, only 'Ain
Ghazal and Wadi Shu'eib appeared to have been relatively large. Now,
however, the expanded excavations at Sha'ar Hagolan further contradict
Gopher's contention that most PN sites were small. Indeed, it is quite possible that Sha'ar Hagolan was a central PN locality and that some sort of
site hierarchy existed. As such, the southern Levant may not have been
so different from other areas of the Near East during the PN.

The People

Unfortunately, there are relatively few PN burials that have been well
studied, especially in the southern Levant. It is likely that diets highly de-

pendent on domesticated cereals and legumes would lead to high rates of caries, dental attrition, and tooth loss, but burials from some PN sites in fact show low incidences of this. The high population densities in the larger communities, plus storage facilities that could attract animal disease vectors, likely increased the rate of communicable diseases, and childhood mortality probably was high. The absence of cemeteries, however, makes these claims difficult to assess (Banning 2002c:41).

If farming assumed an increasingly important role, it is likely that the types of MSM patterns that Peterson (2002) observed for the PPNB were intensified. Unfortunately, she was able to study only two PN individuals (from Newe Yam) (Peterson 2002:35). Some insight may be provided, however, by her analysis of 52 skeletons from the Early Bronze Age I site of Bab edh-Dhra in southern Jordan. By this time, most researchers agree that the economy was firmly based on a mixed agropastoral system, and that animal husbandry was very important, with the use of secondary products being quite significant. Peterson showed a dramatic shift in both the task spectra and sexual organization of labor from earlier periods. This included a pronounced increase in female workload relative to males', with females demonstrating multiple habitual activities. Males, on the other hand, exhibit decreased profiles, perhaps explained by increased male involvement in herding activities. Peterson concludes that males and females had distinctive yet complementary tasks related to increased dependence on domestic animals and their products. These tasks, herding for males and processing for females, placed very different demands on the upper-body musculature of males and females (Peterson 2002:113–125). Certainly the Bronze Age is far removed from the Neolithic, but it is interesting to speculate whether PN populations might exhibit MSM patterns somewhere between those seen on PPN and Bronze Age samples.

Ritual Behavior

Ceramic technology opens up new lines for investigating ritual and symbolic behavior. Pottery carries a wide variety of decorative elements that must have had rich symbolic content, yet analysis of PN ceramics from this perspective are relatively rare (Gopher 1998:218). Orrelle and Gopher (2000) are an exception, and they regard the first pottery in the Levant as fulfilling a social role, treating them as symbolic assemblages.

They believe that triangle, V, and zigzag motifs on Yarmoukian pottery represent vulvae, and that when traces of red occur, they can be interpreted as menstruating vulvae. They argue that these, and figurine representations, are symbols for a social system governing rules of access to women (Orrelle and Gopher 2000:299). They see sexual associations in some Wadi Rabah ceramics as well, although not as pronounced as during the Yarmoukian.

Another exception is Garfinkel's (2003a, b) imaginative analysis of dancing images, primarily on ceramics. He presents evidence from a few Levantine sites in which ceramics and other objects depict images interpreted as dance elements (Garfinkel 2003a:110–124). Much more data are available from Halafian and Samarran contexts, as well as from both Neolithic and Chalcolithic sites in Iran, providing a large amount of information relating to dance, and its ritual and social implications (Garfinkel 2003a:125–203).

Likewise, architectural evidence relating to ritual activity has been addressed throughout this book. Certainly the elaborate structures at Çatalhöyük have long been interpreted as shrines with ceremonial significance. Renewed studies there, however, blur the distinction between "the sacred and the profane," indicating, instead, that ritual activities occurred within household contexts. Other sites, such as 'Ain Ghazal and Sha'ar Hagolan, have evidence for communal buildings, as previously noted, but it is unclear whether these served ritual functions. What we do not seem to have, however, are specialized ritual sites such as those seen during the PPN at Göbekli or Kfar HaHoresh.

Mortuary data are another source of ritual information. For example, burials from Çatalhöyük likely both have ritual significance and relate to concepts of "social memory" (see later discussion). A fair amount of mortuary data are available from the PN of the Zagros Neolithic Complex, where there is considerable variation in burial patterns, with bundled flexed burials, both primary and secondary, being common. Bodies were bundled in reed mats and often covered with ochre. During earlier phases of the Neolithic, individuals often were buried beneath house floors, but during the last phases of occupation at sites such as Ali Kosh, individuals were often interred in open spaces. At Ganj Dareh, individuals were placed in special mud-walled cubicles built into house floors, and in the northern Zagros, groups of individuals, possibly of the same household, were buried in ossuaries after the flesh had decomposed. The ossuaries were either built into or buried under house floors. Burial goods were common, consisting of personal adornment and utilitarian items that may have been used by the deceased during life. Ceramic vessels and baskets were sometimes included in burials, but none of these offerings suggest major social differentiation (Peasnall 2002:225).

As noted earlier, southern Levantine mortuary information is scant, consisting primarily of individuals in a variety of positions. Yarmoukian and Jericho IX burial customs were similar, containing adults in flexed positions with their skulls intact and with no grave goods. Wadi Rabah sites, likewise, have not produced many burials but include three adults below a house floor at 'Ain el Jarba, one adult in a supine position at Hahal Betzet I, and a child with no skull in a flexed position at Nahal Zehora II. A new pattern that emerges at several Wadi Rabah sites is the use of jars for the burial of infants and fetuses (Gopher 1998:219; Gopher and Orrelle 1995).

What this leaves us with in the ritual realm is its remarkably rich figurine tradition. In the southern Levant, graphic figurines and a variety of incised objects are known primarily from Yarmoukian contexts, especially from Sha'ar Hagolan. These are beautifully illustrated by Garfinkel (1999b) and described by Garfinkel et al. (2002). Their symbolic significance has been intensely debated, with considerably different interpretations, as discussed earlier for PPN contexts. The figurines often were explained in sympathetic-magic contexts related to fertility, to Mother Goddess fertility rituals, and to the relationship between obesity and fertility. Garfinkel, however, suggests that many show an underrepresentation of organs related to fertility, and interprets them as objects used in rituals representing different deities (Gopher and Orrelle 1998:222).

Related to their arguments for ceramics, Gopher and Orrelle (1996, 1998) provide a provocative interpretation of both figurines and incised items in sexual contexts. They suggest that two categories of incised pebbles represent "women pebbles" and "vulva pebbles." The "women pebbles" incorporate encoded information on the different ages of women. Gopher and Orrelle argue that narrow, elliptically incised pebbles showing only slits for eyes suggest young women, and the rounder, larger, oval-shaped pebbles with deep incisions indicate hips and buttocks evocative of more mature women. The "vulva pebbles" are believed to portray female genitalia at different reproductive stages. The lines incised on pebbles range from a single slit for young girls to multiple lines indicating more maturity and childbearing. The final elements are net-patterned incised cobbles, reflecting the climax of this process and representing older women who had successfully given birth many times. Notably, some of the pebbles bear red stains, hinting at other stages in the woman's development.

Figurines usually depict seated women, and perhaps some men, and are interpreted as combinations of male and female genitalia. Gopher and Orrelle (1996, 1998) believe these are concerned with duality in the relationships between the sexes, expressed by mixing symbols of both in one artifact. Finally, stone and clay phalli, as well as a small collection of clay figurines of young men, are thought to be related to male initiation rites.

Gopher and Orrelle (1996:275–276) posit that long absences by males, who were engaged in hunting or herding activities, would require the introduction of social devices to control their resources: reproductive women. They believe that access to women must have become difficult. A man acquired status through having a wife, and as she moved through life stages, society used material methods to record reproductive activity. Thus, the women and vulva pebbles may have been overt displays of productive female potential, indicating women's increased societal value. Likewise, the phalli may have signified a form of blood ritual for men. This could have significance for tracing a possible breakdown of traditional female blood ritual, where female rites started to be performed ritually by men. In sum, the imagery presented by the Yarmoukian suggests that several aspects of sexuality were operating alongside each other. These included the encouragement of procreation, an increased male appropriation of female rituals, and symbols of nonproductive sexuality.

There certainly is no lack of imagination in these provocative ideas, even if they seem somewhat male-dominant. Miller (2002) presents a more balanced perspective, believing that the figurines were made by specialists with considerable skills, or even by shamans, while the pebble figurines could have been made by nearly anyone. She also notes that the majority were used in domestic contexts. In interpreting function, a variety of possibilities are suggested, including fertility votives, birthing charms, tokens of individual identity, or emblems of group identity. She does, albeit somewhat reluctantly, conclude that the figurines are

identified with a specific ancestral deity, a matron goddess. Such Yarmoukian goddesses served a variety of functions, such as protecting the
home and its occupants, ensuring their continued success and economic
"fertility," and, foremost, being an emblem of Yarmoukian society, en-
couraging group cohesion (Miller 2002:232).

Social Structure and Organization

The layout and size of PN houses is usually consistent with nuclear
families, and settlement organization suggests the possibility of clans.
Larger houses and compounds, however, indicate extended families, and
large structures that might have served as storage facilities suggest re-
distributive economies. Trade and the growing importance of agricultural
territory hint that some type of tribal organizations may have integrated
large regions by the end of the PN. There is also evidence for craft specialization, something to be expected with the advent of ceramic technology.
The presence of stamp seals hints at either private property or the use of
"contracts." There is, however, no evidence for formal political status of
individuals, with the possible exception of mace heads, perhaps reflecting
status (Banning 2002c:42).

Mortuary data are an indicator of social structure, but as already
noted there is relatively little PN burial evidence, particularly in the southern Levant. Treatment of the dead seems to vary widely. One pattern that
does appear clear is the gradual cessation of decapitation, suggesting that
this practice was no longer relevant. There also is an increased number
of group burials, both trends first observed during the PPNC. At Çatalhöyük, however, mortuary elaboration continued, with both decapitated
burials and ones with their crania intact (Hodder and Cessford 2004:32–
35), so the abandonment of this practice was by no means universal.

Gopher (1998:219–22) and Gopher and Orrelle (1995) summarize
the scant database for southern Levantine mortuary data and its social
significance by noting that graves in the southern Levant tend to be on-
site. Off-site cemeteries only become common during the Chalcolithic.
PN burials generally contain one individual, are mostly primary, and only
rarely contain grave goods. Furthermore, the use of jars for infant burials suggests a change in their place in society, and that the social status
of both children and adults was now dictated by affinity lines. Thus, "the

use of pottery containers for burial . . . may be an early manifestation relating women, pottery, houses and death in symbolic association" (Gopher
1998:220).

Let us look at two specific examples that reflect on PN social organization. One might expect to find elaborate hierarchal examples of social structure at the largest, most populous sites. However, even at Çatalhöyük, Hodder and Cessford (2004) present a strong argument that
households were still the primary social grouping. They are somewhat
critical of theories implying that these large settlements required some
sort of centralized power to deal with regulation and coordination, although Mellaart (1998:36) believes that the site had "established rulers."
Instead, Hodder and Cessford focus on how patterns of social rules,
meanings, and power relations are embedded within the more mundane
aspects of daily practices and how they relate to the centralization of
power. They point out the importance of the house at Çatalhöyük, noting
that even the most elaborate structures, formerly (and still? — see Mellaart 1998:38) interpreted as "shrines," represent a wide range of domestic activities. In other words, all buildings acted as domestic houses with
varying degrees of symbolic elaboration (Hodder and Cessford 2004:21).

Their analysis deals with how social rules learned in daily practice
within the house contributed to the patterns of recurrent construction and
use activities within domestic space. This regulation of social practices
created village-wide social rules, but habituated behavior also was commemorative and involved the construction of social memory. Part of the
concept of social memory involves burial patterns, especially related to
dominant houses that contained up to 60 interments. They document both
site-wide and house-based specific memories but believe "that the politics of memory . . . were house based, and perhaps that dominant houses
invested particularly in the construction and control of social memory"
(Hodder and Cessford 2004:36).

The second example relates to the division of society into villagers
and pastoral nomads — the "desert and sown" distinction. This is explicitly
addressed in an innovative archaeological "ethnography" by Verhoeven
(1999) at the "burnt village" at Tel Sabi Abyad in the Balikh Valley of
northern Syria. Like many other parts of the Near East, the Balikh Valley witnessed the apparent abandonment of late PPN sites (Akkermans
1993:170), but during the PN population density again increased.

During the Level 6 occupation of Sabi Abyad, at ca. 7200 BP, Verhoeven (1999:231–232) argues, a nonhierarchical community was organized on a dual basis of nomads and residents. He estimates a nomadic
population of ca. 400 to 670 people, with the residential group compris-
ing ca. 60 to 120. Rectangular architecture at the site would have housed
residents, while round structures housed nomads. He makes a distinction
between individual household economies and a village economy involved
with the production of goods for the nomads, who had a pastoral economy.
He further proposes that two mechanisms existed for binding together
the dual society and creating a sense of identity. First, and more important, was a rite-of-passage system that expressed fundamental social rules
and values to both the residents and nomads. Second was the deliberate destruction of figurines, interpreted as an act of symbolized economic
transactions between both groups. He believes that Sabi Abyad was a
central place where different but related groups came together and reinforced ideas, rules, identity, ideology, and social solidarity (Verhoeven
1999:232). The Level 6 settlement ultimately was destroyed in a violent
fire. Rather than attributing this to either accident or violence, Verhoeven
(1999:201–202) believes that parts of the village already were abandoned
before the fire and that it may have been deliberately set as a form of
ritual closing prior to total abandonment. While speculative, Verhoeven
presents a compelling argument that is still reflected in the importance of
tribal ties in modern Near Eastern society.

What then, can we conclude of PN social organization? We are seeing societies in transition, undergoing changes that resulted in different
trajectories. In some instances, such as the Hassunan and Samarran subtraditions, these had spectacular consequences: the development of true
urban societies. Similar examples may have occurred in Turkey. In other
cases, such as the southern Levant, there is a more mundane transition,
although recent investigations at sites such as Sha'ar Hagolan and 'Ain
Ghazal suggest much more complexity than originally believed.

Gopher (1998:220–221) feels that for material culture there is no significant breakthrough between the PN and PPN. He believes that differences between these two periods are more in the social and economic
realms, with the PN representing a reorganization into a more efficient
economy. PN communities appear to reflect an established system of
agricultural villages in small territories with technological innovations ad-

justing to new needs. Initially, during the Yarmoukian, there is the establishment of a new village pattern consisting primarily of small communities, although much larger ones, such as Sha'ar Hagolan and 'Ain Ghazal
still existed. By the Wadi Rabah, however, this pattern had developed
into a rural agricultural system (Gopher and Gophna 1993:345–346).
Land use during the PN changed with the reduction in hunting and the
concentration on agriculture and animal husbandry. This likely was reflected in internal politics and power systems. Gopher feels that during
the PPNB, long-range contacts may have been in the hands of a select
group of hunters, and that by the PN, this pattern no longer existed. It
was probably replaced by a different political system based on partner-
ships or alliances aimed at controlling resources such as land, water, and
pasture for agriculture and animal management. Such systems, based on
kin groups, would emphasize the role of women as a resource both in reproductive terms and politically. If this was the case, it must have had
a significant influence on social structuring, resulting in the full departure from systems of egalitarian principles to those tending toward more
complexity within a larger-scale Neolithic world, or what Gopher terms
a "koine" (1998:221).

The relationship of the southern Levant to this larger "koine" is not
clearly understood, but the marginal character of the region may have
resulted in it having less influence. According to Gopher, small PN entities in the southern Levant likely absorbed ideologies from other regions.
The early PN in the southern Levant did not show great innovation and
growth, but rather an accumulative process of steady internal change
based on more efficient economic and social organization, as well as a
potential to accept and absorb change and innovation. In effect, this, then,
is a stage in the reestablishment of a population that suffered a crisis at
the end of the PPN and was slowly recovering (Gopher 1998:221).

Of course, understanding what caused this change is not clear. Gopher believes that the common retreat to climate change as a trigger may
not be valid for most of the PN, as there is limited information for this
(although see earlier discussion in chapter 7 on dating problems of some
paleoclimatic data for this time period). A second explanation may relate to external influences, primarily from contacts with Mesopotamia and
Syria. This need not involve actual population immigration or political
dominance, but rather the development of a general cultural willingness

that accepted change. These regions must have had an influence on the southern Levant, even if it was indirect. Gopher, however, prefers a third explanation, that of emphasizing internal changes and readjustments to new conditions. He acknowledges the peripherality of the southern Levant during the PN as a major cultural characteristic, one that was retained in later periods when the region increasingly came under the influence of Mesopotamian and Egyptian "superpowers" (Gopher 1998:221).

Regional Interaction

Most resources used by PN people were locally abundant. There was, however, exchange in obsidian, shells, bitumen, semiprecious stones, pottery, and other goods. In general, most evidence for trade suggests that materials moved through informal, down-the-line exchange networks. Most exchange was likely conducted by individuals and may have been characterized by a form of balanced reciprocity (Peasnall 2002:218). Despite relatively limited evidence for intense trading, exchange systems likely became increasingly important in some areas, especially those that went on to develop more complex societies.

In the southern Levant, there appears to have been a decrease in long-distance trade for materials like Anatolian obsidian, which occurs in small quantities, mainly in Wadi Rabah sites. Wadi Rabah ceramics also exhibit some similarities to the Halafian, and both Yarmoukian and Wadi Rabah pottery have features similar to materials from Byblos and other Lebanese sites. These could indicate some degree of relatively long-distance exchange (Banning 1998:215–216). Gopher makes the important distinction of long-distance trade of small quantities and medium- to short-range trade systems involving the day-to-day economy. Local, short-distance trade and exchange networks cannot be precisely reconstructed, but they likely existed primarily for food and craft items, perhaps including pottery and basketry (Gopher 1998:218). There is limited evidence for contacts with the Nile Valley during the PN, but documenting this is elusive. Such contacts likely involved the diffusion of a "package" of domesticated plants and animals from the Levant (Kuijt and Goring-Morris 2002:428). This is a complex issue, however; for example, mitochondrial DNA evidence suggests that cattle may have been domesticated independently in Africa rather than imported from the Levant (Bradley et al. 1996).

Summary

The PN was a time of considerable change, particularly in some regions. In the northern reaches of much of the Near East, PN developments continued the elaboration first seen during the PPN. In some areas, there may have been a period of late PPN abandonment, but this was soon followed by substantial PN communities. Many of these were on a cultural trajectory that led to the development of some of the world's first urban societies, especially in Mesopotamia. Other regions, particularly the southern Levant, were more marginalized and peripheral. There, most PN communities did not reflect the cultural elaboration seen during the earlier PPN. Salient aspects of the PN are summarized below.

1. Architectural and village variability during the PN is heterogeneous. Huge and elaborate settlements consisting of densely packed architecture occur in Turkey, and large villages also occur throughout most of the Near East. With the notable exception of a few sites, however, most PN communities in the southern Levant were considerably smaller than their PPN counterparts.

2. Despite some of these large communities, social organization still appears to be primarily at the household level. Likewise, few data exist supporting highly structured social stratification.

3. Economically, the PN consisted of mixed strategies with an increased reliance on domesticated plants and animals. Most communities reflect a growing agropastoral system. There also is evidence suggesting the incorporation of true pastoralism within the wider economic picture.

4. Ceramics obviously become important components in the material cultural inventory. There is some thought that ceramics may have initially served ceremonial functions rather than purely utilitarian ones.

5. Chipped-stone artifacts generally reflect an expedient flake-based technology. A deemphasis on hunting may be one reason for the decrease in both the abundance and size of projectile points.

6. Mortuary patterns, particularly in the southern Levant, represent a change from the PPNB, especially in the abandonment of the practice of postmortem decapitation and in the way in which infants are treated.

7. Ritual or symbolic behavior is especially expressed through elaborate figurine imagery, particularly of corpulent females.

8. In the southern Levant, trade appears concentrated at regional levels, while elsewhere it may have been more widespread.

9. The PPNB interaction sphere appears to have been replaced by more regionally distinctive cultures.

10. The "Great Neolithic Gap" between the PPN and PN is largely unverified. There may have been some localized abandonments and population relocations, but at several Levantine sites the documentation of the PPNC shows an unbroken linkage between the PPN and the PN.

11. Earlier claims of cultural deterioration during the PN are unsubstantiated. While parts of the region, such as the southern Levant, did not reach the elaborateness of the megasites, this may simply reflect an efficient readaptation to new conditions rather than a cultural regression.

12. To some scholars, the distinctions between the PN, especially its later aspects, and the Chalcolithic are semantic.

13. Overall, the PN may be characterized as an adaptation of local settlements with strong tribal ties, forming a pattern that has endured in the Near East over several millennia.

Case Study 6 Tel Wadi Feinan

My research interests have focused more on chipped stone than ceramics. After excavating at sites such as ʿAin Ghazal, Wadi Shuʿeib, and Ghwair I, however, it became apparent that the boundary between the PPN and PN was somewhat blurred. After our excavations at Ghwair I, Mohammad Najjar and I undertook a brief test season at the large PN site of Tel Wadi Feinan, located some 5 km away.

Tel Wadi Feinan is important, because it is one of the southernmost PN sites known (others include Drhaʿ [Bennett 1980] and the adjacent ʿAin Waidaʿ [Kuijt and Chesson 2002], both some 50 km north of Tel Wadi Feinan). It had already undergone extensive testing by Najjar, who demonstrated Chalcolithic and abundant PN remains. Despite severe erosion, architectural features of well-preserved rectangular buildings show that Tel Wadi Feinan was a substantial settlement. The reason for our brief test season was to obtain chipped stone and economic data that were recovered using the same methodology as at Ghwair I, thereby assuring directly comparable materials.

We spent about 10 days at Tel Wadi Feinan during July of 2000. This was not a pleasant experience. The Wadi Feinan is one of the hottest and driest places on Earth, and the old saying about "mad dogs and Englishmen" seemed appropriate here. I do not think I can recall ever being so hot, and there was no air-conditioned camp to escape to. Even our Bedouin assistants thought we were mad to be doing physical labor during this time, when most reasonable people (that is, Bedouins) had retreated to the cooler Jordanian Plateau. This is in stark contrast to the same area during the winter, when we excavated at Ghwair I and were often very cold! Thus, even in an environment that appears as foreboding as the Wadi Feinan, seasonal variation can make huge differences, a point that undoubtedly was not lost on the Neolithic residents of this area.

In spite of this thermal hardship, our brief season was productive and yielded valuable comparative chipped stone and economic data, as well as additional radiocarbon dates, adding badly needed chronological control to the PN (Simmons and Najjar 2002). Flotation recovered limited amounts of botanical materials, consisting of domestic cereals with a dominance of glume wheat (einkorn and/or emmer) chaff and a few other species. Wood charcoal showed a wide range of taxa represented, including *Juniperus* and *Quercus* as possible timber trees, while economically important plants included caper, olive, fig, pistachio nut, acorn, and jujube. The limited faunal assemblage was dominated by sheep, followed by cattle and wolf. The chipped stone is largely consistent with expected PN patterns, although a relatively high number of blades were recovered. Ground stone included a variety of querns and handstones, as well as limestone bowl fragments.

The Wadi Feinan is unique in Jordan in that this spectacular if foreboding landscape contains the remains of all the major Neolithic phases, from PPNA (WF-16) through PPNB (Ghwair I and other sites at the western end of the wadi) and PN; only the PPNC is thus far missing. Once analyses from ongoing projects in the region are complete, our understanding of the trajectory of early village life in this remote area of Jordan will be greatly enhanced.

Chapter 9

And on the Islands

The Colonization of Cyprus

Overview

The Mediterranean islands produced some of the most sophisticated ancient cultures in the world, and yet we know relatively little about their early prehistory. Although examining how pristine island environments were colonized is nothing new (e.g., Keegan and Diamond 1987; Kirch 1988), explicit anthropological approaches to the processes and consequences of the colonization of the Mediterranean are relatively recent developments (Patton 1996). These islands include not only those close to the Greek and Anatolian mainlands, such as the Aegean, where two-thirds have Neolithic settlements (Broodbank 1999:19), but also the more remote insular islands (e.g., Broodbank 1999, 2000; Cherry 1990; Swiny 2001).

The traditional view is that the islands were late recipients of Neolithic colonists who left few material linkages to their continental homelands. Many believed that the island Neolithic was little more than a footnote to mainland developments. Exciting new research on the eastern Mediterranean island of Cyprus, however, is challenging traditional paradigms about when, how, and why the Neolithic spread, and have placed the island on the forefront of research in the circum-Mediterranean (Guilaine and LeBrun 2003; Peltenburg and Wasse 2004; Swiny 2001).

How Were the Islands Colonized?

One obvious aspect of proposing human visits to any island is the need for an adequate seafaring technology. Marine travel as early as ca. 12,000 BP already was known in the Mediterranean, based on obsidian from the island of Melos recovered at Franchthi Cave in mainland Greece (Perlès 2001:36). Melos, however, is not a great distance from the mainland, and several interspersed islands could have provided convenient "stepping stones." Voyaging to oceanic islands such as Cyprus was a more difficult task. Subsequent to the late Miocene, Cyprus always has been isolated by open sea. During the maximum sea-level recession, there was a gap of at least 30–60 km between Cyprus and Anatolia. Slightly over 100 km today separates Cyprus from Latakia in Syria, and in clear weather, the island is visible from the mainland (Simmons 1999:18–19 and citations therein). Despite modest distances, however, Held (1989a:15, 1989b:78–104) concludes that Cyprus was a rather difficult and isolated target, partially due to a lack of stepping-stone islands. While this may be true, in perspective Cyprus was certainly no more difficult a target than Australia, which was reached as early as 50,000 years ago (Bowler et al. 2003), presumably with far less sophisticated seacraft than were available during the Neolithic.

Cherry (1981:45–64, 1990:198–199) makes an important distinction between actual colonization of an island, resulting in permanent settlement and potential founder populations, as opposed to mere utilization of an island's resources on a temporary or seasonal basis. He notes that *colonization* is perhaps a misleading term, since it implies well-planned expeditions by groups intending to establish a permanent base. He believes that a more realistic perspective views early seafaring in the Mediterranean as "many, tentative, impermanent, short-distance reciprocal movements by mere handfuls of individuals" (Cherry 1981:60). Such groups would result in ephemeral, low-visibility sites, which have a history of not receiving much research attention on most of the islands (cf. Simmons 1991, 1998a).

In critically examining early occupation, Evans (1977:14–15) and Cherry (1981:58–59) note that the Mediterranean islands are generally unsuitable as home bases for hunters and gatherers. This is due to the islands' small sizes and limited resources. Cherry (1981:59) notes that only with the inception of agriculture, allowing increased production from decreased amounts of land, would the islands be perceived as appropriate places for *permanent* settlement. He has, however, somewhat modified this view (Cherry 1990), which also is questioned by Watkins (2004:23–24).

Pre-Neolithic Occupations of the
Mediterranean Islands?

With few exceptions, there are only limited data supporting pre-Neolithic occupation on most of the islands. Claims for earlier occupations, including Cyprus, are unsubstantiated. There is evidence for Paleolithic use in the western Mediterranean, on Sicily, but that island likely was either connected to or in close proximity to the mainland during much of the Pleistocene. Likewise, pre-Neolithic claims for other Mediterranean islands are based on weak data; while there are Epipaleolithic occurrences of some Aegean islands, these are relatively late in time. Furthermore, these islands are close to the mainland (summarized in Brookbank 2000:110–117; Cherry 1990, 1992; Patton 1996:66–72; Simmons 1999:14–27). Despite the lack of evidence for true Paleolithic occupations, however, some scholars have suggested that low-visibility "para-Neolithic" or "proto-Neolithic" phases might exist, at least for Cyprus (Held 1989a:8; Watkins 1980:139), a claim that has proven prescient.

Akrotiri *Aetokremnos* ("Vulture Cliff") on the southern coast of Cyprus challenged conventional dogma, documenting an occupation at ca. 10,530 BP (11,775 cal. BP). This small, collapsed rock shelter ranks among the earliest well-documented evidence for a human presence on any of the insular Mediterranean islands. Not only is *Aetokremnos* the oldest site on Cyprus (this occupation is now termed the Akrotiri Phase), but more controversially, it is associated with a huge (over 500 individuals) assemblage of the endemic and extinct Cypriot pygmy hippopotamus, as well as smaller numbers of other animals. The evidence suggests that humans were instrumental in finalizing the extinction of these unique animals. Skeptics dispute this (e.g., Binford 2000; Bunimovitz and Barkai 1996), but we argue that the constellation of evidence strongly supports the direct association of hippopotami with cultural activities. A small group could have been the trigger to eradicate remnant hippopotami populations that were already suffering ecological stress due to climatic change, and were thus on the verge of extinction (Reese 1996, Simmons 1996, 1999, 2001, 2002, 2004a). Although *Aetokremnos* is the sole well-defined representative of the Akrotiri Phase, recent investigations suggest the likelihood of contemporary sites (Ammerman and Noller 2005; Sorabji and Ammerman 2005), although these lack absolute dates at the time of this writing. Ongoing studies should clarify this situation.

Aetokremnos supports a "two-stage" migration/colonization model, representing the first stage in which "explorers" or "scouts" assessed the suitability of colonizing pristine and unfamiliar landscapes (cf. Peltenburg et al. 2000; Rockman and Steele 2003). The second stage is effective colonization and settlement by a wider range of people (Fiedel and Anthony 2003:153). Those responsible for *Aetokremnos* could have been generalized Late Natufian or early Neolithic (PPNA) people who arrived on an unoccupied island, found residual herds of a unique fauna, hunted them into extinction, and then left. But they did not forget Cyprus. And it is here where exciting new research has added to the complexity of the Near Eastern Neolithic.

The Cypriot Neolithic

Research Context

While the transmission of the Neolithic from the Near East to Europe often is thought to have been overland through Anatolia (cf. Bellwood 2005:68; Van Andel and Runnels 1995), colonization and exploratory forays by various marine routes also have been suggested (e.g., Broodbank 2000; Cherry 1981, 1990; Patton 1996:35–62; Perlès 2001:52–63). Early marine travel likely involved stops on islands, and new investigations on Cyprus (fig. 9.1) fuel arguments surrounding how and why the Neolithic spread. These studies have implications for a network of alternate routes from the Near East, suggesting that interactions between Cyprus and the mainland were more of a "two-way street" than previously believed.

Earlier research suggested that these first Neolithic settlers, both to Cyprus and to other Mediterranean islands, were relatively late, ceramic-bearing Neolithic peoples who developed relatively isolated, and in many ways impoverished, insular cultures, compared to their mainland neighbors. Cyprus was the exception to this, being the only island with a substantial early Neolithic (that is, Pre-Pottery) component (Knapp et al. 1994), but even this was thought to be later than similar mainland developments.

Prior to recent discoveries, the PPN of Cyprus was represented by

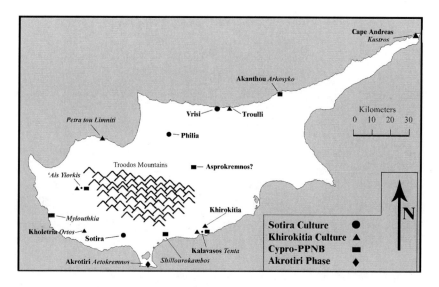

9.1 Map of major Cypriot Neolithic sites.

the Khirokitia Culture (KC). The Akrotiri Phase apparently was not ancestral to the KC, and before the discovery of *Aetokremnos*, it was believed that the KC represented the island's earliest occupation, starting
around 8000 BP and ending about 6500 BP (Peltenburg, Croft, Jackson, McCartney, and Murray 2001:65). Thus, approximately 2,500 years
separated the Akrotiri Phase from the PPN. Similar to the mainland, the
KC is followed, after another apparent hiatus, by the PN (Sotira Culture,
or SC), starting around 6100 BP and ending about 5000 BP (Knapp et al.
1994:381).

The perception that the Cypriot Neolithic was a late phenomenon has
disappeared in light of intriguing new data. These document an earlier
component, usually termed the Cypro–PPNB (CPPNB here), although
not everyone is happy with the usage of "PPNB" (e.g., Watkins 2004:30).
The CPPNB suggests complex economic strategies utilizing a wide array
of landscapes. These new discoveries must be evaluated not only in a Cypriot context, but also from a broader perspective assessing the transmission and subsequent interactions of a "Neolithic Package" from the mainland. This new research repudiates earlier prejudices, demonstrating that
the Cypriot PPN was more sophisticated and of a longer duration than
previously believed. The CPPNB exhibits some similarities to mainland

Table 9.1 Chronology for the Cypriot Neolithic

Period	Conventional (Uncalibrated) BP	Calibrated BP
Akrotiri Phase	?10,800–10,200	?12,000–11,500
Possible PPNA?	?10,200–9500	?11,500–10,500
Early CPPNB	?9500–9100	?10,500–10,200
Middle CPPNB	9100–8500	10,100–9500
Late CPPNB	8500–8000	9500–9000
Khirokitia Culture	8000–6500	9000/8500–7800/7500
Gap?		
Sotira Culture	6100–5000	6900/6500–5900/5700

Sources: Compiled from several sources, including Bolger (2003:214); Hood (personal communication 2004); Peltenburg (2003b:99); and Peltenburg et al. (2001a:65).
Note: Calibrated and uncalibrated equivalents are rounded and approximate.

PPNB cultures, is roughly contemporary with the late EPPNB and early MPPNB, and is at least 1,000 years older than the KC (Peltenburg et al. 2000, 2001; Peltenburg, Croft, Jackson, McCartney, and Murray 2001). The relationship of the Cypro–PPNB to the earlier Akrotiri Phase is as yet unclear, although new dates shorten the chronological gap between the two. Indeed, if recent investigations by McCartney (2005) suggesting upland PPNA sites are confirmed, there may be no gap. Thus far, however, her conclusions are largely based on chipped stone typological and technological variables. These new studies have resulted in a substantially revised early chronology for Cyprus (table 9.1).

The Cypro–PPNB

The CPPNB presently consists of at least four newly investigated sites and an early component of Kalavasos *Tenta*, a KC site. Of these, Parekklisha *Shillourokambos* and Kissonerga *Mylouthkia* presently are the best documented.

Parekklisha *Shillourokambos*. *Shillourokambos* is ca. 10 km from the coast in south-central Cyprus. The following summary is taken primarily from Guilaine (2003a) and Guilaine and Briois (2001). Four phases (Early Phase A and B, Transition B/Middle, and Late) are dated by a

series of radiocarbon determinations. These range from 9310 ± 80 to 8125
± 70 BP, the latter of which is close to the beginnings of the KC. A final,
PN, phase has no radiocarbon dates yet.

The earliest occupation has been disturbed by erosion, but substantial deposits still occur on the bedrock. There are three wells with ca. 1 m
diameters and depths ranging from 4.4 to 5.1 m. There also is a series of
postholes, whose arrangement in one instance likely reflects an animal enclosure. In other cases, these are roughly circular and may be the remains
of round wood or daub structures. There also are several shallow circular depressions. A series of long (up to 30 m) trenches cut into the havara
(a secondary limestone that covers much of the true bedrock in Cyprus)
contains irregularly spaced holes that likely served as postholes, as well
as several openings that could have been doorways. These trenches could
also have been foundations for livestock enclosures as well as habitation
or domestic activity areas.

During Early Phase B, a 150 m² area of densely packed cobbles contains numerous chipped stone, ground stone vessels, and faunal remains.
The excavators interpreted this as a subfloor, and from this phase onward, stone built houses had rubble foundations with mud-plastered floor
or walls. Additionally, the wells continue to be used. During the Middle
Phase, constructions of hardened earth and rubble are associated with
domestic activities. A major feature (Structure 23) is a large (ca. 4–5 m
diameter) pit with a depth up to 6 m. This was rich in chipped stone and
fauna, but is most notable for its mortuary data. There is a funerary deposit
of an aged adult male in a contracted position. Following this, Structure 23
served as a collective grave, with more than 20 skulls; another individual
burial was placed at the top of the fill (Crubézy et al. 2003). The Late
Phase contains the remains of a large (7.2 m diameter) circular rubble
structure with an outer ring and the remains of collapsed walls. The fifth
phase consists of a scatter of silos cut into the PPN deposits. These are
filled with a variety of artifacts, including Combed Ware ceramics, typical
of the SC.

In the Early Phases, there are some direct mainland parallels in the
chipped stone, something not previously demonstrated in Cyprus. Most
materials are of a high-quality translucent chert. While flakes are dominant, three *chaînes opératoires* related to blade production have been identified, including a bipolar technology (similar to the mainland naviform

technology). Tools are varied, and include rare projectile points of both generalized Amuq and Byblos forms (e.g., Briois 2003:129, fig. 4; Guilaine and Briois 2001:48–47, figs. 6:3–7 and 7:9). This is significant, since prior to these investigations, projectile points were virtually absent from the Cypriot Neolithic. Obsidian makes up about 2 percent of the assemblage, and most appears to have come from Cappadocia in Turkey. During the Middle and Late Phases, there is a shift to more locally available opaque cherts. Bipolar core reduction continues but is "profoundly modified" (Guilaine and Briois 2001:47), and projectile points have disappeared. Essentially, typical KC elements are now represented. Briois (2003) and Briois et al. (1997) provide detailed analyses of these materials. Ground stone shows little change through the sequence. Items include pounders, rubbing stones, and querns. Axes are rare. Bowls and thick-walled, shallow basins were manufactured from limestone (Guilaine and Briois 2001:47).

Shillourokambos also yielded evidence for cultic or symbolic behavior (Guilaine 2003b). This is especially apparent in the Early Phase occupations, which include a few pebbles with checkerboard patterns. This is important, since these relatively rare artifacts have previously been found only at two KC sites, Khirokitia and Kholetria *Ortos*, although they now are also reported from Akanthou, another CPPNB site. In addition, a lime-plaster figurine with a slightly rounded face connected to a cylindrical neck, reminiscent of later Early Bronze Age Cycladic figurines, was recovered, as were several small picrolite (a local type of serpentinite) objects. Even more interesting is the presence of a feline head carved from serpentinite (Guilaine et al. 1999).

The feline head assumes even more importance given the recent discovery of a probable cat burial (fig. 9.2) dating to ca. 9500 BP. This is an intentionally prepared burial pit next to a human grave with several offerings. The grave's occupant was 30 years or older, in a semisitting position, and probably buried in a bag. The cat was a roughly eight-month-old individual. Since cats do not occur in the endemic fauna, they had to have been imported to Cyprus, possibly as mousers. While not morphologically domesticated, this find indicates, minimally, taming, and the close personal role of cats to humans (Vigne et al. 2004). Prior to this discovery, most cat remains from Cyprus had been restricted to the KC, and were not in-

9.2 Cat and human burial from *Shillourokambos*. Courtesy Jean Guilaine.

tentional burials; however, cat also has been recovered from *Aɨ Yiorkiɨ*, another CPPNB site.

Finally, the economic data from *Shillourokamboɨ* are very important and indicate an agropastoral economy. Animals typically associated with the PPN in Cyprus were recovered. These include domesticated pigs and dogs, Mesopotamian fallow deer, and "pre-domesticated" sheep, goat, and, significantly, cattle. Thus, both hunting of feral species and management of domesticated species is indicated (Vigne et al. 2003:249). Prior to the *Shillourokamboɨ* excavations, there was no evidence for cattle in Cyprus until the Bronze Age (Croft 1991:63; Knapp et al. 1994:418). Now, however, cattle also occur at *Aɨ Yiorkiɨ* and, possibly, Akanthou, and clearly indicate an economic strategy far more complex than previously believed.

Cattle account for only a small amount (less than 1 percent, but still under analysis) of the fauna. The bones come from adults, young adults, and juveniles. They occur primarily in the earlier phases. The presence of a wide range of body parts eliminates the possibility that cattle were brought to Cyprus as joints of meat (Vigne et al. 2000:94–95, 2003:240, 248). Their appearance on Cyprus this early, in presumably domestic or "pre-domestic" (e.g., Vigne et al. 2000:100–101) form, is extremely important, given that some of the earliest domesticated cattle on the mainland, from Halula and possibly Dja'de (Helmer et al. 2005), are roughly contemporary.

Although paleobotanical data are not well preserved, barley and einkorn/emmer wheat grains are present. These are wild types, rather than domesticated. Wild barley is native to the island, and this is the first time it has been found in an archaeological context. Wild fruits also may have been exploited. Wilcox (2003) believes that these data indicate preagricultural cultivation, with the implication that wild cereals were introduced along with the practice of cultivation.

Kissonerga *Mylouthkia*. The other well-documented early PPN site is Kissonerga *Mylouthkia* on the western coast of the island (Peltenburg, ed. 2003). The most striking features of Neolithic *Mylouthkia* are three deep (5.3–8.5 m) wells (fig. 9.3) cut into the havara (three additional wells believed to be CPPNB are presently under investigation [Peltenburg 2003a:18–21]). Coupled with the wells from *Shillourokamboɨ* (as well as those from the mainland, such as Atlit-Yam), these represent very early and sophisticated water management systems. In addition to the wells

9.3   Section of *Mylouthkia* wells.

are a series of pits and a badly damaged structure (Croft 2003a). This, and other evidence, such as the presence of commensals, leads Peltenburg (2003b:87–93) to believe that *Mylouthkia* was a sedentary settlement.

There are two CPPNB phases separated by ca. 1,000 years. Period 1A is represented by Well 116 and is chronologically secured by three radiocarbon determinations ranging from 9315 ± to 9110 ± 70 BP, placing it within the Early CPPNB. Period 1B (Well 133) has two radiocarbon determinations ranging from 8185 ± 55 and 8025 ± 65 BP, falling within the Late CPPNB. Three additional dates are clearly too old and are explained as anomalies (Peltenburg 2003b:83–84).

Well 116 contains a relatively small amount of animal and human bone, as well as chipped and ground stone. Well 113 has much more interesting remains, including complete caprine skeletons consisting of one mature and eight immature sheep carcasses and twelve immature and two mature goat skeletons. Other materials include deer, pig, caprines, pigeons, fish bones, and a crab claw. Human remains also are scattered throughout the wells. These include an incomplete person of fetal age from Well 116 and at least five individuals from Well 133, consisting of three adults and two adolescents. One individual exhibits a paleopathology in the form of healed cribra orbitalia, indicative of anemia (Cerón-Carrasco 2003; Croft 2003a, b; Fox et al. 2003).

The chipped stone from *Mylouthkia* consists of 828 artifacts (McCartney 2003:135–140; McCartney and Gratuze 2003). During Period 1A, most of the raw material was a high-quality translucent chert, while during Period 1B the material was more varied. Although cores are rare, McCartney argues for the use of a naviform technology during Period 1A, based on bidirectional dorsal scars on blades and, especially, on several examples of cresting on some blades. These are not seen in Period 1B.

A variety of tools are present, with Period 1A being dominated by burins and utilized blades and flakes. The tool sample from Period 1B shows greater variety, including scrapers, notches, and denticulates, essentially mirroring later KC tools. Obsidian is restricted to 22 pieces, 21 from Well 116 and one from Well 133 (McCartney and Gratuze 2003). Notably, 3 tangs from Period 1A may represent the remains of projectile points, two of which are classified as Byblos types. The third has a pair of asymmetrical inverse notches just above the tang (perhaps reminiscent of early mainland el-Khiam forms?). The presence of presumed projectile points is important, although the case would be more convincing if complete specimens had been found. McCartney (2004:113-114), however, considers that true projectile points always were rare and may have had symbolic roles related to status or ethnic identity rather than functional significance. They also may have represented cultural associations with the mainland. Both *Mylouthkia* and *Shillourokambos* show technological and typological similarity to the Levantine PPNB and appear to fall within the "Big Arrowhead Industries" technocomplex (Peltenburg, Croft, Jackson, McCartney, and Murray 2001:78). Ground stone is relatively abundant and varied. Well 133 contained a minimum of 120 vessels, including a finely made macehead (Jackson 2003).

Botanical remains include domesticated einkorn, emmer, hulled barley and wild or domesticated lentil, other large-seeded legumes, fig, pistachio, and linseed/flax. Barley was the most common. Overall, the composition of remains between periods is the same and suggests an autumn or early winter sowing, with a spring harvest. These remains are similar to what is found in later contexts and indicates that the KC agricultural tradition was in place by the CPPNB. Colledge's (2004) metrical analysis of these materials concurs with Murray's morphological study, reaching the conclusion that they represented domestic glume wheat and hulled barley. It is notable that these remains represent some of the earliest domesticates not only in Cyprus but in the Near East (Murray 2003).

Kritou Marottou *Ais Yiorkis*. A third CPPNB site is Kritou Marottou *Ais Yiorkis*. This site located in the foothills of the Troodos Mountains east of Paphos was originally recorded as a KC period locality (Fox 1987). The survey also recorded another nearby KC site, Kannaviou *Kochina*. Both were unusual, since most known Neolithic settlements are located closer to the coast although some newly documented sites also are inland (McCartney 2005). Based on survey data, *Ais Yiorkis* was intriguing because it possibly reflected a temporary camp or small hamlet, likely related to deer and pig exploitation. Thus, it was of particular interest since it appeared to be a small, specialized site—precisely the type that has been under-studied in Cyprus. *Ais Yiorkis* is presently under excavation, and has provided surprising results. Thirteen radiocarbon determinations indicate an occupation between 8720 and 6840 ± 40 BP, placing it within the MCPPNB and LCPPNB, and suggesting a transition to the KC (Simmons 1998b, 2003a, plus five unpublished determinations).

A large chipped-stone assemblage of over 150,000 artifacts contains an abundance of finely made blades and bladelets, including over two dozen obsidian bladelets. A large variety of tool classes are represented, including seven complete probable projectile points. Two of these are crudely shaped, while four have general Byblos morphologies and another is undiagnostic. By mainland standards these are not impressive, but they add to the slowly growing corpus of points from the CPPNB. Several tangs that may represent broken points also occur. Out of several hundred cores, only a few naviform or subnaviform types were recovered, although, as at other CPPNB sites, blade morphology suggests the use of this technology. Several ground stone artifacts also were retrieved, including large platter fragments and numerous handstones. Stone vessels also occur. In 2005, a complete stone vessel was recovered adjacent to a complete plaster bowl, similar to the *vaisselle blanche* vessels found on the mainland. This ranks among the earliest example of this type of technology on Cyprus. A limited number of picrolite artifacts also are present, including two incised "thimbles" and large platter/bowl fragments.

Although architectural remains are rare, they are present. Most significant is a large, circular stone platform, or "rotunda," about 4 m in diameter (fig. 9.4). This is an unusual feature, and nothing like it has been documented in Cyprus. This feature is next to an ashy midden deposit. A cache of finely manufactured blades also was found adjacent to it. The feature's function is presently unknown: it could have served as a residence, a tower, a platform, a corral or "holding pen," or the foundation of a building. In addition to this feature, several deep pits are present, as are a plastered surface bounded on at least one side by a stone wall (another "rotunda"?), and at least two other cobble-topped features. The presence of these structures indicates that *Ais Yiorkis* likely was not a temporary camp.

Finally, the economic data from *Ais Yiorkis* are extremely important. Flotation yielded a rich assemblage of extremely abundant and well-preserved remains, which included domestic cereals (e.g., einkorn and hulled barley grains) and also several wild species. The radiocarbon dates on some of these materials range from 8600 ± 40 to 8480 ± 40 BP, placing them roughly contemporary with *Mylouthkia*, Period 1B. A large number of fauna are present, and, significantly, this includes small numbers of cattle and cat. Deer and pig predominate, followed by caprines. The figures for cattle are consistent with those from this taxon at *Shillourokambos*.

9.4   "Rotunda" structure at *Ais Yiorkis*.

These results demonstrate that *Ais Yiorkis* is far more complex than surface data indicated. Ongoing investigations will determine if additional
features and economic and artifactual diversity indicate that the site was
an upland village rather than the limited-activity locus it initially was believed to represent.

   Kalavasos *Tenta*. Kalavasos *Tenta* is a well-known KC site (Todd
1987), located between Khirokitia and *Shillourokambos*. Its early radiocarbon dates, long dismissed as inaccurate, now fit quite nicely into the
picture of a pre-KC occupation. The oldest date is 9240 ± 130 BP, and
several others fall within the ninth millennium BP, thereby indicating an
occupation throughout the CPPNB. The earliest occupation (Period 5) is
characterized by a series of postholes and pits cut into the natural deposits,
suggesting a lack of solid standing architecture, a situation that parallels
both *Mylouthkia* and *Shillourokambos* (Todd 2001, 2003). This scenario,
however, may be incorrect. The "Top of Site" area, presumably dating
to the KC, had some early dates falling in the CPPNB. If this context is
accurate, as Peltenburg (2003b:86) believes, it would indicate substantial
CPPNB architectural development consisting of what he (2004a:78–79)
refers to as the Circular Radial Building, common on the mainland during

the PPNA. Todd (2003) is somewhat more cautious on this chronological placement but does not discount it. *Tenta*'s CPPNB placement is further supported by chipped stone similarities identified by McCartney (2001, 2003:140–145).

Akanthou *Arkoyako*. Another site, Akanthou *Arkoayko* (also known as Tatlisu-Çiftlikdüzü) was, somewhat ironically, initially recorded by the Cyprus Survey in 1931. Renewed studies by Şevketoğlu (2000:75–79, 2002) indicate that it also dates to the CPPNB, based on several radiocarbon dates.

Akanthou has intriguing if difficult-to-define architecture, including features cut into bedrock and outdoor plastered areas. The remains of three "subsquare" houses and possibly one square structure are especially interesting, since they do not conform to the standard Cypriot Neolithic architectural pattern of circular structures. All the houses have plastered floors, and the walls also were plastered and painted with red and brown pigments (Şevketoğlu 2002:103). A large plastered area with "built-in" pits, possibly an outdoor work surface, surrounds these structures, and a deep ditch also may enclose part of the settlement.

There is a rich obsidian assemblage at Akanthou, consisting of over 2,000 artifacts, by far the largest in Cyprus. These primarily are bladelets, and indicate a bidirectional technology. A large variety of other artifacts also is present, including an incised cobble and numerous picrolite items, such as small "thimbles" or "cups" similar to those from *Aia Yiorkia*, and tokens. The ground stone is fragmentary and rare (Şevketoğlu 2000:75–79, 2002:103–105, personal communication 2005).

A relatively large faunal assemblage has been recovered, including the usual animals, such as sheep/goat, fallow deer, pig, and dog. Of considerable interest is a small number of cattle bones, but contextual issues are yet to be clearly resolved (Frame 2002:235). If this placement is correct, however, Akanthou would be the third CPPNB site with cattle.

Other Possible CPPNB Sites. Three other sites also may date to the CPPNB. These are Ayia Varvara *Aaprokremnoa*, Politico *Kelaïdhoni*, and Agrokipia *Palaeokamina*, all in the central portion of the island. These sites have not yet been excavated, but McCartney's analysis of surface chipped stone suggests the same kind of technological shift as seen from the CPPNB to the KC (McCartney and Gratuze 2003:19; McCartney 2001:432, 2004). However, she more recently notes that these sites could fill the gap between the Akrotiri Phase and the CPPNB and thus represent PPNA occupations (McCartney 2005). It is likely that additional systematic survey with thorough analysis such as McCartney's will document more early sites and that excavations will yield datable materials, which ultimately will resolve the chronological issue. Recall that Akanthou was originally recorded in 1931 but not recognized as a potential early site until nearly 70 years later! Likewise, *Aetokremnos*, with its remote location and limited surface visibility, was not even considered to be an intact archaeological site until excavation proved otherwise.

The Khirokitia Culture

During the KC considerable changes occurred. One of these is that now, despite the presence of substantial villages, there were few Levantine or Anatolian parallels. Overall the KC was often viewed as less sophisticated than its mainland counterparts, representing an increasingly isolated insular character (Steel 2004:45). This is expressed by an unrefined chipped-stone technology and typology, by the presence of circular structures rather than a transformation to rectangular ones, and by limited evidence of substantial ritual or symbolic behavior. Some of these characteristics seem particularly analogous to the mainland late PPNB/PPNC and early PN, where we see a decrease in chipped-stone sophistication and the use of circular dwellings in some areas. In many ways, the Cypriot Neolithic, as with other islands, appeared to be something of a cultural backwater that failed to keep pace with developments within the wider Neolithic world. Indeed, older characterizations of the Cypriot Neolithic, such as "a bizarre and insular anachronism" (Watkins 1980:139) or even as "retarded" (Held 1990:24, both citing then common opinion) were rather uncomplimentary and, as we now know, simply incorrect. There is, however, no denying that the KC is quite distinctive from what came before it.

Khirokitia peoples settled in various locations, but major communities were situated within 10 km of the Mediterranean Sea. There are at least a dozen sites (Stanley-Price 1977, 1979), although Watkins (1973:38) claims that this number is closer to 20, and Held (1982:8) believes that over 50 sites may belong to the KC. The most up-to-date summary of the KC (and SC) may be found in Steel's (2004:45–82) recent synthesis.

Fewer than 20 of these sites are believed to be actual settlements (Cherry 1990:154). Only Khirokitia *Vounoi*, Kalavasos *Tenta*, Kholetria *Ortos*, Rizokarpaso Cape Andreas *Kastros* and Limnitis *Petra tou Limniti* have been excavated or intensively sampled, with the first three representing substantial villages. Limited test excavations and/or surface collections have been conducted at a few other sites (Knapp et al. 1994:404–405). Most research has focused on habitation sites, but modern surveys have confirmed nonarchitectural sites as well (e.g., Rupp et al. 1984).

KC buildings were relatively small circular or subcircular structures. Roofs were conical or, more likely, flat, and some buildings contained lofts. Interior features include hearths, platforms along walls, and frequently a central post or set of pillars. Such structures usually are densely packed within settlements. Hearths and other evidence for domestic activities frequently occur outside of structures. However, at Khirokitia such features regularly occur inside of buildings, suggesting that dwellings may have been central areas for domestic activities (Bolger 2003:217; Knapp et al. 1994:405; LeBrun et al. 1987:293; Steel 2004:46–52).

Larger settlements seem located in defensive positions, or at least have commanding views of the surrounding countryside. As on the mainland, however, there is little evidence for conflict, although three individuals from Khirokitia show injuries consistent with violence (Angel 1953:422). At Khirokitia, the settlement was initially enclosed by a wall (originally interpreted as a road). As the settlement expanded, a second wall was built, with an elaborate entrance system, indicating substantial community effort. LeBrun (2001:114–115) makes a convincing argument that that this structure relates to social space use, rather than defense, creating "human catchment areas" that may have divided the settlement into different membership groups. LeBrun (2002:25) believes that small (ca. 2–3 m in diameter) circular structures were residential areas for nuclear families and that their clustering around a common courtyard or work area reflects an aggregation of social groups. Bolger (2003:26), however, feels that such structures were too small to have housed families. She believes that their size, and burial data, points to a situation in which adults may have lived alone or with their children.

In this context, it is important to note that although Khirokitia was substantial (nearly four acres) and likely housed 300–600 people (LeBrun

1984:71), it is quite distinct from its mainland counterparts. This is particularly apparent in its lack of multiroomed residential units, which usually are viewed as indicating increased household autonomy and storage.
Khirokitia, as well as other KC sites, also has limited evidence for public
or ritual structures. One relatively unusual and large structure, however,
contains several floor-context materials, including caprines and deer, and
LeBrun (2003) has interpreted this is as a symbolic closure of the building. Peltenburg (2004a:85), however, believes that Khirokitia, overall, is
atypical for the KC, and that its large "size exceeded the socio-economic
basis of traditional Neolithic society on the island."

Burials, which emphasize individuals, occur either outside of structures or, more frequently, beneath floors, and do not clearly reflect rank
and status. The deceased usually were buried in contracted positions.
Often a large stone was placed on their chests. Burial goods, such as a
variety of ornaments, were common. At Khirokitia, over 250 burials include all ages, from newborn through adult, and exhibit no unequal treatment. A high infant mortality and pathologies suggest a genetic form of
anemia. The population appears to have resulted from in situ evolution
of groups who arrived on the island much earlier (Knapp et al. 1994:405;
LeBrun et al. 1987:294; LeMort 2003). Physically, this population appears to be distinct from that of the PN, as reflected from Sotira (Angel
1961; Harper 2003), but it probably is unwise to make too much of this
(Knapp et al. 1994:408).

Gender issues have not been addressed in much detail for the KC, although both LeBrun (2002) and McCartney (2002) have made attempts
to do so. There is little evidence for a sexual division of labor during the
Neolithic, with the initial hints for low levels of economic and social division first seen in the Chalcolithic (Bolger 2003:60). Most researchers
posit that the KC essentially represented an egalitarian society (Peltenburg 2004a:84–85). There are, however, some gender distinctions in burials, with necklaces and ground stone occurring more frequently with
females. Steel (2004:54) suggests that females had a certain degree of
mobility for exogamic relations, necessary for maintaining the population
levels.

KC chipped-stone assemblages frequently are referred to as non-
descript, "unremarkable" (Held 1989b:59, 1990:21), or not very creative

(Cauvin 1984:86). Systematic studies, however, have been rare and the lack of such analyses is a major research gap (Held 1990:17–18), although this deficiency is beginning to be rectified (e.g. Astruc 2003; McCartney 2001, 2003; Simmons 1994:4–8). Other stone artifacts are more impressive. Elaborate polished ground stone artifacts, including axes, and a very sophisticated vessel industry, frequently consisting of geometrically decorated pieces, are characteristic of the KC. These consist of two major types: coarse vessels (often large trays or basins) of breccia or hard limestone and finer vessels (often spouted bowls or basins) carved from soft limestone or diabase. The latter are often associated with female burials. Ornaments such as beads or pendants made of picrolite or other polished stone, including imported carnelian, also are common (Steel 2004:56).

Compared to the mainland, evidence for symbolic or ritual behavior throughout the Cypriot Neolithic is scarce. There are, however, figurines, ritual treatment of the dead, and the enigmatic wall painting from *Tenta* (interpreted by Garfinkel 2003a:124 as another example of Neolithic dancing) for the KC. CPPNB evidence for ritual includes some of the contents from the *Mylouthkia* wells and the human and cat burial, as well as likely symbolic objects, from *Shillourokambos*. Rare incised cobbles, usually in checkerboard patterns, are found only at Khirokitia and *Ortos* during the KC, and at *Shillourokambos* and Akanthou during the CPPNB, and have parallels during the later PN on the mainland. Their function is unknown. Scholars have speculated that they could have been models of bread loaves, buildings, or female breasts, stamping devices, gaming pieces, animal branding devices, "hot stamps" used on young boys in initiation rites, objects used in "rain calling" rites (with the geometric incisions representing rain), calendars, and female sexual organs, as summarized by Eirikh-Rose (2004:151–152), who prefers to view them as identity seals representing persons or families. Stewart and Rupp (2004) also provide a number of interpretative possibilities, from common utilitarian items such as food graters or toys, laundry scrubbers, remnants from an initial settlement, or links to exchange between Cyprus and the mainland, seeming to prefer the latter. Given their late appearance on the mainland, it is tempting to speculate that the idea for these unique objects originated in Cyprus. If so, this would be a rare case for the transmission of a cultural item *from* Cyprus to the mainland.

As opposed to the mainland, figurines here are rare, highly stylized, and usually sexually ambiguous, although many have phallic aspects (Steel 2004:58–59). If Cauvin's Mother Goddess concept as a principal driver for the Neolithic Revolution was so important, it is unusual that such figurines do not occur in more abundance during the colonization of an unknown territory. Overall, Cyprus appears not to have witnessed the extraordinary devotion to ritual paraphernalia present on the mainland. The addition of cattle to the Neolithic inventory (although absent by the KC) could have some ritual significance, as it did on the mainland, but this has not yet been fully explored.

Researchers know less about KC subsistence than might be expected. The impression is one of an economy that was agricultural, supplemented by herding, hunting, and, in some cases, fishing. Indirect evidence suggests that individual households worked their own land. Farming was based on several domesticates, while faunal use included both domestic animals and the hunting, and possible managed control of, Persian fallow deer. Various subsidiary food resources also were exploited, such as wild plants and fruits, fish, marine invertebrates, and birds (Croft 1989; Davis 2003; Hansen 2001; Steel 2004:59–62).

There is relatively little systematically collected paleobotanical information available for the KC. There are several reasons for this, including traditionally poor preservation of botanical remains, but early excavations also were conducted without benefit of state-of-the-art data recovery methods. Only five KC sites have yielded any appreciable paleobotanical materials, with Khirokitia having the largest sample. None has produced a wide variety of material, with einkorn and emmer wheat being fairly equally represented, and barley occurring less often. Other species that consistently appear in varying quantities include bitter vetch, broadbean, fig, lentil, olive, pea, pistachio, and ryegrass (Hansen 1991, 2001). Pollen analysis also has been limited, although one study at Khirokitia provided important information on vegetation reconstruction and human impacts (Renault-Miskovsky 1989), if not paleoeconomy.

Fauna from KC sites are better preserved than are botanical remains (Davis 2003). The fauna is all introduced and contains not only presumably domesticated species, but also fallow deer. In addition, there are sheep, goat, and an early breed of domestic pig. Notably, cattle are now absent. Mouse, shrew, dog, and cat also occur (Croft 1989; Davis 2003).

Horwitz et al. (2004) provide an intriguing alternate interpretation of the Cypriot fauna. They question the domestic status of all species on the island until the early Chalcolithic. Part of their argument is that the earliest introduced animals comprise species for which there is no evidence of their earlier or contemporary domestication on the mainland. They feel that these animals were captured and transported to Cyprus as wild forms, citing ethnographic examples where economically or culturally favored captive wild animals ("ethnotramps") were used as food, as pets, or for trade or ritual purposes. In the case of Cyprus, these animals may have been intended as provisions of fresh food for the voyage. Once on the island, they either were deliberately released as a future food resource or accidentally escaped, providing a source of protein on an island with limited animal resources. They further argue that later multiple colonizing events brought fresh stock to the island, which interbred with feral founder animals. Ducos (2000) makes a similar argument as well.

Regardless of specific interpretations, both chronological and regional variations of fauna are apparent (Croft 2003c; Davis 2003:268). For example, at Khirokitia, there is an apparent shift from pig and fallow deer to sheep (Davis 2003:262–263), and sheep are more common than goat, while the reverse situation occurs at Cape *Andreas Kastros*. Both sites exhibit contrasting trends in the percentages of fallow deer and caprines. These distinctions may be due to differing ecological conditions. The sizes of pigs, deer, and goat did not markedly change throughout the occupation of both sites, although there is a slight increase in sheep at Khirokitia (Davis 2003:268). There is also the presence of marine resources at some sites, with an emphasis on fishing at coastal Cape *Andreas Kastros* (Desse and Desse-Berset 2003). Perhaps the biggest change from the CPPNB to the KC is the apparent abandonment of cattle.

The presence of deer during the Cypriot Neolithic has been, to me at least, curious. These animals apparently are not endemic to Cyprus (although see Kassapis 2001), and thus were imported along with the domestic species. Since the settlers already had an array of domesticated animals, a common assumption is that deer were set loose as free-living animals and subjected to controlled hunting within a system of game management (Croft 2003b:57). This is a logical interpretation, despite the lack of projectile points in Neolithic assemblages. One can speculate, however, why hunting was so important if other (domestic) animals were plentiful. Perhaps the urge to hunt, and the social ramifications that go with it (e.g., male bonding?), was so embedded in Neolithic culture on the mainland that the settlers of Cyprus also needed this as a part of their identity.

The Sotira Culture (or Late Neolithic)

The KC is followed by an apparent cultural hiatus, after which the PN, or Sotira culture (SC), is documented. This presumed disconnect, or "Dark Age" (Peltenburg 2004a:85), of ca. 500–1,000 years, has been the subject of some controversy (Knapp et al. 1994:406–409) and clearly has important implications for the origin of the PN and later cultures. While some SC settlements were built over KC remains, there is little evidence for cultural continuity, and this, coupled with the presumed gap, has led some researchers to posit recolonization of the island (Cherry 1981:60–61; Stanley-Price 1977:34–37, 1979:77–78). I am cautious in giving too much credence to a total recolonization model, although certainly infusions of "booster immigrations" (cf. Knapp et al. 1994:408) are not unreasonable. Likewise, Peltenburg (2004a:84–85) does not believe that the island was abandoned after the "extinction" of the KC, but rather that different, low-density settlement strategies were adopted, resulting in low-visibility archaeological sites. Given the degree to which new research has changed our perceptions of the initial colonization of Cyprus, it is likely that similar studies on the SC may show that the gap is more apparent than real.

The SC is widespread and is characterized by substantial uniformity, although ceramic decoration exhibits spatial variations (Clarke 2003: 205). The cultural landscape consists of small (ca. 1–4 acre), similarly organized villages. These are usually made up of crowded single-room structures, most with a circular configuration, although subrectangular forms also occur. There also are subterranean structures. Some settlements, such as Ayios Epiktitos *Vryʃi* and Philia *Drakoʃ* A, have defensive works. In general, several occupational episodes are reflected, followed by abandonment (Bolger 2003:218–219; Cherry 1990:157; Dikaios 1961; Knapp et al. 1994:406–409; Peltenburg 1978; Steel 2004:66–74).

At *Vryʃi*, most of the buildings were identical multipurpose structures. The overall settlement plan shows spatial division that may reflect corporate kinship groups (Peltenburg 1982). At SC (and Chalcolithic) sites, there are abundant on-floor artifact assemblages, in contrast to settlements from either the KC or Bronze Ages. This leads Peltenburg (2003c) to wonder if one reason for SC house replacement may have been the death of an important individual who was buried outside of these buildings but whose material possessions were largely retained, becoming a memorial. The abundance of house-floor materials also could have served as foundation deposits for replicate houses.

Bolger (2003:26–27) suggests that a shift to multiple functions may be associated with the introduction of ceramics and believes that industrial activities could have been performed by small, household groups. There is little evidence for any social stratification, although some socioeconomic distinctions were observed at *Vrysi*. Most sites are relatively standard in size compared to the KC, perhaps due to a deliberate resistance to adopting hierarchical social structures (Bolger 2003:219; Peltenburg 1993).

SC economic patterns are similar to those of the KC, representing a mixed subsistence. New species cultivated include bread wheat, chickpeas, oats, and rye. A variety of fruits likely represents use of wild species rather than orchard farming. The incidence of pigs decreases and may reflect a move toward open farmland (Steel 2004:79). Relatively little is known of the chipped stone, but overall it exhibits the same tendencies as do KC materials. Abundant axes, adzes, and chisels suggest woodworking and clearance of woodlands. Ground stone includes a variety of forms, although the elaborations of the KC no longer are common. Picrolite ornaments continue to be common as well, but figurines nearly disappear (Steel 2004:74–76). Mortuary data are quite limited. When burials occur, they tend to be in separate spaces close to, but outside of, buildings—a major contrast to the KC. This may indicate a desire to remove the dead from the habitation space of the living (Steel 2004:78–79).

While some clay receptacles were recovered at Khirokitia, presaging the introduction of ceramics, ceramics are ubiquitous at SC sites, which are comprised of small- to medium-sized vessels in both painted and monochrome styles. The range of forms is limited and includes bowls, jugs, bottles, holemouth jars, and trays. Local clays were used for simple coil-made vessels, consistent with household production (Steel 2004:74–76). An initial but short-lived monochrome tradition is replaced by vessels with combed and broad line red on white (RW) decorations. There also is evidence for regional styles (Bolger 2003:218–219). Clarke's ceramic analysis (2003:214) suggests that SC society was structured to "portray an external image of homogeneity and cohesiveness to the outside world [i.e., the mainland]. Within an internal social system, this homogeneity exists to protect the social structures of the community while still allowing for individual expression through the use of highly stylized socio-cultural symbolism."

There is considerable discussion over the end of the SC and the beginning of the Chalcolithic, just as there is on the mainland. There appears to have been a major disruption with abandonment of SC sites and another gap, this time around 600 years, before the establishment of the Chalcolithic. However, this scenario is based on limited data and an unclear understanding of the nature of the early Chalcolithic. Not unexpectedly, much debate centers around whether an influx of populations was responsible for the Chalcolithic or if there is an indigenous transition (Peltenburg 2003d; Steel 2004:83–86).

Discussion

What, then, can we say about the Neolithic in Cyprus? The most exciting current developments are in the still-emerging definition of the CPPNB, but the KC and PN should not be neglected. While less research is presently being conducted on these periods, the exemplary research of the LeBruns and their team at Khirokitia and the interdisciplinary investigations of the Kalavasos Project by the Todds have contributed substantially to a better understanding of the later PPN on the island, at a time when its insular idiosyncrasies seem to have been fully formed. Studies on the PN are rarer still, although investigations such as Clarke's (2001, 2003), Flourentzos's (2003), Mantzourani's (2003), and Peltenburg's (2003d) are adding to our understanding of that period as well. But better defining the island's earliest colonization is now receiving the most attention. Several relevant topics are summarized below.

Why Colonize Cyprus in the First Place?

Islands can, of course, be colonized simply due to human curiosity. After all, Cyprus is visible from some mainland vantage points. Thus, why Cyprus was initially colonized may never be fully resolved, but it has not stopped archaeologists from speculating. In this context, Finlayson

(2004) urges that we consider Cyprus as part of the PPNB interaction sphere, and that we stop seeing seafaring as an obstacle. Alternately, I (Simmons 1999:319–323) argued that those responsible for *Aetokremnos* may have been traditionalists not wishing to participate in the Neolithic Revolution (and by extension, the interaction sphere). Likewise, Ronen (1995), in a provocative if unsubstantiated article, refers to the early colonists of Cyprus as "Asprots," comparing them to modern and conservative Hutterites. While Ronen may be stretching ethnographic analogy, he does present some tantalizing ideas. He views the Cypriot Neolithic as a closed society, and certainly there are parallels among, for example, prison populations or religious sects (Rainbird 1999:230).

There also are more functional scenarios. For example, Davis (2003: 258) notes that marine transgression resulting in long-term loss of subsistence resources and ecological stress for mainland Neolithic coastal populations may have contributed to local migration to Cyprus. He suggests that people "came to Cyprus for the same reason that they began husbanding animals—they were looking to increase their food supply" (Davis 2003:258).

Peltenburg (2003b:96–99) provides a related scenario, noting that early Holocene shorelines in the eastern Mediterranean were generally lower than today's. The diminishing littoral, he feels, ultimately had to be abandoned, and coastal Neolithic groups who subsisted on mixed farming, fishing, herding, and hunting economies may have been forced to move. Inland movement would have been difficult due to the relatively high populations already living there. Hence, the alternate decision of colonizing Cyprus, already known from earlier visits, may have been attractive.

In this context Galili et al.'s (2004) discussion on the traditional "Mediterranean Fishing Village" (MFV) is relevant. This expands on the concept of the traditional Mediterranean subsistence system (cf. Butzer 1996) by incorporating marine resources. On the mainland, the MFV was not established until the PPNC and is, therefore, later that the CPPNB, which Galili et al. (2004:97) feel did not emphasize marine resources. They believe that the MFV did not develop on Cyprus until after the eighth millennium BP, after its mainland appearance. They do allow, however, that local hunter-gatherers who used marine resources and lived on the Levantine shores could have served as "ferrymen" to transport Neo-

lithic populations to Cyprus (Galili et al. 2004:97). The reasons for the
late emergence of the MFV, in their view, is that fishing was a low mode of
production, turned to only once terrestrial resources became restricted.

There clearly are many models to explain the colonization of Cyprus,
and many more are likely to be generated as new data become available.
Peltenburg (2003b:99, table 11.6) has thus far proposed perhaps the most
thoughtful and detailed. His model is one of initial exploration, as represented by *Aetokremnos*, followed by an extended period of, first, colonization by agropastoralists and then by consolidation and continual mainland contact. During the LCPPNB, expansion on the island may have
resulted in less external contact and started the unique island character
of Cyprus. This was followed by a florescence for the PPN, as reflected
by the idiosyncratic KC.

Origins

Where did these people come from? Their seafaring abilities must
have been considerable. Given that there were virtually no endemic species on the island, the Neolithic colonizers of Cyprus must have arrived,
likely in successive waves, with veritable "Noah's arks" containing subsistence items that they enjoyed on the mainland. Peltenburg (2003b:93–99;
2004b, with comments by others) again provides some of the most provocative discussion on Cyprus's first colonists. He considers three competing origin models, the first of which proposes that islanders who had
already colonized Cyprus independently invented a settled way of life.
The second involves islanders and newcomers, a combination of native
foragers and more recent arrivals who had started the sedentary process.
The third model is that of the migration of mainland farmer colonists,
recent arrivals who used information from earlier visits to settle a landscape essentially devoid of human populations. This was accomplished by
a series of population movements during a circumscribed period of time.
He prefers the mainland migration model, since "the multiple, close parallels in subsistence, technology, settlement organization, ideological indicators, and participation in the PPNB interaction sphere are best interpreted as evidence for the presence of mainland farmers who emigrated
to the island" (Peltenburg 2003b:96).

The actual geographic point of origin for these people is unknown.

Many, including Cauvin (2000a:164–170, 218–219) and Stordeur (2003b), prefer an inland Middle Euphrates source, based on architectural, artifactual, and ideological similarities to the PPNA and EPPNB. But even Cauvin (2000a:154, 164) equivocates: he seems to want the "homeland" to be the Syro-Cilician coastland but admits to the lack of early Neolithic sites there.

Peltenburg (Peltenburg et al. 2000; Peltenburg, Croft, Jackson, McCartney, and Murray 2001) first hinted at an inland origin as well, acknowledging that supporting data were limited (e.g., McCartney and Peltenburg 2000). He points to many Middle Euphrates similarities but also draws on other evidence, especially fauna and Anatolian obsidian, that suggests linkage with central and southern Turkey. In recent thoughts on this issue, he (Peltenburg 2004b) believes that the coastal Syro-Cilician area was instrumental in communicating with Cyprus. But coastal sites are relatively rare, especially in the northern and Cilician regions. It is not until the PPNC and late PN that substantial coastal communities, such as Ras Shamra or Atlit-Yam, are documented (Galili et al. 2004: 93–94). New research, however, suggests earlier settlements in the north (Stordeur 2004). At this stage, we simply do not yet have enough data to come to an informed conclusion. Certainly Peltenburg's (2004b:4) statement that "only they [Syro-Cilician peoples] had the local expertise for initial seagoing enterprises, coupled with an awareness of the arable potential of Cyprus" seems somewhat premature.

In summary, chronologically the CPPNB falls into the EPPNB through the LPPNB, and by this time, many mainland areas could have served as points of origin. I suspect that several Neolithic groups had the expertise for seagoing voyages as well as an awareness of the potential of Cyprus for permanent agrarian settlement. Ultimately, perhaps what is more interesting is not the origins of the CPPNB, but rather what these people did once they arrived in Cyprus.

The Nature of the CPPNB

What can we say of the nature of the CPPNB, before the formation of the KC with its standardized patterns? Although baseline data are still being established, we know that CPPNB sites were relatively small, and that the economy was mixed, consisting of animal husbandry, farming, hunting, and in some cases, fishing (Peltenburg 2003b). What clearly stands out is that none of the CPPNB sites are similar. *Shillourokambos* appears to have been a small village with relatively ephemeral architecture, and *Mylouthkia* also may have functioned as a village, although supporting data are sparse. Early *Tenta* has some features similar to *Shillourokambos*, but we do not know the full composition and extent of its CPPNB occupation. *Ais Yiorkis* also may be a village, albeit an upland one. Akantou seems to represent a small settlement with subrectangular architecture that does not fit into the Cyprus scheme at all. Other potential CPPNB sites appear not to contain architecture, although excavation could disprove this. While many sites are coastal, inland CPPNB localities also are known, but poorly investigated, excepting *Ais Yiorkis*.

Economic Strategies

Of particular importance are the economic implications of the CPPNB, and the new investigations have posed more questions than they answer. From a pan–Near Eastern perspective, Cyprus greatly complicates the matter by having both domesticated plants and animals during the CPPNB at a time when evidence of morphological domestication on the mainland is limited. It is unlikely that independent domestication occurred in Cyprus, since relevant species are not endemic (but see Wilcox 2003:237). The only exception to this is the wild progenitor of domestic barley (Peltenburg, Croft, Jackson, McCartney, and Murray 2001:71; Wilcox 2003:234). It is clear that principal economic animals were under enough human control to be transported across the sea (Vigne 2001:57). Certainly the cattle from *Ais Yiorkis* and *Shillourokambos* are among the earliest evidence of domesticated (or "predomesticated") cattle in the Near East. As noted in chapter 5, Vigne has suggested that researchers must reevaluate how domestication is determined, emphasizing non-morphological variables as well as morphological criteria. Vigne et al. (2003:250–251) also have suggested that the term *predomestic* is ambiguous and should be abandoned, with the understanding that these animals were anthropologically domesticated even if morphological changes had not yet occurred.

The economic picture is far from clear on the island itself. One emerging aspect of the increasingly diverse Cypriot Neolithic economy that is especially compelling, however, relates to early herding (cf. Vigne 2001; Vigne et al. 1999). The relationship between pastoralists and farmers is an issue rarely addressed for Neolithic Cyprus, with few exceptions (e.g., Marks 1999). In general, two contrasting models are often presented for the Mediterranean region. The first proposes long-distance transhumance divorced from farming villages, while the second envisions mixed farming and herding systems, where herders kept animals close to villages (summarized by Chang 1994:353–354).

Where the CPPNB fits into this scenario remains to be demonstrated, and the presence of cattle, with very different herding requirements than caprines or pigs, has confused the matter. Cattle have been found at sites that are not traditional villages. This may indicate an economic dichotomy selecting against keeping them in large villages and hinting at different types of land use strategies in which herds were rotated to pastures, thus supporting the first model. Cattle may not have been compatible with villages, where forage could have been quickly depleted. On the other hand, most of the limited cattle remains predate the establishment of large villages. Perhaps by the KC, cattle simply were not part of the economic suite.

Perhaps the questions to ask are: why have cattle *not* been previously recovered from Neolithic Cyprus and, now that they have been, why did they not persist? After all, cattle were common in mainland faunal Neolithic assemblages and also occur during the Neolithic on other Mediterranean islands (Simmons 2004b, c), albeit in later contexts. It seems that once established on these islands, cattle remained significant. In Cyprus, however, current data indicate an early withdrawal or die-off during the KC. The timing and reasons for this are not clear: what mechanisms contributed to this apparent disappearance until the Bronze Age? The low numbers of cattle could be nothing more than a factor of their large size: one cow will provide more meat and secondary products, such as milk, and thus feed more people than will several sheep. Issues relating to the relationship of cattle to other domesticates in terms of feeding and forage requirements, for example, may also be relevant and help explain why cattle apparently did not thrive on Cyprus after the CPPNB. Horwitz et al. (2004:39) suggest that perhaps not enough fresh stock was brought over from the mainland to replenish and maintain the founder herds. Others argue that by the KC, people may have chosen not to maintain cattle because they already had a successful economy based on agropastoralism and deer hunting (Rainbird 1999:228). Davis (2003:263) suggests that a reason for the demise of cattle may have been the appearance of a bovine disease, or simply that by the KC, people may have tired of maintaining such large animals.

Were there perhaps some ritual reasons for their appearance, and subsequent disappearance? After all, on the mainland, cattle figured prominently in ritual behavior. Perhaps the earliest colonizers of Cyprus were attempting to retreat from the formalized life that was becoming standardized on the mainland. This could well have included the avoidance of increasingly formalized religious activities. They chose to colonize a new geographic area where they could maintain their traditional lifestyles and ultimately establish their own unique identities. However, they may not have wished to entirely sever their mainland identities. Cattle (along with the rudimentary projectile points?) could have been one ritual element, one which also had economic benefits, that was imported to ensure some symbolic ties with the homeland. Once their island identity was established by the KC, perhaps there no longer was a need to retain cattle (or points) as a material symbol of the ritual world. Such scenarios, of course, are speculative, and at this point, the role of cattle in Cyprus cannot be adequately evaluated (Simmons 2004b).

The KC–SC Interface

Peltenburg's (2003b:99–103, 2004a, b) observation that Cyprus gradually dropped out of the Levantine interaction sphere by the KC represents a fruitful avenue for future studies. Why did this happen, and why did Cyprus, from essentially the KC onward, develop its unique trajectory? Did it have to do with the establishment of a collective island identity that increasingly made distinctions between itself and "the other" (that is, the mainland) (cf. Clarke 2003)? If so, what were the processes causing this transition? Or was the island in fact resettled by new colonists bearing ceramics? These certainly are areas future research will address.

Ecological Implications

Ecological degradation, which likely figured prominently on the mainland, does not appear to have been too significant on Cyprus during the Neolithic. Perhaps herds were properly managed to avoid the type of overgrazing so common in much of the Near East. Additionally, population levels may have been sufficiently low during the CPPNB to minimize impacts. But even if the CPPNB occupation was relatively limited, why is there so little evidence for accelerated impacts during the subsequent KC, when more sites are documented? The decline of pigs and deer and the increase of pine at Khirokitia could indicate local anthropogenic degradation (Davis 2003:263), but on the island as a whole there is limited evidence for this. With the exception of Khirokitia and *Tenta*, most KC sites are relatively small, and thus population growth still may have been low enough to avoid the ecological havoc witnessed on the mainland. Certainly the earliest occupants of Cyprus had a more dramatic impact, helping to drive the endemic fauna to extinction. As populations grew in post-Neolithic times, the consequences of agriculture and animal husbandry also took their toll. By practicing diverse economic strategies, however, Neolithic peoples may have been offered a respite from the ecological deterioration seen in both earlier and later periods (Simmons 2004c).

The Significance of Cyprus in the Neolithic World

What does the Cypriot Neolithic tell us of its role within the wider Neolithic world? By the KC and the SC, mainland contacts were minimized and the island assumed its uniquely insular persona, but Cyprus was a Neolithic "colony" far earlier and longer than initially believed. This points to the island's role as part of the wider PPNB cultural expression (Finlayson 2004), and indeed, the concept of a Mediterranean interaction sphere (cf. Peltenburg 2004b; Simmons 2004d) should be seriously considered. Watkins (2004:32), however, believes that Cyprus was never fully integrated in the PPNB interaction sphere and that over time the need for what links did exist with the mainland increasingly declined. As we have seen in previous chapters, many researchers now acknowledge multiple core-centers for the agricultural transition. It now seems likely that there also were multiple maritime journeys to Cyprus over a relatively long period of time that resulted in the establishment of a permanent Neolithic presence.

It is conceivable that Cyprus was a staging ground for exploration farther west, such as the Aegean Islands or even the Greek mainland, although extremely early Neolithic manifestations in those regions remain elusive (Runnels 1995). Clearly, this new research requires a dramatic reinterpretation of the diffusion and migration of Neolithic peoples and ideas within a wide circum-Mediterranean region. There is no longer reason to believe in one vast Neolithic colonization attempt, and the concept of multiple "pioneer colonizers" (Perlès 2001:62) is more likely.

In conclusion, Neolithic Cyprus has shed its image as an isolated cultural backwater. The island's Neolithic can no longer be considered peripheral to the wider Neolithic world. Rather, from at least the late Epipaleolithic, it was part of the dynamic processes that were occurring over a huge geographic range during this tumultuous time. Cyprus, with its strategic Mediterranean location, was a key component in a world on the cusp of the Neolithic Revolution (cf. Bar-Yosef 2001b). Exciting new studies on the island have literally rewritten our understanding of the turbulent events defining the Neolithic. This research has greatly expanded our understanding of the ways in which humans colonized the Mediterranean islands, ultimately developing some of the most unique cultural systems known in the ancient world.

Summary

The past several years of research on Cyprus have radically transformed the interpretative landscape of the Near Eastern Neolithic. Previously Cyprus was believed not to have been occupied prior to the Neolithic. The first residents of the island, as reflected by the KC, were thought to have been relatively late PPN immigrants who established an isolated and somewhat impoverished insular adaptation with few links to their homelands. Among some of the more salient aspects resulting from new studies are the following points.

1. The island's earliest occupation, as represented by *Aetokremnos* predates the Neolithic by some 2,000 years. The occupants of this site likely were very late (Natufian-equivalent) or very early Neolithic peoples who did not possess a domestic economy. They were hunters who likely contributed to the eradication of the endemic fauna.

2. The limits of the PPN on the island have now been extended with the establishment of the Cypro–PPNB (CPPNB). This shortens the gap

between the Akrotiri Phase and the PPN. There also are hints of an even earlier, PPNA, occupation, which would question the very existence of this supposed gap.

3. The CPPNB shows some material linkages with the mainland, unlike the KC. These are primarily in the form of chipped stone technological similarities.

4. CPPNB sites thus far documented are quite distinct from one another. They appear to represent small settlements occupied by people with a mixed agropastoral economic strategy.

5. Cattle were used by some CPPNB peoples; this is surprising since these animals have not previously been recovered on the island prior to the Bronze Age. Their apparent disappearance during the subsequent KC and SC cultures is presently unexplained.

6. Some of the Near East's earliest domesticates have now been recovered in CPPNB contexts. These were not domesticated on Cyprus and had to have been imported, suggesting established communication patterns between the island and the mainland.

7. The gap between the PPN and the PN, as on the mainland, may be more apparent than real.

8. Cyprus now must be considered as part of an ever-expanding Neolithic interaction sphere that was established earlier than previously believed. By the KC, however, the island appears to have had fewer mainland contacts and assumed an increasingly insular character.

Case Study 7   **Research in Cyprus**

None of the archaeological sites I have worked on in Cyprus is "typical." My first experience was at *Aetokremnos*, and it came about largely by serendipity. The potential significance of the site had been long known, but its location on a secure British Royal Air Force base made access difficult. Stuart Swiny, who was then director of the Cyprus American Archaeological Research Institute (CAARI), felt *Aetokremnos* was important, despite limited evidence that it even was an intact site. During a visit after having worked at megasites in Jordan, I met Stuart, largely arranged through Gary Rollefson, and visited *Aetokremnos*, which is spectacularly but precariously located halfway down a steep cliff with a sharp drop to the Mediterranean Sea. I initially was not convinced that it had much potential, but I was intrigued by the possibilities and thus set about making arrangements for a test excavation.

This was not easy, since I had to obtain permits not only from the Cyprus Department of Antiquities, but also from the British, due to Aetokremnos's RAF location. But, since the site had already generated a considerable amount of controversy (and continues to do so, e.g., Ammerman and Noller 2005), the Department of Antiquities wanted someone to investigate it who did not have a vested interest in whether or not the site was pre-Neolithic, someone who had not previously worked in Cyprus, and I fit the bill. We conducted a very brief season in 1987, demonstrating the presence of intact deposits and the site's significance. Despite this, obtaining funding was a challenge. First, we were rejected by agencies that felt that Aetokremnos was not a site. When this was demonstrated, we then were rejected because we had already proven it was a site! As an insight into the sometimes pettiness of archaeological funding, one reviewer accused me of wanting to work in a scenic place, and many confused Cyprus with Crete! Ultimately, though, we prevailed and obtained adequate funding to fully investigate this important site. The Aetokremnos project is memorable not only because of the intense archaeological discussion it still engenders, but also because it introduced me to the hospitality of the Cypriot people. Furthermore, being on an RAF base had its benefits, including delightful pilot's lunches prepared for us by the officers' club!

After Aetokremnos, I became fascinated with the island's early prehistory and was fortunate enough to investigate two other sites, this time Neolithic ones. Both were outside of the conventional envelope of what was expected during this time period. Kholetria Ortos is a large KC culture site strategically located on top of a hill. Despite its size, however, Ortos lacks architecture, a situation only partially explained by erosion. It was, however, rich in chipped stone and faunal materials, and contributed to our understanding of Neolithic site diversity (Simmons 2003b).

The site that I presently am involved with, Ais Yiorkis, again is out of the ordinary, and our research here was discussed earlier. This, too, is a locality that is substantially altering our perceptions of how the island was colonized and how these early farmers and herders adapted to the unique constraints of an island environment (Simmons 1998b). I feel very fortunate in having had a part in this revisionary movement on early island archaeology in the Mediterranean.

Chapter 10

The Path to the Present

Genesis and Exodus — The Neolithic Experience

Throughout this book, I have attempted a narrative expressing the amazing diversity and complexity of the Near Eastern Neolithic. We have examined its genesis during the Natufian, its subsequent development and florescence during the PPNB, and its exodus, the termination of a long and successful adaptation, during the PN. Or was this really the end of the Neolithic? Certainly it set the stage for the development of some of the most sophisticated urban societies in the ancient world. In this final chapter, I address two broad topics. The first is the current and future state of research on the Neolithic, and the second is resource management, preservation, and presentation.

Contemporary Neolithic Research:
What Do We Know, and What Do We Not Know?

Theoretical and Methodological Improvements

Archaeological theory evolves. What is trendy in one decade will be passé in another. Research on the Neolithic has gone through a series of theoretical paradigms that generally reflect the discipline as a whole. Initial studies focused on establishing baseline data, the "nuts and bolts" of any archaeological endeavor in establishing a chronological and cultural historic record of a given region. Subsequent research, in many ways first starting with the Braidwoods' Iraqi work, was more problem-oriented, usually focused on nothing less than finding "the origins of agriculture" or "the oldest Neolithic settlement." Theory now has become more refined, and several processual perspectives characterize much contemporary research. These include middle-range critical theoretical examinations of site structure, mortuary and ritual practices, regional interaction, household composition, gender, and artifact analyses. While the social realm is receiving much attention, there is a continuing emphasis on clarifying human and environmental interactions. Much of this has to do with achieving a better understanding of climatic changes and geomorphic positioning on the landscape. Finally, it would be a mistake to omit the more prosaic studies that characterize Neolithic research. These relate to the ever-present detailed analysis of both chipped and ground stone, as well as architectural patterning. These "pure data" elements are now often integrated into explicit theoretical models.

The theoretical directions of many contemporary studies have increasingly incorporated postprocessual orientations focusing on social agency and symbolic issues. As one example, consider Cauvin's (2000a, b) view of the Neolithic as nothing less than the birth of religion, or, on a more specific level, his belief that the ubiquitous projectile points were prestige objects (Cauvin 2000a:126). Perhaps the best-known examples are the re-excavations at Çatalhöyük (Hodder 2006). While a broad-ranging spectrum of theoretical orientations characterizes this project, much of the actual on-the-ground excavation is simply good archaeology, with meticulous attention to fine-grained detail to be envied by many projects. For example, single buildings are now often excavated over one season, as opposed to Mellaart's original research in which over 200 buildings were excavated in four years. While such an approach is laudable, one might wonder whether too much information is being retrieved, which adds to analyses and curation issues, and raises the specter of what constitutes "relevant data," a tricky issue indeed. Furthermore, on a pragmatic level, such melding of theory with detailed field research is an expensive endeavor requiring resources that not many projects have. Overall, though, postprocessual approaches to the Near Eastern Neolithic have generally been tempered with a healthy respect for carefully retrieved data.

Coupled with increased theoretical sophistication, methodological refinements have greatly enhanced our understanding of the Neolithic. Over the past hundred years, many of these have been ones that affected the entire discipline and involve more careful excavation and data-recovery procedures. Advances in other disciplines also have immensely benefited archaeology, confirming the need for true interdisciplinary collaboration. In particular, chronological improvements have allowed for better dating of specific entities, sites, and even individual artifacts or ecofacts (such as seeds). The revolution in data recovery has allowed for the retrieval of higher-resolution information. This is particularly significant in relation to plant remains. Residue analysis from ground stone and other artifacts has provided considerable new insights into specific economic and social patterns. Likewise, genetic studies of both floral and faunal remains have allowed for a much more precise understanding of processes involved in domestication. Specifically, DNA studies are opening up exciting new vistas relating to specific domesticates and their spread. Similar genetic analyses on human remains promise considerable insight into population movement and biological inquiries. The incorporation of geomorphic analyses into regional models and environmental reconstructions also has resulted in a better comprehension of the Neolithic and how land use practices have altered the environment. This increasingly includes the use of GIS for modeling settlement behavior.

Data Gaps

Despite over a hundred years of investigation and recent refinements, there are still many things we do not know about the Neolithic. These are being whittled down to ever more precise problems, but there also are wider issues. Below are some data gaps I believe future research needs to address.

Economic Data. We need to be aware of Flannery's admonition, made over 30 years ago, that we should not waste our time looking for the oldest or the first domesticated plant or animal. Far more important are trends, and certainly there are many economic issues that remain unanswered. Although refinements are continually being made, a gap remains in pinpointing the likely multiple geographic origins of specific domesticates, understanding how they came to form Neolithic "packages," and tracing their diffusion to other areas.

Another aspect involves just how much domesticates actually contributed to Neolithic subsistence patterns. Perhaps a model along the line summarized by Rowley-Conwy (2004:97) for Europe also has applicability to the Near East. He sees three phases in the transition to fully agricultural economies. These are availability, in which agriculture is available to hunters and gatherers but plays little or no role in their economy; substitution, in which agriculture provides 5–50 percent of the diet; and consolidation, in which agriculture provides over 50 percent of the diet. Such a model would clearly have to be modified for much of the Near East, since agriculture was not introduced to indigenous hunters and gatherers, as it was in Europe, but the concept may provide a fruitful way to evaluate the relative significance of domesticates. Rowley-Conwy notes that the substitution phase is the actual transition to agriculture and was very rapid, since people depend upon agriculture either to a negligible extent or heavily. In the Near East, roughly analogous scenarios might envision the Natufians as experimenting with an availability phase, whereas the PPNA constituted a substitution phase, with consolidation occurring during the PPNB, but not really becoming firmly established until the PN.

Social Structure. Much recent research has addressed the complex issue of social structure and organization. Despite many compelling arguments, we still do not have an adequate understanding of this issue. In particular, there is a lack of understanding relating to hierarchy, household makeup, and leadership roles. Additionally, only limited attention has been given to defining the roles of difficult-to-document "invisible" personalities in archaeology. These include women and, especially, children (cf. Baxter 2005; Moore and Scott 1997). This is all the more surprising given that some scholars believe that the role of women in the Neolithic was a critical variable.

Burial Patterns. The Neolithic is rich in mortuary data, but detailed studies on human remains such as Eshed et al.'s (2004a, b), Peterson's (2002), or Pinhasi and Pluciennik's (2004) are the exception rather than the rule. Genetic studies also would contribute to origins and other human biological issues. Finally, despite hundreds of documented Neolithic burials, it seems likely that off-site cemeteries or mortuary centers, perhaps similar to Kfar HaHoresh, must exist. Concerted efforts must be directed toward locating such sites.

Defining the Neolithic World. We have spoken for years of a PPNB interaction sphere, and recent discussions have addressed how widespread the Neolithic world was. Intriguing data from Cyprus indicate a considerable expansion of Neolithic communication and transportation skills. Refinements must now be made to better define the nature of Neolithic interactions, at both the regional and macroregional scales. This likely will involve the difficult issue of assessing core/periphery relationships and specific tribal or even "ethnic" entities and their spread

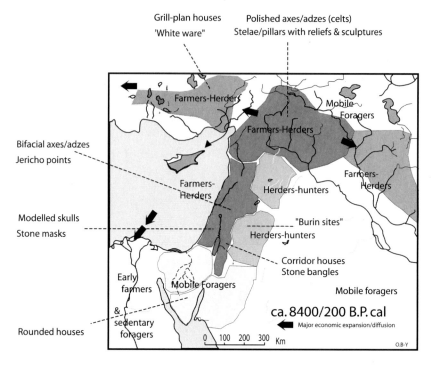

10.1   Map of possible Neolithic "tribes." Note that years are in cal. BP. Courtesy of Ofer Bar-Yosef.

(fig. 10.1). In this context, the current thoughts of many scholars involve a series of "polycentric" Neolithic centers.

Ideology, Ritual, and Symbolism. Interpretations and reconstructions of Neolithic ideology have been at the forefront of much recent research. Much of this remains in the speculative realm and requires rigorous methodologies for better definition.

Chronology. Despite enormous leaps in chronological methods, there are still pressing issues relating to the Neolithic. One is simply in arriving at a consistent use of either calibrated or radiocarbon years. This is complicated by the fact that portions of the Neolithic fall within the calibration "wiggles" that make interpretation particularly difficult.

Sedentism. Although there is an enormous literature regarding sedentism, there is also a clear realization that the Neolithic encompassed a wide range of stability and permanence. More precision is required in establishing criteria for fully evaluating degrees of sedentism.

Communication and Funding. Finally, while not exactly "data gaps," two fundamental and pragmatic problem areas exist relating to communication and funding. There are so many scholars working on the Neolithic that the proliferation of data is difficult to assimilate. Coupled with this is the lack of consistency in analytical techniques and the selective use of data. In addition, while the call to interdisciplinary research has been heeded in contemporary studies, nonarchaeological data are sometimes difficult to successfully integrate. Sometimes a "little knowledge" by either the archaeologist or specialist can lead to unwarranted interpretations. Another observation is that while English, French, and German may be the "lingua franca" of most Near Eastern archaeological outlets, linguistic barriers sometimes exist, since important publications can be in languages, such as Arabic, Hebrew, or Polish, not read by a majority of researchers. Further, the ever-current political conflicts of the region are a barrier to efficient communication. Finally, good archaeological research is expensive. Adequate funding for fieldwork, and, especially, analysis, publication, and site protection and preservation, is increasingly difficult to obtain. This is a critical issue facing future researchers.

Research Trends

Many Neolithic sites have been excavated, and we have a tremendous amount of data to contemplate. But archaeologists are never content with extant information, always wanting to dig more. There will always be new, as well as old, research questions that can be answered only by additional excavations and surveys, although we also need to realize the potential of existing databases. What are some of the research trends that future investigations of the Neolithic will address, in addition to filling in the gaps noted above? While it is difficult to be a seer, the following are certain avenues of research that contemporary scholars are addressing, although I hasten to add that they are not all-inclusive.

In summarizing his important edited volume, Kuijt (2000c) acknowledges that while early research on the Neolithic examined economic aspects, new studies now focus on the social context of Neolithic life at the

household, community, and regional scales. Byrd (2005a), too, empha-
sizes the interplay between social institutions and "human agency" as a
critical element in understanding the Neolithic, and many other researchers similarly are stressing the social dimension, while at the same time
realizing the difficulty in archaeologically documenting this. Such studies
offer what Kuijt (2000c:311–312) calls an alternative perspective on the
Neolithic, and what I would call a complementary perspective. This shifts
emphasis from how and when domestication occurred to examining the
nature of Neolithic social organization and how these frameworks can be
linked with the new economies provided by food production.

Kuijt highlights several specific contemporary trends. He notes that
social processes are incorporated into at least three different research directions: those investigating the initial founding of early agricultural villages, the consolidation of these villages into large aggregate communities,
and the subsequent abandonment of these megasites. On a broader level,
he points to several other contemporary themes. One relates to the coexistence of hierarchical and egalitarian elements. This is important, since it
recognizes that such systems are not mutually exclusive. Another examines the concept of social organization through heterarchy and hierarchy,
while the frameworks of governance and social differentiation in Neolithic society form yet an additional direction for future research. Here
Kuijt admits that we know relatively little about how Neolithic communities were actually led and governed. Finally, he notes the concepts of
Neolithic households, "Houses," and links to economy as fruitful future
research directions.

Garfinkel (2002:258–261) presents a series of specific topics relating to human organization during the PN that have applicability to the
broader Neolithic. At the household level, he cites the following issues:
kinship reorganization, enclosedness, food supplies and storage, food processing and cooking, and accumulation of wealth. At the community level,
the following are relevant: settlement density, formalized passageways,
communal maintenance works, centers and peripheries of villages (with
communal activity occurring in the centers of villages), communal ritual,
central storage and redistribution, formalized cemeteries, craft specialization, and trade.

In a similar vein, Belfer-Cohen and Goring-Morris (2002) provide
one of the most current assessments of the Neolithic. Much of their dis-

cussion focuses on summarizing a recent (2002) conference held at the University of Toronto entitled "Domesticating Space: Landscape and Site Structure in the Prehistoric Near East." They note that the eternal questions of how and why sedentism emerged continue to vex researchers. While this is still of concern, a current emphasis is on the concept of space and human responses to it. This is often addressed by detailed analyses of architectural plans to better understand the social implications of spatial patterning, but there are also broader attempts at integrating the social and symbolic significance of space within and between sites. Much of this relates to nondomestic architectural features, such as the stairway/"theater" at Ghwair I or the claimed temples at 'Ain Ghazal. Other aspects relate to entire sites that are nondomestic, such as Göbekli or Kfar HaHoresh.

Some scholars working with the Neolithic now talk about the domestication not only of plants and animals, but also of the landscape, with an assumption that with the advent of the Neolithic nothing was "natural" anymore. Coupled with this are more sophisticated questions being asked about increasing social complexity and the inevitable tensions that were created by expanding populations. Along these lines, Belfer-Cohen and Goring-Morris note that much research has in a sense gone full circle with the renewed emphasis on ritual and symbolism. They go so far as to suggest that analogies to the early Greek religious organization and the notion of amphictyonies — that is, leagues of neighboring communities associated with sacred places — may be appropriate in understanding early Neolithic ritual behavior. They conclude with the observation that "there is a broad consensus of opinion that matters were much more complex from the very beginning of the Neolithic, thus generally accepting the tenets proposed by Jacques Cauvin" (Belfer-Cohen and Goring-Morris 2002:114). Here I might disagree with their observation: having been at the same conference, I did not leave with a feeling that Cauvin's ideas were universally embraced!

After summarizing the conference, Belfer-Cohen and Goring-Morris discuss their thoughts on current trends. While acknowledging that the Neolithic was tied to environmental variables and involved a dramatic economic shift, they feel that ultimately it should be viewed in terms of social processes. They note that these involved a series of trials and errors, of successes and failures. They strongly emphasize the strains and tensions that larger communities placed on individual and community memory systems. These stresses resulted in changes in social relationships and in coping with daily experiences, requiring various forms of regulatory systems. Sometimes these were reflected in architecture, such as storage features, but Belfer-Cohen and Goring-Morris believe that an intensification of ceremonies and repetitive rituals to reinforce a sense of cohesion were important as well. They also emphasize growing tensions brought about by increased community sizes, citing Flannery's (2002) contention that scalar stress was a significant mechanism to account for the change from communal sharing to individual ownership.

Belfer-Cohen and Goring-Morris argue that we can see the material ramifications of such changes throughout the course of the Neolithic, primarily by architectural distinctions within and between private and communal spaces and by changes in ground stone usage (see also Wright 2000). They invoke ethnographic data, emphasizing that alternate responses to these stresses were likely. Finally, they note that previously unknown diseases may have had a significant impact on many settlements. They conclude that different Neolithic groups likely confronted these stresses with different responses, and they wisely caution against assuming too much from the archaeological record alone. We must be aware that some responses were not adaptive and failed in the long run. They believe, however, that during troubling and unstable times, what I have called "a tumultuous time" in this book, the "most effective regulatory mechanisms are likely to be those found within the realms of symbolic behaviours rather than in profane domains, i.e., in ceremonies, rites, cultic practices, and the like" (Belfer-Cohen and Goring-Morris 2002:146-147). They point to the emergence of sites whose primary functions were not devoted to daily subsistence, localities that became beacons that served as focal points for Neolithic settlements. It is likely that complex kinship ties, exchange networks, land issues relating to shared access ("the Commons"), and land ownership rights and boundaries all contributed to tensions, and that sacred sites belonging to all could have helped to alleviate some of the stresses brought about by this radical new way of living.

I believe that Belfer-Cohen and Goring-Morris have provided a convincing argument for one direction that future research on the Neolithic will take. At the same time, they may be overemphasizing the ritual world and the role of stresses brought about by large communities. The "bea-

con" nonresidential sites they refer to are rare. Furthermore, the over-
crowding brought about by megasite living may not accurately reflect the
entire range of Neolithic settlement patterns. While there is an increase
in large communities during the LPPNB that continued into the PN in
some regions, let us not forget the successful fragmentation into smaller
PN communities in the Levant. Of course this could be one of the successful responses taken by some LPPNB groups, supporting the concept
of flexibility that Belfer-Cohen and Goring-Morris argue for.

Finally, it should come as no surprise that Ofer Bar-Yosef (2004) has
considerable thoughts on what he calls "targets" of current Neolithic research. He notes that the use of analogies (e.g., ethnoarchaeology, ethno-
history, ethnobotany, etc.) and controlled replicative experiments complete what we cannot find through excavation. He uses the formation
of states as a point of departure, linking this to increased populations
that began during the Neolithic. Roughly 4,000 years passed from the
PPNA to the formation of early chiefdoms, as reflected, for example, by
the Halafian. During this time, substantial organizational and economic
shifts occurred, and Bar-Yosef feels that many social decisions were made
in the face of a variety of situations. Some of these are defined as "climatic
surprises," reinforcing his belief that environmental variables cannot be
neglected if one is to properly understand the Neolithic. With increased
populations, adaptive decisions in the face of natural disasters (as well as
other events) become more complex, and Bar-Yosef feels that larger villages may have assumed increasingly defined ethnic identities. He therefore calls for the mapping of Neolithic tribal territories, an approach literally undertaken by Kozłowski and Aurenche (2005). He notes that data
on defining Neolithic "chiefdoms" are currently lacking, but that some
events, such as the colonization of Cyprus, likely involved some sort of
leaders. He also believes that the stratigraphic gap between the PPNB
and PN is well established (but see discussion elsewhere in this book) and
attributes it to a series of droughts that affected Neolithic tribes. This required a reorientation from larger to smaller settlements that included the
reliance on more flexible subsistence strategies related to pastoral nomadism. In some regions such as Mesopotamia, recovery was relatively rapid,
with local populations well on their way toward becoming early chiefdoms.

Bar-Yosef concludes with several questions for future investigations.

How does the archaeological record inform us on whether population growth drove the evolution of farming societies and the need to absorb new lands? Can we map out territories of social entities during the PPNA, the PPNB, and the PN, and should this guide where future excavations are conducted, especially in areas affected by modern development? What was the location of the original "core area" (if indeed there was one — see previous comments on multiple-core concepts), and did centers of socio-economic change move from one core to others? Was the transmission of the Neolithic driven by demic diffusion or the transmission of ideas? Did the spread of the Neolithic depend on geographic constraints or axes? Finally, can linguistics interact with archaeology in determining the origin of Indo-European and Afro-Asiatic languages?

In summary, several research domains will guide contemporary and future scholars in their investigations into the Neolithic. There is no doubt that one trend will be toward achieving a better understanding of the new social order that arose during the Neolithic. A related topic will be the refinement of Neolithic "interaction spheres" or "polycentric" zones of influence, including establishing the role that diffusions of both people and ideas played in an ever-expanding Neolithic world. In this context, we can hope for more studies such as Colledge et al.'s (2004) comprehensive archaeobotanical investigations from several sites that inform us of this process. They convincingly show that there are vegetational "signatures" characterizing the different geographic regions occupied by Neolithic peoples, and that similarities of the crop packages between regions are indicative of both the routes of demic migration and early agricultural practices. In a similar vein, Pinhasi and Pluciennik's (2004) biological investigations on human skeletal remains also are aiding our understanding of demic diffusion from the Near East into Europe.

Certainly the Mediterranean islands' role in this Neolithic world are rewriting our understanding of many issues. Continued investigations on Cyprus will clarify the early colonization of this island and stimulate the search for similar reflections on other islands. Other scholars will concentrate on more mundane tasks of ever more precise definitions of "baseline" data characterizing individual sites and artifact assemblages. While we know much about some regions, there still are many parts of the Near East that have not been well investigated, and the establishment of such elementary data will remain an important priority. So, while we know more about the Neolithic now than we did even 20 years ago, there is still a lot to be learned.

Preservation and Presentation

There is an important issue that I have not yet addressed: protecting the fragile heritage that Neolithic peoples left to the modern world. Many books deal with heritage management, and I do not provide great detail here, but site preservation, as well as how sites are presented to the public, have not received much attention in a Neolithic context (excepting Çatalhöyük). The antiquities services of most Near Eastern countries have limited budgets, and preservation funds tend to be devoted to large, impressive sites belonging to periods later than the Neolithic. Even spectacular sites, such as Jericho, are not as well protected or preserved as they should be. Certainly, more mundane, but more typical, Neolithic settlements have received limited attention.

When many sites were excavated, preservation and conservation were not major issues. Even today, with limited research funds, these topics tend to be shortchanged. One need only visit Beidha to see how much decades of neglect have affected these precious ruins. 'Ain Ghazal is perhaps an even more tragic example. It is located within the bustling Jordanian capital of Amman, and despite its world-class status, its neglect is apparent. Funding for excavation, let alone preservation, was always limited. At least we backfilled much of what we excavated, so erosion is not as apparent as at Beidha. But given Amman's rapid development, the site is endangered, despite the government's sincere attempts at conservation. Visiting today, one is greeted by fields of weeds that belie the site's significance. Even more remote sites such as Ghwair I suffer, not just from the ravages of visitors, but from the forces of nature. Years of severe winter rains have taken their toll.

I do not have a ready answer to this dilemma. Certainly one obvious solution is simply not to excavate any more until sufficient funding for preservation can be obtained. Given the tightening of research budgets, this is unlikely to occur soon. While not conducting any new excavations and instead focusing on previously excavated materials is an attractive option, I do not think that it is a viable one. If sites such as Ghwair I, Ba'ja, *Shillourokambos*, or innumerable others had not been excavated, we would know far less of the diversity of the Neolithic. If 'Ain Ghazal had not been excavated, the megasite phenomenon might never have been documented. Certainly this is a major challenge to future generations of scholars.

There are some positive attempts at both preservation and presentation, however. While tourism in the Near East has suffered due to recent political events, it nonetheless is one avenue for increasing preservation funding. While many tourists may prefer to see the spectacular remains of antiquity, with the right "advertising" less spectacular remains can be made just as interesting. Of course, this is a mixed blessing. The last thing that most archaeologists want to see are masses of tourists clambering over fragile ruins, disrupting the tranquility that so many of us find in working at remote and often beautiful places.

It is, however, our obligation to share our findings with the public. With the increase of eco-tourism, as opposed to mass tourism, there is the opportunity to tailor a wide range of sites to an educated lay population. One such proposal has been made for the remote Wadi Feinan of Jordan, which contains not only the entire Neolithic sequence, but impressive remains of ancient mining as well. This region is well suited for sustainable eco-tourism development that will protect the cultural resources and benefit indigenous peoples (e.g., Simmons and Corona 2000). To this end, we have recently established a simple archaeological park at Ghwair I, taking advantage of the spectacularly preserved architectural remains to convey to visitors the impressive, yet fragile, nature of this community. Another example is at Beidha, where Dennis's (2003) reconstruction of Neolithic structures (fig. 10.2) is coupled with signage and simple trails to the site. This was all accomplished at a relatively low cost and could be seen as a model for future studies.

Concluding Remarks—Setting the Path to the Present?

Archaeologists can be pessimists, perhaps due to their documenting the ultimate collapse of so many societies over time. Diamond (2005) presents a compelling argument that past societies have fallen due to a recurring pattern of catastrophe brought about by reproducing too fast, squandering resources, and ignoring warning signs given by the environment. Add increased social stratification, the development of complex political entities, religious fervor, and warfare, and one has a potent mix that has much

10.2   Modern reconstruction of Beidha Neolithic houses. Courtesy of Samantha Dennis.

to do with many of the woes of humankind. Overpopulation, hunger, disease, ethnic and religious strife, ecological degradation: all of these may be the legacy of food production and sedentism. Given a big-picture perspective, it is tempting to blame the Neolithic. After all, hunters and gatherers rarely are guilty of massive destruction and genocide.

Witnessing the heart-wrenching misery of starvation in Africa makes one ask why one of the very principles of the Neolithic, surplus, cannot feed so many desperate people. Surely a society that now has the technology to explore space can produce increased food yields. Indeed, most of the world today is fed by genetically modified crops. Yet, as Diamond (2002:706) points out, "providing undernourished people with more food would be a laudable goal if it were inexorably linked to reducing our numbers, but in the past more food has always resulted in more people." The ultimate solution to such tragedies must lie in political, not technological, solutions.

Likewise, politics have severely affected the very region where the Neolithic first began. I find it tremendously sad that the Near East, a land of austere beauty, is also the scene of so much conflict, tragedy, and suffering. Is this also the result of tribalism that likely developed during the Neolithic?

It is easy to wonder if the Neolithic Revolution has been worth it. Was it an improvement for humanity or a harbinger of the strife that affects so much of the world today? I cannot imagine that the first villagers themselves brought about these problems, but certainly they set the stage for subsequent population increase and conflict. While studying the Neolithic in remote places where few people now live, and working with indigenous people, such as the Bedouin, I have always been impressed by their honest hospitality and seemingly low-stress lives. In many ways, their lifestyles may not be too far from those of Neolithic pastoralists, and it is easy to yearn for a return to simpler times. After all, how could Neolithic people possibly have foreseen what trajectory humanity would take? But this is misleading — it is far too easy to wish for the "good old days" without realizing the benefits and triumphs of modern society as well. For better or worse, we cannot reverse the legacy of the Neolithic. And even Diamond (2005:525) has reason for optimism: "My remaining cause for hope is another consequence of the globalized modern world's interconnectedness. Past societies lacked archaeologists and television." That is, contemporary society has global communications and 24-hour news: there is no excuse to claim ignorance. The modern world also has people who are dedicated to studying the past and, trite though it may sound, to informing us of previous mistakes in the hopes that we may avoid them.

If the Neolithic had never occurred, this book would not have been written. While not belittling the undisputed success of hunting and gathering for most of humankind's existence, without the security and surplus provided by food production, subsequent cultural achievements, reflected by the development of urban cultures of the Near East and elsewhere, but ultimately culminating in contemporary society, would simply never have occurred. These remains of classical antiquity used to be called the "civilizations" of the Near East, as exemplified by the Sumerians, the Babylonians, and others. In this more enlightened time, however, the word *civilization* often is avoided, even if not by modern politicians, as being too biased and conveying a set of value judgments that suggest earlier cultures were not "civilized." In fact, Ofer Bar-Yosef (2001b) has begun using *civilization* to refer to the PPNB—perhaps this is a refreshing change. We should not become too obsessed with any particular term—what is more important is that so many aspects of life that we now take for granted had their origins in the Neolithic.

One might reasonably argue that we are still living the benefits, as well as the liabilities, of a Neolithic lifestyle. And this is why it is so critical that we continue to investigate this crucial stage of the human experience wherever it occurs, using the most modern and sophisticated methodological and theoretical approaches. The results of the past several years of investigations on the Neolithic in the Near East, many of which have been chronicled in this book, are proof positive of why now is such an exciting time to be conducting research on this milestone in human history, this "bold experiment."

References Cited

Abay, Eşref
  2003   The Neolithic Figurines from Ulucak Höyuk: Reconsideration of the Figurine Issue by Contextual Evidence. *Neolithics* 2:16–22.
Abbès, Frédéric
  1994   Techniques de débitage et gestion de silex sur le Moyen-Euphrate (Syrie) au PPNA final et au PPNB ancien. In *Neolithic Chipped Stone Industries of the Fertile Crescent*, edited by Hans Georg Gebel and Stefan Kozłowski, pp. 299–312. SENEPSE 1, Ex Oriente, Berlin.
Agelarakis, Anagnostis
  2004   The Shanidar Cave Proto-Neolithic Human Condition as Reflected Through Osteology and Palaeopathology. In *The Proto-Neolithic Cemetery in Shanidar Cave*, by Ralph Solecki, Rose Solecki, and Anagnostis Agelarakis, pp. 159–184. Texas A&M University Press, College Station.
Akkermans, Peter
  1993   *Villages in the Steppe: Late Neolithic Settlement and Subsistence in the Balikh Valley, Northern Syria*. International Monographs in Prehistory, Ann Arbor.
Akkermans, Peter, and Glenn Schwartz
  2003   *The Archaeology of Syria: From Complex Hunter-Gatherers to Early Urban Societies (ca. 16,000–300 BC)*. Cambridge University Press, Cambridge.
Algaze, Guillermo
  1989   The Uruk Expansion: Cross-Cultural Exchange in Early Mesopotamian Civilization. *Current Anthropology* 30:571–608.
Alley, Richard B., Jochem Marotzke, William D. Nordhaus, Jonathan T. Overpeck, Dorothy M. Peteet, Roger A. Pielke, Jr., Raymond T. Pierrehumbert, Peter B. Rhines, Thomas F. Stocker, Lynne D. Talley, and J. Michael Wallace
  2003   Abrupt Climate Change. *Science* 299:2005–2010.
Ammerman, Albert, and Jay Noller
  2005   New Light on Aetokremnos. *World Archaeology* 37:533–543.
Anati, Emmanuel
  1962   Prehistoric Trade and the Puzzle of Jericho. *Bulletin of the American Schools of Oriental Research* 167:25–31.
Anderson, Patricia
  1991   Harvesting of Wild Cereals During the Natufian as Seen from the Ex-

perimental Cultivation and Harvest of Wild Einkorn Wheat and Micro-wear Analysis of Stone Tools. In Ofer Bar-Yosef and François Valla (eds.), pp. 521–556.

Anderson, Patricia (editor)
1999   *Prehistory of Agriculture: New Experimental and Ethnographic Approaches*. Monograph 40, Institute of Archaeology, University of California, Los Angeles.

Anderson-Gerfaud, Patricia
1983   Consideration of the Uses of Certain Backed and "Lustred" Stone Tools from the Late Mesolithic and Natufian Levels of Abu Hureyra and Mu-reybet (Syria). In *Traces d'utilisation sur les outiles néolithiques de Proche Ori-ent*, edited by M.-C. Cauvin, pp. 77–105. GIS-Maison de l'Orient, Lyon.

Angel, Lawrence
1953   The Human Remains from Khirokitia. In *Khirokitia*, by Porphyrios Dikaios, pp. 416–430. Oxford University Press, Oxford.
1961   The Neolithic Crania from Sotira. In *Sotira*, by Porphyrios Dikaios, pp. 223–229. University Museum Monograph No. 4, University of Pennsyl-vania, Philadelphia.

Araus, José Luis, Ana Maria Febrero, Maria Catala, Miquel Molist, Jordi Voltas, and Ignacio Romagosa
1999   Crop Water Availability in Early Agriculture: Evidence from Carbon Isotope Discrimination of Seeds from a Tenth Millennium BP Site on the Euphrates. *Global Change Biology* 5:201–212.

Arensburg, Baruch, and Israel Hershkovitz
1988   Nahal Hemar Cave: Neolithic Human Remains. *'Atiqot* 18:50–63.

Arensburg, Baruch, and Yoel Rak
1979   The Search for Early Man in Israel. In *The Quaternary of Israel*, edited by Aharon Horowitz, pp. 201–209. Academic Press, New York.

Arsebük, Güven
1998   A Review of the Current Status of Pleistocene Archaeology in Turkey. In *Light on Top of the Black Hill: Studies Presented to Halet Çambel*, edited by Güven Arsebük, Machteld Mellink, and Wulf Schirmer, pp. 71–76. Ege Yayınları, Istanbul.

Astruc, Laurence
2003   L'outillage lithique taillé de Khirokitia (Néolithique Pré-Céramique Ré-cent, VIIe millénaire av. J.-C. cal.): caractéristiques générales et particu-larités. In Jean Guilaine and Alain LeBrun (eds.), pp. 161–173.

Aurenche, Olivier
1981   *La maison orientale. L'architecture de Proche-Orient ancien des origines au milieu du quatrième millénaire*. Maison de l'Orient, Paris.

Aurenche, Olivier, Philippe Galet, Emmanuelle Régagnon-Caroline, and Jacques Évin
2001   Proto-Neolithic and Neolithic Cultures in the Middle East — The Birth

of Agriculture, Livestock Farming, and Ceramics: A Calibrated [14]C Chronology 12,500–5,500 cal BC. *Radiocarbon* 43:1191–1202.

Aurenche, Olivier, and Stefan Kozłowski
1999   *La naissance du Néolithique au Proche-Orient*. Éditions Errance, Paris.

Balkan-Atli, Nur, Didier Binder, and Marie-Claire Cauvin
1999   Obsidian: Sources, Workshops, and Trade in Central Anatolia. In Mehmet Özdoğan and Nezih Başgelen (eds.), pp. 133–145.

Balter, Michael
2005   *The Goddess and the Bull — Çatalhöyük: An Archaeological Journey to the Dawn of Civilization*. Free Press/Simon and Schuster, New York.

Banning, Edward
1998   The Neolithic Period: Triumphs of Architecture, Agriculture, and Art. *Near Eastern Archaeology* 61:188–237.
2002a   Aceramic Neolithic: Pre-Pottery Neolithic. In *Encyclopedia of Prehistory: 8. South and Southwest Asia*, edited by Peter Peregrine and Melvin Ember, pp. 1–20. Kluwer Academic/Plenum, New York.
2002b   Consensus and Debate on the Late Neolithic and Chalcolithic of the Southern Levant. *Paléorient* 28:143–156.
2002c   Ceramic Neolithic — Late or Pottery Neolithic. In *Encyclopedia of Prehistory: 8. South and Southwest Asia*, edited by Peter Peregrine and Melvin Ember, pp. 40–55. Kluwer Academic/Plenum, New York.
2003   Housing Neolithic Farmers. *Near Eastern Archaeology* 66:4–21.

Banning, Edward, and Brian Byrd
1989   Alternative Approaches for Exploring Levantine Neolithic Architecture. *Paléorient* 15:154–160.

Banning, Edward, Dan Rahimi, and Julian Siggers
1994   The Late Neolithic of the Southern Levant: Hiatus, Settlement Shift or Observer Bias? The Perspective from Wadi Ziqlab. *Paléorient* 20:151–164.

Bar-Gal, G. Kahila, H. Khalaily, O. Mader, Pierre Ducos, and Liora Kolska Horwitz
2002   Ancient DNA Evidence for the Transition from Wild to Domestic Status in Neolithic Goats: A Case Study from the Site of Abu Gosh, Israel. *Ancient Biomolecules* 4:9–17.

Bar-Mathews, Miryam, Avner Ayalon, and Aaron Kaufman
1997   Late Quaternary Paleoclimate in the Eastern Mediterranean Region from Stable Isotope Analysis of Speleothems at Soreq Cave, Israel. *Quaternary Research* 47:155–168.

Bar-Mathews, Miryam, Avner Ayalon, Aaron Kaufman, and Gerald Wasserburg
1999   The Eastern Mediterranean Paleoclimate as a Reflection of Regional Events: Soreq Cave, Israel. *Earth and Planetary Science Letters* 166:85–95.

Bar-Oz, Guy, Tamar Dayan, Daniel Kaufman, and Mina Weinstein-Evron
2004   The Natufian Economy at el-Wad Terrace with Special Reference to Gazelle Exploitation. *Journal of Archaeological Science* 31:217–231.

Bar-Yosef, Danielle

1989   Late Palaeolithic and Neolithic Marine Shells in the Southern Levant as
        Cultural Markers. In *Proceedings of the 1986 Shell Bead Conference*, edited by
        Charles F. Hayes, pp. 169–174. Rochester Museum and Science Center,
        Rochester, NY.

1991   Changes in the Selection of Marine Shells from the Natufian to the Neo-
        lithic. In Ofer Bar-Yosef and François Valla (eds.), pp. 629–636.

Bar-Yosef, Ofer

1983   The Natufian of the Southern Levant. In *The Hilly Flanks and Beyond*,
        edited by T. Cuyler Young, Phillip Smith, and Peder Mortensen, pp. 11–
        42. Studies in Ancient Oriental Civilizations No. 36, Oriental Institute
        of the University of Chicago, Chicago.

1984   Seasonality Among Neolithic Hunter-Gatherers in Southern Sinai. In
        Animals and Archaeology: 3. Early Herders and Their Flocks, edited by Juliet
        Clutton-Brock and Caroline Grigson, pp. 145–160. International Series
        202, British Archaeological Reports, Oxford.

1985   The Stone Age of the Sinai Peninsula. In *Studi di paletnologia in onore di
        Salvador M. Puglisi*, edited by Mario Liverani, Alba Palmieri, and Renato
        Peroni, pp. 107–122. Università di Roma "La Sapienzia," Dipartimento
        di scienze storiche, archeologiche e antropologiche dell'antichità, Rome.

1986   The Walls of Jericho: An Alternative Interpretation. *Current Anthropology*
        27:157–162.

1995   The Role of Climate in the Interpretation of Human Movements and
        Cultural Transformations in Western Asia. In *Paleoclimate and Evolution,
        with Emphasis on Human Origins*, edited by Elisabeth S. Vrba, George H.
        Denton, Timothy C. Partridge, and Lloyd H. Burckle, pp. 507–523. Yale
        University Press, New Haven.

1996   Late Pleistocene Lithic Traditions in the Near East and Their Expres-
        sions in Early Neolithic Assemblages. In *Neolithic Chipped Stone Industries
        of the Fertile Crescent, and Their Contemporaries in Adjacent Regions: Proceedings
        of the Second Workshop on PPN Chipped Lithic Industries, Warsaw University,
        3rd–7th April 1995*, edited by Stefan Kozłowski and Hans Georg Gebel,
        pp. 207–216. SENEPSE 3, Ex Oriente, Berlin.

1997   Symbolic Expressions in the Later Prehistory of the Levant: Why Are
        They So Few? In *Beyond Art: Pleistocene Image and Symbol*, edited by Mar-
        garet W. Conkey, Olga Soffer, Deborah Stratmann, and Nina G. Jablon-
        ski, pp. 161–187. Memoir No. 23, California Academy of Sciences, San
        Francisco.

1998a   The Natufian Culture in the Levant, Threshold to the Origins of Agri-
        culture. *Evolutionary Anthropology* 6:159–177.

1998b   Earliest Food Producers—Pre-Pottery Neolithic (8000–5000). In *The
        Archaeology of the Holy Land*, edited by Thomas Levy, pp. 190–204. Leices-
        ter University Press, London and Washington.

2001a   From Sedentary Foragers to Village Hierarchies: The Emergence of Social Institutions. In *The Origin of Human Social Institutions*, edited by Wal-
ter Garrison Runciman, pp. 1–38. Published for the British Academy by
Oxford University Press, Oxford.

2001b   The World Around Cyprus: From Epi-Paleolithic Foragers to the Collapse of the PPNB Civilization. In Stuart Swiny (ed.), pp. 129–164.

2002a   Natufian: A Complex Society of Foragers. In *Beyond Foraging and Collect-
ing: Evolutionary Change in Hunter-Gatherer Settlement Systems*, edited by
Ben Fitzhugh and Junko Habu, pp. 91–147. Kluwer Academic/Plenum,
New York.

2002b   The Natufian Culture and the Early Neolithic: Social and Economic
Trends in Southwestern Asia. In *Examining the Farming/Language Dispersal Hypothesis*, edited by Peter Belwood and Colin Renfrew, pp. 113–126.
McDonald Institute for Archaeological Research, University of Cambridge, Cambridge.

2004   Targets of Current Neolithic Research in Southwestern Asia. *Neolithics*
1:24–27.

Bar-Yosef, Ofer, and David Alon
1988   Excavations in the Nahal Hemar Cave. *'Atiqot* 18.

Bar-Yosef, Ofer, and Daniella Bar-Yosef Mayer
2002   Early Neolithic Tribes in the Levant. In *The Archaeology of Tribal Societies*, edited by William Parkinson, pp. 340–371. Archaeological Series
15, International Monographs in Prehistory, Ann Arbor.

Bar-Yosef, Ofer, and Anna Belfer-Cohen
1989a   The Origins of Sedentism and Farming Communities in the Levant. *Journal of World Prehistory* 3:447–498.

1989b   The Levantine "PPNB" Interaction Sphere. In *People and Culture in
Change*, edited by Israel Hershkovitz, pp. 59–72. International Series
508(i), British Archaeological Reports, Oxford.

1992   From Foraging to Farming in the Mediterranean Levant. In *Transitions
to Agriculture in Prehistory*, edited by Anne Gebauer and T. Douglas Price,
pp. 21–48. Monographs in World Archaeology No. 4, Prehistory Press,
Madison.

1999   Encoding Information: Unique Natufian Objects from Hayonim Cave,
Western Galilee, Israel. *Antiquity* 73:402–410.

2000   Early Sedentism in the Near East: A Bumpy Ride to Village Life. In Ian
Kuijt (ed.), pp. 19–37.

2002   Facing Environmental Crisis: Societal and Cultural Changes at the Transition from the Younger Dryas to the Holocene in the Levant. In René
T. J. Cappers and Sytze Bottema (eds.), pp. 55–66.

Bar-Yosef, Ofer, Paul Goldberg, and T. Leveson
1974   Late Quaternary Stratigraphy and Prehistory of Wadi Fazael, Lower
Jordan Valley. *Paléorient* 2:415–428.

Bar-Yosef, Ofer, and Avi Gopher

1997   The Excavations of Netiv Hagdud: Stratigraphy and Architectural Re-
        mains. In *An Early Neolithic Village in the Jordan Valley: Part I. The Ar-
        chaeology of Netiv Hagdud*, edited by Ofer Bar-Yosef and Avi Gopher,
        pp. 41–69. American School of Prehistoric Research Bulletin No. 43,
        Peabody Museum of Archaeology and Ethnology, Harvard University,
        Cambridge.

Bar-Yosef, Ofer, and Anatoly Khazanov

1992   *Pastoralism in the Levant.* Monographs in World Archaeology No. 10, Pre-
        history Press, Madison.

Bar-Yosef, Ofer, and Renée S. Kra (editors)

1994   *Late Quaternary Chronology and Paleoclimates of the Eastern Mediterranean.*
        Radiocarbon, University of Arizona, Tucson.

Bar-Yosef, Ofer, and Giles Martin

1979   La problème de la "Sortie des Grottes" au Natoufien: répartition et local-
        ization des gisements épipaléolithiques du Levant Méditerranée. *Bulletin
        de la Société Préhistorique Française* 78:178–192.

Bar-Yosef, Ofer, and Richard Meadow

1995   The Origins of Agriculture in the Near East. In *Last Hunters, First
        Farmers: New Perspectives on the Prehistoric Transition to Agriculture*, edited
        by T. Douglas Price and Anne Gebauer, pp. 39–94. School of American
        Research Press, Santa Fe.

Bar-Yosef, Ofer, and François Valla (editors)

1991   *The Natufian Culture in the Levant.* Archaeological Series 1, International
        Monographs in Prehistory, Ann Arbor.

Bar-Yosef Mayer, Daniella

1997   Miscellaneous Finds: The Marine Shells from Netiv Hagdud. In *An Early
        Neolithic Village in the Jordan Valley: Part I. The Archaeology of Netiv Hagdud*,
        edited by Ofer Bar-Yosef and Avi Gopher, pp. 189–192. American School
        of Prehistoric Research Bulletin 43, Peabody Museum of Archaeology
        and Ethnology, Harvard University, Cambridge.

Barlow, K. Renee, and Melissa Heck

2002   More on Acorn Eating During the Natufian: Expected Patterning in
        Diet and the Archaeological Record of Subsistence. In *Hunter-Gatherer
        Archaeobotany: Perspectives from the Northern Temperate Zone*, edited by Sarah
        Mason and Jon Gather, pp. 128–145. Institute of Archaeology, Univer-
        sity College London, London.

Baxter, Jane (editor)

2005   *Children in Action: Perspectives on the Archaeology of Childhood.* Archaeological
        Papers No. 15, American Anthropological Association, Washington, DC.

Belfer-Cohen, Anna

1991a   The Natufian in the Levant. *Annual Review of Anthropology* 20:167–186.

1991b   Art Items from Layer B, Hayonim Cave: A Case Study of Art in a Natu-
        fian Context. In Ofer Bar-Yosef and François Valla (eds.), pp. 569–588.

1995 Rethinking Social Stratification in the Natufian Culture: The Evidence from Burials. In *Archaeology of Death in the Ancient Near East: Proceedings of the Manchester Conference, 16th–20th December 1992*, edited by Stuart Campbell and Anthony Green, pp. 9–16. Oxbow Monograph No. 51, Oxbow Books, Oxford.

Belfer-Cohen, Anna, and Baruch Arensburg
1997 The Human Remains from Netiv Hagdud. In *An Early Neolithic Village in the Jordan Valley: Part I. The Archaeology of Netiv Hagdud*, edited by Ofer Bar-Yosef and Avi Gopher, pp. 201–208. American School of Prehistoric Research Bulletin No. 43, Peabody Museum of Archaeology and Ethnology, Harvard University, Cambridge.

Belfer-Cohen, Anna, and Nigel Goring-Morris
1996 The Late Epipaleolithic as the Precursor of the Neolithic: The Lithic Evidence. In *Neolithic Chipped Stone Industries of the Fertile Crescent, and Their Contemporaries in Adjacent Regions: Proceedings of the Second Workshop on PPN Chipped Lithic Industries, Warsaw University, 3rd–7th April 1995*, edited by Stefan Kozłowski and Hans Georg Gebel, pp. 217–225. SENEPSE 3, Ex Oriente, Berlin.

2002 Recent Developments in Near Eastern Neolithic Research. *Paléorient* 28:143–156.

Belfer-Cohen, Anna, L. Schepartz, and Baruch Arensburg
1991 New Biological Data for the Natufian Populations in Israel. In Ofer Bar-Yosef and François Valla (eds.), pp. 411–424.

Bellwood, Peter
2005 *The First Farmers: The Origins of Agricultural Societies*. Blackwell, Oxford.

Bender, Barbara
1978 Gatherer-Hunter to Farmer: A Social Perspective. *World Archaeology* 10: 204–222.

Bennett, Crystal
1980 Soundings at Dhra', Jordan. *Levant* 12:30–39.

Betts, Alison
1988 The Black Desert Survey: Prehistoric Sites and Subsistence Strategies in Eastern Jordan. In *The Prehistory of Jordan: The State of Research in 1986*, edited by Andrew Garrard and Hans Georg Gebel, pp. 369–392. International Series 396(ii), British Archaeological Reports, Oxford.

1989 The Pre-Pottery Neolithic B Period in Eastern Jordan. *Paléorient* 15:147–153.

1991 The Late Epipaleolithic in the Black Desert, Eastern Jordan. In Ofer Bar-Yosef and François Valla (eds.), pp. 217–234.

Biçakçi, Erhan
1998 An Essay on the Chronology of the Pre-Pottery Neolithic Settlement of the East-Taurus Region (Turkey). In *Light on Top of the Black Hill: Studies Presented to Halet Çambel*, edited by Güven Arsebük, Machteld Mellink, and Wulf Schirmer, pp. 137–150. Ege Yayınları, Istanbul.

Bienert, Hans-Dieter

1991   Skull Cult in the Prehistoric Near East. *Journal of Prehistoric Religion* 5:9–23.

2001   The Pre-Pottery Neolithic B (PPNB) of Jordan: A First Step Towards Proto-Urbanism? In *Studies in the History and Archaeology of Jordan VII*, edited by Ghazi Bisheh, pp. 107–119. Department of Antiquities, Amman.

Bienert, Hans-Dieter, Hans Georg Gebel, and Reinder Neef

2004   *Central Settlements in Neolithic Jordan*. SENEPSE 5, Ex Oriente, Berlin.

Binder, Didier

2002   Stones Making Sense: What Obsidian Could Tell About the Origins of the Central Anatolian Neolithic. In *The Neolithic of Central Turkey*, edited by Frédéric Gérard and Laurens Thissen, pp. 79–90. British Institute of Archaeology at Ankara, Ege Yayınları, Istanbul.

Binford, Lewis

1968   Post-Pleistocene Adaptations. In *New Perspectives in Archaeology*, edited by Sally Binford and Lewis Binford, pp. 313–341. Aldine, Chicago.

1980   Willow Smoke and Dogs' Tails: Hunter-Gatherer Settlement Systems and Site Formation. *American Antiquity* 45:4–20.

2000   Review of *Faunal Extinctions in an Island Society: Pygmy Hippopotamus Hunters of the Akrotiri Peninsula, Cyprus* by Alan H. Simmons. *American Antiquity* 65:771.

Boekschoten, G. J., and Paul Sondaar

1972   On the Fossil Mammals of Cyprus. *Proceedings of the Koninklijke Nederlandse Akademie van Wetenschappen, Series B* 75:306–338.

Bolger, Diane

2003   *Gender in Ancient Cyprus: Narratives of Social Change on a Mediterranean Island*. AltaMira, Walnut Creek, CA.

Bonogofsky, Michelle

2001a   Cranial Modeling and Neolithic Bone Modification at 'Ain Ghazal: New Interpretations. *Paléorient* 272:141–146.

2001b   An Osteo-Archaeological Examination of the Ancestor Cult During the Pre-Pottery Neolithic B Period in the Levant. PhD dissertation, University of California, Berkeley.

Boserup, Ester

1965   *The Conditions of Agricultural Growth*. Allen and Unwin, London.

Bottema, Sytze

2002   The Use of Palynology in Tracing Early Agriculture. In René T. J. Cappers and Sytze Bottema (eds.), pp. 27–38.

Bowler, James, Harvey Johnston, Jon Olley, Robert Prescott, Richard Roberts, Wilfred Shawcross, and Nigel Spooner

2003   New Ages for Human Occupation and Climatic Change at Lake Mungo, Australia. *Nature* 421:837–840.

Boyd, B.
1995   Houses and Hearths, Pits and Burials: Natufian Mortuary Practices at
            Mallaha (Eynan), Upper Jordan Valley. In *Archaeology of Death in the An-
            cient Near East*, edited by Stuart Campbell and Anthony Green, pp. 17–
            23. Oxbow Monograph 51, Oxbow Books, Oxford.

Boyd, Brian, and Jill Cook
1993   A Reconsideration of the 'Ain Sakhri Figurine. *Proceedings of the Prehistoric
            Society* 59:399–405.

Bradley, Daniel, David MacHugh, Patrick Cunningham, and Ronan Loftus
1996   Mitochondrial Diversity and the Origins of African and European Cat-
            tle. *Proceedings of the National Academy of Sciences of the United States of
            America* 93:5131–5135.

Braidwood, Robert
1957   Jericho and Its Setting in Near Eastern History. *Antiquity* 31:73–81.
1960   The Agricultural Revolution. *Scientific American* 203:130–141.
1975   *Prehistoric Men*. Scott, Foresman, Glenview, IL. Originally published
            1948, Chicago Natural History Museum Popular Series, Anthropology
            No. 37, Chicago.

Braidwood, Robert, and Bruce Howe
1960   *Prehistoric Investigations in Iraqi Kurdistan*. Studies in Ancient Oriental
            Civilization No. 31. Oriental Institute of the University of Chicago, Chi-
            cago.

Braidwood, Robert, Jonathan Sauer, Hans Helbaek, Paul Mangelsdorf, Hugh Cutler,
Carleton Coon, Ralph Linton, Julian Steward, and A. Leo Oppenheim
1953   Symposium: Did Man Once Live by Beer Alone? *American Anthropologist*
            55: 515–526.

Braidwood, Robert, and Gordon Willey
1962   *Courses Toward Urban Life: Archaeological Considerations of Some Cultural
            Alternates*. Aldine, Chicago.

Briois, François
2003   Nature et évolution des industries lithiques de *Shillourokambos*. In Jean
            Guilaine and Alain LeBrun (eds.), pp. 121–133.

Briois, François, B. Gratuze, and Jean Guilaine
1997   Obsidiennes du site néolithique précéramique de *Shillourokambos*, Chy-
            pre. *Paléorient* 23:95–112.

Broodbank, Cyprian
1999   Colonization and Configuration in the Insular Neolithic of the Aegean.
            In *Neolithic Society in Greece*, edited by Paul Halstead, pp. 15–41. Sheffield
            Studies in Aegean Archaeology 2, Sheffield Academic Press, Sheffield.
2000   *An Island Archaeology of the Early Cyclades*. Cambridge University Press,
            Cambridge.

Bunimovitz, Shlomo, and Ran Barkai
1996   Ancient Bones and Modern Myths: Ninth Millennium BC Hippopota-

mus Hunters at Akrotiri Aetokremnos, Cyprus? *Journal of Mediterranean Archaeology* 9:85–96.

Butzer, Karl
    1996   Ecology in the Long View: Settlement Histories, Agrosystemic Strategies, and Ecological Performance. *Journal of Field Archaeology* 23:141–150.

Buzy, D.
    1928   Une industrie mésolithique en Palestine. *Revue Biblique* 37:558–578.

Byrd, Brian
    1984   Late Quaternary Hunter-Gatherer Complexes in the Levant Between 20,000 and 10,000 B.P. In *Late Quaternary Chronology and Paleoclimates of the Eastern Mediterranean*, edited by Ofer Bar-Yosef and Renée S. Kra, pp. 205–226. Radiocarbon, Tucson.

    1989a   The Natufian: Settlement Variability and Economic Adaptations in the Levant at the End of the Pleistocene. *Journal of World Prehistory* 3:159–197.

    1989b   *The Natufian Encampment at Beidha: Late Pleistocene Adaptation in the Southern Levant*. Jutland Archeological Society Publications 23:1, Jysk arkæologisk selskab, Højbjerg, Denmark.

    1992   The Dispersal of Food Production Across the Levant. In *Transitions to Agriculture in Prehistory*, edited by Anne Gebauer and T. Douglas Price, pp. 49–61. Monographs in World Archaeology No. 4, Prehistory Press, Madison.

    1994   Public and Private, Domestic and Corporate: The Emergence of the Southwest Asian Village. *American Antiquity* 59:639–666.

    2000   Households in Transition: Neolithic Social Organization Within Southwest Asia. In Ian Kuijt (ed.), pp. 63–98.

    2005a   Reassessing the Emergence of Village Life in the Near East. *Journal of Archaeological Research* 13:231–290.

    2005b   *Early Village Life at Beidha, Jordan: Neolithic Spatial Organization and Vernacular Architecture*. British Academy Monographs in Archaeology No. 14, Oxford University Press, Oxford.

Byrd, Brian, and Edward Banning
    1988   Southern Levantine Pier Houses: Intersite Architectural Patterning During the Pre-Pottery Neolithic B. *Paléorient* 14:65–72.

Byrd, Brian, and Susan Colledge
    1991   Early Natufian Occupation Along the Edge of the Southern Jordanian Steppe. In Ofer Bar-Yosef and François Valla (eds.), pp. 265–276.

Byrd, Brian, and Christopher Monahan
    1995   Death, Mortuary Ritual, and Natufian Social Structure. *Journal of Anthropological Archaeology* 14:251–287.

Caneva, Isabella, Cristini Lemorini, Daniela Zampetti, and Paolo Biagi
    2001   *Beyond Tools: Redefining the PPN Lithic Assemblages of the Levant*. SENEPSE 9, Ex Oriente, Berlin.

Cappers, René T. J., and Sytze Bottema (editors)

2002   *The Dawn of Farming in the Near East.* Studies in Early Near Eastern Production, Subsistence, and Environment 6, 1999, Ex Oriente, Berlin.

Cauvin, Jacques

2000a   *The Birth of the Gods and the Origins of Agriculture.* Translated by Trevor
Watkins. Cambridge University Press, Cambridge. Originally published
1994, *Naissance des divinités, naissance de l'agriculture*, CNRS, Paris.

2000b   The Symbolic Foundations of the Neolithic Revolution in the Near East.
In Ian Kuijt (ed.), pp. 235-251.

Cauvin, Marie-Claire

1984   L'outillage lithique de Khirokitia (Chypre) et le Levant. In *Fouilles récentes à Khirokitia (Chypre), 1977-1981*, edited by Alain LeBrun, pp. 85-87.
Mémoire No. 41, Éditions Recherche sur les civilisations, Paris.

1991   Du Natoufien au Levant nord? Jayroud et Mureybet (Syrie). In Ofer
Bar-Yosef and François Valla (eds.), pp. 295-314.

1994   Synthèses sur les industries lithiques Néolithique Précéramique en
Syrie. In *Neolithic Chipped Stone Industries of the Fertile Crescent*, edited by
Hans Georg Gebel and Stefan Kozłowski, pp. 279-297. SENEPSE 1,
Ex Oriente, Berlin.

Cerón-Carrasco, Ruby

2003   Fish Remains. In Edgar Peltenburg (ed.), pp. 81-82.

Chang, Claudia

1994   Sheep for the Ancestors: Ethnoarchaeology and the Study of Ancient
Pastoralism. In *Beyond the Site: Regional Studies in the Aegean Area*, edited
by Nicholas Kardulias, pp. 353-371. University Press of America, Lan-
ham, MD.

Chapman, J.

1991   The Creation of Social Arenas in the Neolithic and Copper Age of SE
Europe: The Case of Varna. In *Sacred and Profane*, edited by Paul Gar-
wood, David Jennings, R. G. Skeates, and Judith Toms, pp. 152-171.
Oxford University Committee for Archaeology Monograph 32, Institute
of Archaeology, Oxford.

Chataigner, Christine, Jean-Louis Poidevin, and N. O. Arnaud

1998   Turkish Occurrences of Obsidian and Use by Prehistoric Peoples in the
Near East from 14,000 to 6000 BP. *Journal of Volcanology and Geothermal
Research* 85:517-537.

Cherry, John

1981   Pattern and Process in the Earliest Colonisation of the Mediterranean
Islands. *Proceedings of the Prehistoric Society* 47:41-68.

1990   The First Colonization of the Mediterranean Islands: A Review of Recent Research. *Journal of Mediterranean Archaeology* 3:145-221.

1992   Paleolithic Sardinians? Some Questions of Evidence and Method. In
Sardinia in the Mediterranean: A Footprint in the Sea, edited by Robert H.

Tykot and Tamsey K. Andrews, pp. 29–39. Monographs in Mediterranean Archaeology 3, Sheffield Academic Press, Oxford.

Childe, V. Gordon
    1936   *Man Makes Himself.* Watts, London.

Clarke, Joanne
    2001   Style and Society in Ceramic Neolithic Cyprus. *Levant* 33:65–80.
    2003   Insularity and Identity in Prehistoric Cyprus. In Jean Guilaine and Alain LeBrun (eds.), pp. 203–218.

Cohen, Mark
    1977   *The Food Crisis in Prehistory: Overpopulation and the Origins of Agriculture.* Yale University Press, New Haven.

Cohen, Mark, and George Armelagos
    1984   *Paleopathology at the Origins of Agriculture.* Academic Press, New York.

Colledge, Sue
    2001   *Plant Exploitation on Epipaleolithic and Early Neolithic Sites in the Levant.* International Series No. 986, British Archaeological Reports, Oxford.
    2002   Identifying Pre-Domestication Cultivation in the Archaeobotanical Record Using Multivariate Analysis: Presenting the Case for Quantification. In René T. J. Cappers and Sytze Bottema (eds.), pp. 141–152.
    2004   Reappraisal of the Archaeobotanical Evidence for the Emergence and Dispersal of the "Founder Crops." In Edgar Peltenburg and Alexander Wasse (eds.), pp. 49–60.

Colledge, Sue, James Conolly, and Stephen Shennan
    2004   Archaeobotanical Evidence for the Spread of Farming in the Eastern Mediterranean [and comments]. *Current Anthropology* 45 (supp.):35–58.

Cooperative Holocene Mapping Project (COHMAP)
    1988   Climatic Changes of the Last 18,000 Years: Observations and Model Simulation. *Science* 241:1043–1052.

Cope, Carol
    1991   Gazelle Hunting Strategies in the Southern Levant. In Ofer Bar-Yosef and François Valla (eds.), pp. 341–358.

Copeland, Lorraine
    1991   Natufian Sites in Lebanon. In Ofer Bar-Yosef and François Valla (eds.), pp. 27–42.

Coppa, Alfredo, Luca Bondioli, Andrea Cucina, David W. Frayer, Catherine Jarrige, Jean-François Jarrige, Gonzague Quivron, Massimo Rossi, M. Vidale, and Roberto Macchiarelli
    2006   Early Neolithic Tradition of Dentistry. *Nature* 440:755–776.

Coqueugniot, Éric
    1983   Analyse tracéologique d'une série de grattoirs et herminettes de Mureybet, Syrie (IXe–IVVe millénaires). In *Traces d'utilisation sur les outiles néolithiques du Proche-Orient*, Marie-Claire Cauvin, ed., pp. 139–172. Travaux de la Maison de l'Orient 3, Maison de l'Orient, Lyon.

Cornwall, Ian
  1981   The Pre-Pottery Neolithic Burials. In *Excavations at Jericho: 3. The Archi-
            tecture and Stratigraphy of the Tell*, edited by Thomas Holland, pp. 395–406.
            British School of Archaeology in Jerusalem, London.
Cowan, C. Wesley, and Patty Jo Watson (editors)
  1992   *The Origins of Agriculture: An International Perspective*. Smithsonian Institu-
            tion Press, Washington, DC, and London.
Crabtree, Pamela
  1991   Gender Hierarchies and the Sexual Division of Labor in the Natufian
            Culture of the Southern Levant. In *The Archaeology of Gender*, edited by
            Dale Walde and Noreen D. Willows, pp. 384–391. University of Calgary
            Archaeological Association, Calgary.
Cressey, George
  1960   *Crossroads: Land and Life in Southwest Asia*. Lippincott, Chicago.
Croft, Paul
  1989   The Osteology of Neolithic and Chalcolithic Cyprus. Unpublished Ph.D.
            dissertation, University of Cambridge, Cambridge.
  1991   Man and Beast in Chalcolithic Cyprus. *Bulletin of the American Schools of
            Oriental Research* 282/283:63–79.
  2003a   The Wells and Other Vestiges. In Edgar Peltenburg (ed.), pp. 3–9.
  2003b   The Animal Bones. In Edgar Peltenburg (ed.), pp. 49–58.
  2003c   Water-Holes and Cowboys—Animal Remains from the Paphian Neo-
            lithic. In Jean Guilaine and Alain LeBrun (eds.), pp. 269–278.
Crowfoot-Payne, Joan
  1983   The Flint Industries of Jericho. In *Excavations at Jericho*, edited by Kath-
            leen M. Kenyon and Thomas A. Holland, pp. 622–759. British School
            of Archaeology in Jerusalem, London.
Crubézy, Éric, Jean-Denis Vigne, Jean Guilaine, Thierry Giraud, Patrice Gérard,
  and François Briois
  2003   Aux origines des sépultures collectives: la structure 23 de *Shillourokambos*
            (Chypre, 7500 B.C.). In Jean Guilaine and Alain LeBrun (eds.), pp.
            295–311.
Davies, William, and Ruth Charles (editors)
  1999   *Dorothy Garrod and the Progress of the Palaeolithic*. Oxbow, Oxford.
Davis, Jonathan, Alan Simmons, Rolfe Mandel, Gary Rollefson, and Zeidan Kafafi
  1990   A Postulated Early Holocene Summer Precipitation Episode in the Le-
            vant: Effects on Neolithic Adaptations. Paper presented at the 55th An-
            nual Meeting of the Society for American Archaeology, Las Vegas.
Davis, Simon
  1983   The Age Profiles of Gazelles Predated by Ancient Man in Israel: Pos-
            sible Evidence for a Shift from Seasonality to Sedentism in the Natufian.
            Paléorient 9:55–62.
  2003   The Zooarchaeology of Khirokitia (Neolithic Cyprus), Including a View

from the Mainland. In Jean Guilaine and Alain LeBrun (eds.), pp. 253–268.

Davis, Simon, and François Valla
1978   Evidence for the Domestication of the Dog 12,000 Years Ago in the Natufian of Israel. *Nature* 276:608–610.

Dayan, Tamar
1994   Early Domesticated Dogs of the Near East. *Journal of Archaeological Sciences* 21:633–640.

Dayan, Tamar, and Daniel Simberloff
1995   Natufian Gazelles: Proto-Domestication Reconsidered. *Journal of Archaeological Sciences* 22:671–675.

De Cupere, Bea, and Refik Duru
2003   Faunal Remains from Neolithic Höyüek (SW-Turkey) and the Presence of Early Domestic Cattle in Anatolia. *Paléorient* 291:107–120.

Delage, Christophe (editor)
2004   *The Last Hunter-Gatherers in the Near East*. International Series 1320, British Archaeological Reports, Oxford.

Dennis, Samantha
2003   The Experimental Reconstruction of a Pre-Pottery Neolithic B Structure at Beidha — A Visual Introduction. *Levant* 35:39–48.

Desse, Jean, and Nathalie Desse-Bersert
2003   Les premiers pêcheurs de Chypre. In Jean Guilaine and Alain LeBrun (eds.), pp. 279–291.

Diamond, Jared
1997   *Guns, Germs, and Steel: The Fates of Human Societies*. Norton, New York.
2002   Evolution, Consequences and Future of Plant and Animal Domestication. *Nature* 418:700–707.
2005   *Collapse: How Societies Choose to Fail or Succeed*. Viking Penguin, New York.

Diamond, Jared, and Peter Bellwood
2003   Farmers and Their Languages: The First Expansions. *Science* 300:597–603.

Dikaios, Porphyrios
1961   *Sotira*. Museum Monograph 4, University Museum, University of Pennsylvania, Philadelphia.

Dubreuil, Laure
2004   Long-Term Trends in Natufian Subsistence: A Use-Wear Analysis of Ground Stone Tools. *Journal of Archaeological Science* 31:1613–1629.

Ducos, Pierre
1968   *L'origine des animaux domestiques en Palestine*. Mémoire No. 6, Institut de préhistoire de l'Université de Bordeaux, Bordeaux.
2000   The Introduction of Animals by Man in Cyprus: An Alternative to the Noah's Ark Model. In *Archaeozoology of the Near East IVA*, edited by Marjan Mashkour, Alice M. Choyke, Hijlke Buitenhuis, and François Poplin, pp. 74–82. Publication 32, Archaeological Research Center, Groningen.

Echegaray, Gomez
  1966   *Excavation en la terraza de El-Khiam (Jordania)*, part II. Casa Espanola de Santiago en Jerusalem, Madrid.
Edwards, Phillip
  1989   Revising the Broad Spectrum Revolution: Its Role in the Origins of Southwest Asian Food Production. *Antiquity* 68:225-246.
  1991   Wadi Hammeh 27: An Early Natufian Site at Pella, Jordan. In Ofer Bar-Yosef and François Valla (eds.), pp. 123-148.
Edwards, Phillip, and Tom Higham
  2001   Zahrat adh-Drha‘ 2 and the Dead Sea Plain at the Dawn of the Holocene. In *Australians Uncovering Ancient Jordan: Fifty Years of Middle Eastern Archaeology*, edited by Alan Walmsley, pp. 139-152. Research Institute for Humanities and Social Sciences, University of Sydney, Sydney.
Edwards, Phillip, John Meadows, Ghattas Sayej, and Mary Metzer
  2002   Zahrat Adh-Dhra‘ 2: A New Pre-Pottery Neolithic A Site on the Dead Sea Plain. *Bulletin of the American Schools of Oriental Research* 327:1-15.
Eirikh-Rose, Anna
  2004   Geometric Patterns on Pebbles: Early Identity Symbols? In Edgar Peltenburg and Alexander Wasse (eds.), pp. 145-162.
El-Najjar, Mohammad, Abdel Halim Al-Shiyab, and I. Al-Sarie
  1997   Cases of Tuberculosis at ‘Ain Ghazal, Jordan. *Paléorient* 22:123-128.
Eshed, Vered, Avi Gopher, Timothy Gage, and Israel Hershkovitz
  2004   Has the Transition to Agriculture Reshaped the Demographic Structure of Prehistoric Populations? New Evidence from the Levant. *American Journal of Physical Anthropology* 124:315-329.
Eshed, Vered, Avi Gopher, Ehud Galili, and Israel Hershkovitz
  2004   Musculoskeletal Stress Markers in Natufian Hunter-Gatherers and Neolithic Farmers in the Levant: The Upper Limb. *American Journal of Physical Anthropology* 123:303-315.
Esin, Ufuk
  1999   Introduction—The Neolithic in Turkey: A General Review. In Mehmet Özdoğan and Nezih Başgelen (eds.), pp. 13-23.
Evans, John
  1977   Island Archaeology in the Mediterranean: Problems and Opportunities. *World Archaeology* 9:12-26.
Fagan, Brian
  2004   *The Long Summer: How Climate Changed Civilization*. Basic Books, New York.
Fiedel, Stuart, and David Anthony
  2003   Deerslayers, Pathfinders, and Icemen: Origins of the European Neolithic as Seen from the Frontier. In *Colonization of Unfamiliar Landscapes: The Archaeology of Adaptation*, edited by Marcy Rockman and James Steele, pp. 144-168. Routledge, London and New York.

Finlayson, Bill
    2004   Island Colonization, Insularity or Mainstream? In Edgar Peltenburg
        and Alexander Wasse (eds.), pp. 15–22.
Finlayson, Bill, Ian Kuijt, Trina Arpin, Meredith S. Chesson, Samantha Dennis,
    Nathan Goodale, Seiji Kadowaki, Lisa Maher, Samuel Smith, Mark Schurr, and
    Jode McKay
    2003   Dhra, Excavation Project, 2002 Interim Report. *Levant* 35:1–38.
Finlayson, Bill, Steven Mithen, Denise Carruthers, Amanda Kennedy, Anne Pirie,
    and Richard Tipping
    2000   The Dana-Faynan-Ghuwayr Early Prehistory Project. *Levant* 32:1–26.
Fish, Suzanne, and Paul Fish
    1991   Comparative Aspects of Paradigms for the Neolithic Transition in the
        Levant and the American Southwest. In *Perspectives on the Past: Theoreti-*
        cal Biases in Mediterranean Hunter-Gatherer Research, edited by Geoffrey
        Clark, pp. 396–410. University of Pennsylvania Press, Philadelphia.
Flannery, Kent
    1968   Archaeological Systems Theory and Early Meso-America. In *Anthropo-*
        logical Archaeology in the Americas, edited by Betty Meggars, pp. 67–87.
        Anthropological Society of Washington, Washington, DC.
    1969   Origins and Ecological Effects of Early Domestication in Iran and the
        Near East. In *The Domestication and Exploitation of Plants and Animals*,
        edited by Peter Ucko and George Dimbleby, pp. 73–100. Aldine, Lon-
        don.
    1972   The Origins of the Village as a Settlement Type in Mesoamerica and
        the Near East: A Comparative Study. In *Man, Settlement and Urbanism*,
        edited by Peter Ucko, Ruth Tringham, and George Dimbleby, pp. 23–53.
        Duckworth, London.
    1973   The Origins of Agriculture. *Annual Review of Anthropology* 2:271–301.
    1993   Will the Real Model Please Stand Up: Comments on Saidel's "Round
        House or Square?" *Journal of Mediterranean Archaeology* 6:109–117.
    2002   The Origins of the Village Revisited: From Nuclear to Extended House-
        holds. *American Antiquity* 67:417–433.
Flourentzos, Pavlos
    2003   Paralimni-Nissia: A Unique Neolithic Settlement in Cyprus. In Jean
        Guilaine and Alain LeBrun (eds.), pp. 73–83.
Fox, Sherry, Dorothy Lunt, and Marie Watt
    2003   Human Remains. In Edgar Peltenburg (ed.), pp. 43–47.
Fox, William
    1987   The Neolithic Occupation of Western Cyprus. In *Western Cyprus: Con-*
        nections, edited by David Rupp, pp. 19–44. Studies in Mediterranean Ar-
        chaeology Vol. 77. Paul Åströms Förlag, Göteborg.
Frame, Sheilagh
    2002   Island Neolithics: Animal Exploitation in the Aceramic Neolithic of Cy-
        prus. In *World Islands in Prehistory*, edited by William Waldren and J. A.

Ensenyat, pp. 233–238. International Series 1095, British Archaeological Reports, Oxford.

Galili, Ehud, Avi Gopher, Baruch Rosen, and Liora Kolska Horwitz
2004   The Emergence of the Mediterranean Fishing Village in the Levant and the Anomaly of Neolithic Cyprus. In Edgar Peltenburg and Alexander Wasse (eds.), pp. 91–101.

Galili, Ehud, Mina Weinstein-Evron, Israel Hershkovitz, Avi Gopher, Mordecai Kislev, Omri Lernau, Liora Kolska-Horwitz, and Hanan Lernau
1993   Atlit-Yam: A Prehistoric Site on the Sea Floor off the Israeli Coast. *Journal of Field Archaeology* 20:133–157.

Garfinkel, Yosef
1994   Ritual Burial of Cultic Objects: The Earliest Evidence. *Cambridge Archaeological Journal* 4:159–188.

1996   Critical Observations on the So-Called Khiamian Flint Industry. In *Neolithic Chipped Stone Industries of the Fertile Crescent, and Their Contemporaries in Adjacent Regions: Proceedings of the Second Workshop on PPN Chipped Lithic Industries, Warsaw University, 3rd–7th April 1995*, edited by Stefan Kozłowski and Hans Georg Gebel, pp. 15–21. SENEPSE 3, Ex Oriente, Berlin.

1999a   *Neolithic and Chalcolithic Pottery of the Southern Levant.* QEDEM 39, Institute of Archaeology, Hebrew University of Jerusalem, Jerusalem.

1999b   *The Yarmukians: Neolithic Art from Sha'ar Hagolan.* Bible Lands Museum, Jerusalem.

2002   Conclusions: The Effect of Population Size on the Human Organization at Sha'ar Hagolan. In Yosef Garfinkel and Michele Miller 2002b, pp. 257–262.

2003a   *Dancing at the Dawn of Agriculture.* University of Texas Press, Austin.

2003b   The Earliest Dancing Scenes in the Near East. *Near Eastern Archaeology* 66:84–95.

Garfinkel, Yosef, and David Ben-Shlomo
2002a   Architecture and Village Planning in Area E. In Yosef Garfinkel and Michele Miller 2002b, pp. 55–70.

2002b   Sha'ar Hagolan Architecture in Its Near Eastern Context. In Yosef Garfinkel and Michele Miller 2002b, pp. 71–84.

Garfinkel, Yosef, Naomi Korn, and Michele Miller
2002   Art from Sha'ar Hagolan: Visions of a Neolithic Village in the Levant. In Yosef Garfinkel and Michele Miller 2002b, pp. 188–208.

Garfinkel, Yosef, and Michele Miller
2002a   Introduction. In *Sha'ar Hagolan 1: Neolithic Art in Context*, by Yosef Garfinkel and Michele Miller, pp. 1–9. Oxbow Books, Oxford.

2002b   *Sha'ar Hagolan 1: Neolithic Art in Context.* Oxbow Books, Oxford.

Garrard, Andrew
1991   Natufian Settlement in the Azraq Basin, Eastern Jordan. In Ofer Bar-Yosef and François Valla (eds.), pp. 235–244.

1999   Charting the Emergence of Cereal and Pulse Domestication in South-
           West Asia. *Environmental Archaeology* 18:47–62.

Garrard, Andrew, Douglas Baird, and Brian Byrd
1994   The Chronological Basis and Significance of the Late Paleolithic and
           Neolithic Sequence in the Azraq Basin, Jordan. In *Late Quaternary Chro-
           nology and Paleoclimates of the Eastern Mediterranean*, edited by Ofer Bar-
           Yosef and Renée S. Kra, pp. 177–199. Radiocarbon, University of Ari-
           zona, Tucson.

Garrard, Andrew, Susan Colledge, and Louise Martin
1996   The Emergence of Crop Cultivation and Caprine Herding in the "Mar-
           ginal Zone" of the Southern Levant. In *The Origins and Spread of Agri-
           culture and Pastoralism in Eurasia*, edited by David Harris, pp. 204–226.
           Smithsonian Press, Washington, DC.

Garrod, Dorothy
1932   A New Mesolithic Industry: The Natufian of Palestine. *Journal of the
           Royal Anthropological Institute* 62:257–269.
1957   The Natufian Culture: The Life and Economy of a Mesolithic People in
           the Near East. *Proceedings of the British Academy* 43:211–227.

Garrod, Dorothy, and Dorothea Bate
1937   *The Stone Age of Mount Carmel.* Clarendon Press, Oxford.

Garstang, John, and J. B. E. Garstang
1940   *The Story of Jericho.* Hodder and Stoughton, London.

Gebauer, Anne, and T. Douglas Price (editors)
1992   *Transitions to Agriculture in Prehistory.* Monographs in World Archaeology
           No. 4, Prehistory Press, Madison.

Gebel, Hans Georg
2002   Walls. Loci of Forces. In *Magic Practices and Ritual in the Near Eastern Neo-
           lithic*, edited by Hans Georg Gebel, Bo Hermansen, and Charlott Jensen,
           pp. 119–132. SENEPSE 8, Ex Oriente, Berlin.

Gebel, Hans Georg, and Bo Hermansen
1999   Ba'ja Neolithic Project 1999: Short Report on Architectural Findings.
           Neolithics 3:18–21.

Gebel, Hans Georg, Bo Hermansen, and Charlott Jensen (editors)
2002   *Magic Practices and Ritual in the Near Eastern Neolithic.* SENEPSE 8, Ex
           Oriente, Berlin.

Gebel, Hans Georg, and Stefan Kozłowski (editors)
1994   *Neolithic Chipped Stone Industries of the Fertile Crescent.* SENEPSE 1, Ex
           Oriente, Berlin.

Gérard, Frédéric, and Laurens Thissen (editors)
2002   *The Neolithic of Central Turkey.* British Institute of Archaeology at Ankara,
           Ege Yayınları, Istanbul.

Gimbutas, Maria
1982   *The Goddesses and Gods of Old Europe, 6500–3500 B.C.* Thames and Hudson,
           London.

Gopher, Avi

1994   *Arrowheads of the Neolithic Levant.* American Schools of Oriental Research, Dissertation Series Vol. 10, Eisenbrauns, Winona Lake, IN.

1998   Early Pottery-Bearing Groups in Israel — The Pottery Neolithic Period. In *The Archaeology of the Holy Land*, edited by Thomas Levy, pp. 205–225. Leicester University Press, London and Washington.

Gopher, Avi, and Ram Gophna

1993   Cultures of the Eighth and Seventh Millennia BP in the Southern Levant: A Review for the 1990s. *Journal of World Prehistory* 7:297–353.

Gopher, Avi, and Yuval Goren

1998   The Beginning of Pottery. In *The Archaeology of the Holy Land*, edited by Thomas Levy, pp. 224–225. Leicester University Press, London and Washington.

Gopher, Avi, and Nigel Goring-Morris

1998   Abu Salem: A Pre-Pottery Neolithic B Camp in the Central Negev Highlands, Israel. *Bulletin of the American Schools of Oriental Research* 312:1–20.

Gopher, Avi, and Estelle Orrelle

1995   New Data on Burials from the Pottery Neolithic Period (Sixth–Fifth Millennium BC) in Israel. In *The Archaeology of Death in the Ancient Near East*, edited by Stuart Campbell and Anthony Green, pp. 24–28. Oxbow Books, Oxford.

1996   An Alternative Interpretation for the Material Imagery of the Yarmukian, a Neolithic Culture of the Sixth Millennium BC in the Southern Levant. *Cambridge Archaeological Journal* 6:255–279.

1998   Yarmukian Imagery. In *The Archaeology of the Holy Land*, edited by Thomas Levy, pp. 222–223. Leicester University Press, London and Washington.

Goren, Yuval, Nigel Goring-Morris, and Irena Segal

2001   The Technology of Skull Modeling in the Pre-Pottery Neolithic B (PPNB): Regional Variability, the Relation of Technology and Iconography and Their Archaeological Implications. *Journal of Archaeological Science* 28:671–690.

Goring-Morris, Nigel

1991   The Harifian of the Southern Levant. In Ofer Bar-Yosef and François Valla (eds.), pp. 173–216.

1998   Complex Hunter/Gatherers at the End of the Paleolithic (20,000–10,000 BP). In *The Archaeology of the Holy Land*, edited by Thomas Levy, pp. 141–168. Leicester University Press, London and Washington.

2000   The Quick and the Dead: The Social Context of Aceramic Neolithic Mortuary Practices as Seen from Kfar Hahoresh. In Ian Kuijt (ed.), pp. 103–136.

Goring-Morris, Nigel, and Anna Belfer-Cohen

1998   The Articulation of Cultural Processes and Late Quaternary Environmental Changes in Cisjordan. *Paléorient* 23:71–93.

2002   Symbolic Behaviour from the Epipalaeolithic and Early Neolithic of the Near East: Preliminary Observations on Continuity and Change. In *Magic Practices and Ritual in the Near Eastern Neolithic*, edited by Hans Georg Gebel, Bo Hermansen, and Charlott Jensen, pp. 67–79. SENEPSE 8, Ex Oriente, Berlin.

Goring-Morris, Nigel, Rosemary Burns, Angela Davidson, Vered Eshed, Yuval Goren, Israel Hershkovitz, Steve Kangas, and Julija Kelecevic
1998   The 1997 Season of Excavations at the Mortuary Site of Kfar HaHoresh, Galilee, Israel. *Neolithics* 3:1–4.

Grindell, Beth
1998   Unmasked Equalities: An Example of Mortuary Practices and Social Complexity in the Levantine Natufian and Pre-Pottery Neolithic. Ph.D. dissertation, University of Arizona, Tucson. University Microfilms, Ann Arbor.

Grosman, Leore, and Anna Belfer-Cohen
2002   Zooming onto the "Younger Dryas." In René T. J. Cappers and Sytze Bottema (eds.), pp. 49–54.

Groube, Les
1996   The Impact of Disease upon the Emergence of Agriculture. In *The Origins and Spread of Agriculture and Pastoralism in Eurasia*, edited by David Harris, pp. 101–129. Smithsonian Press, Washington, DC.

Guilaine, Jean
2003a   Parekklisha-*Shillourokambos*: périodisation et aménagements domestiques. In Jean Guilaine and Alain LeBrun (eds.), pp. 4–14.
2003b   Objets "symboliques" et parures de Parekklisha-Shillourokambos. In Jean Guilaine and Alain LeBrun (eds.), pp. 329–340.

Guilaine, Jean, and François Briois
2001   Parekklisha *Shillourokambos*: An Early Neolithic Site in Cyprus. In Stuart Swiny (ed.), pp. 37–53.

Guilaine, Jean, P. Devèze, J. Coularou, and François Briois
1999   Tête sculptée en pierre dans le Néolithique Pré-céramique de Shillourokambos (Parekklisha, Chypre). *Report of the Department of Antiquities, Cyprus*: 1–12.

Guilaine, Jean, and Alain LeBrun (editors)
2003   *Le Néolithique de Chypre*. Bulletin de correspondance hellénique supp. 43. École française d'Athènes, Athens.

Guilaine, Jean, and Jean Zammit
2005   *The Origins of War: Violence in Prehistory*. Blackwell, Oxford.

Haak, Wolfgang, Peter Forster, Barbara Bramanti, Schichi Matsumura, Guido Brandt, Marc Tänzer, Richard Villems, Colin Renfrew, Detlef Gronenborn, Kurt Werner Alt, and Joachim Burger
2005   Ancient DNA from the First European Farmers in 7500-Year-Old Neolithic Sites. *Science* 310:1016–1018.

Hahn, Eduard
1896 *Die Haustiere und ihre Beziehungen zur Wirtschaft des Menschen*. Duncker and Humblot, Leipzig.
Hansen, Julie
1991 Paleoethnobotany in Cyprus: Recent Developments. In *New Light on Early Farming: Recent Developments in Paleoethnobotany*, edited by Jane Renfrew, pp. 225–236. Edinburgh University Press, Edinburgh.
2001 Aceramic Neolithic Plant Remains in Cyprus: Clues to Their Origins? In Stuart Swiny (ed.), pp. 119–128.
Harlan, Jack
1967 A Wild Wheat Harvest in Turkey. *Archaeology* 20:197–201.
Harlan, Jack, and Daniel Zohary
1966 Distribution of Wild Wheats and Barley. *Science* 153:1075–1080.
Harper, Nathan
2003 A Multivariate Analysis of Archaeological Cypriot Populations: Relative Biological Relationships in the Eastern Mediterranean. Master's thesis, Dept. of Anthropology, Wichita State University, Wichita.
Harris, David
1989 An Evolutionary Continuum of People-Plant Interaction. In *Foraging and Farming: The Evolution of Plant Exploitation*, edited by David Harris and Gordon Hillman, pp. 11–26. Unwin Hyman, London.
1990 *Settling Down and Breaking Ground: Rethinking the Neolithic Revolution*. Twaalfe Kroon-Voordracht, Amsterdam.
Harris, David (editor)
1996 *The Origins and Spread of Agriculture and Pastoralism in Eurasia*. Smithsonian Press, Washington, DC.
Harris, David, and Gordon Hillman (editors)
1989 *Foraging and Farming: The Evolution of Plant Exploitation*. Unwin Hyman, London.
Hassan, Fekri
1981 *Demographic Archaeology*. Academic Press, New York.
Hayden, Brian
1981 Research and Development in the Stone Age: Technological Transitions Among Hunter-Gatherers. *Current Anthropology* 22:519–548.
1990 Nimrods, Piscators, Pluckers, and Planters: The Emergence of Food Production. *Journal of Anthropological Archaeology* 9:31–69.
1992 Models of Domestication. In *Transitions to Agriculture in Prehistory*, edited by Anne Gebauer and T. Douglas Price, pp. 11–19. Monographs in World Archaeology No. 4, Prehistory Press, Madison.
1995 An Overview of Domestication. In *Last Hunters, First Farmers: New Perspectives on the Prehistoric Transition to Agriculture*, edited by T. Douglas Price and Anne Gebauer, pp. 273–299. School of American Research Press, Santa Fe.

2001   Fabulous Feasts: A Prolegomenon to the Importance of Feasting. In
            Feasts: Archaeological Perspectives on Food, Politics, and Power, edited by
            Michael Dietler and Brian Hayden, pp. 3–64. Smithsonian Institution
            Press, Washington, DC.

2003   Were Luxury Foods the First Domesticates? Ethnoarchaeological Per-
            spectives from Southeast Asia. *World Archaeology* 34:458–469.

Held, Steve
    1982   The Earliest Prehistory of Cyprus. In *An Archaeological Guide to the Ancient
            Kourion Area and the Akrotiri Peninsula*, edited by Helena Swiny, pp. 6–11.
            Department of Antiquities, Cyprus, Nicosia.

    1989a   Colonization Cycles on Cyprus, 1: The Biogeographic and Paleontologi-
            cal Foundations of Early Prehistoric Settlement. *Report of the Department
            of Antiquities, Cyprus, 1989*: 7–28.

    1989b   Early Prehistoric Island Archaeology in Cyprus: Configurations of For-
            mative Culture Growth from the Pleistocene/Holocene Boundary to the
            Mid-3rd Millennium B.C. Unpublished Ph.D. dissertation, Institute of
            Archaeology, University College, University of London.

    1990   Back to What Future? New Directions for Cypriot Early Prehistoric Re-
            search in the 1990s. *Report of the Department of Antiquities, Cyprus, 1990*:
            1–43.

Helmer, Daniel, Lionel Gourichon, Hervé Monchot, Joris Peters, and Maria Saña
Segui
    2005   Identifying Early Domestic Cattle from Pre-Pottery Neolithic Sites on
            the Middle Euphrates Using Sexual Dimorphism. In *The First Steps of
            Animal Domestication*, edited by Jean-Denis Vigne, Joris Peters, and
            Daniel Helmer, pp. 86–95. Oxbow Books, Oxford.

Henry, Donald
    1975   The Fauna in Near Eastern Archaeological Deposits. In *Problems in Pre-
            history: North Africa and the Levant*, edited by Fred Wendorf and Anthony
            Marks, pp. 379–385. Southern Methodist University Press, Dallas.

    1983   Adaptive Evolution Within the Epipaleolithic of the Near East. In *Ad-
            vances in World Archaeology*, vol. 2, edited by Fred Wendorf and Angela
            Close, pp. 99–160. Academic Press, London.

    1989   *From Foraging to Agriculture: The Levant at the End of the Ice Age*. University
            of Pennsylvania Press, Philadelphia.

    2002   Models of Agricultural Origins and Proxy Measures of Prehistoric
            Demographics. In René T. J. Cappers and Sytze Bottema (eds.), pp. 15–
            25.

Henry, Donald, Carlos Cordova, Joel White, Rebecca Dean, Joseph Beaver, Heidi
Ekstrom, Seiji Kadowaki, Joy McCorriston, April Nowell, and Linda Scott-
Cummings
    2003   The Early Neolithic Site of Ayn Abū Nukhayla, Southern Jordan. *Bul-
            letin of the American Schools of Oriental Research* 330:1–30.

Hermansen, Bo, and Charlott Jensen
2002   Notes on Some Features of Possible Ritual Significance at MPPNB
        Shararat Mazyad, Southern Jordan. In *Magic Practices and Ritual in the
        Near Eastern Neolithic*, edited by Hans Georg Gebel, Bo Hermansen, and
        Charlott Jensen, pp. 91–101. SENEPSE 8, Ex Oriente, Berlin.
Hershkovitz, Israel, and Ehud Galili
1990   8,000-Year-Old Human Remains on the Sea Floor near Atlit, Israel.
        Human Evolution 5:319–358.
Hershkovitz, Israel, Ofer Bar-Yosef, and Baruch Arensburg
1994   The Pre-Pottery Neolithic Populations of South Sinai and Their Re-
        lations to Other Circum-Mediterranean Groups: An Anthropological
        Study. *Paléorient* 20:59–84.
Hershkovitz, Israel, Ehud Galili, and B. Ring
1991   Des squelettes humains 8000 ans sous la mer: indications sur la vie so-
        ciale et économique des habitants de la Côte Sud du Levant à période
        Néolithique Pré-Céramique. *L'Anthropologie* 95:639–650.
Hershkovitz, Israel, Irit Zohar, I. Segal, M. Speirs, O. Meirav, U. Sherter, H. Feld-
        man, and Nigel Goring-Morris
1995   Remedy for an 8,500-Year-Old Plastered Human Skull from Kfar
        HaHoresh, Israel. *Journal of Archaeological Science* 22:779–788.
Heun, Manfred, Ralf Schäfer-Pregl, Dieter Klawan, Renato Castagna, Monica Ac-
        cerbi, Basilio Borghi, and Francesco Salamini
1997   Site of Einkorn Wheat Domestication Identified by DNA Fingerprint-
        ing. *Science* 278:1312–1314.
Hillman, Gordon
2000a   Abu Hureyra 1: The Epipaleolithic. In Andrew Moore, Gordon Hillman,
        and Anthony Legge, pp. 327–399.
2000b   Overview: The Plant-Based Components of Subsistence in Abu Hu-
        reyra 1 and 2. In Andrew Moore, Gordon Hillman, and Anthony Legge,
        pp. 416–422.
Hillman, Gordon, and M. Stuart Davies
1990   Measured Domestication Rates in Wild Wheats and Barley Under
        Primitive Cultivation, and Their Archeological Implications. *Journal of
        World Prehistory* 4:157–222.
Hillman, Gordon, Robert Hedges, Andrew Moore, Sue Colledge, and Paul Pettitt
2001   New Evidence for Late Glacial Cereal Cultivation at Abu Hureyra on
        the Euphrates. *Holocene* 11:383–393.
Hodder, Ian
1990   *The Domestication of Europe: Structure and Contingency in Neolithic Societies.*
        Blackwell, Oxford.
2001   Symbolism and the Origins of Agriculture in the Near East. *Cambridge
        Archaeological Journal* 11:107–112.
Hodder, Ian (editor)
2006   *Çatalhöyük Perspectives: Themes from the 1995-99 Seasons.* McDonald Insti-

tute of Archaeological Research, Çatalhöyük Research Project 6, David Brown, Oxford.

Hodder, Ian, and Craig Cessford

2004   Daily Practice and Social Memory at Çatalhöyük. *American Antiquity* 69:17–40.

Hole, Frank

2000   Is Size Important? Function and Hierarchy in Neolithic Settlements. In Ian Kuijt (ed.), pp. 191–209.

2003   Centers in the Neolithic? *Neolithics* 2:33–35.

Hole, Frank, Kent Flannery, and James Neely

1969   *Prehistory and Human Ecology of the Deh Luran Plain*. Memoirs of the Museum of Anthropology No. 1, University of Michigan, Ann Arbor.

Hopf, Maria

1983   Appendix B. Jericho Plant Remains. In *Jericho: 5. The Pottery Phases of the Tell and Other Finds*, edited by Kathleen Kenyon and Thomas A. Holland, pp. 576–621. British School of Archaeology in Jerusalem, London.

Horowitz, Aharon

1979   *The Quaternary of Israel*. Academic Press, New York.

Horwitz, Liora, Eitan Tchernov, Pierre Ducos, Cornelia Becker, Angela von den Driesch, Louise Martin, and Andrew Garrard

1999   Animal Domestication in the Southern Levant. *Paléorient* 25:63–80.

Horwitz, Liora, Eitan Tchernov, Hitomi Hongo

2004   The Domestic Status of the Early Neolithic Fauna of Cyprus: A View From the Mainland. In Edgar Peltenburg and Alexander Wasse (eds.), pp. 35–48.

Jackson, Adam

2003   The Ground Stone Industry. In Edgar Peltenburg (ed.), pp. 35–40.

Jobling, W. and D. Tangri

1991   A Pre-Pottery Neolithic Site in the Hisma Basin, Southern Jordan. *Paléorient* 17:141–148.

Jones, Martin, Terry Brown, and Robin Allaby

1996   Tracking Early Crops and Early Farmers: The Potential of Biomolecular Archaeology. In *The Origins and Spread of Agriculture and Pastoralism in Eurasia*, edited by David Harris, pp. 93–100. Smithsonian Press, Washington, DC.

Kafafi, Zeidan

1987   The Pottery Neolithic in Jordan in Connection with Other Near Eastern Regions. In *Studies in the History and Archaeology of Jordan III*, edited by Adnan Hadidi, pp. 33–39. Department of Antiquities, Amman.

1992   Pottery Neolithic Settlement Patterns in Jordan. In *Studies in the History and Archaeology of Jordan IV*, pp. 115–122. Department of Antiquities, Amman.

2001   *Jebel Abu Thawwab (Er-Rumman), Central Jordan: The Late Neolithic and Early Bronze Age Occupations*. Monograph of the Institute of Archaeology and Anthropology Vol. 3, Yarmouk University, Yarmouk, Jordan, and Ex Oriente, Berlin.

Kaplan, Jacob
1958   Excavations at Wadi Raba. *Israel Exploration Journal* 8:149–160.

Kassapis, Herodotos
2001   A New Persian Fallow Deer (*Dama mesopotamica*) Fossil Site in Cyprus: A Preliminary Report. *Wildlife Management in the 21st Century, Abstracts*. XXVth International Congress of the International Union of Game Biologists I.U.G.G. and IXth International Symposium Perdix, Limassol, Cyprus.

Katz, Solomon, and Mary Voigt
1986   Bread and Beer: The Early Use of Cereals in Human Diet. *Expedition* 28:23–34.

Keegan, William, and Jared Diamond
1987   Colonization of Islands by Humans: A Biogeographical Perspective. In *Advances in Archaeological Method and Theory*, vol. 10, edited by Michael Schiffer, pp. 49–92. Academic Press, New York.

Kenyon, Kathleen
1957a   Reply to Professor Braidwood. *Antiquity* 31:83–84.
1957b   *Digging Up Jericho*. Benn, London.
1960   *Archaeology of the Holy Land*. Frederick A. Praeger, New York.
1981   *Excavations at Jericho: 3. The Architecture and Stratigraphy of the Tell*. British School of Archaeology in Jerusalem, London.

Kirch, Patrick (editor)
1988   *Island Societies: Archaeological Approaches to Evolution and Transformation*. Cambridge University Press, Cambridge.

Kirkbride, Diana
1966   Five Seasons at the Pre-Pottery Neolithic Village of Beidha in Jordan. *Palestine Exploration Quarterly* 98:8–72.

Kislev, Mordechai
1992   Agriculture in the Near East in the VIIth Millennium BC. In *Préhistoire d'agriculture: nouvelles approches expérimentales et ethnographiques*, edited by Patricia Anderson, pp. 87–93. CRA Monographies 6, CNRS, Valbonne.

Kislev, Mordechai, Anat Hartmann, and Ehud Galili
2004   Archaeobotanical and Archaeoentomological Evidence from a Well at Atlit-Yam Indicates Colder, More Humid Climate on the Israeli Coast During the PPNC Period. *Journal of Archaeological Science* 31:1301–1310.

Knapp, A. Bernard, Steve Held, and Stuart Manning
1994   The Prehistory of Cyprus: Problems and Prospects. *Journal of World Prehistory* 8:377–453.

Köhler-Rollefson, Ilse
1988   The Aftermath of the Levantine Neolithic Revolution in Light of Ecologic and Ethnographic Evidence. *Paléorient* 14:87–93.
1992   A Mode for the Development of Nomadic Pastoralism on the Trans-

jordanian Plateau. In *Pastoralism in the Levant*, edited by Ofer Bar-Yosef and Anatoly Khazanov, pp. 11–18. Monographs in World Archaeology No. 10, Prehistory Press, Madison.

Köhler-Rollefson, Ilse, William Gillespie, and Mary Metzger
1988   The Fauna from Neolithic 'Ain Ghazal. In *The Prehistory of Jordan. The State of Research in 1986*, edited by Andrew Garrard and Hans Georg Gebel, pp. 423–430. International Series, No. 396, British Archaeological Reports, Oxford.

Köhler-Rollefson, Ilse, and Gary Rollefson
1990   The Impact of Neolithic Subsistence Strategies on the Environment: The Case of 'Ain Ghazal, Jordan. In *Man's Role in the Shaping of the Eastern Mediterranean Landscape*, edited by Sytze Bottema, G. Entjes-Nieborg, and Willem Van Zeist, pp. 3–14. Balkema, Rotterdam.

Kozłowski, Stefan
1999   *The Eastern Wing of the Fertile Crescent: Late Prehistory of Greater Mesopotamian Lithic Industries*. International Series 760, British Archaeological Reports, Oxford.

2002   *Nemrik: An Aceramic Village in Northern Iraq*. Światowit Supplement Series P: Prehistory and Middle Ages Vol. 8, Institute of Archaeology, Warsaw University, Warsaw.

Kozłowski, Stefan, and Olivier Aurenche
2005   *Territories, Boundaries and Cultures in the Neolithic Near East*. International Series 1362, British Archaeological Reports, Oxford.

Kozłowski, Stefan, and Hans Georg Gebel (editors)
1996   *Neolithic Chipped Stone Industries of the Fertile Crescent, and Their Contemporaries in Adjacent Regions: Proceedings of the Second Workshop on PPN Chipped Lithic Industries, Warsaw University, 3rd–7th April 1995*. SENEPSE 3, Ex Oriente, Berlin.

Kuijt, Ian
1994   Pre-Pottery Neolithic A Period Settlement Systems of the Southern Levant: New Data, Archaeological Visibility, and Regional Site Hierarchies. *Journal of Mediterranean Archaeology* 7:165–192.

1996   Negotiating Equality Through Ritual: A Consideration of Late Natufian and Prepottery Neolithic A Period Mortuary Practices. *Journal of Anthropological Archaeology* 15:313–336.

1997   Trying to Fit Round Houses into Square Holes: Reexamining the Timing of the South-Central Levantine Pre-Pottery Neolithic A and Pre-Pottery Neolithic B Cultural Transition. In *The Prehistory of Jordan II: Perspectives from 1997*, edited by Hans Georg Gebel, Zeidan Kafafi, and Gary Rollefson, pp. 193–202. Ex Oriente, Berlin.

2000a   People and Space in Early Agricultural Villages: Exploring Daily Lives, Community Size, and Architecture in the Late Pre-Pottery Neolithic. *Journal of Anthropological Archaeology* 19:75–102.

2000b   Keeping the Peace: Ritual, Skull Caching, and Community Integration in the Levantine Neolithic. In Ian Kuijt (ed.), pp. 137–164.

2000c   Near Eastern Neolithic Research: Directions and Trends. In Ian Kuijt (ed.), pp. 311–322.

2001   Meaningful Masks: Place, Death, and the Transmission of Social Memory in Early Agricultural Communities of the Near Eastern Pre-Pottery Neolithic. In *Social Memory, Identity, and Death: Intradisciplinary Perspectives on Mortuary Rituals*, edited by Meredith Chesson, pp. 80–99. Archaeological Papers No. 10, American Anthropological Association, Washington, DC.

Kuijt, Ian (editor)

2000   *Life in Neolithic Farming Communities: Social Organization, Identity, and Differentiation*. Kluwer Academic/Plenum, New York.

Kuijt, Ian, and Ofer Bar-Yosef

1994   Radiocarbon Chronology for the Levantine Neolithic: Observations and Data. In *Late Quaternary Chronology and Paleoclimates of the Eastern Mediterranean*, edited by Ofer Bar-Yosef and Renée S. Kra, pp. 227–245. Radiocarbon, University of Arizona, Tucson.

Kuijt, Ian, and Meredith Chesson

2002   Excavations at 'Ain Waida', Jordan: New Insights into Pottery Neolithic Lifeways in the Southern Levant. *Paléorient* 282:109–122.

2005   Lumps of Clay and Pieces of Stone: Ambiguity, Bodies, and Identity as Portrayed in Neolithic Figurines. In *Archaeologies of the Middle East: Critical Perspectives*, edited by Reinhard Bernbeck and Susan Pollock, pp. 152–183. Blackwell, Oxford.

Kuijt, Ian, and Nigel Goring-Morris

2002   Foraging, Farming, and Social Complexity in the Pre-Pottery Neolithic of the Southern Levant: A Review and Synthesis. *Journal of World Prehistory* 16:361–440.

Kuijt, Ian, and Hamzeh Mahasneh

1998   Dhra': An Early Neolithic Village in the Southern Jordan Valley. *Journal of Field Archaeology* 25:153–161.

Kutzbach, John, and Peter Guetter

1986   The Influence of Changing Orbital Parameters and Surface Boundary Conditions on Climate Simulations for the Past 18,000 Years. *Journal of Atmospheric Science* 43:1726–1759.

Kutzbach, John, Peter Guetter, Pat Behling, and Rich Selin

1993   Simulated Climatic Changes: Results of the COHMAP Climate-Model Experiments. In *Global Climates Since the Last Glacial Maximum*, edited by Herbert E. Wright, Jr., John E. Kutzbach, Thompson Webb III, William F. Ruddiman, F. Alayne Street-Perrott, and Patrick J. Bartlein, pp. 24–93. University of Minnesota Press, Minneapolis and London.

LeBrun, Alain

1984   *Fouilles récentes à Khirokitia (Chypre), 1977–1981*. Éditions Recherche sur les civilisations Mémoire 41, ADPF, Paris.

2001   At the Other End of the Sequence: The Cypriot Neolithic as Seen from Khirokitia. In Stuart Swiny (ed.), pp. 109–118.

2002   Neolithic Society in Cyprus: A Tentative Analysis. In *Engendering Aphrodite: Women and Society in Ancient Cyprus*, edited by Diane Bolger and Nancy Serwint, pp. 23–31. CAARI Monographs vol. 3, American Schools of Oriental Research, Boston.

2003   Idéologie et symboles à Khirokitia: la "fermeture" d'un bâtiment et sa mise en scène. In Jean Guilaine and Alain LeBrun (eds.), pp. 341–349.

LeBrun, Alain, Sophie Cluzan, Simon Davis, Julie Hansen, and Josephine Renault-Miskovsky

1987   Le Néolithique Précéramique de Chypre. *L'Anthropologie* 91:283–316.

Legge, Anthony

1972   Prehistoric Exploitation of the Gazelle in Palestine. In *Papers in Economic Prehistory*, edited by Eric Higgs, pp. 119–124. University of Cambridge Press, Cambridge.

Legge, Anthony, and Peter Rowley-Conwy

2000   The Exploitation of Animals. In Andrew Moore, Gordon Hillman, and Anthony Legge, pp. 423–471.

LeMort, Françoise

2003   Les restes humains de Khirokitia: particularités et interprétations. In Jean Guilaine and Alain LeBrun (eds.), pp. 313–325.

Lev-Yadun, Simcha, Avi Gopher, and Shahal Abbo

2000   The Cradle of Agriculture. *Science* 288:1602–1603.

Lieberman, Daniel, and Ofer Bar-Yosef

1994   On Sedentism and Cereal Gathering in the Natufian. *Current Anthropology* 35:431–434.

Mabry, Jonathan

2003   The Birth of the Ancestors: The Meanings of Human Figurines in Near Eastern Neolithic Villages. In *The Near East in the Southwest: Essays in Honor of William G. Dever*, edited by Beth Alpert Nakhai, pp. 85–116. Annual, Vol. 58, American Schools of Oriental Research, Boston.

Mantzourani, Eleni

2003   Kantou-Kouphovounos: A Late Neolithic Site in the Limassol District. In Jean Guilaine and Alain LeBrun (eds.), pp. 85–98.

Marks, Sherry

1999   Rethinking the Aceramic Neolithic: Insights from an Ethnoarchaeological Study on Cyprus. Unpublished master's thesis, Department of Anthropology and Ethnic Studies, University of Nevada, Las Vegas.

Marshack, Alexander

1997   Paleolithic Image Making and Symboling in Europe and the Middle

East: A Comparative Review. In *Beyond Art: Pleistocene Image and Symbol*, edited by Margaret W. Conkey, Olga Soffer, Deborah Stratmann, and Nina G. Jablonski, pp. 53–91. California Academy of Sciences, San Francisco.

Martin, Louise

2000   Gazelle (*Gazella* spp.) Behavioural Ecology: Predicting Animal Behaviour for Prehistoric Environments in South-West Asia. *Journal of Zoology, London* 250:13–30.

Matthews, Roger

1996   Surface Scraping and Planning. In *On the Surface: Catalhoyuk 1993–95*, edited by Ian Hodder. British Institute of Archaeology at Ankara and McDonald Institute for Archaeological Research, London and Cambridge.

Mazurowski, Ryszard F.

1997   *Ground and Pecked Stone Industry in the Pre-Pottery Neolithic of Northern Iraq.* Nemrik 9, Vol. 3, Institute of Archaeology, University of Warsaw, Warsaw.

2000   Tell Qaramel — Preliminary Report on the First Season, 1999. *Polish Archaeology in the Mediterranean* 11:285–296.

McCartney, Carole

2001   The Chipped Stone Assemblage from *Tenta* (Cyprus), Cultural and Chronological Implications. In *Beyond Tools: Redefining the PPN Lithic Assemblages of the Levant*, edited by Isabella Caneva, Cristini Lemorini, Daniela Zampetti, and Paolo Biagi, pp. 427–436. SENEPSE 9, Ex Oriente, Berlin.

2002   Women's Knives. In *Engendering Aphrodite: Women and Society in Ancient Cyprus*, edited by Diane Bolger and Nancy Serwint, pp. 237–249. CAARI Monographs Vol. 3, American Schools of Oriental Research, Boston.

2003   The Mylouthkia and Tenta Chipped Stone Industries and Their Interpretation Within a Redefined Cypriot Aceramic Neolithic. In Jean Guilaine and Alain LeBrun (eds.), pp. 135–146.

2004   Cypriot Neolithic Chipped Stone Industries and the Progress of Regionalization. In Edgar Peltenburg and Alexander Wasse (eds.), pp. 103–122.

2005   Preliminary Report on the Re-survey of Three Early Neolithic Sites in Cyprus. *Report of the Department of Antiquities, Cyprus*: 1–21.

McCartney, Carole, and Bernard Gratuze

2003   The Chipped Stone. In Edgar Peltenburg (ed.), pp. 11–34.

McCartney, Carole, and Edgar Peltenburg

2000   The Colonization of Cyprus: Questions of Origins and Isolation. *Neolithics* 1:8–11.

McCorriston, Joyce

1994   Acorn Eating and Agricultural Origins: California Ethnographies as Analogies for the Ancient Near East. *Antiquity* 68:97–107.

McCorriston, Joyce, and Frank Hole
    1991   The Ecology of Seasonal Stress and the Origins of Agriculture in the
            Near East. *American Anthropologist* 93:46–69.
McGovern, Patrick
    2003   *Ancient Wine: The Search for the Origins of Viniculture.* Princeton University
            Press, Princeton and Oxford.
Mellaart, James
    1975   *The Neolithic of the Near East.* Thames and Hudson, London.
    1998   Çatal Höyük: The 1960s Seasons. In *Ancient Anatolia*, edited by Roger
            Matthews, pp. 35–41. British Institute of Archaeology at Ankara, Lon-
            don.
Miller, Michele
    2002   The Function of the Anthropomorphic Figurines: A Preliminary Analy-
            sis. In Yosef Garfinkel and Michele Miller 2002b, pp. 221–233.
Miller, Naomi
    2003   Food, Fodder, or Fuel? *Expedition* 44:5–6.
Mithen, Steve, Bill Finlayson, Anne Pirie, Denise Carruthers, and Amanda Kennedy
    2000   New Evidence for Economic and Technological Diversity in the Pre-
            Pottery Neolithic A: Wadi Feinan 16. *Current Anthropology* 41:655–663.
Molleson, Theya
    2000   The People of Abu Hureyra. In Andrew Moore, Gordon Hillman, and
            Anthony Legge, pp. 301–324.
Moore, Andrew
    1985   The Development of Neolithic Societies in the Near East. In *Advances
            in World Archaeology*, edited by Fred Wendorf and Angela E. Close, pp.
            1–69. Academic Press, New York.
    1991   Abu Hureyra 1 and the Antecedents of Agriculture on the Middle Eu-
            phrates. In Ofer Bar-Yosef and François Valla (eds.), pp. 277–294.
    2000a   Stone and Other Artifacts. In Andrew Moore, Gordon Hillman, and
            Anthony Legge, pp. 165–186.
    2000b   The Excavation of Abu Hureyra 1. In Andrew Moore, Gordon Hillman,
            and Anthony Legge, pp. 105–131.
Moore, Andrew, and Gordon Hillman
    1992   The Pleistocene to Holocene Transition and Human Economy in South-
            west Asia: The Impact of the Younger Dryas. *American Antiquity* 57:482–
            494.
Moore, Andrew, Gordon Hillman, and Anthony Legge
    2000   *Village on the Euphrates: From Foraging to Farming at Abu Hureyra.* Oxford
            University Press, Oxford.
Moore, Jenny, and Eleanor Scott (editors)
    1997   *Invisible People and Processes: Writing Gender and Childhood into European Pre-
            history.* Leicester University Press, London and New York.

Moulins, Dominique de

    2000   Abu Hureyra 2: Plant Remains from the Neolithic. In Andrew Moore, Gordon Hillman, and Anthony Legge, pp. 399–416.

Munro, Natalie

    2004   Zooarchaeological Measures of Hunting Pressure and Occupation Intensity in the Natufian [and comments]. *Current Anthropology* 45 (supp.): 5–33.

Murray, Mary Anne

    2003   The Plant Remains. In Edgar Peltenburg (ed.), pp. 59–71.

Nadel, Daniel

    1994   New Symmetry of Early Neolithic Tools: Arrowheads and Truncated Elements. In *Neolithic Chipped Stone Industries of the Fertile Crescent*, edited by Hans Georg Gebel and Stefan Kozłowski, pp. 407–421. SENEPSE 1, Ex Oriente, Berlin.

Nadel, Daniel, Ofer Bar-Yosef, and Avi Gopher

    1991   Early Neolithic Arrowhead Types in the Southern Levant: A Typological Suggestion. *Paléorient* 17:109–119.

Nadel, Daniel, and Israel Hershkovitz

    1991   New Subsistence Data and Human Remains from the Earliest Epipaleolithic in Israel. *Current Anthropology* 32:631–635.

Nadel, Daniel, and Ella Werker

    1999   The Oldest Ever Brush Hut Plant Remains from Ohalo II, Jordan Valley, Israel (19,000 BP). *Antiquity* 73:755–764.

Naveh, Danny

    2003   PPNA Jericho: A Socio-Political Perspective. *Cambridge Archaeological Journal* 13:83–96.

Neef, Reinder

    2003   Overlooking the Steppe-Forest: A Preliminary Report on the Botanical Remains from Early Neolithic Göbekli Tepe (Southeastern Turkey). *Neolithics* 2:13–16.

Neeley, Michael, and Geoffrey Clark

    1993   The Human Food Niche in the Levant over the Past 150,000 Years. In *Hunting and Animal Exploitation in the Later Palaeolithic and Mesolithic of Eurasia*, edited by Gail Larsen Peterkin, Harvey M. Bricker, and Paul Mellars, pp. 221–240. Archaeological Papers No. 4, American Anthropological Association, Washington, DC.

Neolithics

    1997   Symposium: Central Settlements in Neolithic of Jordan. *Neolithics* 2/97.

    2003   Supra-Regional Concepts I. *Neolithics* 2:32–37.

    2004   Supra-Regional Concepts II. *Neolithics* 2:21–52.

    2005   The Early Neolithic Origins of Ritual Centers. *Neolithics* 2/05.

Nesbitt, Mark

    2002   When and Where Did Domesticated Cereals First Occur in Southwest Asia? In René T. J. Cappers and Sytze Bottema (eds.), pp. 113–132.

Neuville, René
1933   Statue érotique du désert de Judée. *L'Anthropologie* 43:558–560.
1934   Le préhistoire de Palestine. *Revue Biblique* 43:237–259.
1951   *Le Paléolithique et le Mésolithique du désert de Judée.* Archives de L'Institut de Paléontologie Humaine Mémoire 24. Masson, Editeurs, Paris.
Nissen, Hans, Mujahed Muheisen, and Hans Georg Gebel
1991   Report of the Excavations at Basta 1988. *Annual of the Jordanian Department of Antiquities* 35:13–40.
Noy, Tamar
1989   Gilgal 1: A Pre-Pottery Neolithic A Site, Israel: The 1985–1987 Seasons. *Paléorient* 15:11–18.
1991   Art and Decoration of the Natufian at Nahal Oren. In Ofer Bar-Yosef and François Valla (eds.), pp. 557–568.
Olsen, Stanley
1985   *Origins of the Domestic Dog.* University of Arizona Press, Tucson.
Olszewski, Deborah
1986   *The North Syrian Late Epipaleolithic: The Earliest Occupation at Tell Abu Hureyra in the Context of the Levantine Late Epipaleolithic.* International Series 309, British Archaeological Reports, Oxford.
1991   Social Complexity in the Natufian? Assessing the Relationship of Ideas and Data. In *Perspectives on the Past: Theoretical Biases in Mediterranean Hunter-Gatherer Research*, edited by Geoffrey Clark, pp. 322–340. University of Pennsylvania Press, Philadelphia.
1993a   The Zarzian Occupation at Warwasi Rockshelter, Iran. In *The Paleolithic Prehistory of the Zagros-Taurus*, edited by Deborah I. Olszewski and Harold L. Dibble, pp. 207–236. Monograph 83, University Museum, University of Pennsylvania, Philadelphia.
1993b   Zarzian Microliths from Warwasi Rockshelter, Iran: Scalene Triangles as Arrow Components. In *Hunting and Animal Exploitation in the Later Palaeolithic and Mesolithic of Eurasia*, edited by Gail Larsen Peterkin, Harvey M. Bricker, and Paul Mellars, pp. 199–205. American Anthropological Association, Washington, DC.
1993c   Subsistence Ecology in the Mediterranean Forest: Implications for the Origins of Cultivation in the Epipaleolithic Southern Levant. *American Anthropologist* 95:420–435.
Orrelle, Estelle, and Avi Gopher
2000   The Pottery Neolithic Period: Questions About Pottery Decoration, Symbolism, and Meaning. In Ian Kuijt (ed.), pp. 295–308.
Özdoğan, Asli
1999   Çayönü. In Mehmet Özdoğan and Nezih Başgelen (eds.), pp. 35–63.
Özdoğan, Mehmet
1999   Concluding Remarks. In Mehmet Özdoğan and Nezih Başgelen (eds.), pp. 225–236.

Özdoğan, Mehmet, and Nezih Başgelen (editors)
1999   *Neolithic in Turkey: The Cradle of Civilization.* Arkeoloji ve Sanat Yayınları, Istanbul.

Özdoğan, Mehmet, and Asli Özdoğan
1998   Building of Cult and the Cult of Buildings. In *Light on Top of the Black Hill: Studies Presented to Halet Çambel,* edited by Güven Arsebük, Machteld Mellink, and Wulf Schirmer, pp. 581–601. Ege Yayınları, Istanbul.

Patton, Mark
1996   *Islands in Time: Island Sociogeography and Mediterranean Prehistory.* Routledge, London and New York.

Peasnall, Brian
2002   Iranian Neolithic. In *Encyclopedia of Prehistory: 8. South and Southwest Asia,* edited by Peter Peregrine and Melvin Ember, pp. 215–235. Kluwer Academic/Plenum, New York.

Peltenburg, Edgar
1978   The Sotira Culture: Regional Diversity and Cultural Unity in Late Neolithic Cyprus. *Levant* 10:55–74.

1982   *Vrysi: A Subterranean Settlement in Cyprus. Excavations at Prehistoric Ayios Epiktitos-Vrysi 1969-73.* Aris and Phillips, Warminster.

1993   Settlement Continuity and Resistance to Complexity in Cyprus, ca. 4500-2500 B.C.E. *Bulletin of the American Schools of Oriental Research* 292:9–23.

2003a   Identifying Settlement of the Xth–IXth Millennium B.P. in Cyprus from the Contents of Kissonerga-Mylouthkia Wells. In Jean Guilaine and Alain LeBrun (eds.), pp. 15–33.

2003b   Conclusions: Mylouthkia I and the Early Colonists of Cyprus. In Edgar Peltenburg (ed.), pp. 83–103.

2003c   Incorporated Houses, Memory and Identity in Prehistoric Cyprus: Inferences from Ayios Epiktitos-*Vrysi.* In Jean Guilaine and Alain LeBrun (eds.), pp. 99–118.

2003d   Post-Colonisation Settlement Patterns: The Late Neolithic-Chalcolithic Transition. In Edgar Peltenburg (ed.), pp. 257–276.

2004a   Social Space in Early Sedentary Communities of Southwest Asia and Cyprus. In Edgar Peltenburg and Alexander Wasse (eds.), pp. 71–89.

2004b   Cyprus—A Regional Component of the Levantine PPN. *Neolithics* 1:3–7.

Peltenburg, Edgar (editor)
2003   *The Colonisation and Settlement of Cyprus. Investigations at Kissonerga-Mylouthkia, 1976-1996.* Studies in Mediterranean Archaeology vol. 70:4. Paul Aströms Förlag, Sävedalen.

Peltenburg, Edgar, Sue Colledge, Paul Croft, Adam Jackson, Carole McCartney, and Mary Anne Murray
2000   Agro-Pastoralist Colonization of Cyprus in the 10th Millennium BP: Initial Assessments. *Antiquity* 74: 844–53.

2001   Neolithic Dispersals from the Levantine Corridor: A Mediterranean
            Perspective. *Levant* 33:35–64.

Peltenburg, Edgar, Paul Croft, Adam Jackson, Carole McCartney, and Mary Anne
    Murray
2001   Well-Established Colonists: Mylouthkia 1 and the Cypro-Pre-Pottery
            Neolithic B. In Stuart Swiny (ed.), pp. 61–93.

Peltenburg, Edgar, and Alexander Wasse (editors)
2004   *Neolithic Revolution: New Perspectives on Southwest Asia in Light of Recent Dis-
            coveries on Cyprus.* Levant Supplementary Series Vol. 1, Oxbow Books,
            Oxford.

Perlès, Catherine
2001   *The Early Neolithic in Greece.* Cambridge University Press, Cambridge.

Perlès, Catherine, and James Phillips
1991   The Natufian Conference — Discussion. In Ofer Bar-Yosef and François
            Valla (eds.), pp. 637–644.

Perrot, Jean
1966a   Le gisement Natoufien de Mallaha (Eynan), Israel. *L'Anthropologie* 70:
            437–484.
1966b   La troisième campagne de fouilles à Munhatta (1964). *Syria* 63:49–63.
1968   La préhistoire palestinienne. In *Supplément au Dictionnaire de la Bible*,
            vol. 8, pp. 286–446. Letouzey and Ané, Paris.

Peters, Joris, Daniel Helmer, Angela von den Driesch, and Maria Saña Segui
1999   Early Animal Husbandry in the Northern Levant. *Paléorient* 25:27–47.

Peterson, Jane
1994   Changes in the Sexual Division of Labor in the Prehistory of the South-
            ern Levant. Ph.D. dissertation, Department of Anthropology, Arizona
            State University, Tempe. University Microfilms, Ann Arbor.
1998   The Natufian Hunting Conundrum: Spears, Atlatls, or Bows? Musculo-
            skeletal and Armature Evidence. *International Journal of Osteoarchaeology*
            8:378–389.
2002   *Sexual Revolutions: Gender and Labor at the Dawn of Agriculture.* AltaMira,
            Walnut Creek, CA.

Pinhasi, Ron, and Mark Pluciennik
2004   A Regional Biological Approach to the Spread of Farming in Europe
            [and comments]. *Current Anthropology* 45 (supp.): 59–82.

Piperno, Dolores, Ehud Weiss, Irene Holst, and Dani Nadel
2004   Processing of Wild Cereal Grains in the Upper Paleolithic Revealed by
            Starch Grain Analysis. *Nature* 430:670–673.

Pirie, Anne
2001   A Brief Note on the Chipped Stone Assemblage from PPNA Nachcha-
            rini Cave, Lebanon. *Neolithics* 2:10–12.

Prausnitz, Moshe
1966   The Kebaran, the Natufian and the Tahunian: A Study in Terminology.
            Israel Exploration Journal 16:220–230.

1970 *From Hunter to Farmer and Trader*. Sivan Press, Jerusalem.

Price, T. Douglas, and Anne Gebauer

1995 *Last Hunters, First Farmers: New Perspectives on the Prehistoric Transition to Agriculture*. School of American Research Press, Santa Fe.

Pringle, Heather

1998 The Slow Birth of Agriculture. *Science* 282:1446–1450.

Quintero, Leslie, and Ilse Köhler-Rollefson

1997 The 'Ain Ghazal Dog: A Case for the Neolithic Origin of *Canis familiaris* in the Near East. In *The Prehistory of Jordan II: Perspectives from 1997*, edited by Hans Georg Gebel, Zeidan Kafafi, and Gary Rollefson, pp. 567–574. SENEPSE 4, Ex Oriente, Berlin.

Quintero, Leslie, and Philip Wilke

1995 Evolution and Economic Significance of Naviform Core-and-Blade Technology in the Southern Levant. *Paléorient* 21:17–33.

Rainbird, Paul

1999 Islands Out of Time: Towards a Critique of Island Archaeology. *Journal of Mediterranean Archaeology* 12:216–234.

Redding, Richard

1988 A General Explanation of Subsistence Change: From Hunting and Gathering to Food Production. *Journal of Anthropological Archaeology* 7:56–97.

Redman, Charles

1978 *The Rise of Civilization*. Freeman, San Francisco.

Reed, Charles (editor)

1977 *Origins of Agriculture*. Mouton, The Hague.

Reese, David

1996 Cypriot Hippo Hunters No Myth. *Journal of Mediterranean Archaeology* 9:107–112.

Renault-Miskovsky, Josephine

1989 Étude paléobotanique, paléoclimatique et palethnographique du site néolithique de Khirokitia dans le sud-ouest de l'île de Chypre. In *Fouilles récentes à Khirokitia (Chypre) 1983–1986*, edited by Alain LeBrun, pp. 251–263. Éditions Recherche sur les civilisations Mémoire 81, ADPF, Paris.

Renfrew, Colin

1975 Trade as Action at a Distance: Questions of Integration and Communication. In *Ancient Civilization and Trade*, edited by Jeremy A. Sabloff and C. C. Lamberg-Karlovsky, pp. 3–59. University of New Mexico Press, Albuquerque.

Rice, Glen

1975 A Systematic Explanation of a Change in Mogollon Settlement Patterns. Ph.D. dissertation, University of Washington. University Microfilms, Ann Arbor.

Richerson, Peter, Robert Boyd, and Robert Bettiner

2001 Was Agriculture Impossible During the Pleistocene but Mandatory During the Holocene? A Climate Change Hypothesis. *American Antiquity* 66:387–411.

Rindos, David
 1984   *The Origins of Agriculture: An Evolutionary Perspective*. Academic Press, New York.

Roberts, Neil, and H. Wright
 1993   Vegetational, Lake-Level, and Climatic History of the Near East and Southwest Asia. In *Global Climates Since the Last Glacial Maximum*, edited by H. E. Wright, Jr., John E. Kutzbach, Thompson Webb III, William F. Ruddiman, F. Alayne Street-Perrott, and Patrick J. Bartlein, pp. 194–220. University of Minnesota Press, Minneapolis and London.

Rockman, Marcy, and James Steele (editors)
 2003   *Colonization of Unfamiliar Landscapes: The Archaeology of Adaptation*. Routledge, London and New York.

Roehrer-Ertl, Olav, and Kurt-Walter Frey
 1987   Two Cases of Homicide from the Pre-Pottery Neolithic of Arabia Petraea. *Gegenbaurs morphologisches Jahrbuch* 133:507–537.

Roehrer-Ertl, Olav, Kurt-Walter Frey, and Heinrich Newesely
 1988   Preliminary Note on Early Neolithic Human Remains from Basta and Sabra. In *The Prehistory of Jordan: The State of Research in 1986*, edited by Andrew Garrard and Hans Georg Gebel, pp. 135–136. International Series 396(i), British Archaeological Reports, Oxford.

Rollefson, Gary
 1983   Ritual and Ceremony at Neolithic 'Ain Ghazal. *Paléorient* 9:29–38.
 1986   Neolithic 'Ain Ghazal (Jordan): Ritual and Ceremony II. *Paléorient* 12:45–52.
 1987   Local and External Relations in the Levantine PPN Period: 'Ain Ghazal (Jordan) as a Regional Center. In *Studies in the History and Archaeology of Jordan III*, edited by Adnan Hadidi, pp. 29–32. Department of Antiquities, Amman.
 1989   The Late Aceramic Neolithic of the Levant: A Synthesis. *Paléorient* 15:168–173.
 1992   Neolithic Settlement Patterns in Northern Jordan and Palestine. In *Studies in the History and Archaeology of Jordan IV*, pp. 123–127. Department of Antiquities, Amman.
 1993   Neolithic Chipped Stone Technology at 'Ain Ghazal, Jordan: The Status of the PPNC. *Paléorient* 16:119–124.
 1996   The Neolithic Devolution: Ecological Impact and Cultural Compensation at 'Ain Ghazal, Jordan. In *Retrieving the Past*, edited by Joseph Seger, pp. 219–229. Cobb Institute of Archaeology, Mississippi State University.
 1997a Changes in Architecture and Social Organization at 'Ain Ghazal. In *The Prehistory of Jordan II: Perspectives from 1997*, edited by Hans Georg Gebel, Zeidan Kafafi, and Gary Rollefson, pp. 287–307. Ex Oriente, Berlin.

1997b   Neolithic 'Ayn Ghazal in Its Landscape. In *Studies in the History and Archaeology of Jordan VI*, edited by Ghazi Bisheh, Muna Zaghloul, and Ina Kehrberg, pp. 241–244. Department of Antiquities, Amman.

1998a   The Aceramic Neolithic. In *The Prehistoric Archaeology of Jordan*, edited by Donald O. Henry, pp. 102–126. International Series 705, British Archaeological Reports, Oxford.

1998b   Invoking the Spirit: Prehistoric Religion at 'Ain Ghazal. *Odyssey* 1:55–63.

2000   Ritual and Social Structure at Neolithic 'Ain Ghazal. In Ian Kuijt (ed.), pp. 165–190.

2001a   An Archaeological Odyssey. *Cambridge Archaeological Journal* 11:112–114.

2001b   Jordan in the Seventh and Sixth Millennia BC. In *Studies in the History and Archaeology of Jordan VII*, edited by Ghazi Bisheh, pp. 95–100. Department of Antiquities, Amman.

Rollefson, Gary, and Ilse Köhler-Rollefson

1989   The Collapse of Early Neolithic Settlements in the Southern Levant. In *People and Culture in Change: Proceedings of the Second Symposium on Upper Palaeolithic, Mesolithic, and Neolithic Populations of Europe and the Mediterranean Basin*, edited by Israel Hershkovitz, pp. 73–89. International Series 508(i), British Archaeological Reports, Oxford.

1992   Early Neolithic Exploitation Patterns in the Levant: Cultural Impact on the Environment. *Population and Environment* 13:243–254.

Rollefson, Gary, Alan Simmons, and Zeidan Kafafi

1992   Neolithic Cultures at 'Ain Ghazal, Jordan. *Journal of Field Archaeology* 19:443–471.

Ronen, Avraham

1995   Core, Periphery and Ideology in Aceramic Cyprus. *Quartär* 45–46:178–206.

Ronen, Avraham, and Dan Adler

2001   The Walls of Jericho Were Magical. *Archaeology, Ethnology and Anthropology of Eurasia* 2:97–103.

Ronen, Avraham, and Monique Lechevallier

1999   Save the Khiamian! *Neolithics* 1:6–7.

Rosenberg, Michael

1998   Cheating at Musical Chairs: Territoriality and Sedentism in an Evolutionary Context. *Current Anthropology* 39:653–664.

1999   Hallan Çemi. In Mehmet Özdoğan and Nezih Başgelen (eds.), pp. 25–33.

Rosenberg, Michael, Mark Nesbitt, Richard Redding, and Brian Peasnall

1998   Hallan Çemi, Pig Husbandry, and Post-Pleistocene Adaptations Along the Taurus-Zagros Arc (Turkey). *Paléorient* 24:25–41.

Rosenberg, Michael, and Brian Peasnall

1998   A Report on Soundings at Demirköy Höyük: An Aceramic Neolithic Site in Eastern Anatolia. *Anatolica* 24:195–207.

Rosenberg, Michael, and Richard Redding
    2000   Hallan Çemi and Early Village Organization in Eastern Anatolia. In Ian
              Kuijt (ed.), pp. 39–61.
Rossignol-Strick, Martine
    1993   Late Quaternary Climate in the Eastern Mediterranean Region. *Paléo-
              rient* 19:135–152.
Rowley-Conwy, Peter
    2004   How the West Was Lost [and comments]. *Current Anthropology* 45
              (supp.): 83–113.
Runnels, Curtis
    1995   Review of Aegean Prehistory IV: The Stone Age of Greece from the
              Palaeolithic to the Advent of the Neolithic. *American Journal of Archaeology*
              99:699–728.
Rupp, David W. (editor)
    1987   *Western Cyprus: Connections.* Studies in Mediterranean Archaeology 77.
              Paul Åströms Förlag, Göteborg.
Rupp, David W., Lone Wriedt Sørensen, Roger H. King, and William A. Fox
    1984   Canadian Palaipaphos (Cyprus) Survey Project: Second Preliminary
              Report, 1980–1982. *Journal of Field Archaeology* 11:133–154.
Rust, Alfred
    1950   *Die Hohlenfunde von Jabrud (Syrien).* Karl Wachholz, Neumunster.
Saidel, Benjamin
    1993   Round House or Square? Architectural Form and Socio-Economic Or-
              ganization in the PPNB. *Journal of Mediterranean Archaeology* 6:65–108.
Sauer, Carl
    1952   *Agricultural Origins and Dispersals.* American Geographical Society, New
              York.
Sayej, Ghattas
    2001   A New Pre-Pottery Neolithic A Cultural Region in Jordan: The Dead
              Sea Basin. In *Australians Uncovering Ancient Jordan: Fifty Years of Middle
              Eastern Archaeology,* edited by Alan Walmsley, pp. 225–232. Research
              Institute for Humanities and Social Sciences, University of Sydney,
              Sydney.
Schmandt-Besserat, Denise
    1992   *Before Writing: 1. From Counting to Cuneiform.* University of Texas Press,
              Austin.
    1998a   A Stone Metaphor of Creation. *Near Eastern Archaeology* 61:109–117.
    1998b   'Ain Ghazal "Monumental" Figures. *Bulletin of the American Schools of Ori-
              ental Research* 310:1–17.
Schmidt, Klaus
    2001a   Göbekli Tepe and Early Neolithic Sites of the Urfa Region: A Synopsis
              of New Results and Current Views. *Neolithics* 1:9–11.
    2001b   Göbekli Tepe, Southeastern Turkey, A Preliminary Report on the 1995–
              1999 Excavations. *Paléorient* 26:45–54.

2002a   Göbekli Tepe — Southeastern Turkey. The Seventh Campaign 2001. *Neolithics* 1:23–25.

2002b   The 2002 Excavations at Göbekli Tepe (Southeastern Turkey)–Impressions from an Enigmatic Site. *Neolithics* 2:8–13.

2003   Göbekli Tepe 2003. *Neolithics* 2:3–8.

Schroeder, Bruce

1991   Natufian in the Central Béqaa Valley, Lebanon. In Ofer Bar-Yosef and François Valla (eds.), pp. 43–80.

Scott, Thomas

1977   The Harifian of the Central Negev, Israel. In *Prehistory and Paleoenvironments in the Central Negev, Israel*, vol. 2, edited by Anthony Marks, pp. 271–322. Southern Methodist University Press, Dallas.

Servello, Frank

1976   Nahal Divshon: A Pre-Pottery Neolithic B Hunting Camp. In *Prehistory and Paleoenvironments in the Central Negev, Israel: 1. The Avdat/Aqez Area, Part 1*, edited by Anthony E. Marks, pp. 349–370. Institute for the Study of Early Man, Reports of Investigations 2, Southern Methodist University Press, Dallas.

Severinghaus, Jeff, and Edward Brook

1999   Abrupt Climate Change at the End of the Last Glacial Period Inferred from Trapped Air in Polar Ice. *Science* 286:930–934.

Şevketoğlu, Muge

2000   *Archaeological Field Survey of the Neolithic and Chalcolithic Settlement Sites in Kyrenia District, North Cyprus*. International Series 834, British Archaeological Reports, Oxford.

2002   Akanthou-Arkosyko (Tatlisu-Çiftlikdüzü): The Anatolian Connections in the 9th Millennium BC. In *World Islands in Prehistory*, edited by William Waldren and J. A. Ensenyat, pp. 98–106. International Series 1095, British Archaeological Reports, Oxford.

Sherratt, Andrew

1983   The Secondary Exploitation of Animals in the Old World. *World Archaeology* 15:90–102.

Siggers, Julian

1997   The Lithic Assemblages from Tabaqat al-Bûrma: A Late Neolithic Site in Wadi Ziqlab. Unpublished Ph.D. dissertation, University of Toronto.

Sillen, Andrew, and Julia Lee-Thorp

1991   Dietary Change in the Late Natufian. In Ofer Bar-Yosef and François Valla (eds.), pp. 399–410.

Simmons, Alan

1980   Early Neolithic Settlement and Economic Behavior in the Western Negev Desert of the Southern Levant. Unpublished Ph.D. dissertation, Department of Anthropology, Southern Methodist University, Dallas.

1981   A Paleosubsistence Model for Early Neolithic Occupation of the Western Negev Desert. *Bulletin of the American Schools of Oriental Research* 242: 31–49.

1986   New Evidence for the Early Use of Cultigens in the American Southwest. *American Antiquity* 51:73–89.

1991   One Flew over the Hippo's Nest: Extinct Pleistocene Fauna, Early Man, and Conservative Archaeology in Cyprus. In *Perspectives on the Past*, edited by Geoffrey Clark, pp. 282–304. University of Pennsylvania Press, Philadelphia.

1994   Early Neolithic Settlement in Western Cyprus: Preliminary Report on the 1992–1993 Test Excavations at Kholetria *Ortos. Bulletin of the American Schools of Oriental Research* 295:1–14.

1995   Town Planning in the Neolithic—Is 'Ayn Ghazal "Normal"? In *Studies in the History and Archaeology of Jordan V*, edited by Khairieh 'Amr, Fawzi Zayadine, and Muna Zaghloul, pp. 119–122. Department of Antiquities, Amman.

1996   Whose Myth? Archaeological Data, Interpretations, and Implications for the Human Association with Extinct Pleistocene Fauna at Akrotiri *Aetokremnos. Journal of Mediterranean Archaeology* 9:97–105.

1998a   Exposed Fragments, Buried Hippos: Assessing Surface Archaeology. In *Surface Archaeology*, edited by Alan Sullivan, pp. 159–167. University of New Mexico Press, Albuquerque.

1998b   Of Tiny Hippos, Large Cows, and Early Colonists in Cyprus. *Journal of Mediterranean Archaeology* 11:232–241.

1999   *Faunal Extinctions in an Island Society: Pygmy Hippopotamus Hunters of Cyprus.* Kluwer Academic/Plenum, New York.

2000   Villages on the Edge: Regional Settlement Change and the End of the Levantine Pre-Pottery Neolithic. In Ian Kuijt (ed.), pp. 211–230.

2001   The First Humans and Last Pygmy Hippopotami of Cyprus. In Stuart Swiny (ed.), pp. 1–18.

2002   The Role of Islands in Pushing the Pleistocene Extinction Envelope: The Strange Case of the Cypriot Pygmy Hippos. In *World Islands in Prehistory*, edited by William Waldren and J. A. Ensenyat, pp. 406–414. International Series 1095, British Archaeological Reports, Oxford.

2003a   2003 Excavations at Kritou Marottou *Ais Yiorkis*, An Early Neolithic Site in Western Cyprus: Preliminary Report. *Neolithics* 2:8–12.

2003b   Villages Without Walls, Cows Without Corrals. In Jean Guilaine and Alain LeBrun, pp. 61–70.

2004a   Bitter Hippos of Cyprus: The Island's First Occupants and Last Endemic Animals—Setting the Stage for Colonization. In Edgar Peltenburg and Alexander Wasse, pp. 1–14.

2004b   Cows for the Ancestors: The Initial Colonization of Cyprus. Paper presented at The Creation of Symbolic Worlds conference, BANEA, University of Reading.

2004c   The Earliest Residents of Cyprus: Ecological Pariahs or Harmonious Settlers? Paper presented at the 69th Annual Meeting of the Society for American Archaeology, Montreal.

2004d   The Mediterranean PPNB Interaction Sphere? *Neolithics* 1:16–18.

Simmons, Alan, and Renée Corona

2000   A Proposal for the Wadi Faynan Archaeological Park: Issues and Suggestions. Invited paper presented at the Wadi Faynan Conference, Amman.

Simmons, Alan, and Giora Ilany

1975–1977   What Mean These Bones?–Behavioral Implications of Gazelles' Remains from Archaeological Sites. *Paléorient* 3:269–274.

Simmons, Alan, and Rolfe Mandel

1988   A Preliminary Assessment of the Geomorphology of 'Ain Ghazal. In *The Prehistory of Jordan: The State of Research in 1986*, pp. 431–436, edited by Andrew Garrard and Hans Georg Gebel. International Series 396, British Archaeological Reports, Oxford.

Simmons, Alan, Ilse Köhler-Rollefson, Gary Rollefson, Rolfe Mandel, and Zeidan Kafafi

1988   'Ain Ghazal: A Major Neolithic Settlement in Central Jordan. *Science* 240:35–39.

Simmons, Alan, and Mohammad Najjar

2002   Preliminary Report on the Tell Wadi Feinan Testing Project. *Neolithics* 1:19–21.

2003   Ghuwayr I, A Pre-Pottery Neolithic B Settlement in Southern Jordan: Report of the 1996–2000 Campaigns. *Annual of the Department of Antiquities of Jordan* 47:407–430.

2006   Ghwair I, a Small but Complex Neolithic Community in Southern Jordan. *Journal of Field Archaeology* 31:77–95.

Simmons, Alan, Gary Rollefson, Zeidan Kafafi, Rolfe Mandel, Maysoon Al-Nahar, Jason Cooper, Ilse Köhler-Rollefson, and Kathy Roler Durand

2001   Wadi Shu'eib, a Large Neolithic Community in Central Jordan: Final Report of Test Investigations. *Bulletin of the American Schools of Oriental Research* 321:1–39.

Singh, Purushottam

1974   *Neolithic Cultures of Western Asia*. Seminar Press, London and New York.

Smith, Bruce

1995   *Emergence of Agriculture*. Scientific American Library, New York.

2001   The Transition to Food Production. In *Archaeology at the Millennium: A Sourcebook*, edited by Gary Feinman and T. Douglas Price, pp. 199–229. Kluwer Academic/Plenum, New York.

Smith, Patricia

1991   The Dental Evidence for Nutritional Status in the Natufians. In Ofer Bar-Yosef and François Valla (eds.), pp. 425–432.

1998   People of the Holy Land from Prehistory to the Recent Past. In *The Ar-*

chaeology of the Holy Land, edited by Thomas Levy, pp. 58–74. Leicester University Press, London and Washington.

Smith, Phillip
1976   *Food Production and Its Consequences*. Cummings, Menlo Park, CA.

Smith, Phillip, and T. Cuyler Young
1983   The Force of Numbers: Population Pressure in the Central Western Zagros 12,000–4,500 B.C. In *The Hilly Flanks and Beyond*, edited by T. Cuyler Young, Phillip Smith, and Peder Mortensen, University of Chicago Press, Chicago.

Solecki, Ralph, Rose Solecki, and Anagnostis Agelarakis
2004   *The Proto-Neolithic Cemetery in Shanidar Cave*. Texas A&M University Press, College Station.

Solecki, Rose, and Ralph Solecki
2004   Burial Offerings and Other Goods from the Proto-Neolithic Graves. In *The Proto-Neolithic Cemetery in Shanidar Cave*, by Ralph Solecki, Rose Solecki, and Anagnostis Agelarakis, pp. 48–63. Texas A&M University Press, College Station.

Sorabji, Daniel, and Albert Ammerman
2005   New Evidence on Early Sites in Cyprus. Paper presented at the 23rd Annual CAARI Archaeological Workshop, Nicosia.

Stanley-Price, Nicholas
1977   Colonisation and Continuity in the Early Prehistory of Cyprus. *World Archaeology* 9:27–41.

1979   *Early Prehistoric Settlement in Cyprus: A Review and Gazetteer of Sites, c. 6500–3000 B.C.* International Series No. 65, British Archaeological Reports, Oxford.

Steel, Louise
2004   *Cyprus Before History*. Duckworth, London.

Stekelis, Moshe
1951   A New Neolithic Industry: The Yarmukian of Palestine. *Israel Exploration Journal* 1:1–19.

1972   *The Yarmukian Culture of the Neolithic Period*. Magnes Press, Jerusalem.

Stewart, Sarah, and David Rupp
2004   Tools and Toys or Traces of Trade: The Problem of the Enigmatic Incised Objects from Cyprus and the Levant. In Edgar Peltenburg and Alexander Wasse (eds.), pp. 163–173.

Stiner, Mary, and Natalie Munro
2002   Approaches to Prehistoric Diet Breadth, Demography, and Prey Ranking Systems in Time and Space. *Journal of Archaeological Method and Theory* 9:175–208.

Stordeur, Danielle
2000   New Discoveries in Architecture and Symbolism at Jerf el Ahmr (Syria), 1997–1999. *Neolithics* 1:1–4.

2003a Tell Aswad 2001 et 2002. *Neolithics* 1:7–15.

2003b De la vallée de L'Euphrate à Chypre? À la recherche d'indices de relations au Néolithique. In Jean Guilaine and Alain LeBrun, pp. 353–371.

2004 New Insights and Concepts: Two Themes of the Neolithic in Syria and South-East Anatolia. *Neolithics* 1:49–51.

Stordeur, Danielle, Bassam Jammous, Daniel Helmer, and George Wilcox

1996 Jerf el Ahmr: A New Mureybetian Site (PPNA) on the Middle Euphrates. *Neolithics* 2:1–2.

Street, F. Alayne, and A. T. Grove

1979 Global Maps of Lake-Level Fluctuations since 30,000 Years BP. *Quaternary Research* 12:83–118.

Stutz, Aaron

2004 The Natufian in Real Time? Radiocarbon Date Calibration as a Tool for Understanding Natufian Societies and Their Long-Term Prehistoric Context. In *The Last Hunter-Gatherers in the Near East*, edited by Christophe Delage, pp. 13–37. International Series 1320, British Archaeological Reports, Oxford.

Swiny, Stuart

1988 The Pleistocene Fauna of Cyprus and Recent Discoveries on the Akrotiri Peninsula. *Report of the Department of Antiquities, Cyprus 1988*, 1–14.

Swiny, Stuart (editor)

2001 *The Earliest Prehistory of Cyprus: From Colonization to Exploitation*. Archaeological Reports No. 5, American Schools of Oriental Research, Boston.

Tchernov, Eitan

1994 *An Early Neolithic Village in the Jordan Valley, Part II: The Fauna of Netiv Hagdud*. American School of Prehistoric Research Bulletin 44, Peabody Museum of Archaeology and Ethnology, Harvard University, Cambridge.

1998 Are Late Pleistocene Environmental Factors, Faunal Changes and Cultural Transformations Causally Connected? The Case of the Southern Levant. *Paléorient* 23:209–228.

Tchernov, Eitan, and Ofer Bar-Yosef

1982 Animal Exploitation in the Pre-Pottery Neolithic B Period at Wadi Tbeik, Southern Sinai. *Paléorient* 8:17–37.

Tchernov, Eitan, and François Valla

1997 Two New Dogs, and Other Natufian Dogs, from the Southern Levant. *Journal of Archaeological Science* 24:65–95.

Tilley, Christopher

1996 *An Ethnography of the Neolithic: Early Prehistoric Societies in Southern Scandinavia*. Cambridge University Press, Cambridge.

Todd, Ian (editor)

1987 *Vasilikos Valley Project 6: Excavations at Kalavasos Tenta*, vol. 2. Studies in Mediterranean Archaeology Vol. 71:6, Paul Åströms Förlag, Göteborg.

2001 Kalavasos Tenta Revisited. In Stuart Swiny (ed.), pp. 95–107.

2003   Kalavasos-Tenta: A Reappraisal. In Jean Guilaine and Alain LeBrun (eds.), pp. 35–44.

Tubb, Katherine, and Carol Grissom

1995   'Ain Ghazal: A Comparative Study of the 1983 and 1985 Statuary Caches. In *Studies in the History and Archaeology of Jordan V*, edited by Khairieh 'Amr, Fawzi Zayadin, and Muna Zaghloul, pp. 437–447. Department of Antiquities, Amman.

Turville-Petre, Francis

1932   Excavations in the Mugharet el-Kebarah. *Journal of the Royal Anthropological Institute* 62:271–276.

Ucko, Peter, and George Dimbleby (editors)

1969   *The Domestication and Exploitation of Plants and Animals*. Aldine, London.

Unger-Hamilton, Romana

1991   Natufian Plant Husbandry in the Southern Levant and Comparison with That of the Neolithic Periods: The Lithic Perspective. In Ofer Bar-Yosef and François Valla (eds.), pp. 483–520.

1999   Harvesting Wild Cereals and Other Plants: Experimental Observations. In *Prehistory of Agriculture: New Experimental and Ethnographic Approaches*, edited by Patricia Anderson, pp. 145–152. Monograph 40, Institute of Archaeology, University of California, Los Angeles.

Valla, François

1984   *Les industries de silex de Mallaha (Eynan) et du Natoufien dans le Levant*. Mémoires et travaux du Centre de recherche français de Jérusalem No. 3, Association Paléorient, Paris.

1987   Les Natoufiens connaissent-ils l'Arc? In *La Main et l'outil, manches et emmanchements préhistoriques*, edited by Danielle Stordeur, pp. 165–174. Travaux de la Maison de l'Orient No. 15, Boccard, Paris.

1998   The First Settled Societies—Natufian (12,500–10,200 BP). In *The Archaeology of the Holy Land*, edited by Thomas Levy, pp. 169–187. Leicester University Press, London and Washington.

Van Andel, Tjeerd, and Curtis Runnels

1995   The Earliest Farmers in Europe. *Antiquity* 69:481–500.

Van Zeist, Willem, and J. A. H. Bakker-Heeres

1985   Archaeobotanical Studies in the Levant. 1. Neolithic Sites in the Damascus Basin: Aswad, Ghoraifé, Ramad. *Palaeohistoria* 24:165–256.

Verhoeven, Marc

1999   *An Archaeological Ethnography of a Neolithic Community: Space, Place, and Social Relations in the Burnt Village at Tell Sabri Abyad, Syria*. Nederlands Historisch-Archaeologisch Instituut, Istanbul.

2002   Ritual and Ideology in the Pre-Pottery Neolithic B of the Levant and Southeast Anatolia. *Cambridge Archaeological Journal* 12:2233–2258.

Vigne, Jean-Denis

2001   Large Mammals of Early Aceramic Neolithic Cyprus: Preliminary Results from Parekklisha *Shillourokambos*. In Stuart Swiny (ed.), pp. 55–60.

Vigne, Jean-Denis, Isabelle Carrère, and Jean Guilaine
  2003   Unstable Status of Early Domestic Ungulates in the Near East: The Ex-
            ample of Shillourokambos (Cyprus, IX–VIIIth Millennia Cal. B.C.). In
            Jean Guilaine and Alain LeBrun (eds.), pp. 239–251.
Vigne, Jean-Denis, Isabelle Carrère, Jean-François Saliège, Alain Person, Hervé Bo-
cherens, Jean Guilaine, and François Briois
  2000   Predomestic Cattle, Sheep, Goat and Pig During the Late 9th and the
            8th Millennium Cal. BC on Cyprus: Preliminary Results of *Shillouro-
            kambos* (Parekklisha, Limassol). In *Archaeozoology of the Near East IVA*,
            edited by Marjan Mashkour, Alice M. Choyke, Hijlke Buitenhuis, and
            François Poplin, pp. 83–106. Publication 32, Archaeological Research
            Center, Groningen.
Vigne, Jean-Denis, Geneviève Dollfus, and Joris Peters
  1999   The Beginning of Herding in the Near East: New Data and New Ideas.
            Paléorient 25:9–10.
Vigne, Jean-Denis, Jean Guilaine, Karyne Debue, Laurent Haye, and Patrice Gérard
  2004   Early Taming of the Cat in Cyprus. *Science* 304:259.
Vigne, Jean-Denis, Daniel Helmer, and Joris Peters
  2005   New Archaeological Approaches to Trace the First Steps of Animal Do-
            mestication: General Presentation, Reflections and Proposals. In *The
            First Steps of Animal Domestication*, edited by Jean-Denis Vigne, Joris
            Peters, and Daniel Helmer, pp. 1–16. Oxbow Books, Oxford.
Vita-Finzi, Claudio, and Eric Higgs
  1970   Prehistoric Economy in the Mount Carmel Area of Palestine: Site Catch-
            ment Analysis. *Proceedings of the Prehistoric Society* 36:1–37.
Voigt, Mary
  2000   Çatal Höyük in Context: Ritual at Early Neolithic Sites in Central and
            Eastern Turkey. In Ian Kuijt (ed.), pp. 253–293.
Wallach, Janet
  1999   *Desert Queen — The Extraordinary Life of Gertrude Bell: Adventurer, Advisor to
            Kings, Ally of Lawrence of Arabia*. Anchor Books, New York.
Wasse, Alexander
  2000   The Development of Goat and Sheep Herding During the Levantine
            Neolithic. Unpublished Ph.D. dissertation, University of London.
  2002   Final Results of an Analysis of the Sheep and Goat Bones from Ain Gha-
            zal, Jordan. *Levant* 34:59–82.
Wasse, Alexander, and Anne Pirie
  2001   The Anti-Lebanon Highlands Archaeological Project: Preliminary Re-
            port on the 2001 Survey Season. Report for the Directorate General of
            Antiquities of Lebanon, Beirut.
Watkins, Trevor
  1973   Some Problems of the Neolithic and Chalcolithic Periods in Cyprus. *Re-
            port of the Department of Antiquities, Cyprus*: 34–61.

1980   The Economic Status of the Aceramic Neolithic Culture of Cyprus. *Jour-
        nal of Mediterranean Anthropology and Archaeology* 1:139–149.
1998   The Human Environment. *Paléorient* 23:263–270.
2003   Developing Socio-Cultural Networks. *Neolithics* 2:36–37.
2004   Putting the Colonization of Cyprus into Context. In Edgar Peltenburg
        and Alexander Wasse (eds.), pp. 23–34.

Watkins, Trevor, Douglas Baird, and Alison Betts
1989   Qermez Dere and the Early Aceramic Neolithic of N. Iraq. *Paléorient*
        15:19–24.

Watson, Patty Jo
1995   Explaining the Transition to Agriculture. In *Last Hunters, First Farmers:
        New Perspectives on the Prehistoric Transition to Agriculture*, edited by
        T. Douglas Price and Anne Gebauer, pp. 21–37. School of American Re-
        search Press, Santa Fe.

Weinstein-Evron, Mina, and Anna Belfer-Cohen
1993   Natufian Figurines from the New Excavations of the El-Wad Cave, Mt.
        Carmel, Israel. *Rock Art Research* 10:102–106.

Weinstein-Evron, Mina, Daniel Kaufman, and Nurit Bird-David
2001   Rolling Stones: Basalt Implements as Evidence for Trade/Exchange in
        the Levantine Epipaleolithic. *Journal of the Israel Prehistoric Society* 31:25–
        42.

Weinstein-Evron, Mina, B. Lang, and Shimon Ilani
1999   Natufian Trade/Exchange in Basalt Implements: Evidence from North-
        ern Israel. *Archaeometry* 41:267–273.

Weiss, Harvey
2000   Beyond the Younger Dryas: Collapse as Adaptation to Abrupt Cli-
        mate Change in Ancient West Asia and the Eastern Mediterranean. In
        Environmental Disaster and the Archaeology of Human Response, edited by
        Garth Bawden and Richard Martin Reycraft, pp. 75–98. Anthropologi-
        cal Papers No. 7, Maxwell Museum of Anthropology, University of New
        Mexico, Albuquerque.

Whitcher, Sarah, Joel Janetski, and Richard Meadow
2000   Animal Bones from Wadi Mataha (Petra Basin, Jordan): The Initial
        Analysis. In *Archaeozoology of the Near East IVA*, edited by Marjan Mash-
        kour, Alice M. Choyke, Hijlke Buitenhuis, and François Poplin, pp. 39–
        48. Publication 32, Archaeological Research Center, Groningen.

Wilcox, George
2002   Geographical Variation in Major Cereal Components and Evidence for
        Independent Domestication Events in Western Asia. In René T. J. Cap-
        pers and Sytze Bottema (eds.), pp. 133–140.
2003   The Origins of Cypriot Farming. In Jean Guilaine and Alain LeBrun,
        pp. 231–238.

Wilkinson, Tony
    2003   *Archaeological Landscapes of the Near East.* University of Arizona Press, Tucson.
Wilson, Peter
    1988   *The Domestication of the Human Species.* Yale University Press, New Haven and London.
Wood, Andrée
    1998   Revisited: Blood Residue Investigations at Çayönü. In *Light on Top of the Black Hill: Studies Presented to Halet Çambel,* edited by Güven Arsebük, Machteld Mellink, and Wulf Schirmer, pp. 763–764. Ege Yayınları, Istanbul.
Wright, Gary
    1971   Origins of Food Production in Southwestern Asia: A Survey of Ideas. *Current Anthropology* 12:447–477.
    1978   Social Differentiation in the Early Natufian. In *Social Archaeology: Beyond Subsistence and Dating,* edited by Charles L. Redman, Mary Jane Berman, Edward V. Curtin, William T. Langhorne, Jr., Nina M. Versaggi, and Jeffery C. Wanser, pp. 201–233. Academic Press, New York.
Wright, Herbert E., Jr.
    1993   Environmental Determinism in Near Eastern Prehistory. *Current Anthropology* 34:458–469.
Wright, Katherine I.
    1994   Ground Stone Tools and Hunter-Gatherer Subsistence in Southwest Asia: Implications for the Transition to Farming. *American Antiquity* 59:238–263.
    2000   The Social Origins of Cooking and Dining in Early Villages of Western Asia. *Proceedings of the Prehistoric Society* 66:89–121.
Zeder, Melinda, and Brian Hesse
    2000   The Initial Domestication of Goats (*Capra hircus*) in the Zagros Mountains 10,000 Years Ago. *Science* 287:2254–2257.
Zeuner, Frederick
    1963   *A History of Domesticated Animals.* Hutchinson, London.
Ziegler, Matthew
    2003   Excavating a Neolithic Peace at Dhra (Jordan). *Near Eastern Archaeology* 66:140–142.
Zohary, Daniel
    1969   The Progenitors of Wheat and Barley in Relation to Domestication and Agricultural Dispersal in the Old World. In *The Domestication and Exploitation of Plants and Animals,* edited by Peter Ucko and George Dimbleby, pp. 47–66. Aldine, Chicago and New York.
    1996   The Mode of Domestication of the Founder Crops of Southwest Asian Agriculture. In *The Origins and Spread of Agriculture and Pastoralism in Eur-*

asia, edited by David Harris, pp. 142–158. Smithsonian Press, Washington, DC.

1999   Domestication of the Neolithic Near Eastern Crop Assemblage. In *Prehistory of Agriculture: New Experimental and Ethnographic Approaches*, edited by Patricia Anderson, pp. 42–50. Monograph 40, Institute of Archaeology, University of California, Los Angeles.

Zohary, Daniel, and Maria Hopf

2000   *Domestication of Plants in the Old World*. 3rd ed. Oxford University Press, Oxford.

Zohary, Michael

1962   *Plant Life of Palestine*. Ronald Press, New York.

1973   *Geobotanical Foundations of the Middle East*. Gustav Fischer, Stuttgart.

Index

subsistence, 16, 17–18, 26–27, 266–67.
See also economy
Sultanian, 87, 88, 91–92
symbolism, 27, 226, 268; fertility, 219–
20; mortuary contexts, 221–22;
PPNB, 158–59, 167–68
Syria, ix, 24, 66, 123, 176, 224, 230;
Natufian in, 49, 51; PN in, 199, 201;
PPNB in, 122, 126, 128, 129
Syrian Desert, 31, 32

Tahunian, 121–22
Tatlisu-Çiftlikdüzü, 244, 248
Taurus Mountains, 30, 31, 91, 137–38,
142, 143
Tel Abu Hureyra. See Abu Hureyra, Tel
Tel Aswad. See Aswad, Tel
Tel Halula. See Halula, Tel
Tel Judaidah. See Judaidah, Tel
Tel Ramad. See Ramad, Tel
Tel Sabi Abyad. See Sabi Abyad, Tel
Tel Wadi Feinan. See Wadi Feinan, Tel
Tepe Guran, 128
territoriality: PPNB, 164–65
Tiberias, Lake, 32, 36
Tigris River, 66, 199, 212
tokens: clay, 155, 157
trade, xii; obsidian, 229–30; PN, 225,
227; PPNA, 115–16, 118; PPNB, 128,
164, 165
Trialetian, 53, 91
Troodos Mountains, 34, 241
Turkey, ix, xii, 13, 30, 31, 51, 176; do-
mestication in, 66, 141–42, 143;
obsidian from, 116, 236; PN, 200,
201, 226; PPNA, 91, 98; PPNB in,
122–23, 126, 128, 134, 140

Ubaidian, 200
Umm Dabaghiyah, 214

Van, Lake, 41, 116
villages, xi–xii, 5, 270; climate, 42–43;

early, ix–x, 13; fishing, 254–55;
Natufian, 46–47, 59, 67, 78–79; and
nomads, 222–23; organization of,
159–60; origins of, 16–17; PN, 215,
223–24, 226; population of, 78–79;
PPNA, 89, 106, 112, 117; PPNB,
127–28, 144–46, 164, 167, 170–74
violence, 73, 149, 164, 188
vulva pebbles, 219–20

Wad, el-, 67, 72, 75, 80, 126
Wadi Feinan, Tel, 227–28
Wadi Feinan 16: 90, 276
Wadi Hammeh 27: 56, 63, 76
Wadi Mataha, 67, 68
Wadi Rabah, 199, 200, 201, 212, 216, 219,
225; chipped stone from, 207, 208;
pottery from, 206, 218
Wadi Shu'eib, 44, 128, 185, 186, 212, 216;
archaeology of, 194, 196, 197 (fig.);
as megasite, 176, 178–79
wells: on Cyprus, 235, 238–40
wheat: on Cyprus, 238, 241; domestication of, 15–16, 60, 102–3; einkorn and
emmer, 66, 103, 140; wild, 61, 238
wine making: PN, 213–14
women, 148; figurines of, 157–58, 226;
symbolic importance of, 114–15, 219.
See also Goddess

Yarmoukian culture, 199, 200, 201, 214,
219, 221, 225; architecture, 210–12;
pottery, 204, 218; settlement pattern
of, 215, 216, 224
Yiftahel, 129, 161
Younger Dryas, 20, 24, 38–39, 63, 69,
83, 85

Zagros Mountains, 13, 30, 31, 49, 53, 91,
141, 142, 218–19
Zagros Neolithic Complex, 200, 218
Zahrat Adh-Dhra' 2: 90
Zarzian culture, 49, 53

About the Author

Alan H. Simmons is Distinguished Professor in the Department of Anthropology at the University of Nevada, Las Vegas. He also served as departmental chair from 2004–2008 and has been at UNLV since 1993. Prior to that he held positions at the Desert Research Institute in Reno, Nevada; the Museum of Anthropology at the University of Kansas in Lawrence; Professional Analysts in Eugene, Oregon; the Navajo Nation Cultural Resource Management Program in Window Rock, Arizona; and the Arizona State Museum at the University of Arizona in Tucson. He has worked on a variety of archaeological sites in the United States, Canada, and several Near Eastern and eastern Mediterranean countries, including Egypt, Cyprus, Israel, Jordan, and Lebanon.

Simmons received his B.A. at the University of Colorado, Boulder; M.A.s from the University of Toronto and Southern Methodist University; and his Ph.D. from Southern Methodist University.

He has published numerous articles and book chapters on his research, including pieces in *Science, Nature, Antiquity, American Antiquity, Proceedings of the National Academy of Sciences,* and the *Journal of Field Archaeology.* He has authored or edited numerous monographs and published a book in 1999 on the extinction of indigenous pygmy hippopotami in Cyprus and the first settlers of the island.

Simmons's research has been supported by grants from the National Science Foundation and the National Endowment for the Humanities, and a variety of private agencies, including the National Geographic Society, the Brennan Foundation, and the Institute for Aegean Prehistory. In 2007 he received the American Schools of Oriental Research's P.E. MacAllister Field Archaeology Award, and in 2009 the present book received ASOR's G. Ernest Wright Award.

His research interests include the origins and consequences of food production, lithic analyses, human adaptations to harsh environments, aleoeconomy, and archaeological ethics. His most recent fieldwork has been in Jordan and, currently, in Cyprus.